Lecture Notes in Computer Sci

Commenced Publication in 1973
Founding and Former Series Editors:
Gerhard Goos, Juris Hartmanis, and Jan van Leeuw

Adam Smith (Ed.)

Information Theoretic Security

6th International Conference, ICITS 2012
Montreal, QC, Canada, August 15-17, 2012
Proceedings

 Springer

Volume Editor

Adam Smith
Pennsylvania State University
Department of Computer Science and Engineering
University Park, PA 16802, USA
E-mail: asmith@psu.edu

ISSN 0302-9743   e-ISSN 1611-3349
ISBN 978-3-642-32283-9   e-ISBN 978-3-642-32284-6
DOI 10.1007/978-3-642-32284-6
Springer Heidelberg Dordrecht London New York

Library of Congress Control Number: 2012943067

CR Subject Classification (1998): K.6.5, E.3, E.4, K.4.4, F.2.1

LNCS Sublibrary: SL 4 – Security and Cryptology

Typesetting: Camera-ready by author, data conversion by Scientific Publishing Services, Chennai, India

Printed on acid-free paper

Springer is part of Springer Science+Business Media (www.springer.com)

Preface

ICITS 2012 was the 6th International Conference of Information-theoretic Security, held at the Université de Montréal in Montreal, Quebec, Canada, during August 15–17, 2012. ICITS 2012 was held in cooperation with the International Association for Cryptologic Research (IACR). The General Chair of the conference was Jürg Wullschleger. He was helped by two local Co-chairs, Claude Crépeau and Alain Tapp.

The Program Committee, consisting of 14 members, received 46 submissions to two tracks. Twenty-two papers were ultimately accepted, 11 from each track. The quality of the submissions to both tracks was high, making the selection process challenging.

The two-track format was new to ICITS this year, and represented an experiment in bringing together researchers from three communities — information theory, cryptography, quantum computing — with very different publication cultures. Submissions to both tracks were reviewed by the committee, and in some cases external reviewers, to assess their quality and suitability. The two tracks differed in how accepted submissions were handled. The first, "conference", track was set up as a traditional computer science conference: submissions had to be original, and revised versions of the 11 accepted papers appear in this volume. (Revisions were not checked as to their contents, and the authors bear full responsibility for the contents of their papers.)

In contrast, papers accepted to the second, "workshop", track do not appear in these proceedings except, at the discretion of the authors, as one-page abstracts (authors of seven of the 11 papers decided to contribute abstracts). Workshop-track papers represent recently published or as-yet unpublished research. A full list of the workshop-track papers presented at the conference appears before the table of contents.

The goal of the two-track format was to encourage participation from researchers from communities where a conference publication may preclude publication in a top journal, and to draw participants who normally publish in other conferences (CRYPTO and ISIT, for example). I believe that in this respect the format was very successful.

Finally, I note that it was up to authors to decide which track they would submit to—each paper was only considered for one track—and the same review process applied to papers from both tracks.

In addition to the 22 contributed presentations, there were seven invited talks:

- "Reconstruction of a Shared Secret in the Presence of Faults," by Serge Fehr of CWI Amsterdam
- "Timing Side Channels: Quantifying and Mitigating the Threat," by Negar Kiyavash of the University of Illinois at Urbana-Champaign

- "Non-malleable Extractors, Non-malleable Condensers and Their Applications," by Xin Li of the University of Washington
- "How to Fake Auxiliary Input," by Krzysztof Pietrzak of IST Austria
- "The Many Entropies of One-Way Functions," by Salil Vadhan of Harvard
- "Information Locking from Asymptotic Geometry," by Patrick Hayden of McGill University
- "Semantic Security in the Physical Layer," by Alexander Vardy of the University of California, San Diego

I am grateful to the many people who contributed to the success of ICITS 2012. Above all, I thank the authors who submitted papers. ICITS exists to disseminate their research. I also thank the extremely hard-working committee members, who devoted many hours of their time and enthusiastically engaged with the new format, and the external reviewers who assisted the committee. Jürg Wullshleger deserves special thanks since he served both as a committee member and as the General Chair. His advice and help with the format and program were invaluable.

The two-track format came about after discussions with a wide range of people, including the members of the Program Committee and the ICITS Steering Committee, chaired by Yvo Desmedt. Their suggestions deserve the credit for the success of the two-track format (though I deserve the blame for any deficiencies in its implementation). I would particularly like to thank Christian Schaffner and Stephanie Wehner for a conversation at QIP during which the two-track idea was conceived (exactly nine months before ICITS!). The Steering Committee also provided useful general advice on my role as Program Committee chair. I am especially grateful to Rei Safavi-Naini, the ICITS 2008 Program Chair, for several helpful conversations.

Finally, I would like to thank Alfred Hofmann, Christine Reiss and Anna Kramer and the rest of the LNCS staff at Springer for their help preparing the proceedings.

June 2012

Adam Smith
Program Chair
ICITS 2012

ICITS 2012

**The 6th International Conference on
Information-theoretic Security**
Montréal, Québec, Canada, August 15–17, 2012

Organized in cooperation with the
International Association for Cryptologic Research

General Chair	Jürg Wullschleger (Université de Montréal)
Local Co-chairs	Alain Tapp (Université de Montréal) Claude Crépeau (McGill University)
Program Chair	Adam Smith (Pennsylvania State University)

Program Committee

Anne Broadbent	University of Waterloo, Canada
Thomas Holenstein	ETH Zürich, Switzerland
Yuval Ishai	Technion – Israel Institute of Technology, Israel
Sidarth Jaggi	Chinese University of Hong Kong, SAR China
Bhavana Kanukurthi	University of California, Los Angeles, USA
Ashish Khisti	University of Toronto, Canada
Yingbin Liang	Syracuse University, USA
Prakash Narayan	University of Maryland, USA
Louis Salvail	Université de Montréal, Canada
Anand Sarwate	Toyota Technological Institute at Chicago, USA
Christian Schaffner	University of Amsterdam, The Netherlands
Stephanie Wehner	National University of Singapore, Singapore
Daniel Wichs	IBM Research, USA
Jürg Wullschleger	Université de Montréal, Canada

ICITS Steering Committee

Carlo Blundo	University of Salerno, Italy
Ronald Cramer	CWI & Leiden University, The Netherlands
Yvo Desmedt (Chair)	University College London, UK
Hideki Imai	University of Tokyo, Japan
Kaoru Kurosawa	Ibaraki University, Japan
Ueli Maurer	ETH Zürich, Switzerland
C. Pandu Rangan	Indian Institute of Technology, Madras, India
Rei Safavi-Naini	University of Calgary, Canada
Moti Yung	Google & Columbia University, USA
Yulian Zheng	University of North Carolina, USA

External Reviewers

Prabhanjan Ananth
Mattias Andersson
Gilad Asharov
Raef Bassily
Amos Beimel
Mario Berta
Andrej Bogdanov
Niek Bouman
David Cash
Rafael Dowsley
Serge Fehr

Eiichiro Fujisaki
Benjamin Fuller
Esther Hänggi
Ariel Gabizon
Adriana Lopez-Alt
Samuel Ranellucci
Florian Speelman
Marco Tomamichel
Dominique Unruh
Mark Wilde
Stefan Wolf

Sponsors

Centre de recherches mathématiques, Université de Montréal
Institute for Quantum Computing, University of Waterloo
INstitute for Transdisciplinary Research In Quantum computing (INTRIQ), a strategic cluster of the *Fonds de recherche du Québec – Nature et technologies*

Workshop Track Papers

The following papers, accepted to the "workshop track," were presented at ICITS 2012 but do not appear as long papers in these proceedings. Authors could opt to include a one-page abstract. Abstracts of the papers marked with an asterisk appear at the end of the proceedings.

(In contrast, submissions accepted to the conference track appear as long papers. They are listed in the table of contents.)

Table of Contents

Guessing Secrecy

Mohsen Alimomeni and Reihaneh Safavi-Naini

University of Calgary, Department of Computer Science

Abstract. Shannon's definition of perfect secrecy captures the strongest notion of security for an encryption system and requires that the ciphertext leaks no information about the plaintext to an eavesdropper with unbounded computational power. The only known system with perfect secrecy in this model is one-time pad. Two important limitations of one-time pad in practice are, (i) the size of key space must not be less than the size of plaintext space, and (ii) the key must be chosen uniformly at random for each message to be encrypted. A number of follow up work attempt to relax these limitations by introducing relaxed or new definitions of secrecy.

In this paper we propose a new relaxation of secrecy that we call perfect guessing secrecy, or guessing secrecy for short. This is a natural definition that requires that the adversary's success chance of the plaintext using his best guessing strategy does not change after seeing the ciphertext. Unlike perfect secrecy, guessing secrecy does allow some leakage of information but requires that the best guess of the plaintext remain the same after seeing the ciphertext. We define guessing secrecy and prove a number of results. We show that similar to perfect secrecy, in guessing secrecy the size of the key space can not be less than the size of plaintext space. Moreover, when the two sets are of equal size, one can find two families of distributions on the plaintext space and key space, such that perfect guessing secrecy is guaranteed for any pair of distributions, one from each family. In other words, perfect guessing secrecy can be guaranteed with non-uniform keys also. We also show the relation between perfect secrecy and perfect guessing secrecy. We discuss our results and propose direction of future research.

Keywords: Guessing secrecy, randomness, perfect secrecy, Information theoretic security, imperfect randomness.

1 Introduction

Consider the classical scenario of symmetric cryptography: Alice, wants to send a message X securely to Bob, over a reliable communication channel that is eavesdropped by Eve who has unlimited computational power. The goal of secrecy systems is to prevent Eve from learning the message, given her view of the communication channel. Without giving any advantage to Alice and Bob, providing secrecy against Eve in the above setting is impossible. In Shannon's model of secrecy system [1], Alice and Bob share a secret key K that is unknown to

A. Smith (Ed.): ICITS 2012, LNCS 7412, pp. 1–13, 2012.

Eve. Alice and Bob use a symmetric key encryption system that consists of two functions: an encryption function that takes the message X and the key K, and generates a ciphertext Y, and a decryption function that takes the ciphertext Y and the same key K, and recovers the message X back. Alice and Bob use the encryption and decryption functions, respectively. Eve who sees the ciphertext Y, without the knowledge of the key K cannot recover X. Other models assume other types of advantage, such as noisy view of communication channel [2], or bounded storage for Eve [3].

In this paper we follow Shannon's model and consider the case that Alice and Bob share a realization of a random variable (key). Shannon's definition of perfect secrecy, requires that no information about the plaintext be leaked from the ciphertext. Perfect secrecy requires that the distribution of ciphertexts and plaintexts be statistically independent and so the adversary's information about the plaintext will not be affected by having access to the ciphertext. The only system with perfect secrecy is one-time pad. One-time pad requires a new key to be selected for encryption of each message. Shannon proved that for any encryption scheme with perfect secrecy, entropy of the key distribution must be at least equal to the entropy of the plaintext. He also proved that for perfect secrecy the size of the key space must be at least as large as the size of plaintext space. For the case that the two sizes are equal to the size of ciphertexts, that is the system has the best possible key efficiency, the distribution on the key space must be uniform. These requirements are hard, if not impossible, to satisfy since even if one could tolerate using a new key for every message, guaranteeing uniformity of the key is a real challenge in practice. This is because there is no known source of randomness with guaranteed uniform output, and in almost all cases the output of a randomness source is likely to have biases.

1.1 Previous Work

A number of authors considered alternative models to achieve more practical cryptosystems:

ϵ-**Secrecy.** One of the first attempts to relax the requirement on the independence of plaintext and ciphertext distribution, led to the definition of ϵ-secrecy that allows small amount of information leakage about the plaintext after viewing the ciphertext.

A number of papers [4,5,6] considered whether ϵ-secrecy is possible if the key is not chosen uniformly at random. Bosely and Dodis [7] considered this problem and proved that for practical key lengths (not exponential in plaintext length) either encryption is impossible, or the key is deterministically extractable to a uniform key with the same length as the plaintext. That is there is a deterministic function that takes the key as input and generates a random string of the size at least equal to the message. The generated random string can then be used in one-time pad to provide secrecy. In other words, they proved that any encryption function that provides ϵ-secrecy is essentially one-time pad.

Entropic Security. Russel and Wang [8] built upon a notion of secrecy, called semantic security, and assumed a bound on the prior knowledge of the adversary about the plaintexts. With this restriction, they could reduce the length of the key, depending on the amount of adversary's prior knowledge about plaintexts. Dodis and Smith [9] introduced entropic security based on Russel and Wang definition and provided simpler constructions that achieved entropic security. Although compared to perfect secrecy, their notion of secrecy needs smaller key size, but their schemes require the key to be uniformly distributed.

Bounded Storage Model. Another direction proposed was to limit the memory of the computationally unbounded adversary. Maurer [3] introduced Bounded Storage Model, and proved that a constant size key can be used to provide unconditional security in this model [10]. Aumann and Robin [11] defined the notion of everlasting security using the Bounded Storage Model, and showed that a key can be reused to send an exponential number of plaintexts [12].

In these models the key is either deterministically extractable, or is almost uniformly distributed. Moreover the assumption of bounded storage is challenged in many real life scenarios.

1.2 Our Contribution

We propose a new notion of secrecy that we call guessing secrecy that is similar to Shannon's formulation of perfect secrecy, but uses min-entropy and conditional min-entropy instead of corresponding Shannon entropies. Pefect guessing secrecy, referred to as guessing secrecy for simplicity, requires that the best chance of the adversary in guessing the plaintext does not change after viewing the ciphertext. In other words, it requires that the conditional min-entropy of the plaintext distribution given ciphertext, be equal to the min-entropy of the plaintext distribution.

We show that similar to perfect secrecy, perfect guessing secrecy requires the size of the key space to be at least equal to the size of plaintext space. If the sizes are the same however, unlike Shannon secrecy, it may be possible to obtain perfect guessing secrecy using non-uniform keys. We show two concrete families of distributions, on the message space and key space respectively, with the property that perfect guessing secrecy is guaranteed for any distribution on messages from the former family, together with any distribution on the keys, from the latter family. Ideally one would like to have both families to be large: that is perfect guessing secrecy be obtained for many plaintext distributions, using a large family of distributions on the keys. We however show that for the any family of distributions on the message space that contains uniform distribution, one must choose the key to be uniformly random, and the only encryption system that provides guessing secrecy is one-time pad. That is the family of distributions on the key space reduces to a single element. We leave the problem of finding larger families of distribution for message and key space that satisfy perfect guessing secrecy as an open problem.

We also show the relationship between perfect secrecy and perfect guessing secrecy.

1.3   Motivation

Guessing secrecy preserves the min-entropy of a random variable by using the randomness from a shared key. This provides sufficient level of security in some scenarios for example when the communicated random variable is used as the input to an extractor to generate a uniformly distributed key. Reducing randomness requirement of the shared key (not requiring the key to be uniformly distributed and/or the key length be the same as the plaintext length) for guessing secrecy might help us to improve such scenarios in practice.

2   Notations and Preliminaries

We denote random variables by capital letter, such as X. If not stated otherwise, a random variable X induces a probability distribution P_X over a set which is denoted by the corresponding calligraphic letter $\mathcal{X}$. The cardinality, or size of a set $\mathcal{X}$ is denoted by $|\mathcal{X}|$, and by length of an instance $x \in \mathcal{X}$ we mean the length of the bit-string representation of it, i.e. $\log(|\mathcal{X}|)$. Uniform distribution over a set $\mathcal{X}$ is denoted by $U_{\mathcal{X}}$ or U_n if $\mathcal{X} = \{0, 1\}^n$. The logarithms will be in base 2 throughout the paper.

2.1   Information Measures

Shannon [13] defined the entropy (or average uncertainty) of a random variable as the information that is gained after observing a realization of the random variable.

Shannon Entropy. The *Shannon entropy* $H(X)$ of a random variable X is given by $H(X) = \mathbb{E}[-\log P_X]$. The *conditional Shannon entropy* $H(X|Y)$ of the random variable X given Y is the average value of $H(X|Y = y)$ over all possible values of y, i.e. $H(X|Y) = -\sum_{y \in \mathcal{Y}} P_Y(y)H(X|Y = y)$. The *mutual information* between two random variables measures the mutual dependence of them and is given by $I(X;Y) = H(X) - H(X|Y)$.

Statistical Distance. The *statistical distance* $\Delta(X, Y)$ between two random variables X and Y over the same range $\mathcal{A}$ with probability distributions P_X and P_Y respectively, is given by $\Delta(X, Y) = \frac{1}{2} \sum_{a \in \mathcal{A}} |P_X(a) - P_Y(a)|$. If $\Delta(X, U_{\mathcal{X}}) \leq \epsilon$ for sufficiently small ϵ, then we say X is almost uniformly distributed.

Min-Entropy. The min-entropy $H_\infty(X)$ of a random variable X is given by

$$H_\infty(X) = \min_x \left\{ \log \frac{1}{\Pr[X=x]} \right\} = -\log \max_x P_X(x).$$

A comprehensive study of information measures can be found in [14,15].

2.2   Shannon Secrecy

In this section, we recall some of the classical results in secrecy.

Encryption System. Let $\mathcal{X}$ be the set of plaintexts that is encrypted using a key from the set $\mathcal{K}$. Let $\mathcal{Y}$ the set of all ciphertexts. An *encryption system* is a pair of functions enc : $\mathcal{X} \times \mathcal{K} \to \mathcal{Y}$ and dec : $\mathcal{Y} \times \mathcal{K} \to \mathcal{X}$ such that for every $x \in \mathcal{X}$ and $k \in \mathcal{K}$ it holds that dec(enc($x, k), k) = x$, i.e. the decryption has no errors.

A realistic assumption here is that the adversary may have some prior information about the plaintext even before observing the ciphertext. For example if the adversary knows that the plaintext is English text, then this information may help her to better guess the plaintext after observing the ciphertext. The adversaries prior knowledge about the plaintext can be modeled as an random variable X over the set of plaintexts $\mathcal{X}$ with probability distribution P_X. We also assume that there is a random variable K over the set of keys $\mathcal{K}$ with probability distribution P_K. It is assumed that random variables X and K are independent. We also consider the random variable Y over ciphertexts $\mathcal{Y}$ with probability distribution P_Y that is determined by P_X and P_K and the encryption function enc.

Remark 1. From now on, without loss of generality, we only consider probability distributions that assign nonzero values to elements of their underlying space, unless otherwise stated. This is because we often need to consider conditional probabilities and this assumption simplifies the expression of theorems.

Remark 2. When we refer to an encryption system we assume there are probability distributions P_X and P_K on the plaintext and key space respectively.

Shannon's definition of secrecy, which is the strongest definition of security against an eavesdropping adversary for encryption systems, requires that the ciphertext gives no information about the plaintexts. In the language of probability theory this means that the probability distribution over the plaintexts P_X does not change even given a ciphertext y, i.e. $P_X = P_{X|Y=y}$ for all $y \in \mathcal{Y}$. In terms of entropy, this is equivalent to saying that $H(X|Y) = H(X)$. If an encryption system satisfies this property, then we say it is *perfectly secure*, or it satisfies perfect secrecy:

Perfect Secrecy. An encryption system provides *perfect secrecy* if the ciphertext reveals no information about the plaintext, i.e., $I(X; Y) = 0$.

One-Time Pad. Shannon showed that one-time pad scheme achieves perfect secrecy. One-time pad encrypts a plaintext x which is an element of a group G by selecting a key k which is another group element that is selected uniformly at random, and outputs $x + k$ where $+$ is the group operation. One-time pad requires that for encryption of each message, the key to be chosen uniformly at random from a set of keys, and the size of the key space be as large as the size of plaintext space. This requirement make the system no applicable in real world applications.

Shannon proved that perfect secrecy, in general, needs the key entropy to be higher than the plaintext entropy; i.e. $H(K) \geq H(X)$. It is also proved that perfect secrecy requires that the size of the key space be at least equal to the size of the plaintext space. Shannon also proved that if the size of plaintexts, keys and ciphertexts are the same, i.e. $|\mathcal{X}| = |\mathcal{Y}| = |\mathcal{K}|$, then any encryption scheme with perfect secrecy is essentially one-time pad, i.e. i) The distribution over keys, P_K, is uniform. ii) For every $x \in \mathcal{X}$ and every $y \in \mathcal{Y}$, there exists a unique key $k \in \mathcal{K}$ such that $\mathsf{enc}(x, k) = y$.

Shannon's result motivated a line of research to relax the notion of perfect secrecy in order to achieve more realistic encryption schemes.

3 Secrecy Based on Guessing Probability

We propose a new relaxation of perfect secrecy, that we call perfect guessing secrecy, or for simplicity guessing secrecy. We prove that an encryption scheme with guessing secrecy still needs a key of length at least as large as the plaintext, but we show that depending on the distribution of the plaintexts, it is possible to provide guessing secrecy with non-uniform distributions on the key space.

Guessing secrecy allows some information leakage to the adversary but requires that the leaked information not change the best chance of adversary's guess of the plaintext.

3.1 Basic Definitions

The *guessing probability* of a random variable X with probability distribution P_X, denoted by $G(X)$, and is given by:

$$G(X) = \max_x P_X(x).$$

This is, the success probability of correctly guessing the value of a realization of variable when using the best guessing strategy (guessing the most probable value of the range as the guess). Guessing probability is related to min-entropy as $H_\infty(X) = -\log G(X)$. Min-entropy is a measure of success chance of guessing X, or in other words, predictability of a random variable by an adversary. It can also be viewed as the worst case entropy compared to Shannon entropy which is an average entropy.

The *conditional guessing probability* of X given a random variable Y with a joint probability distribution P_{XY} is given by:

$$G(X|Y) = \sum_y P_Y(y) G(X|Y = y),$$

and measures the average unpredictability of X, averaged over all realization of the random variable Y. Note that $H_\infty(X|Y) = -\log G(X|Y)$.

The concept of guessing probability is also related (but not equivalent) to *guessing entropy* introduced in [16]. Guessing entropy measures the expected number of guesses required to determine a realization of a random variable, assuming the guessing strategy is by asking the elements of the set in decreasing order of probabilities, starting from the element with the highest probability. Guessing entropy of random variable X is defined by $\sum i p_i$ where p_i values are probability values in X sorted in decreasing order ($i = 1$ to $|X|$). Guessing probability however is the probability of a single best guess at X which is equal to p_1 and so guessing probability is always less than the guessing entropy.

3.2   Guessing Secrecy

The definition of guessing secrecy is the following:

Definition 1. *Let X be a random variable over plaintexts $\mathcal{X}$ with probability distribution P_X, and K a random variable over keys $\mathcal{K}$ with probability distribution P_K independent and assume the two variables are independent. An encryption scheme* enc $: \mathcal{X} \times \mathcal{K} \to \mathcal{Y}$ *satisfies* weak perfect guessing secrecy *for distributions P_X and P_K if $G(X|Y) = G(X)$. The scheme satisfies* strong perfect guessing secrecy *for distributions P_X and P_K if for any $y \in \mathcal{Y}$, we have $G(X|Y = y) = G(X)$.*

Clearly a scheme with strong guessing security satisfies the weak guessing secrecy requirement. However the converse is not true in general. From now on, we will use *guessing secrecy* to refer to weak perfect guessing secrecy, unless otherwise mentioned. (We previously used guessing secrecy in lieu of perfect guessing secrecy.)

Remark. Min-entropy has been commonly used to measure the randomness in a random variable. In this paper we use min-entropy to measure secrecy. Using guessing probability instead of min-entropy allows us to remove $-\log$ and provides a natural way of capturing security.

The next theorem states that if the size of key space must be at least the size of plaintext space, and this is regardless of plaintext distribution.

Theorem 1. *If an encryption function* enc $: \mathcal{X} \times \mathcal{K} \to \mathcal{Y}$ *satisfies guessing secrecy for distributions P_X and P_K over plaintexts and keys respectively, then we have $|\mathcal{K}| \geq |\mathcal{X}|$.*

Proof. Assume there is an encryption function that provides guessing secrecy and $|\mathcal{K}| < |\mathcal{X}|$. Let $Z_x = \{y \in \mathcal{Y} | P_{Y|X}(y|x) = 0\}$. For each $x \in \mathcal{X}$, Z_x is non-empty, i.e. $|Z_x| > 0$. This is because the size of the key space is less than the size of plaintext space, and so, the image of x under encryption function using all keys will be not be equal to $\mathcal{Y}$. Let x^* be an element of $\mathcal{X}$ with the highest probability. Now from the definition of conditional guessing secrecy we have:

$$G(X|Y) = \sum_y \max_x P_X(x)P_{Y|X}(y|x) \tag{3.1}$$

$$= \underbrace{\sum_{y \notin Z_{x^*}} \max_x P_X(x)P_{Y|X}(y|x)}_{S_1} + \underbrace{\sum_{y \in Z_{x^*}} \max_x P_X(x)P_{Y|X}(y|x)}_{S_2} \tag{3.2}$$

For the first summand we have:

$$S_1 \geq \sum_{y \notin Z_{x^*}} P_X(x^*)P_{Y|X}(y|x^*) \tag{3.3}$$

$$= P_X(x^*) \sum_y P_{Y|X}(y|x^*) = G(X) \tag{3.4}$$

It is easy to verify that $S_2 > 0$ since $|\mathcal{Y}| \geq |\mathcal{X}|$. Therefore $G(X|Y) = S_1 + S_2 > G(X)$ which contradicts guessing secrecy. $\qquad\qquad\square$

The following theorem states that to have guessing secrecy, the min-entropy of the key distribution must be at least the min-entropy of the plaintext distribution. This is very similar to the result of Shannon for perfect secrecy where the Shannon entropy of the key distribution must be at least the Shannon entropy of the plaintext distribution.

Theorem 2. *If an encryption function* enc $: \mathcal{X} \times \mathcal{K} \to \mathcal{Y}$ *satisfies guessing secrecy, then* $G(K) \leq G(X)$ *or* $H_\infty(K) \geq H_\infty(X)$.

Proof. First see that from the definition of conditional guessing probability we have:

$$G(X|Y) = \sum_y P_Y(y) \max_x P_{X|Y}(x|y)$$

$$= \sum_y \max_x P_X(x)P_{Y|X}(y|x) \tag{3.5}$$

$$= \sum_y \max_x \{P_X(x) \sum_k P_K(k) \Pr(\text{enc}(x,k) = y)\} \tag{3.6}$$

$$= \sum_y \max_x \{P_X(x) \sum_{k \in K_{x,y}} P_K(k)\} \tag{3.7}$$

where $K_{x,y} = \{k|\text{enc}(x,k) = y\}$. Note that $\Pr(\text{enc}(x,k) = y)$ is an indicator function, i.e. its value is zero or 1, so we have the last equality. Considering the encryption function as a table with columns representing plaintexts and rows representing keys, then we take the last summation 3.7 only in one row of the table, namely the row corresponding to the key with highest probability, i.e. k^*. Then continuing from the last equality we have:

$$G(X|Y) \geq \sum_x P_X(x)P_K(k^*) \qquad (3.8)$$

$$= \max_k P_K(k) \qquad (3.9)$$

Finally from the definition of guessing secrecy we have: $G(X) = G(X|Y) \geq G(K)$. □

We can define guessing secrecy for a family of distributions over keys as defined for perfect secrecy in the following way:

Definition 2. *An encryption system with a probability distribution on the message space provides guessing secrecy for a family of distributions D over the key space if for all distributions in the family D, it satisfies guessing secrecy.*

For example, let D_t be the family of distributions that have min-entropy at least t. This family of distributions is called a *weak random source or t-source* [17]. Then we say an encryption scheme satisfies guessing secrecy for the family of distributions D_t, if it satisfies guessing secrecy for all distributions in the family, i.e. all distributions that have min-entropy at least t.

We can also require secrecy for a family of distributions over plaintext space. For example, the definition of secrecy in [8], requires security only if the plaintext is sampled from a family of distributions that have sufficiently high min entropy. Here to compare Perfect secrecy and guessing secrecy, we define the notion of secrecy for a family of distributions over the plaintext space. We use the following notations and abbreviations.

Notation. For a secrecy definition T, we say that a function enc satisfies $\mathbb{F}$-T.Secrecy if enc satisfies the definition of T secrecy for a family of distributions $\mathbb{F}$ over the plaintext space. We will abbreviate $\mathbb{F}$-Guessing.Secrecy by $\mathbb{F}$-G.S.

We are interested in finding families of distributions over the key and the plaintext spaces such any pair of distributions, one from each families, guarantee guessing secrecy. Using D_t as the family of plaintext distributions, we can prove a theorem similar to Shannon's theorem for perfect secrecy as follows:

Corollary 1. *If $|\mathcal{X}| = |\mathcal{Y}| = |\mathcal{K}|$, an encryption function enc satisfies D_t-G.S for some t, if and only if,*

(1) $\forall x, y, k_{x,y} = 1$;
(2) the distribution over K is uniform, that is $P_K(k) = \frac{1}{|\mathcal{K}|}$.

Proof. enc has guessing secrecy if and only if $\sum_y \max_x\{P_X(x)\sum_{k \in K_{x,y}} P_K(k)\} = \max_x P_X(x)$. Now consider the uniform distribution over $\mathcal{X}$. Then we have

$\sum_y \max_x \{\sum_{k \in K_{x,y}} P_K(k)\} = 1$. On the other hand, from theorem 2, when $\mathcal{X}$ is uniformly distributed, the key must be uniformly distributed also.

Now for uniform distribution over keys, if there exists x_0, y_0 such that $k_{x_0,y_0} > 1$, then,

$$\sum_y \max_x \{\sum_{k \in K_{x,y}} P_K(k)\} > |\mathcal{Y}| \max_k P_K(k) = 1,$$

which is a contradiction.   □

The above corllary implies that any encryption system that provides guessing secrecy for a family of distributions over plaintexts that contains the uniform distribution, is essentially one-time pad and this implies guessing secrecy is equivalent to perfect secrecy in these cases. However, the question of whether there exists an encryption function providing guessing secrecy for a family of distribution over keys remains open when a family of distributions is considered over plaintexts that do no contain uniform distribution.

3.3   Guessing Secrecy with Imperfect Randomness

In this section, we investigate whether guessing secrecy is possible when keys that are not uniformly distributed. This questions is particularly interesting when the key distribution is from a weak random source. Although we cannot give a direct answer to this question, we can show that guessing secrecy is possible with non-uniform keys if plaintexts are coming from certain distributions.

We need the following definition to state the main theorem of this section:

Definition 3. *For a random variable X with probability distribution P_X, let P_2 be the probability of the second highest probable value of X. Note that $P_2(X)$ may be equal to $G(X)$. Let*

$$S(X) = \frac{G(X)}{P_2(X)}$$

and

$$U(X) = \max_{x_0,x_1} \frac{P_X(x_0)}{P_X(x_1)}.$$

where $x_0, x_1 \in \mathcal{X}$ and x_0 can be equal to x_1. $U(X)$ is actually the highest probability of P_X divided by the minimum probability of P_X. This can be used to measure the uniformity of a distribution and was used in other works in different context (as an example see [18]).

For a set of distributions over plaintexts such that the first and second highest probabilities are "far" from each other, we show that there exists encryption schemes with guessing secrecy if the distribution over keys are such that the maximum and minimum probabilities are " close".

Theorem 3. *Let X be any random variable over $\mathcal{X} = \{0,1\}^n$ with $S(X) \geq m \geq 1$. For a family of distributions $\mathbb{F}$ over keys defined as $\mathbb{F} = \{K \mid U(K) \leq m\}$, there exists an encryption function $\mathsf{enc} : \mathcal{X} \times \mathcal{K} \to \mathcal{Y}$ satisfying guessing secrecy for $\mathbb{F}$ such that $|\mathcal{X}| = |\mathcal{Y}| = |\mathcal{K}|$.*

Proof. Let x^* be a value in $\mathcal{X}$ with the highest probability, i.e. $P_X(x^*) = G(X)$. Then $U(K) \le m \le S(X)$ implies that for all $y \in \mathcal{Y}$ we have:

$$P_X(x^*)P_K(k) \ge P_X(x')P_K(k')$$

for all $x' \in \mathcal{X}$ and $k' \in \mathcal{K}$, where k is the key that encrypts x^* to y. Thus we have

$$\max_x \{P_X(x)P_K(k)\} = G(X)P_K(k)$$

Now for an encryption function f such that $\forall x \in \mathcal{X}, y \in \mathcal{Y} : k_{x,y} = 1$, we have:

$$G(X|Y) = \sum_y \max_x \{P_X(x) \sum_{k \in K_{x,y}} P_K(k)\} \qquad (3.10)$$

$$= \sum_y \max_x \{P_X(x)P_K(k) \mid f(x,k) = y\} \qquad (3.11)$$

$$= G(X) \sum_y \{P_K(k) \mid f(x^*,k) = y\} \qquad (3.12)$$

$$= G(X) \qquad (3.13)$$

The last equality is because by summing over values of y, $P_K(k)$ will take all values of P_K which sum to one. □

In the above theorem, $U(K)$ is a measure of closeness of K to uniform distribution. For example if $m = 1$, then the key must be chosen uniformly at random. As m grows larger, the keys distribution further deviates from uniform distribution in terms of statistical distance. This implies that the farther the second highest probability in P_X is from $G(X)$, the farther $G(K)$ can get from the lowest probability of P_K and the more non-uniform distributions can be used for guessing secrecy, which is desirable for our purpose.

3.4   Relation with Perfect Secrecy

We first consider the following notions of secrecy: Guessing Secrecy (G.S), D_t-G.S, Perfect-Secrecy (P.S) and all-Perfect-Secrecy (all-P.S). Definitions of these notions follow from previous definitions and the notations. With all-P.S we mean perfect secrecy for family of all distributions over plaintexts.

The following relations follow from the definitions of these notions:

$$\text{all-P.S} \implies D_t\text{-G.S}$$
$$\Downarrow \qquad\qquad \Downarrow$$
$$\text{P.S} \implies \text{G.S}$$

where $a \Rightarrow b$ means if a function has property a, then it will also have property b. Based on theorem 2.7 in [19] and theorem 1, for all these notions of security, we must have $|\mathcal{K}| \ge |\mathcal{X}|$.

$$\text{all-P.S} \overset{(2)}{\leftarrow} D_t\text{-G.S}$$
$$\uparrow_{(1)} \qquad \mspace{-20mu} \Updownarrow_{(3)}$$
$$\text{P.S} \overset{(4)}{\nleftrightarrow} \text{G.S}$$

where $a \to b$ means a implies b under certain conditions.

(1) If $|\mathcal{X}| = |\mathcal{Y}| = |\mathcal{K}|$, then P.S $\to$ all-P.S ([19] Theorem 2.8).
(2) If $|\mathcal{X}| = |\mathcal{Y}| = |\mathcal{K}|$, then D_t-G.S $\to$ all-P.S (Theorem 1).
(3, 4) There exists an encryption scheme providing guessing secrecy for a family of distributions over plaintexts and keys but it does not provide D_t-G.S (Theorem 3).

Points 3 and 4, are the main advantages of guessing secrecy over perfect secrecy (and ϵ-secrecy) in terms of randomness requirements.

4   Concluding Remarks

We proposed a new definition of secrecy that provides sufficient security guarantee in some realistic application scenario and matches the intuition that for a good secrecy system it should be hard to "guess" the plaintext. Although our current results might not provide a direct practical implication, but our initial results highlights an important aspect of guessing secrecy that is not present in other known relaxations of secrecy: it is possible to use non-uniform keys to provide perfect guessing secrecy. In all other definitions of secrecy, keys must be uniformly selected. We showed families of distributions on messages and keys that provide perfect guessing secrecy. Finding encryption systems that provide perfect guessing secrecy for larger families of distributions, is an interesting open question. Investigating randomness requirements of ϵ-guessing secrecy defined as $H_\infty(X) - H_\infty(X|Y) \le \epsilon$, is also a natural generalization of our work.

Acknowledgement. We are grateful to Hadi Ahmadi for helpful discussions we had about this work. We would also like to thank the anonymous referees for useful comments. Financial support for this work is in part provided by Alberta Innovates Technology Future.

References

1. Shannon, C.: Communication theory of secrecy systems. Bell System Technical Journal 28, 656–715 (1949)
2. Wyner, A.D.: The wire-tap channel. Bell Syst. Tech. J. 54(8), 1355–1367 (1975)
3. Maurer, U.M.: Conditionally-perfect secrecy and a provably-secure randomized cipher. J. Cryptol. 5(1), 53–66 (1992)
4. McInnes, J.L., Pinkas, B.: On the Impossibility of Private Key Cryptography with Weakly Random Keys. In: Menezes, A., Vanstone, S.A. (eds.) CRYPTO 1990. LNCS, vol. 537, pp. 421–435. Springer, Heidelberg (1991)

5. Dodis, Y., Spencer, J.: On the (non)universality of the one-time pad. In: Proceedings of the 43rd Symposium on Foundations of Computer Science, FOCS 2002, pp. 376–388. IEEE Computer Society, Washington, DC (2002)

6. Dodis, Y., Ong, S.J., Prabhakaran, M., Sahai, A.: On the (im)possibility of cryptography with imperfect randomness. In: Proceedings of the 45th Annual IEEE Symposium on Foundations of Computer Science, pp. 196–205. IEEE Computer Society, Washington, DC (2004)

7. Bosley, C., Dodis, Y.: Does Privacy Require True Randomness? In: Vadhan, S.P. (ed.) TCC 2007. LNCS, vol. 4392, pp. 1–20. Springer, Heidelberg (2007)

8. Russell, A., Wang, H.: How to Fool an Unbounded Adversary with a Short Key. In: Knudsen, L.R. (ed.) EUROCRYPT 2002. LNCS, vol. 2332, pp. 133–148. Springer, Heidelberg (2002)

9. Dodis, Y., Smith, A.: Entropic Security and the Encryption of High Entropy Messages. In: Kilian, J. (ed.) TCC 2005. LNCS, vol. 3378, pp. 556–577. Springer, Heidelberg (2005)

10. Cachin, C., Maurer, U.M.: Unconditional Security against Memory-Bounded Adversaries. In: Kaliski Jr., B.S. (ed.) CRYPTO 1997. LNCS, vol. 1294, pp. 292–306. Springer, Heidelberg (1997)

11. Aumann, Y., Rabin, M.O.: Information Theoretically Secure Communication in the Limited Storage Space Model. In: Wiener, M. (ed.) CRYPTO 1999. LNCS, vol. 1666, pp. 65–79. Springer, Heidelberg (1999)

12. Ding, Y.Z., Rabin, M.O.: Hyper-Encryption and Everlasting Security. In: Alt, H., Ferreira, A. (eds.) STACS 2002. LNCS, vol. 2285, pp. 1–26. Springer, Heidelberg (2002)

13. Shannon, C.: A mathematical theory of communication. Bell System Technical Journal 27, 379–423 (1948)

14. Cover, T.M., Thomas, J.A.: Elements of Information Theory, 2nd edn. Wiley Series in Telecommunications. John Wiley & Sons, Inc. (1991)

15. Cachin, C., Maurer, U.: Entropy measures and unconditional security in cryptography (1997)

16. Massey, J.L.: Guessing and entropy. In: Proceedings of the 1994 IEEE International Symposium on Information Theory, p. 204 (1994)

17. Zuckerman, D.: General weak random sources. In: Proceedings of the 31st Annual Symposium on Foundations of Computer Science, SFCS 1990, vol. 2, pp. 534–543. IEEE Computer Society, Washington, DC (1990)

18. Csiszar, I., Korner, J.: Broadcast channels with confidential messages. IEEE Transactions on Information Theory 24(3), 339–348 (1978)

19. Katz, J., Lindell, Y.: Introduction to Modern Cryptography (Chapman & Hall/Crc Cryptography and Network Security Series). Chapman & Hall/CRC (2007)

Trading Robustness for Correctness and Privacy in Certain Multiparty Computations, beyond an Honest Majority

Anne Broadbent[1,2], Stacey Jeffery[1,2], Samuel Ranellucci[3], and Alain Tapp[3]

[1] Institute for Quantum Computing, University of Waterloo, Ontario, Canada
[2] School of Computer Science, University of Waterloo, Ontario, Canada
[3] DIRO, Université de Montréal, Quebec, Canada

Abstract. We improve on the classical results in information-theoretically secure multiparty computation among a set of n participants, by considering the special case of the computation of the *addition* function over binary inputs in the secure channels model with a *simultaneous* broadcast channel. This simple function is a useful building block for other applications. The classical results in multiparty computation show that in this model, every function can be computed with information-theoretic security if and only if less than $n/2$ participants are corrupt. In this article we show that, under certain conditions, this bound can be overcome.

More precisely, let $t^{(p)}, t^{(r)}$ and $t^{(c)}$ be the *privacy*, *robustness* and *correctness* thresholds; that is, the minimum number of participants that must be actively corrupted in order for privacy, robustness or correctness, respectively, to be compromised. We show a series of novel tradeoffs applicable to the multiparty computation of $f(x_1, \ldots, x_n) = x_1 + \ldots + x_n$ for $x_i \in \{0, 1\}$, culminating in the most general tradeoff: $t^{(p)} + t^{(r)} = n + 1$ and $t^{(c)} + t^{(r)} = n + 1$. These tradeoffs are applicable as long as $t^{(r)} < n/2$, which implies that, at the cost of reducing robustness, privacy and correctness are achievable despite a dishonest majority (as an example, setting the robustness threshold to $n/3$ yields privacy and correctness thresholds of $2n/3 + 1$).

We give applications to information-theoretically secure voting and anonymous message transmission, yielding protocols with the same tradeoffs.

Keywords: multiparty computation, secret sharing, information-theoretic security, simultaneous broadcast, addition, voting, anonymous communication.

1 Introduction

Secure multiparty computation [1] enables a group of n participants to collaborate in order to compute a global function on their private inputs. Assuming that private random keys are shared between each pair of participants, every function can be securely computed if and only if less than $\frac{n}{3}$ participants are corrupt. This

A. Smith (Ed.): ICITS 2012, LNCS 7412, pp. 14–36, 2012.

fundamental result is due to Chaum, Crépeau and Damgård [2] and to Ben-Or, Goldwasser and Wigderson [3]. When a broadcast channel is available, the results of Rabin and Ben-Or [4] tell us that this proportion can be improved to $\frac{n}{2}$.

In [5] and [6], Broadbent and Tapp presented multiparty protocols for voting and anonymous message transmission that are information-theoretically secure even in the presence of a dishonest majority. Along with the use of authenticated private communication, the protocol uses a simultaneous broadcast channel. In this paper we present a new approach in the same model that achieves better functionality.

In this article we show how to achieve tradeoffs between the privacy, correctness, and robustness thresholds for certain multiparty functions. In most multiparty computation results to date, the approach has been to define a model in which bounds on the numbers of corrupt players are known, and to define protocols that work in that model. In another approach, sometimes called hybrid security or multiple threshold security, no assumptions are made on the number or type of adversaries, but rather, various thresholds are given for different adversarial situations. This model reflects reality — it is never known in practice how many participants are honest. It is simply hoped that enough are honest for the security properties of the protocol to hold, some of which may be more important than others.

One way to accomplish this is to differentiate between various types of corrupt participants as is done by Fitzi, Hirt, Holenstein and Wullschleger in [7] and Fitzi, Hirt and Maurer in [8]. In the latter model, there are t_a actively corrupt players, whose behaviour is entirely controlled by the adversary, t_p passively corrupt players, whose entire information is known to the adversary, and t_f fail-corrupt players, who can be made to cease all participation in the protocol by the adversary, but are otherwise honest. Their results state that multiparty computation with zero failure probability can be done if and only if $3t_a + 2t_p + t_f < n$ (whether or not a broadcast channel is available), and multiparty computation with exponentially small failure probability is achievable given a broadcast if and only if $2t_a + 2t_p + t_f < n$; if no broadcast is available, the additional condition $3t_a + t_f < n$ is necessary and sufficient.

In a recent result by Lucas, Raub and Maurer [9], tradeoffs were given between information-theoretically secure robustness and computationally secure correctness and privacy for general multiparty computation, achieving the bounds established in [10]. We achieve a similar tradeoff, with information-theoretic correctness and privacy, that can be applied to a limited number of multiparty computation problems. The result of [9] is achieved using a technique called *virtual players*, where a set of participants simulate a new participant. We use another kind of virtual player called a *ghost* to achieve our tradeoffs.

1.1   Contributions

We define the function SUM : $\{0,1\}^n \to \{0,\ldots,n\}$ by SUM$(x_1,\ldots,x_n) = x_1 + \cdots + x_n$, the *integer* sum of n bits. If the input is regarded as an n-bit string, this function is the Hamming weight. We present three protocols for multiparty computation of SUM. Our protocols have the property that the outcome is always correct if all participants are honest.

The protocols can be trivially generalized to allow each participant an input in $\{0, \dots, k\}$ for arbitrary k by having each participant simulate k participants. Each of our protocols for multiparty sum yields protocols for voting and anonymous message transmission with the same security properties.

The first protocol achieves privacy and correctness in the presence of a dishonest majority of up to $n - 1$ actively corrupt participants, but has low robustness: a single participant can make the protocol abort. The corresponding voting protocol improves over the one from [5] and [6] by having an exact tally.

The second protocol trades privacy for correctness and robustness. For any $t \in [0, \frac{n}{2})$, the protocol is private whenever there are less than $n - t$ corrupt participants, and also correct and robust whenever there are less than $t + 1$ corrupt participants. This tradeoff is also applicable to the computation of *any* multiparty linear function. The third protocol achieves a similar but slightly improved tradeoff: privacy and correctness for robustness. For any $t \in [0, \frac{n}{2})$, the protocol is private *and correct* whenever there are less than $n - t$ corrupt participants, and also robust whenever there are less than $t + 1$ corrupt participants. The corresponding voting and anonymous message transmission protocols are an improvement over [5] and [6] in that robustness can be improved at the cost of a slight decrease in privacy and correctness. It may certainly be the case, particularly in an application such as voting, that privacy and correctness are much more important than robustness, however a robustness threshold greater than 1 may be desirable.

We begin by describing our model in Section 2. We then give some preliminaries, followed by our three protocols for multiparty sum in Sections 4, 5, and 6. Finally we show in Section 7 how those protocols can be generalized to larger inputs and how they can be turned into protocols for voting and anonymous message transmission. Due to lack of space, proofs are given in the Appendix.

2   Model and Definitions

In this section, we describe our model and give basic security definitions. For all our security definitions we assume an active adversary that completely controls a certain number of participants. We assume that all pairs of participants are connected by a private authenticated channel, which is equivalent to the assumption that they share a polynomial-sized private random key. We also assume that the participants have access to a simultaneous broadcast channel.

Definition 1. *An n participant simultaneous broadcast channel is a collection of n broadcast channels, one for each participant, such that each participant chooses his input to the broadcast before receiving the value of any other participant's broadcast.*

It is not uncommon in multiparty computation to allow additional resources, even if those resources cannot be implemented with the threshold on the honest participants (the results of [4], which combine a broadcast channel with $\frac{n}{2}$ honest participants being one example). Our work suggests that a simultaneous broadcast channel is an interesting primitive to study in this context. Sealed bid envelopes that are opened publicly are an example of a practical implementation of a simultaneous broadcast channel. Our protocols then provide *everlasting* security: as long as the computational assumptions are not broken *during* the execution of the protocol (more precisely, during the execution of the simultaneous broadcast), the security of the protocols is perfect. Note that breaking the computational assumption is not sufficient on its own to compromise privacy of the protocols.

Note that under the assumption that trapdoor one-way permutations exist, [11] gives a protocol for secure multiparty computation in our model; the advantage of our scheme is that we only require simultaneous broadcast.

Throughout this paper, we assume that n is even. We will use calligraphic script letters to denote the players involved in various schemes, such as $\mathcal{A}, \mathcal{B}, \mathcal{C}, \ldots$. Arrays will be denoted using standard vector notation $\boldsymbol{x}$ and array elements will be denoted with superscripts: $\boldsymbol{x} = (\boldsymbol{x}^{(1)}, \ldots, \boldsymbol{x}^{(\ell)})$. The notation $[y_1, \ldots, y_n] = $ SCHEME-Stage$[\mathcal{P}_1(x_1), \ldots, \mathcal{P}_n(x_n)]$ means that some stage, Stage, of some scheme, SCHEME, is being carried out, with players $\mathcal{P}_1, \ldots, \mathcal{P}_n$. Player i uses input x_i, and receives output y_i.

We will now present the main security definitions.

Definition 2. *A multiparty protocol for computing f is* private *if a group of corrupt participants, C, can learn no more about $x_1, \ldots, x_n$ than they would learn from $f(x_1, \ldots, x_n)$ for some choice of $\{x_i : i \in C\}$.*

The following two security properties, correctness and robustness, are generally both included in correctness. However, we view them as separate properties in light of the fact that obtaining an incorrect answer is often more problematic than aborting.

Definition 3. *A multiparty protocol for computing f is* correct *if (except with exponentially small probability), whenever the protocol does not abort, the output is consistent with the inputs of the honest participants and some fixed inputs for the dishonest participants, known to them before they learn the outcome of the protocol.*

Definition 4. *A multiparty protocol for computing f is* robust *if it is correct and does not abort except with exponentially small probability.*

In the case of a protocol aborting, we can view the output as NULL. If a subprotocol aborts, then by default the calling protocol aborts unless otherwise specified. Note that aborting conditional on some honest player's input is considered to be breaking privacy.

Definition 5. *We denote by $t^{(c)}$ the* correctness threshold, *or the minimum number of corrupt participants that can compromise correctness. Similarly, $t^{(p)}$ denotes the* privacy threshold, *and $t^{(r)}$ the* robustness threshold.

Unlike in [8], we only consider an active adversary; one with complete control over the actions of each player it corrupts. We do not consider an adversary who actively corrupts some amount of players and then passively corrupts some additional players. Additionally, though our notation is similar to [8], the meaning is quite different. In [8], the meaning of t_p is the number of participants that are passively corrupted, whereas in our model, $t^{(p)}$ is the minimum number of participants that must be actively corrupted for privacy to be lost.

We do not place any restrictions on the dishonest participants, though we assume that all corrupt participants are part of a single collusion, called the adversary.

3 Preliminaries

3.1 Sharing a Secret

All of our protocols are based on secret sharing [12], and derive their security properties in part from the secret sharing scheme used. A secret sharing scheme is a multiparty computational primitive, whereby a secret can be distributed over a group of participants such that an authorized group of participants can reconstruct the secret (correctness), and any unauthorized group of participants can learn nothing about the secret (privacy).

Note that the notions of privacy and correctness for secret sharing are slightly different than those for general multiparty computation, however we still use $t^{(p)}$, $t^{(c)}$, and later $t^{(r)}$, to denote the thresholds for privacy, correctness and robustness, respectively.

What defines an authorized group varies between secret sharing schemes. For instance, in some secret sharing schemes, an authorized subset of participants is defined to be any set of more than t participants, for some $t \leq n$. Such a secret sharing scheme is called a t-out-of-n threshold secret sharing scheme.

The first protocol, $\mathsf{SS}_{p,n}$ (see **Scheme 1**), uses a very basic n-out-of-n threshold secret sharing scheme. A secret sharing scheme has two phases, *distribute* and *reconstruct*. The distribution phase is a protocol for constructing shares of the secret and distributing them to the receivers. The reconstruction phase is a protocol by which an authorized set of receivers can reconstruct the secret.

Privacy in $\mathsf{SS}_{p,n}$ follows from the fact that, given any group of $n-1$ participants $\{\mathcal{P}_1, \ldots, \mathcal{P}_n\} \setminus \mathcal{P}_j$, there are p equiprobable possibilities for $\mathcal{P}_j$'s share, each corresponding to a distinct possibility for the secret $m = m_j + \sum_{i \neq j} m_i$ (mod p). Therefore, given $n-1$ shares, the secret is still completely unknown.

Definition 6. *We say that a secret sharing scheme* SCHEME *is linear if, for a publicly known integer a and any two secrets m and m' shared among $\mathcal{P}_1, \ldots, \mathcal{P}_n$, with shares $m_1, \ldots, m_n$ and $m'_1, \ldots, m'_n$ respectively, if $\{\mathcal{P}_{i_1}, \ldots, \mathcal{P}_{i_t}\}$ is an authorized subset of receivers, then* SCHEME-Rec$[\mathcal{P}_{i_1}(am_{i_1} + m'_{i_1}), \ldots, \mathcal{P}_{i_t}(am_{i_t} + m'_{i_t})]$ *outputs $am + m'$ to each $\mathcal{P}_{i_j}$.*

It is easy to see that $\mathsf{SS}_{p,n}$ is a linear secret sharing scheme.

Scheme 1. $SS_{p,n}$

Players: a sender S

$\qquad$ n receivers $R_1, \ldots, R_n$

Distribute: $[\emptyset, m_1, \ldots, m_n] = SS_{p,n}\text{Dist}[S(m), R_1, \ldots, R_n]$

$\quad$ **Input:** m, the secret, input by sender S

$\quad$ **Output:** m_i, the ith share, output to R_i for each i, such that $\sum_{i=1}^n m_i = m$ (mod p)

$\qquad$ 1. S chooses $m_i \in_R \mathbb{Z}_p$ for $i = 1, \ldots, n-1$, and sets $m_n = m - \sum_{i=1}^{n-1} m_i$ (mod p)

$\qquad$ 2. S sends m_i to R_i

Reconstruct: $[m, \ldots, m] = SS_{p,n}\text{Rec}[R_1(m_1), \ldots, R_n(m_n)]$

$\quad$ **Input:** m_i input by R_i for $i = 1, \ldots, n$

$\quad$ **Output:** m output to R_i for $i = 1, \ldots, n$

$\qquad$ 1. Each R_i for $i = 1, \ldots, n$, inputs m_i into the simultaneous broadcast channel.

$\qquad$ 2. Each R_i constructs $m = \sum_{j=1}^n m_j$ (mod p)

Definition 7. *A linear distributed secret,* $\text{LDS}[P_1, \ldots, P_n](m)$ *is a list of shares* (m_i), *each in possession of player* P_i, *such that* $[m_1, \ldots, m_n] = \text{SCHEME-Dist}[m]$ *for some linear secret sharing scheme* **SCHEME**.

3.2 Sub-protocols Used

Given a set of two or more linear distributed secrets $\text{LDS}[R_1, \ldots, R_n](m^{(j)})$, relative to any linear secret sharing scheme, the participants can always create a new linear distributed secret by the following: each R_i adds all his shares to get a share of $\sum_j m^{(j)}$. This simple procedure does not involve any interaction between participants, but allows them to generate a new shared secret: the sum of two or more previously shared secrets.

Procedure 1. shows how to generate randomness in a group of participants $\{P_1, \ldots, P_n\}$ with a simultaneous broadcast. As long as one participant is honest, the output is an unbiased integer between 0 and $p - 1$.

Procedure 1. $[a, \ldots, a] = \text{RANDOM}_{n,p}[P_1, \ldots, P_n]$

Players: n participants, $P_1, \ldots, P_n$

Output: An unbiased $a \in \mathbb{Z}_p$ is output to all players

---

1. Each participant P_i inputs $a_i \in_R \{0, \ldots, p-1\}$ into the simultaneous broadcast channel.

2. Each participant P_i sets $a = \sum_{i=1}^n a_i$ (mod p).

In order to bias the outcome, a corrupt participant's input would have to depend on the inputs of all other players. The simultaneous broadcast channel makes this impossible.

The following procedure can be used to check the equality of a set of linear distributed secrets, without revealing the values of the individual secrets. If there are two distinct secrets in the set, then the procedure outputs unequal except with exponentially small probability in the security parameter s. This procedure is used in our second and third protocols.

Procedure 2. EQUALITY$_s$

Players: n participants $\mathcal{P}_1, \ldots, \mathcal{P}_n$
Input: $\{X^j\}_{j=1}^{2s}$ a set of $2s$ LDSs, $X^j = \mathsf{LDS}(v_j)$
Output: equal or unequal

Repeat the following s times in parallel:

1. The participants use RANDOM to choose a random partition $\{P, Q\}$ of $\{X^j\}$ with $|P| = |Q| = s$.
2. The participants compute $Y = \sum_{j \in P} X^j - \sum_{j \in Q} X^j$.
3. The participants reconstruct the secret Y. If $Y \neq 0$ they output unequal.

If $Y = 0$ in every round, output equal.

---

4 Multiparty Sum with Bins

The first tool we will apply is the use of a concept we call *bins*. The intuitive description that follows makes clear the reason for this name.

The following physical analogy applies to all three of our protocols. The protocols are modelled after the concrete setup of an array of $2n$ bins. A participant may place a ball in any bin, but may not remove a ball from a bin or observe the contents of a bin. If $x_i = 1$, participant $\mathcal{P}_i$ chooses a random bin from $j = 1, \ldots, n$, called the *count bins*, and places his ball in the jth bin. Otherwise, if $x_i = 0$, $\mathcal{P}_i$ chooses a random bin from $j = n+1, \ldots, 2n$, called the *no-count bins*, and places his ball in the jth bin. When all balls have been placed, the totals for each bin are revealed and the sum over all balls in the count bins (the first n bins) is the output $y = \mathsf{SUM}(x_1, \ldots, x_n)$. So far the need for $2n$ bins instead of 2 bins is not clear, but we will soon explain this necessity.

For our protocols, we model each bin as an integer $\pmod{p}$, with an input x_i encoded as a string of $2n$ integers, one integer for each bin ($p \geq 2n + 1$). The ith integer of an encoded input represents the contents of the ith bin. In this case, a well-constructed input encoding has exactly one bin with value 1 and all other bins with value 0. In our protocols, each participant splits his input into shares, each share consisting of $2n$ integers $\pmod{p}$, with the property that each bin of the input array can be reconstructed from the bins of the shares using some secret sharing scheme. For instance, if we use SS, the bin-wise sum $\pmod{p}$ of the shares is equal to the encoded input. Given a set of bin array inputs shared among the n participants, it is easy to compute the tally without revealing any information about the inputs, by simply adding the shares and reconstructing the total. We require only that the secret sharing scheme used be linear.

Without looking at individual bin arrays, we must ensure that all bin arrays are well-constructed. If a participant attempts to contribute more than 1 ball to the total, or negate part of the total by a constant c by putting $p - c$ balls in the n count bins, then the sum over all $2n$ bins in the tally will not be equal to n. Thus, a cheating strategy would be to include $c + 1$ balls in the n count (respectively no-count) bins, and $-c = p - c$ balls in the n no-count (respectively count) bins. However, having $2n$ bins makes it likely that many bins will be empty and a negative number of balls, $p - c$, in an empty bin would be detected, since $p - c > n$. This justifies the need for $2n$ bins, as well as $p = 2n + 1$. A negative number of balls is detected with constant probability and repetition yields exponential security.

4.1   Protocol

Here we present the first protocol for SUM, which makes use of the bins idea. It may be useful to consider the simple secret sharing scheme, SS, but note that any linear secret sharing scheme would work.

The following procedure encodes a bit as described above.

Procedure 3. BIN-ARRAY$_n$

Input: $x \in \{0, 1\}$
Output: $\boldsymbol{x} = (\boldsymbol{x}^{(i)})_{i=1}^{2n}$

---

1. if $x = 1$ choose $j \in_R \{1, \dots, n\}$ otherwise if $x = 0$ chose $j \in_R \{n + 1, \dots, 2n\}$
2. for $i = 1, \dots, 2n$: if $i = j$, $\boldsymbol{x}^{(i)} = 1$, else $\boldsymbol{x}^{(i)} = 0$

We call an array encoding an integer in this way a BIN-ARRAY. We say that a BIN-ARRAY is *well-formed* if each bin is an integer in $\{0, 1\}$ and the sum over all bins is 1. A BIN-ARRAY that is not well-formed is called *ill-formed*.

We will need to distribute BIN-ARRAYs among the n participants. We can easily distribute shares of an array by simply creating shares of each entry. We define the following addition on shares of an array, which follows directly from the addition on the individual shares. Let $\boldsymbol{a}_i = (a_i^{(j)})_{j=1}^{\ell}$ and $\boldsymbol{b}_i = (b_i^{(j)})_{j=1}^{\ell}$ be two array-shares. Then $\boldsymbol{a}_i + \boldsymbol{b}_i = (a_i^{(j)} + b_i^{(j)})_{j=1}^{\ell}$.

We now give our first protocol for SUM.

Since the only way to break privacy is to break the secret sharing scheme, as long as we use a secret sharing scheme with $t^{(p)} = n$, such as SS, we get $t^{(p)}(\text{BIN-SUM}) = n$ (Theorem 1).

The only way for a adversary to make the output inconsistent with the honest inputs is to put more than 1 ball in either the count or the no-count bins. If they use more than 1 ball in total, it will be detected when the total number of balls in y is more than n, and the protocol will abort. To avoid this, the adversary must put -1 in some bin, and hope that it is non-empty. However, any bin is empty with constant probability, and so repetition yields exponential

---

Protocol 1. BIN-SUM$_{n,s}$

Players: n participants $\mathcal{P}_1, \ldots, \mathcal{P}_n$
Input: $\mathcal{P}_i$ inputs $x_i \in \{0,1\}$, for $i = 1, \ldots, n$
Output: Each participant gets output $y = x_1 + \cdots + x_n$

Repeat in parallel s times:

1. Each $\mathcal{P}_i$ creates $\boldsymbol{x}_i = \mathsf{BIN\text{-}ARRAY}_n(x_i)$ and distributes $X_i = \mathsf{LDS}[\mathcal{P}_1, \ldots, \mathcal{P}_n](\boldsymbol{x}_i)$ using some linear secret sharing scheme.
2. Participants create the sum, $Y = \sum_{j=1}^{n} X_j$.
3. Participants input their shares of Y into the simultaneous broadcast channel and reconstructs the value of Y, $\boldsymbol{y}$.
4. If the sum over all bins in $\boldsymbol{y}$ does not equal n, abort.
5. Each participant computes $y = \sum_{j=1}^{n} \boldsymbol{y}^{(j)}$, the total over all count bins of Y.

If the outcome y is not the same in every round, abort.

---

security. Therefore, no dishonest coalition of any size can make an output that is inconsistent with honest inputs, that is, $t^{(c)} = n$ (Theorem 2).

The major downfall of this protocol is that any participant can make the protocol abort. In other words, $t^{(r)} = 1$ (Theorem 3). In many situations, such as voting (see Section 7.1), it may be desirable to have $t^{(p)}$ and $t^{(c)}$ much higher than $t^{(r)}$, however, it is often desirable to have $t^{(r)} > 1$. In our next protocol, we allow $t^{(r)}$ to be as high as $\frac{n}{2}$ at the expense of some privacy and correctness.

5   Multiparty Sum with Bins and Ghosts

The second tool we make use of is the concept of *ghost players*. Given a verifiable secret sharing scheme with privacy, correctness and robustness thresholds $t^{(p)} = t^{(c)} = t^{(r)} = \frac{n}{2}$, we modify the protocol as follows. During the distribution phase, the sender creates $n + g$ shares, distributes n of them, and discards g of them, for some $g \in [0, n)$. This lowers the proportion of actively corrupt participants by adding participants who cannot be actively corrupted. Now $\frac{n+g}{2}$ corrupt players are required to break privacy, and ghost players cannot contribute to this corrupt coalition. Thus we get privacy threshold $t^{(p)} = \frac{n+g}{2}$. In order to prevent the correct reconstruction of a secret, we need $\frac{n+g}{2}$ corrupt players. We can't assume the ghosts do not contribute to such a collusion, so among the real players, we have correctness and robustness thresholds of $t^{(c)} = t^{(r)} = \frac{n+g}{2} - g = \frac{n-g}{2}$. We thus obtain a tradeoff between correctness and robustness, $t = \frac{n-g}{2}$, and privacy, $n - t$, where $t \in [0, \frac{n}{2})$. Again, our protocol implements the multiparty computation of SUM, but we can also use the linearity of the underlying secret sharing scheme to show that this tradeoff can be applied to any *linear* function as well. (Note that our function, SUM is not actually linear, because of the restriction that the input be in $\{0,1\}$). This is accomplished, without the use of bins. Each participant simply distributes his input x_i to some linear function f, using the verifiable secret sharing scheme we now present,

GVSS. Each participant computes f on his shares of the inputs and outputs the resulting share of $f(x_1, \ldots, x_n)$.

We can view the ghosts as a kind of virtual player. Since these ghost players do nothing, they are all fail-corrupt. However, they are honest in every other respect.

We do require that the secret sharing scheme to which we apply the ghost modification be verifiable to gain the desired accuracy and robustness thresholds. We now detail this concept.

5.1   Verifiable Secret Sharing

Verifiable secret sharing is an extension of secret sharing that allows reconstruction of a secret even in the presence of faulty or missing shares. More formally, a verifiable secret sharing scheme is a secret sharing scheme with the following properties:

P1. If the sender is honest, then before the reconstruction phase has been initiated, the adversary has no information about the secret.

C1. The probability that the distribution phase completes successfully and there exist distinct m and m' such that both m and m' have non-negligible probability of being the outcome of the reconstruction phase is exponentially small. If the sender is honest, the unique m that can be the outcome of reconstruction with non-negligible probability is the message input by the sender during the distribution phase.

R1. The probability that the distribution succeeds and the reconstruction phase outputs NULL is exponentially small (even if the sender is corrupted). If the sender is honest, the distribution phase succeeds except with exponentially small probability.

In any verifiable secret sharing scheme, each property will be subject to some threshold of corrupt participants. Property **R1** and **C1** are often combined, but we will find it convenient to discuss them separately.

It is not difficult to see that these properties are necessary to obtain our tradeoff, for otherwise we could not reconstruct a non-NULL secret from the uncorrupted shares.

There exist linear verifiable secret sharing schemes with $t^{(c)} = t^{(r)} = t^{(p)} = \frac{n}{2}$ [13]. We can use such a scheme, in conjunction with the usage of ghost players, to get an improved protocol for SUM. The protocol, which we call GHOST-SUM, is similar to BIN-SUM, but we require the secret sharing scheme used to be a verifiable secret sharing scheme, and we modify the distribution phase slightly. In addition, we add some verification steps to ensure that the inputs are well-formed in order to increase robustness.

Let VSS_n be a black box $\frac{n}{2}$-out-of-n-threshold verifiable secret sharing scheme (satisfying properties **P1**, **C1**, and **R1**) with distribution phase $[\emptyset, m_1, \ldots, m_n] = \mathsf{VSS}_n \mathsf{Dist}[\mathcal{S}(m), \mathcal{R}_1, \ldots, \mathcal{R}_n]$. We define the distribution phase of $\mathsf{GVSS}_{n,g}$ as:

$$\mathsf{GVSS}_{n,g}\mathsf{Dist}[\mathcal{S}(m), \mathcal{R}_1, \ldots, \mathcal{R}_n] = \mathsf{VSS}_{n+g}\mathsf{Dist}[\mathcal{S}(m), \mathcal{R}_1, \ldots, \mathcal{R}_n, \mathcal{S}, \ldots, \mathcal{S}]$$

In words, the distribution phase of $\mathsf{GVSS}_{n,g}$ is just the distribution phase of VSS_{n+g}, where $\mathcal{S}$ does not distribute the last g shares to other players. These shares are considered to be discarded.

In our second protocol, the use of a verifiable secret sharing scheme means that the participants commit to their inputs in some way. In BIN-SUM with SS, a participant can change his input any time he wants in an arbitrary way by simply changing his own share of his input. In contrast, after the distribution stage of a verifiable secret sharing scheme, the sender is committed to his secret. Therefore, in this second protocol, we introduce some verification steps where the participants check that the committed BIN-ARRAYs are well-formed without learning their values. This allows us to raise the robustness threshold by detecting and eliminating ill-formed BIN-ARRAYs.

One tool we will use in the verification is equality testing. This allows participants to check that in every round the inputs from a particular participant have the same value.

Procedure 4. BIN-ARRAY-EQUALITY$_s$

Players: n participants $\mathcal{P}_1, \ldots, \mathcal{P}_n$

Input: $\{X^j\}_{j=1}^{s^2}$, a set of LDSs, with $X^j = \mathsf{LDS}(v_j)$ where $v_j = (v_j^{(\ell)})_{\ell=1}^{2n}$ is a BIN-ARRAY

Output: equal or unequal

For $i = 1, \ldots, s - 1$:

1. For $j = (i-1)s + 1, \ldots, (i+1)s$
   (a) $Y^j = \sum_{\ell=1}^{n} \mathsf{LDS}(v_\ell^{(j)})$
   (b) $N^j = \sum_{\ell=n+1}^{2n} \mathsf{LDS}(v_\ell^{(j)})$
2. Compute $\mathsf{EQUALITY}(\{Y^j\}_{j=(i-1)s+1}^{(i+1)s})$ and $\mathsf{EQUALITY}(\{N^j\}_{j=(i-1)s+1}^{(i+1)s})$. If either outputs unequal, return unequal.

Return equal.

This procedure takes s sets of s shared BIN-ARRAYs and checks that they encode the same value. It does this by equality testing with two sets at a time, testing the equality of the sum over the count bins, Y^j, as well as the sum over the no-count bins, N^j.

The other verification technique involves opening some BIN-ARRAYs to see that they are well-formed. In order to avoid revealing the value of the opened BIN-ARRAYs, each participant shares his BIN-ARRAYs with the bins permuted. Some of the BIN-ARRAYs are selected for opening, and the sender reveals the permutations on his unopened BIN-ARRAYs so that they can be unpermuted before computation takes place.

What we have essentially done here is to throw away the correctness of the first protocol, making it the same property as robustness. We then use the ghost players to establish a tradeoff between privacy and correctness/robustness. The result is a threshold tradeoff $(t^{(p)}, t^{(c)}, t^{(r)}) = (n - t, t + 1, t + 1)$ for any $t \in [0, \frac{n}{2})$,

---

Protocol 2. GHOST-SUM$_{n,s,g}$

Players: n participants $\mathcal{P}_1, \ldots, \mathcal{P}_n$
Input: $\mathcal{P}_i$ inputs $x_i \in \{0,1\}$, for $i = 1, \ldots, n$
Output: Each participant gets output $y = x_1 + \cdots + x_n$

Preparation Each $\mathcal{P}_i$ creates s *sets* of $2s$ copies of identical BIN-ARRAY$_n(x_i)$s. The BIN-ARRAYs should vary randomly over different sets, but be identical within a set. $\mathcal{P}_i$ then applies a random permutation to each BIN-ARRAY.

Distribution Each BIN-ARRAY is distributed among all n participants using GVSS$_{n,g}$Dist. If any call to GVSS$_{n,g}$Dist aborts, the sender is excluded from future steps of the protocol.

Verification 1 For each set of $2s$ BIN-ARRAYs:

1. Half the BIN-ARRAYs are opened (chosen using RANDOM) and checked for well-formedness.

2. For each unopened BIN-ARRAY in this iteration, $\mathcal{P}_i$ broadcasts the permutations on the bins, which each participant applies to his shares of that BIN-ARRAY.

Verification 2 For each participant $\mathcal{P}_i$, all s^2 of $\mathcal{P}_i$'s unopened BIN-ARRAYs are put into BIN-ARRAY-EQUALITY. If it returns unequal then $\mathcal{P}_i$'s shares are discarded and he is excluded from future steps of the protocol.

Computation For each participant $\mathcal{P}_i$, the participants choose the first unopened BIN-ARRAY from each *set* and use these to compute s parallel totals, as in **Protocol 1**. If each repetition does not give the same answer the protocol aborts.

---

by setting $g = n - 2t$ (**Theorem 8** and **9**). However, by using a verifiable secret sharing scheme with certain desirable properties, we can keep correctness fairly high, and then use the ghosts to establish a tradeoff between privacy/correctness and robustness. In our third and final protocol, we do just that.

6 Multiparty Sum with Bins, Ghosts and Commitments

We now present our third and final protocol for SUM. It has the strongest security properties, with $(t^{(p)}, t^{(c)}, t^{(r)}) = (n - t, n - t, t + 1)$.

This new protocol uses the concept of ghosts, just as in the second, but we obtain an improved tradeoff by making use of the particular properties of a specific verifiable secret sharing scheme from [14].

6.1 Verifiable Secret Sharing with Signatures

We will outline the verifiable secret sharing scheme of [14], which we call ICVSS, and show that it has the properties we require to achieve our improved tradeoff.

The scheme makes use of an information-theoretically secure pseudo-signature that has the properties we require. The secret is encoded as $f(0)$ for some degree

$\leq \frac{n}{2}$ polynomial f, with shares $f(i)$ for $i \in \{1, \ldots, n\}$. Each player P_i *commits* to his shares by distributing signed shares of his shares, which we call *subshares*.

The signature scheme involves a signer S, an intermediate receiver I, and several final receivers $R_1, \ldots, R_n$. The three stages are as follows:

Distribute. S sends a message m to I, and some auxiliary signature information to I and each R_i.

Confirm. For each i, I and R_i carry out computations on their auxiliary information to ensure that if R_i is honest, he will accept m in the reveal phase.

Reveal. I reveals m to all R_i and gives each R_i some auxiliary information. Each R_i accepts or rejects m. If more than $t^{(r)}$ receivers accept, then m is considered to be accepted.

The signature scheme has the following properties:

SC1. If S, I, and at least $t^{(r)}$ of $R_1, \ldots, R_n$ are honest, then each honest R_i will accept in the reveal phase.

SC2. If I, R_i, and at least $t^{(r)} - 1$ other receivers are honest, then after the confirm phase, I knows a message m such that R_i will accept m in the reveal phase.

SC3. If S, R_i, and at least $t^{(c)} - 1$ other receivers are honest, then R_i will reject every value $\tilde{m} \neq m$ except with exponentially small probability.

SP1. If S and I are honest, then no R_i can learn any information about m before the reveal phase.

SL1. If c is a publicly known scalar, and σ and σ' represent signatures for messages m and m' respectively, then $c\sigma + \sigma'$ is a signature for $cm + m'$.

A pseudo-signature scheme is a kind of commitment scheme. We say that S *commits to m through I*. Of course, the value of m is only committed to from the perspective of $R_1, \ldots, R_n$, who must have received some auxiliary information during the distribute and confirm phases. However, for simplicity, we will gloss over this fact by saying S commits to m through I and assume that every participant in the calling protocol is implicitly a receiver. When we say that some I *opens a commitment* we mean that he carries out the reveal phase.

A pseudo-signature scheme with the above properties, as well as a verifiable secret sharing scheme based on these signatures can be found in [14]. Both have thresholds $t^{(r)} = t^{(c)} = t^{(p)} = \frac{n}{2}$. We now present their secret sharing scheme, which will form the basis for our third protocol.

Definition 8. *A vector of shares $(m_1, \ldots, m_n)$ is t-consistent if there exists a polynomial f of degree at most t containing every point (i, m_i) for $i = 1, \ldots, n$.*

We can characterize the exact property of ICVSS that allows us to achieve our improved tradeoff for SUM. In order to achieve correctness in SUM, we require that the secret sharing scheme have a weaker version of the correctness property, since some of the correctness of SUM comes from the bin technique and verification steps. The property is as follows:

Scheme 2. ICVSS_n

Players: a sender $\mathcal{S}$
  n receivers $\mathcal{R}_1, \ldots, \mathcal{R}_n$

Distribute: $[\emptyset, m_1, \ldots, m_n] = \mathsf{ICVSS}_n \mathsf{Dist}[\mathcal{S}(m), \mathcal{R}_1, \ldots, \mathcal{R}_n]$
  Input: m, the secret, input by sender $\mathcal{S}$
  Output: m_i, the ith share, output to receiver i, $\mathcal{R}_i$
  1. $\mathcal{S}$ randomly chooses $f \in \mathbb{Z}_p[x][y]$ of degree at most $\frac{n}{2}$ in each variable such that $f(0,0) = m$. Let $m_{ij} = f(i,j)$. For each $i \in \{1, \ldots, n\}$, $\mathcal{S}$ sends $\mathcal{R}_i$ the vectors $\boldsymbol{c}_i = (m_{1i}, \ldots, m_{ni})$ and $\boldsymbol{r}_i = (m_{i1}, \ldots, m_{in})$ $\mathcal{S}$ commits to $\boldsymbol{c}_i$ and $\boldsymbol{r}_i$ through $\mathcal{R}_i$. Set $m_i = (\boldsymbol{c}_i, \boldsymbol{r}_i)$.
  2. Each receiver $\mathcal{R}_i$ checks that the two vectors he received are $\frac{n}{2}$-consistent. If not, $\mathcal{R}_i$ opens the inconsistent vector that $\mathcal{S}$ committed to. If the commitment is accepted, then the protocol aborts.
  3. For $i = 1, \ldots, n$ and $j = 1, \ldots, n$ with $j \neq i$, $\mathcal{R}_i$ sends $\mathcal{R}_j$ the share m_{ji}. $\mathcal{R}_i$ commits to m_{ji} through $\mathcal{R}_j$. $\mathcal{R}_i$ ensures that the value he receives from $\mathcal{R}_j$, $\tilde{m}_{ij}$ matches his m_{ij}. If $m_{ij} \neq \tilde{m}_{ij}$ then $\mathcal{R}_i$ opens the commitment to m_{ij} from $\mathcal{S}$ and the commitment to $\tilde{m}_{ij}$ from $\mathcal{R}_j$. Seeing this, $\mathcal{R}_j$ opens the commitment to $\tilde{m}_{ij}$ from $\mathcal{S}$ (or is disqualified). If all commitments are accepted, then the protocol aborts.

Reconstruct: $[m, \ldots, m] = \mathsf{ICVSS}_n \mathsf{Rec}[\mathcal{R}_1(m_1), \ldots, \mathcal{R}_n(m_n)]$
  Input: m_i input by $\mathcal{R}_i$ for $i = 1, \ldots, n$
  Output: m output to $\mathcal{R}_i$ for $i = 1, \ldots, n$
  1. Each $\mathcal{R}_i$ inputs his row $\boldsymbol{r}_i = (m_{i1}, \ldots, m_{in})$ into the simultaneous broadcast channel, and for each j, opens the commitment from $\mathcal{R}_j$ to m_{ij}. If any of these commitments are rejected, then $\mathcal{R}_i$ is disqualified. All other players check that this row is $\frac{n}{2}$-consistent.
  2. The secret m can be interpolated from the shares of non-disqualified players.

C' Suppose the behaviour of corrupt parties results in the reconstruct phase outputting $\tilde{m}$. Before the reconstruction phase has completed they have exactly as much information about $\tilde{m}$ as they have about the secret.

What this property essentially means is that the corrupt participants, though they may be able to change the output of the reconstruction phase, cannot *control* the outcome if they don't know m. That is, if the number of corrupt participants is less than the privacy threshold, then the corrupt participants cannot control the outcome of the reconstruction phase.

Since ghosts are fail-corrupt participants, we require that fail-corrupt participants can't help break privacy or this weaker correctness of the scheme. For privacy, this is true of any verifiable secret sharing scheme (See Theorem 4).

Any scheme that satisfies these properties can give us the improved tradeoff. By Theorems 4 and 14, ICVSS has the required properties.

6.2   Protocol

We use a secret sharing scheme similar to GVSS called IC-GVSS. It is identical to GVSS except that the underlying verifiable secret sharing scheme is ICVSS.

Protocol 3. IC-GHOST-SUM$_{n,s,g}$

Players: n participants $\mathcal{P}_1, \ldots, \mathcal{P}_n$
Input: $\mathcal{P}_i$ inputs $x_i \in \{0, 1\}$, for $i = 1, \ldots, n$
Output: Each participant gets output $y = x_1 + \cdots + x_n$

Preparation Each $\mathcal{P}_i$ creates s *sets* of $2s$ copies of identical BIN-ARRAY$_n(x_i)$s. The BIN-ARRAYs should vary randomly over different sets, but be identical within a set. $\mathcal{P}_i$ then applies a random permutation to each BIN-ARRAY.

Distribution Each BIN-ARRAY is distributed among all n participants using IC-GVSS-Dist$_{n,g}$. If any call to IC-GVSS-Dist$_{n,g}$ aborts, the sender is excluded from future steps of the protocol.

Verification1 For each set of $2s$ BIN-ARRAYs:
  1. Half the BIN-ARRAYs are opened (chosen using RANDOM), including the commitments by the sender of that set. The opened BIN-ARRAYs are checked for well-formedness. If one of a participant's BIN-ARRAYs is found to be ill-formed, his shares are discarded and he is excluded from future steps.
  2. For each unopened BIN-ARRAY in this iteration, $\mathcal{P}_i$ broadcasts the permutations on the bins, which each participant applies to his shares of that BIN-ARRAY.

Verification2 For each participant $\mathcal{P}_i$, all s^2 of $\mathcal{P}_i$'s unopened BIN-ARRAYs are put into BIN-ARRAY-EQUALITY. If it returns unequal then $\mathcal{P}_i$'s shares are discarded and he is excluded from future steps.

Computation For each participant $\mathcal{P}_i$, the participants choose the first unopened BIN-ARRAY from each *set* and use these to compute s parallel totals, as in **Protocol 1**. If each repetition does not give the same answer the protocol aborts.

In IC-GHOST-SUM we achieve the desired threshold tradeoff $(t^{(p)}, t^{(c)}, t^{(r)}) = (n - t, n - t, t + 1)$ for any $t \in [0, \frac{n}{2})$, by setting $g = n - 2t$ (Theorems 15, 17, 18 and 19). Table 1 summarizes the characteristics of the three protocols.

Table 1. Thresholds on privacy $t^{(p)}$, correctness $t^{(c)}$ and robustness $t^{(r)}$, for our three main protocols that compute addition of binary inputs. The parameter $t \in [0, \frac{n}{2})$ yields various tradeoffs for protocols GHOST-SUM and IC-GHOST-SUM. The tradeoff for protocol GHOST-SUM is also applicable to the computation of any linear function.

	$t^{(p)}$	$t^{(c)}$	$t^{(r)}$
BIN-SUM	n	n	1
GHOST-SUM	$n - t$	$t + 1$	$t + 1$
IC-GHOST-SUM	$n - t$	$n - t$	$t + 1$

7   Applications

The sum of bits is a very basic function that can be useful in several contexts. In this section we present two very distinct applications. The first one, voting, is very natural. The second application is less obvious and regards anonymous transmission of information. We would first like to point out the fact that it is very easy to modify the three SUM protocols to have a more general set of inputs than bits. More precisely, by having each participant simulate k participants, it is possible to perform the sum of integers between 0 and k.

7.1   Voting

The multiparty problem of voting is as follows. Players $\mathcal{P}_i$ for $i = 1, \ldots, n$ input $x_i \in \{0, \ldots, c - 1\}$. The output is $f(x_1, \ldots, x_n) = (t_1, \ldots, t_c)$ where $t_j = |\{i : x_i = j\}|$. Each player inputs a choice in $\{0, \ldots, c-1\}$ and the output is the tally of how many players voted for each of the c choices.

To see how the same ideas applied to multiparty sum can be applied to voting, we can think of SUM as a vote for one of two choices, where submitting your vote to the tally (i.e., putting your ball in one of the first n bins) corresponds to voting for one choice, and withholding your vote from the tally (i.e., putting your ball in one of the last n bins) corresponds to voting for the other choice. In fact, we may regard the first n bins as one tally, and the last set of n bins as a separate tally. We can generalise by considering cn bins, with bins $(i - 1)n + 1, \ldots, in$ corresponding to the ith candidate, or choice. Similar to the protocols for SUM, the total over all bins in the final tally must be equal to n or the protocol aborts.

We can easily extend the voting protocol to allow each voter k votes. This could allow a voter to weigh various candidates as he chooses, for instance, giving several votes to his favourite candidate, who he may feel is unlikely to win, and several votes to his second favourite candidate, who is more likely to win the majority. A further application of multiple votes is a multi-issue ballot, where a voter can divide his votes among issues as he chooses.

Another less straightforward extension of the voting protocol could transform it into a more practical protocol. A set of distinguished players, called voting authorities, can be introduced. Channels would only be required between each participant and each authority, as well as between all authorities. The initial sharing stage would be similar, but all subsequent stages of the protocol would be carried out by the voting authorities. All thresholds now apply to the authorities, including robustness. Note that even if we were to use the simple secret sharing scheme SS, no dishonest coalition of non-authority voters can make the protocol abort. This is true because of the verification stages, which find ill-formed votes except with exponentially small probability.

7.2   Anonymous Message Transmission

The multiparty problem of anonymous message transmission is as follows. One or more players $\mathcal{P}_i$ from $i = 1, \ldots, n$ inputs a message $x_i \in \{0, 1, \perp\}^{\ell}$ and a designated receiver $\mathcal{R}$ receives the multiset of all transmitted messages $M = \{x_i\}$.

We require two privacy properties to hold: if $\mathcal{P}_i$ sends message x_i, then for each $j \neq i$, $\mathcal{P}_j$ learns nothing about x_i; and for each $x_i \in M$, $\mathcal{R}$ has no information about i (the receiver learns nothing about the identity of any sender).

The protocols in [5] and [6] achieve unconditional privacy, but a single participant can cause the protocol to fail. In addition, the protocols abort whenever two players try to send messages simultaneously. In this section, we describe a protocol which trades privacy for robustness and allows any set of messages to be sent. We do this by slightly modifying the voting protocol from Section 7.1 to achieve anonymous message transmission. We get the same security properties in this modified protocol.

Anonymous bit transmission, the case where $\ell = 1$, can be achieved by a three candidate vote. The first candidate represents 0, the second candidate represents 1, and the third candidate represents no message, $\perp$. We call this a BIT-BIN-ARRAY. At the end of the computation, the shares of the total are sent to the receiver, rather than broadcast to all participants. The receiver then knows how many participants sent him the message 0, and how many sent 1.

We can efficiently generalise the above idea to larger ℓ, by defining a MESSAGE as a vector of ℓ BIT-BIN-ARRAYs. (In the case of a message of arbitrary length, we don't need $\perp$, since we can encode the sending of no message as some string, say the all zeros string, but we leave it in for simplicity). We have two additional requirements.

A bin can be defined by a pair of numbers, (c, b), where $c \in \{0, 1, \perp\}$ represents the candidate, or choice, that the bin falls under, and b denotes the bin number *within that candidate*. The first requirement is that every BIT-BIN-ARRAY in a MESSAGE must have a single non-empty bin, as in a standard vote, but the *bin number* (b) of the non-empty bin must be the same in each message. That is, to show that two bits are part of the same message, they must use the same bin (in different BIT-BIN-ARRAYs).

Secondly, in order to distinguish between different messages, we require that two senders don't choose the same bin number b.

The second requirement can be solved by increasing the number of bins in a BIT-BIN-ARRAY from $3n$ to $3n^2$. We then have $b \in [n^2]$, so in each round, the probability that two messages collide is bounded by a constant. Repetition

---

Procedure 5. BIN-NUMBER-EQUALITY$_s$

Players: $\mathcal{P}_1, \ldots, \mathcal{P}_n$
Input: $(X^j)_{j=1}^{\ell}$ a set of s LDSs, $X^j = \text{LDS}(v_j^{(i)})_{i=1}^{6s}$
Output: equal or unequal

For $k = 1, \ldots, n^2$:

1. For $j = 1, \ldots, \ell$, $Y^j = v_j^{(k)} + v_j^{(n^2+k)} + v_j^{(2n^2+k)}$
2. Compute EQUALITY$(\{Y^j\}_{j=1}^{\ell})$. If it outputs unequal, return unequal.

Return equal.

---

yields exponential probability that there will be some round in which no two messages collide.

For the first requirement, we simply need to add an extra step to the second verification phase, where we call the following procedure on each MESSAGE for each sender.

The above protocol simply ensures that, for any MESSAGE and any bin number $b \in [n^2]$, the sum of the values in bins $(0, b)$, $(1, b)$, and $(\perp, b)$ are same in each BIT-BIN-ARRAY throughout the MESSAGE. If that MESSAGE uses bin b, the sums will all be 1 (since exactly one of 0, 1, and $\perp$ was chosen for each bit of the message) and otherwise the sums will all be 0.

References

1. Yao, A.C.: Protocols for secure computations. In: Proceedings of the 23rd Annual Symposium on the Foundations of Computer Science (FOCS 1982), pp. 160–164. IEEE (1982)
2. Chaum, D., Crépeau, C., Damgård, I.: Multiparty unconditionally secure protocols. In: Simon, J. (ed.) Proceedings of the 20th annual ACM Symposium on Theory of Computing (STOC 1988), pp. 11–19. ACM (1988)
3. Ben-Or, M., Goldwasser, S., Wigderson, A.: Completeness theorems for non-cryptographic fault-tolerant distributed computation. In: Simon, J. (ed.) Proceedings of the 20th Annual ACM Symposium on Theory of Computing (STOC 1988), pp. 1–10. ACM (1988)
4. Rabin, T., Ben-Or, M.: Verifiable secret sharing and multiparty protocols with honest majority. In: Johnson, D.S. (ed.) Proceedings of the 21st Annual ACM Symposium on Theory of Computing (STOC 1989), pp. 73–85. ACM (1989)
5. Broadbent, A., Tapp, A.: Information-Theoretic Security Without an Honest Majority. In: Kurosawa, K. (ed.) ASIACRYPT 2007. LNCS, vol. 4833, pp. 410–426. Springer, Heidelberg (2007)
6. Broadbent, A., Tapp, A.: Information-theoretically secure voting without an honest majority. In: Proceedings of the IAVoSS Workshop On Trustworthy Elections, WOTE 2008 (2008), Cryptology ePrint Archive: Report 2008/266
7. Fitzi, M., Hirt, M., Holenstein, T., Wullschleger, J.: Two-Threshold Broadcast and Detectable Multi-party Computation. In: Biham, E. (ed.) EUROCRYPT 2003. LNCS, vol. 2656, pp. 51–67. Springer, Heidelberg (2003)
8. Fitzi, M., Hirt, M., Maurer, U.: Trading Correctness for Privacy in Unconditional Multi-party Computation. In: Krawczyk, H. (ed.) CRYPTO 1998. LNCS, vol. 1462, pp. 121–136. Springer, Heidelberg (1998)
9. Lucas, C., Raub, D., Maurer, U.: Hybrid-secure MPC: Trading information-theoretic robustness for computational privacy. In: Proceedings of the 29th Annual ACM SIGACT-SIGOPS Symposium on Principles of Distributed Computing (PODC 2010), pp. 219–228. ACM (2010)
10. Ishai, Y., Kushilevitz, E., Lindell, Y., Petrank, E.: On Combining Privacy with Guaranteed Output Delivery in Secure Multiparty Computation. In: Dwork, C. (ed.) CRYPTO 2006. LNCS, vol. 4117, pp. 483–500. Springer, Heidelberg (2006)
11. Fitzi, M., Gottesman, D., Hirt, M., Holenstein, T., Smith, A.: Detectable Byzantine agreement secure against faulty majorities. In: Proceedings of the 21st Annual Symposium on Principles of Distributed Computing (PODC 2002), pp. 118–126. ACM (2002)

12. Shamir, A.: How to share a secret. Communications of the ACM 22, 612–613 (1979)
13. Cramer, R., Damgård, I., Maurer, U.: General Secure Multi-party Computation from any Linear Secret-Sharing Scheme. In: Preneel, B. (ed.) EUROCRYPT 2000. LNCS, vol. 1807, pp. 316–334. Springer, Heidelberg (2000)
14. Cramer, R., Damgård, I., Dziembowski, S., Hirt, M., Rabin, T.: Efficient Multiparty Computations Secure against an Adaptive Adversary. In: Stern, J. (ed.) EUROCRYPT 1999. LNCS, vol. 1592, pp. 311–326. Springer, Heidelberg (1999)

A Proofs

A.1 Properties of BIN-SUM

Theorem 1. $t^{(p)}(\text{BIN-SUM}) = n$.

Proof. The privacy threshold of BIN-SUM follows directly from that of the employed secret sharing scheme. If we use a threshold scheme with threshold n, such as SS, then we get $t^{(p)} = n$ in BIN-SUM.

Theorem 2. $t^{(c)}(\text{BIN-SUM}) = n$.

Proof. Suppose a coalition of $c < n$ dishonest voters wishes to cause the sum to be incorrect. If they deposit more than c balls between them, the final tally over all bins will be greater than n and the protocol will abort. Thus, the only way for them to cause the final sum to be inconsistent with the honest inputs is for at least one dishonest participant to put a negative number of balls in at least one bin, say bin b. If no other participant deposits a ball in bin b, then the bin total will be $p - 1 > n$, so the protocol will abort. For a participant to succeed in depositing a negative ball in a count bin (respectively no-count bin), he must put his negative ball in a no-count bin (respectively count bin) with at least one ball in it. Even in the worst case where all $n - 1$ other balls are deposited in the no-count bins, the probability that bin b is empty is $(\frac{n-1}{n})^{n-1}$, which is greater than $\frac{1}{3}$ for all n. By repeating the protocol s times, the probability that a participant successfully deposits a negative ball without the protocol aborting is less than $(\frac{2}{3})^s$.

Theorem 3. $t^{(r)}(\text{BIN-SUM}) = 1$.

Proof. A single participant need only encode a number that is strictly greater than 1 to cause the total number of balls in all bins to be strictly greater than n, making the protocol abort.

A.2 Properties of GVSS

Theorem 4. *Suppose an honest sender has distributed a secret m using any verifiable secret sharing scheme with privacy threshold $t^{(p)}$. Then a coalition of $t^{(p)} - 1$ actively corrupt parties and any number of fail-corrupt participants can't gain any information about m.*

Proof. Suppose the actively corrupt participants could learn some information about m. This information must be a function of the private communication transcript for each corrupt player, as well as the transcript of all public broadcasts. A fail-corrupt participant adds no information to these, since he does not communicate at all. Therefore, if the actively corrupt participants could gain information about m in the presence of fail-corrupt players, they could do so without the fail-corrupt players, contradicting the threshold $t^{(p)}$.

Theorem 5. *Suppose an honest sender has distributed a secret m using* $\mathsf{GVSS}_{n,g}$. *Then a coalition of less than $\frac{n+g}{2}$ dishonest participants can't learn any information about m except with exponentially small probability.*

Proof. There are at most $\frac{n+g}{2} - 1$ actively corrupt participants, out of $n + g$ participants total. The rest are either fail-corrupt (ghosts) or honest. therefore, by Theorem 4, the actively corrupt participants can learn no information about m.

Theorem 6. *Suppose less than $\frac{n-g}{2}$ participants are corrupt. The probability that the distribution phase of* $\mathsf{GVSS}_{n,g}$ *outputs shares $m_1, \ldots, m_n$ to receivers $\mathcal{R}_1, \ldots, \mathcal{R}_n$ and there is no fixed m such that the reconstruction phase will output m is exponentially small.*

Proof. Suppose there are $\frac{n-g}{2} - 1$ corrupt participants. There are $n - (\frac{n-g}{2} - 1) = \frac{n+g}{2} + 1$ honest participants, so with probability exponentially close to 1, the distribution phase aborts, or it succeeds and there exists a fixed value m such that $\mathsf{VSS}_{n+g}\mathsf{Rec}$ will output m except with exponentially small probability, by properties **C1** and **R1** of VSS (with threshold $\frac{n}{2}$ for n participants).

A.3   Properties of **GHOST-SUM**

Theorem 7. EQUALITY *detects inequality* $(\bmod\ p)$ *in* $\{X^i\}$, *except with exponentially small probability.*

Proof. Suppose the input $\{X^j\}$ is unequal. Let P and Q be any partition of $\{X^j\}$ such that $|P| = |Q|$ and $\sum_{i \in P} X^i = \sum_{i \in Q} X^i$. Note that by swapping any two non-equal elements in Q and P respectively, we make the two sums unequal. This observation is not entirely obvious, since we're working $(\bmod\ p)$. Suppose we swap $a \in P$ and $b \in Q$ where $a > b$. This will result in $\sum_{i \in P} X^i$ decreasing by $a - b$ and $\sum_{i \in Q} X^i$ increasing by $a - b$. Since these two sums were equal before the swap, we now have a difference of $2(a - b)$. If $2(a - b) \equiv 0 \pmod{p}$, since p is odd, then we must have $(a - b) \equiv 0 \pmod{p}$, which is a contradiction since a and b are assumed non-equal. So as long as we swap non-equal elements from the partitions, their sums will no longer be equal. From this observation, we will show that there are at least as many partitions with $\sum_{i \in P} X^i \neq \sum_{i \in Q} X^i$ as there are with $\sum_{i \in P} X^i = \sum_{i \in Q} X^i$.

Consider the operation of swapping the first two unequal elements in the sorted sets P and Q. Clearly this operation maps equal sum partitions to unequal sum partitions. In addition, let us specify that the partition where P and Q are identical be mapped to the partition obtained by sorting the set $\{X^i\}$ and setting P equal to the first half; the result will be unequal since $\{X^i\}$ is unequal. We now have a one-to-one mapping from equal sum partitions to unequal partitions, so no more than half of the possible partitions can have the property $\sum_{i\in P} X^i = \sum_{i\in Q} X^i$.

Thus the probability of choosing a partition with this property when two or more elements are unequal is less than $\frac{1}{2}$. With s repetitions, the probability of an unequal set passing EQUALITY is less than $\frac{1}{2^s}$.

Theorem 8. $t^{(p)}(\text{GHOST-SUM}_{n,g}) = \frac{n+g}{2}$.

Proof. Again, the privacy threshold follows directly from that of the employed secret sharing scheme.

Theorem 9. $t^{(c)}(\text{GHOST-SUM}_{n,g}) = t^{(r)}(\text{GHOST-SUM}_{n,g}) = \frac{n-g}{2}$.

Proof. The protocol aborts if and only if:

1. the honest participants fail to reconstruct the total (secret sharing scheme aborts), or
2. the reconstructed total's bins sum to a value other than n.

The first case is not possible, by Theorem 6.

Note that the value of the secret cannot be changed after the distribution phase because the total number of non-honest parties is less than $\frac{n-g}{2} + g = \frac{n+g}{2}$, which is $t^{(c)}(\text{ICVSS}_{n+g})$.

We therefore need only show that if an input is ill-formed it will be found in the verification steps and discarded and if an input differs across the s parallel computation rounds it will be found in the second verification step.

If a participant wants to share an ill-formed BIN-ARRAY in a set, he must create no more than s invalid BIN-ARRAYs in that set, or he is guaranteed to have at least one invalid BIN-ARRAY opened in the first verification phase. If he has $1 \leq x \leq s$ invalid BIN-ARRAYs, then the probability that no invalid BIN-ARRAY is opened is:

$$\frac{\binom{2s-x}{s}}{\binom{2s}{s}} \leq \frac{1}{2}$$

If the participant has at least one invalid BIN-ARRAY per set, the probability that an invalid BIN-ARRAY is not opened is $\leq \frac{1}{2^s}$. If a participant has invalid BIN-ARRAYs in some sets and not others, then his inputs are not equal across all rounds.

If the inputs are not equal across all rounds, then except with exponentially small probability, the input is discarded and the player disqualified in the second verification step.

A.4 Properties of IC-GVSS

Theorem 10. $t^{(p)}(\text{IC-GVSS}_{n,g}) = \frac{n+g}{2}$.

Proof. This follows from Theorem 5.

Theorem 11. $t^{(r)}(\text{IC-GVSS}_{n,g}) = \frac{n-g}{2}$.

Proof. This follows from 6.

Theorem 12. *A set of less than $\frac{n+g}{2}$ dishonest receivers cannot forge a signature. That is, they cannot create a share and a signature that convinces an honest participant that the share came from an honest sender.*

Proof. If the sender and a receiver are honest, then the receiver will reject any value different from the intended share except with exponentially small probability by property **SC3**. Therefore, $\frac{n+g}{2} - 1$ corrupt players cannot convince a single honest player to accept the fake share, therefore they cannot get $\frac{n+g}{2}$ participants to accept the fake share, which is required for it to pass.

Theorem 13. *In IC-GVSS$_{n,g}$, an honest sender cannot be eliminated in the share phase unless at least $\frac{n+g}{2}$ participants are corrupt.*

Proof. A sender can be eliminated in the distribution phase if and only if a participant shows signed shares that are ill-formed and $\frac{n+g}{2}$ participants accept the signature. If a sender is honest, he will give well-formed shares and so any player accepting a signature on an ill-formed share is accepting a forged share, which can't be done by Theorem 12.

Theorem 14. *IC-GVSS$_{n,g}$ has property $\mathbf{C'}$ when simultaneous broadcast is used in the reconstruction phase.*

Proof. Let $m_1, \ldots, m_n$ be shares distributed using IC-GVSS. Suppose the actively corrupt participants, $\mathcal{P}_1, \ldots, \mathcal{P}_c$ change their shares to $m'_1, \ldots, m'_c$. Let g be a polynomial interpolating the actual shares and g' be a polynomial interpolating the changed shares, $m'_1, \ldots, m'_c, m_{c+1}, \ldots, m_n$. If a simultaneous broadcast channel is used, the new shares cannot be a function of any honest shares.

Consider $(g' - g)(0) = a$. The secret reconstructed from the new shares will be $m' = g'(0) = m + a$. The dishonest coalition knows a, since they know $g' - g$ (the shares of honest parties are all 0). Therefore, they have information about m' if and only if they have information about m.

A.5 Properties of IC-GHOST-SUM

Theorem 15. *In $t^{(p)}(\text{IC-GHOST-SUM}_{n,g}) = \frac{n+g}{2}$.*

Proof. Follows from Theorem 8.

Theorem 16. BIN-ARRAY-EQUALITY *will not output* unequal *for an equal set when there are less than* $\frac{n+g}{2}$ *corrupt participants, except with exponentially small probability.*

Proof. It is not difficult to see that this would require dishonest players to forge shares. This is not possible, except with exponentially small probability, by Theorem 12.

Theorem 17. *If less than* $\frac{n+g}{2}$ *participants are corrupt, then no honest participant will be disqualified except with exponentially small probability.*

Proof. In the distribution phase, an honest participant will not be disqualified except with exponentially small probability, by Theorem 13.

In the first verification phase, a participant can only be disqualified if one of his BIN-ARRAYs is opened to an invalid secret. In order to accomplish this, at least one corrupt participant must open an incorrect share with the first participant's signature forged. This cannot be done with less than $\frac{n+g}{2}$ corrupt participants by Theorem 12.

In the second verification phase, a participant can only be disqualified if one round of equality outputs unequal. This can't happen to an honest participant except with exponentially small probability, by Theorem 16.

Theorem 18. $t^{(c)}(\text{IC-GHOST-SUM}_{n,g}) = \frac{n+g}{2}$.

Proof. Suppose a dishonest collusion of $\frac{n+g}{2} - 1$ participants want to cause the total Y to be inconsistent with the inputs of honest participants. They must change the value of some shared BIN-ARRAY, X.

By Theorem 10, nothing is known about X before the computation (and output) phase. By Theorem 14, the dishonest collusion will therefore know nothing about the value of the shared BIN-ARRAY X' that would result from their behaviour. It could be any array of $2n$ integers (mod p). There are p^{2n} of these, and only $2n$ well-formed BIN-ARRAYs. The probability of creating a well-formed BIN-ARRAY is thus less than $\frac{2n}{p^{2n}}$, which is bounded by a constant. Repetition yields exponential security.

Theorem 19. *In* $t^{(r)}(\text{IC-GHOST-SUM}_{n,g}) = \frac{n-g}{2}$.

Proof. This proof is identical to that of Theorem 9.

Two Protocols for Delegation of Computation

Ran Canetti[1,2,*], Ben Riva[2,*], and Guy N. Rothblum[3]

[1] Boston University, Boston, MA, USA
[2] Tel Aviv University, Tel Aviv, Israel
[3] Microsoft Research Silicon Valley, Mountain View, CA, USA

Abstract. Consider a weak client that wishes to delegate computation to an untrusted server and be able to succinctly verify the correctness of the result. We present protocols in two relaxed variants of this problem.

We first consider a model where the client delegates the computation to *two or more* servers, and is guaranteed to output the correct answer as long as even a *single* server is honest. In this model, we show a 1-round statistically sound protocol for any log-space uniform $\mathcal{NC}$ circuit. In contrast, in the single server setting all known one-round succinct delegation protocols are computationally sound. The protocol extends the arithemetization techniques of [Goldwasser-Kalai-Rothblum, STOC 08] and [Feige-Kilian, STOC 97].

Next we consider a simplified view of the protocol of [Goldwasser-Kalai-Rothblum, STOC 08] in the single-server model with a non-succinct, but *public*, offline stage. Using this simplification we construct two computationally sound protocols for delegation of computation of any circuit C with depth d and input length n, *even a non-uniform one*, such that the client runs in time $n \cdot \mathrm{poly}(\log(|C|), d)$. The first protocol is potentially practical and easier to implement for general computations than the full protocol of [Goldwasser-Kalai-Rothblum, STOC 08], and the second is a 1-round protocol with similar complexity, but less efficient server.

1 Introduction

An emerging paradigm in modern computing is *pay-per-use* Cloud Computing, where individuals and companies outsource computations to companies that perform the computations on dedicated servers. This motivates exploring methods for delegating computations reliably, while maintaining the efficiency gains: A weak client delegates his computation to a powerful server; once the server returns the result of the computation, the client should be able to verify the correctness of that result so that (a) the client uses considerably less resources than those required to actually perform the computation from scratch, and (b) the server does not use significantly more resources than those needed for performing the computation.

A classic solution to this problem is to have the server prove correctness of the computation using a universal argument [K92, BG02]. Here the server incurs

---

* Research supported by the Check Point Institute for Information Security, an ISF grant and an EU Marie Curie grant.

A. Smith (Ed.): ICITS 2012, LNCS 7412, pp. 37–61, 2012.

polynomial overhead and the client's complexity is linear in the input length and security parameter, and only polylogarithmic in the complexity of the original computation. This solution is general and applies to any problem in $\mathcal{P}$. It also has the nice property that it is publicly verifiable: The client needs to keep no secret state. However, it has two main drawbacks: First, it is interactive, taking four messages. Second, it is only computationally sound.

Micali [M00] "squashes" Kilian's protocol to one message in the Random Oracle model, while maintaining public verifiability. Further extensions of this construction give a two-message protocol in the plain model, with similar complexity advantages [CL08, BCCR12, GLR11, DFH12]. However, their soundness relies on non-standard hardness assumptions. Furthermore, all of these protocols have only computational soundness. No statistically-sound protocol with a constant number of rounds is known.

An alternative delegation protocol, proposed by Goldwasser, Kalai and Rothblum [GKR08], guarantees statistical soundness. However, the protocol works only for languages that have $\mathcal{L}$-uniform $\mathcal{NC}$ circuits. Furthermore, the number of rounds is quasilinear in the depth of the circuit. Using the technique of Kalai and Raz [KR09] this protocol can be transformed into a one-round protocol, assuming the existence of a computational Private Information Retrieval scheme with polylogarithmic communication. Here, however, soundness is only computational.

Two relaxations of the model have been recently proposed. One relaxation, proposed in [CRR11], lets the client interact with *two or more* servers, and requires that the client outputs the right value as long as there exists *one* server that follows the protocol. That is, the client asks for the value of $f(x)$ from several servers. In case the servers make contradictory claims about $f(x)$, they "play" against each other in a protocol where the weak client can efficiently determine the true claim as long as there is at least *one* honest server. As before, the servers should incur only polynomial overhead, whereas the client's resources should be much smaller than required to compute the function. This model, called the *Refereed Delegation of Computation (RDoC)* model, directly extends the refereed games model of Feige and Kilian [FK97]. It is also somewhat reminiscent of the MIP model of [BGKW88]. However, the MIP model provides different guarantees (e.g., soundness is guaranteed only as long as no two servers collude, and malicious servers can potentially prevent honest ones from convincing the client.) In that model, and assuming collisions resistant hash functions, [CRR11] shows a computationally sound delegation protocol whose number of rounds is logarithmic in the time needed to compute $f(x)$. The protocol is inspired by a protocol of Feige and Kilian [FK97].

Another relaxation, proposed by [GGP10], considers two stages of the protocol, offline and online. In the offline stage we fix a function (or a circuit) f and allow the client to work *harder* (e.g., proportional to the size of f). In the online stage, the client can delegate the computation of $f(x)$ for any input x, and can verify the result in time that independent of the size of f. The assumption that the client can work "hard" during the offline stage is often justified by proposing that the client rely on the assistance of a trusted party to perform the offline stage on the client's behalf. We call this model the *Offline/Online Verifiable Delegation of Computation (OVDoC)* model. Several protocols have been proposed in this model [GGP10, CKV10, AIK10, CKLR11, BGV11].

However, in all the recent protocols in this model the offline stage generates information that must be kept secret and used at the online stage (or else soundness will no longer be guaranteed). Having such secret information is a serious impediment. First, it requires the client to put complete trust in the entity that participates in the offline stage. Furthermore, in some of the protocols soundness is only guaranteed as long as the server does not know which past interactions convinced the client.

1.1 Our Contributions

A statistically sound, 1-roundtrip protocol in the RDoC model. Our main contribution is a *1-roundtrip statistically sound* RDoC protocol for any circuit computable in $\mathcal{L}$-uniform $\mathcal{NC}$. The protocol adapts techniques from a protocol of Feige and Kilian [FK97], where the servers are inefficient even for log-space computations, together with techniques from the work of Goldwasser, Kalai and Rothblum [GKR08], and some new techniques.

We provide a brief overview of the protocol. For the description here we restrict attention to the case when there are exactly two servers, one honest and one malicious (but the referee/client does not know which is honest). We later show how to extend our protocols to more than two servers.

At a high level, our protocol follows the structure of the [GKR08] interactive proof. That is, initially the servers make claims about the output layer of the circuits. Then, a (very efficient) *sum-check* protocol [LFKN92] is used to reduce a claim about a high layer in the circuit, which we call an input claim, into a claim about a lower layer (closer to the circuit's input layer), we call this an output claim. The guarantee is that if the input claim is false, then w.h.p. over the referee's coins the output claim will also be false. They use this sub-protocol to reduce the claim about the circuit's output layer into a claim about the circuit's input layer, and complete the protocol by noting that claims about the input layer can be verified by the referee in quasi-linear time.

However, as in [GKR08], the above protocol is highly interactive: First, each sum-check sub-protocol requires a logarithmic number of rounds. Second, the claim for each layer in the circuit depends on the coins chosen by the referee in the sum-check for the layer above it, so all of these sum check protocols must be run sequentially from the top circuit output layer to the bottom circuit input layer. To eliminate the first source of interaction, we use a variant of the one-round refereed game for the sum check test from [FK97]. This still leaves us with a significant technical obstacle: How can we collapse all of sum-check protocols from the different layers into just one round of interaction? The difficulty comes from the fact that, in order to run the [FK97] protocol, both servers need to know the claim being debated. This claim, however, depends on the referee's (non-public) coins in the sum check for the layer above. Revealing all of those coins to both servers ahead of time would compromise soundness.

We overcome this obstacle (and additional lower-level ones) using techniques tailored to our setting. In a nutshell, the claim for each layer is the value of a low-degree multi-variate polynomial (say p) on a certain secret point (say z) that is known only to the referee. The referee sends to each server a different low-degree parametric curve passing through the point z (but also through many others), and asks for the (low-degree) polynomial q describing p restricted to that server's curve. Essentially, soundness follows because each server (on its own) cannot tell which of the points on its curve is the one that the referee will be checking. If the server cheats and sends $q' \neq q$, then (since q and q' are low degree polynomials over a larger field) with high probability the server must be cheating on the point z that the referee is checking on.

Kol and Raz present an alternative exposition of this protocol [KR11]. They also provide an extension of this protocol that somewhat reduces the workload of the client at the price of a comparable increase in the number of rounds. As far as we know, these results have been obtained independently of ours.

A simplification of the [GKR08] protocol in the OVDoC model with a public offline stage. For our second result, we start by describing the model of OVDoC with a public offline stage. Recall that the offline/online delegation of computation model assumes that the client can work "hard" during the offline stage and that the information generated in the offline stage is kept secret. In our model the entire randomness used in the offline stage is made public. This means that: (1) The correctness of the offline computation can be verified by anyone, and, (2) The output of the offline stage can be used by anyone in the online stage to verify the computation of any input.

For instance, imagine that some well-known company (e.g., Microsoft, Google) publishes short public keys for a set of different circuits. (Or, Microsoft ships these keys as part of its products, as currently done with Certificate Authorities.) Any interested party can also check these values and verify that they are correct. Later on, a (weak) client can take these values and delegate its computation to *any* server, without running the offline stage by itself.

As already mentioned, the [GKR08] protocol works only for $\mathcal{L}$-uniform $\mathcal{NC}$ circuits. This is because the client cannot verify claims about the circuit structure for larger circuits since the explicit circuit is too large (larger than the client running time) and (for general non-uniform circuits) there is no shorter implicit representation.[1] Moreover, the full [GKR08] protocol has a large overhead over the plain execution of the computation.

In the relaxed model of OVDoC with a public offline stage we show that we can combine a lighter version of the [GKR08] protocol (namely, only the *bare-bones* protocol. See Sect. 2) with another efficient computationally-sound protocol in a

---

[1] We note that Cormode, Mitzenmacher and Thaler [CMT12] argue that many useful problems have succinct circuit representation. In those cases a weak client can verify claims about the circuit structure by herself.

way that bypasses the above difficulties. As a result, our protocol can work with *any* circuit C, requiring the client to run in time $n \cdot \text{poly}(\log(|C|), \text{depth}(C))$, where n is the input length. We do not require the circuit to be uniform, resulting in a potentially easier to implement protocol. Furthermore, the simplification reduces the number of executions of the bare-bones protocol by a factor of $O(\text{depth}(C))$, which in practice can be very meaningful. (See [CMT12] for experimental results of a single execution of the bare-bones protocol. Note that they also significantly improve the server's running time using a technique that can be applied to our protocols as well.)

As a more theoretical result, we additionally show that by carefully applying the technique of [KR09] we can construct a 1-round protocol with less efficient server. Previously, assuming standard computational assumptions, it was known how to construct a 1-round protocol only for $\mathcal{L}$-uniform $\mathcal{NC}$ circuits.

1.2 Organization

Section 2 describes the protocol of [GKR08] which we use extensively in our constructions. Section 3 defines the model of refereed delegation of computation, shows a "parallel repetition" theorem of RDoC protocols and describes how to extend RDoC with two servers to any number of servers. It also presents the construction of a one-round RDoC for any $\mathcal{L}$-uniform $\mathcal{NC}$ computation. Section 4 describes the simplified construction of the [GKR08] protocol and the construction of a one-round computationally sound protocol for any circuit.

2 The Protocols of [GKR08, KR09]

Given that our protocols rely heavily on the structure of the [GKR08, KR09] protocols, we start with a brief exposition of these protocols. Also, in Appendix A we describe the protocol of [FK97] that we use in our RDoC construction.

2.1 Preliminaries: Low Degree Extension (LDE)

Given a field F, a subset $H \subseteq F$ and a function $f : H^m \to F$, we let the low degree extension of f, denoted $\tilde{f}$, be the *unique* multi-variate polynomial $\tilde{f} : F^m \to F$ that satisfies: (1) (low-degree) $\deg(\tilde{f}) < |H|$ for each variable; and (2) (extension) $f(x) = \tilde{f}(x)$ for all $x \in H^m$. Such polynomials can be constructed using Lagrange Interpolation.

Similarly we define the low degree extension of a vector. Let $\alpha : H^m \to \{0, \ldots |H|^m - 1\}$ be the lexicographic order of H^m. Given a vector $\boldsymbol{w} = (w_0, \ldots w_{k-1}) \in F^k$, where $k \leq |H|^m$, we can view this vector as a function $f_{\boldsymbol{w}} : H^m \to F$ such that $f_{\boldsymbol{w}}(z) = w_{\alpha(z)}$ when $\alpha(z) \leq k - 1$ and $f_{\boldsymbol{w}}(z) = 0$ otherwise. We define the low degree extension of the vector $\boldsymbol{w}$ to be the low degree extension of $f_{\boldsymbol{w}}$.

2.2   The Bare-Bones [GKR08] Protocol, Given a Circuit Specification Oracle

Notations and Parameters. The protocol is between a server and a client, where both know the input x of length n.

Given an arithmetic circuit $C : \{0,1\}^n \to \{0,1\}$ of fan-in 2 gates, size S and depth d, the players choose the following parameters: 1) An extension field H of $GF[2]$ such that $\max(d, \log(S)) \leq |H| \leq \text{poly}(d, \log(S))$, 2) An integer m such that $S \leq |H|^m \leq \text{poly}(S)$, 3) An extension field F of H such that $|F| \leq \text{poly}(|H|)$. (The size of F influences the soundness of the protocol.).

Using standard techniques, we can transform the arithmetic circuit C to a new arithmetic circuit $C' : F^n \to F^S$ over the field F with the following properties: 1) C' is of size $\text{poly}(S)$ and depth d, with fan-in 2 gates, 2) Each layer, except for the input layer, is of size S (simply by adding dummy gates), 3) For every $(x_1, \ldots, x_n) \in \{0,1\}^n$, $C'(x_1, \ldots, x_n) = (C(x_1, \ldots, x_n), 0, \ldots, 0)$.

Let $\text{spec}_c()$ be the predicate describing a circuit C. That is, $\text{spec}_c(i, b, w_1, w_2, w_3)$ returns 1 if in the i-th layer of C there is a gate that connects wires w_2 and w_3 to wire w_1, and this gate is a b-gate where $b \in \{0 = add, 1 = mult\}$.[2] Let $\widetilde{\text{spec}}_{c(i)}$ be the low degree extension of $\text{spec}_c(i, \cdot, \cdot, \cdot, \cdot)$ with respect to H, F and m, of degree δ (that depends on $\text{spec}_c()$) in each variable. In this section we assume the client has an oracle access to $\widetilde{\text{spec}}_{c'(i)}$.

We denote the output layer as the 0 layer and the other layers according to their distance from the output layer. The input layer is the d-th layer. For $0 \leq i \leq d$ we associate a vector $v_i = (v_{i,0}, \ldots, v_{i,S-1}) \in F^S$ with the values of all gates of the i-th layer in the computation of $C'(x_1, \ldots, x_n)$. v_0 is the circuit result $(C(x_1, \ldots, x_n), 0, \ldots, 0)$ and v_d is the circuit input $(x_1, \ldots, x_n)$. Let $\widetilde{V}_i : F^m \to F$ be the low degree extension of the vector v_i with respect to H, F and m. This polynomial is of degree $\leq |H| - 1$ in each of its variables, and given v_i can be computed in time $\leq \text{poly}(|F|^m) = \text{poly}(S)$. Since v_d is of length n, $\widetilde{V}_d$ can be computed in time $\leq n \cdot \text{poly}(|H|, m)$.

The Protocol. The server claims that $C'(x_1, \ldots, x_n) = (0, \ldots, 0)$. An interactive protocol is executed between the server and the client. In each step the server reduces the correctness of the computation of layer i to the correctness of the computation of layer $i + 1$. Concretely, for layer i, the server claims that $\widetilde{V}_i(u_i) = r_i$ for some randomly chosen u_i that the client picked and sent to the server. Then, the server reduces the correctness of this claim to the correctness of $\widetilde{V}_{i+1}(u_{i+1}) = r_{i+1}$ for some randomly chosen u_{i+1} that the client picked. This process continues until they reach the input layer and then the client verifies the correctness of this layer by himself (as $\widetilde{V}_d$ is small and known to the client).

We now describe in detail the reduction between the layers. [GKR08, R09] show that there exists a $3m$-variate polynomial $f_u^{(i)} : (F^m)^3 \to F$ of size $\leq \text{poly}(S)$ and degree $\leq 2\delta$ defined by

---

[2] In general, it is possible to use any gate that can be expressed as a polynomial of its inputs.

$$f_u^{(i)}(p, w, w') = \widetilde{\beta}(u, p) \cdot [\, \widetilde{\text{spec}}_{c'(i+1)}(0, p, w, w')(\widetilde{V}_{i+1}(w) + \widetilde{V}_{i+1}(w')) \, + $$
$$\widetilde{\text{spec}}_{c'(i+1)}(1, p, w, w')(\widetilde{V}_{i+1}(w) \cdot \widetilde{V}_{i+1}(w')) \,]$$

where $\widetilde{\beta}(u, p)$ is a $|H| - 1$ degree polynomial that depends only on F, H and m, and, can be computed in time $\text{poly}(|H|, m)$. Note that given an oracle access to $\widetilde{\text{spec}}_{c'(i)}$ and the values of $\widetilde{V}_{i+1}(w)$ and $\widetilde{V}_{i+1}(w')$, the polynomial $f_u^{(i)}(p, w, w')$ can be evaluated in time $\text{poly}(|H|, m)$.

[GKR08, R09] proves that $\widetilde{V}_i(u_i) = \sum_{p,w,w' \in H^m} f_u^{(i)}(p, w, w')$. Now, given a claim for layer i that $\widetilde{V}_i(u_i) = r_i$ for some randomly chosen u_i that the client picked and sent to the server, proving that $\widetilde{V}_i(u_i) = r_i$ is equivalent to proving that $r_i = \sum_{p,w,w' \in H^m} f_u^{(i)}(p, w, w')$.

This part is done by a standard *sum-check* interactive protocol between the two players. For each layer of the circuit, the client and the server execute a sum-check interactive protocol that consists of $3m$ rounds. The last step of the sum-check requires a computation of $f_{u_i}^{(i)}(p, w, w')$ by the client. In order to do that, the server sends a low degree polynomial $\widetilde{V}_{i+1}(\gamma(t))$ where $\gamma(t)$ is the 1-degree curve that passes through w and w'. Using this polynomial, the client computes $\widetilde{V}_{i+1}(w)$ and $\widetilde{V}_{i+1}(w')$ and uses that to compute and verify $f_{u_i}^{(i)}(p, w, w')$. Then, the client picks a random point t' on the curve $\gamma(t)$ and continues to the correctness proof of the claimed value of $\widetilde{V}_{i+1}(\gamma(t'))$ (where $u_{i+1} = \gamma(t')$ in the next round).

Complexity. It is shown in [R09] that by taking F such that $|F| \geq 700md\delta = \text{poly}(|H|)$ we get soundness of $\frac{1}{100}$. In addition, the overall running time of the server is $\text{poly}(|F|^m) = \text{poly}(S)$, the running time of the client is $\text{poly}(|F|, m) + n \cdot \text{poly}(|H|, m) = n \cdot \text{poly}(d, \log(S))$ and the communication complexity is $\text{poly}(|F|, m) = \text{poly}(d, \log(S))$.

Cormode, Mitzenmacher and Thaler [CMT12] show that by using a multilinear extension, the running time of the server can be reduced to $O(S \cdot \log(S))$. Their technique can be applied to our constructions as well. They also suggest that by using large fields, e.g. of size 32 bit, performance of many applications can be significantly improved. However, in both of our constructions the players work in time $\geq |F|^m$, thus making this option inefficient.

2.3 Realizing the Oracle for $\mathcal{L}$-Uniform $\mathcal{NC}$ Circuits

The above protocol is presented for any circuit given an oracle access to $\widetilde{\text{spec}}_{c'(i)}$. [GKR08] shows how to realize the protocol without an oracle access but for a more restricted class of languages, $\mathcal{L}$-uniform $\mathcal{NC}$, which is the class of languages that can be computed by circuits of poly-size and poly-logarithmic depth where there is a log-space Turing Machine that generates those circuits.

Specifically, [GKR08] shows the following:

1. For a language L in $\mathcal{NL}$ (i.e., L has a non-deterministic log-space Turing Machine), it is possible to compute the $\widetilde{\text{spec}}_{c(i)}$ (where C is the circuit that computes L) in time polylog(n). Thus, the client can compute it by himself and, as a result, realize the bare-bones protocol.
2. For a language L in $\mathcal{L}$-uniform $\mathcal{NC}$, the client delegates also the computation of the oracle answers to the server. More specifically, let C be the circuit that computes L and let $\text{TM}_{\text{spec}(c)}$ be the Turing Machine that computes $\widetilde{\text{spec}}_{c(i)}$. Since L is $\mathcal{L}$-uniform, $\text{TM}_{\text{spec}(c)}$ is also non-deterministic log-space Turing Machine, and therefore the computation of $\text{TM}_{\text{spec}(c)}$ can be delegated to the server. As a result, the bare-bones protocol is executed once for the delegation of C, and $2d$ times for the delegations of $\text{TM}_{\text{spec}(c)}$.

2.4   The Transformation of [KR09]

Assuming the existence of a poly-logarithmic computational Private Information Retrieval (cPIR) scheme, [KR09] presents a transformation from any public-coin unconditionally-sound proof system into a one-round computationally-sound proof system. In high-level the transformation is as follows. The verifier sends all the random coins together in the same round, hidden inside different cPIR queries. The (honest) prover prepares a database with all the possible answers, and returns the answers to the verifier queries all together. Then, the verifier peels the cPIR answers and feeds the original verifier with the results.

The exact transformation is more subtle, and we refer the reader to [KR09] for more details. We note that the transformation does not change the expressiveness of the underlying protocol, and in particular, transforming the protocol of [GKR08] results in a protocol for $\mathcal{L}$-uniform $\mathcal{NC}$ circuits.

We denote the verifier's message in this protocol by $\text{GKR-KR}_v(S, d, \lambda)$ given the circuit size S, depth d and security parameter λ. Similarly, we denote the prover's response by $\text{GKR-KR}_p(C, x, q)$ for a given circuit C, input x and queries $q = \text{GKR-KR}_v(S, d, \lambda)$.

3   Refereed Delegation of Computation

3.1   The Model

A refereed delegation of computation for a function f is a protocol between a referee/client R and N servers $P_1, P_2, \ldots, P_N$. All parties may use local randomness. The referee and the servers receive an input x. The servers claim different results for the computation of $f(x)$ and the referee should be able to determine the correct answer with high probability. We assume that at least one of the servers is honest.

Definition 1 (Refereed Delegation of Computation). *Let $(P_1, P_2, \ldots, P_N, R)$ be an ε-RDoC with N servers for a function f if the following holds:*

- *For any input x and any i, if server P_i is honest then for any $P_1^*, \ldots, P_{i-1}^*$, $P_{i+1}^*, \ldots, P_N^*$ the output of R is $f(x)$ w.p. at least $1 - \varepsilon$.*
- *The complexity of the referee is at most quasi-linear in $|x|$ and the complexity of the (honest) servers is polynomial in the complexity of evaluating f.*

For completeness of the description, we briefly review the model of Refereed Games [FK97]. A refereed game (RG) for a language L is a protocol between a referee R and two competing *unbounded* servers P_1 and P_2. All three parties may use local randomness. The referee and the servers receive $x \in \{0,1\}^*$. Without loss of generality we can assume P_1 claims that $x \in L$ and P_2 claims that $x \notin L$, and the referee should be able to determine the correct answer with probability at least $2/3$.

Parallel Repetition for RDoC. We have the following "parallel repetition" theorem for RDoC for boolean functions.

Theorem 1 (Parallel Repetition for RDoC). *Let $(P_1, P_2, \ldots, P_N, R)$ be a ε-RDoC for a boolean function f, and let $(P_1^k, P_2^k, \ldots, P_N^k, R^k)$ be a RDoC obtained by running $(P_1, P_2, \ldots, P_N, R)$ k times in parallel and in which R^k accepts if and only if R accepted in the majority of the executions. Then, $(P_1^k, P_2^k, \ldots, P_N^k, R^k)$ is a RDoC with error probability $\varepsilon^{poly(k)}$.*

Proof (sketch). We use the fact that parallel repetition reduces the error probability of any interactive proof system, and we build an interactive proof system (P, V) for the language $L = \{ x \mid f(x) = 1 \}$ from our RDoC $(P_1, P_2, \ldots, P_N, R)$. Without loss of generality, we assume $x \in L$ and P_1 is an honest server. We view the referee R and the honest server P_1 as the verifier V, and the other servers as the prover P. Similarly, we view P_1^k and R^k as the verifier V^k in the parallel repetition version of (P, V). Since $(P_1, P_2, \ldots, P_N, R)$ is a RDoC, the soundness of (P, V) is bounded by ε. Now, if we assume there are malicious servers $P_2^k, \ldots, P_N^k$ that convince the referee in $(P_1^k, P_2^k, \ldots, P_N^k, R^k)$ with probability p, it means there is a prover P^k that can convince V^k with probability p. However, since the parallel repetition of interactive proofs reduced the error probability to $\varepsilon^{poly(k)}$, p is negligible. $\square$

From Two Servers to N Servers. Here we show how, given a RDoC with two servers and negligible error probability, one can construct a RDoC with N servers and negligible error probability, where we only need to assume that at least *one* of them is honest. The idea is to execute the RDoC with two servers between each pair of servers. By the soundness of the RDoC with two servers, with high probability there exists an honest server P_i that convinces the referee in *all* of his "games". The referee outputs the claimed result of P_i.

This solution can be executed in parallel for all pairs, and therefore keeps the number of rounds the same. However, it requires $\frac{N \cdot (N-1)}{2}$ different executions of the protocol.

3.2   One-Round RDoC for Any $\mathcal{L}$-Uniform $\mathcal{NC}$ Computation

Feige and Kilian [FK97] construct a one-round refereed game for the sum-check task. In Appendix A we describe their protocol in detail (though our description below is self-contained).

The Protocol, Given a Circuit Specification Oracle. The intuition behind our protocol is as follows. We assume the referee has an oracle access to $\widetilde{\text{spec}}_{c'(i)}$. We use the idea of [GKR08] to check the entire computation by checking the sum-checks between each two consecutive layers. We use the protocol of [FK97] to run each sum-check in a single round of communication. Ideally, we would like to execute all the sum-checks in parallel, in a single round. But, we cannot do that directly since the protocol of [FK97] assumes the referee can compute $f_{u_i}^{(i)}$ by himself for any point, but here, $f_{u_i}^{(i)}$ itself is too complex for the referee to compute. Thus, we change the "linking" between the layers.

For simplicity, we now describe the protocol as a sequential protocol with several rounds. However, since we are interested in a one-round protocol, all servers actually execute all rounds of the this protocol *together*, in a single round. The referee chooses his messages for all rounds together and sends them to the servers in one message. Then, the servers answer all rounds together. Last, the referee reads all answers, starting from the input layer towards the output layer, and checks the servers' answers until he finds who is the honest server. (In our protocol the direction of the "linking" reductions is different than in [GKR08].) We denote this protocol by (P_1, P_2, R).

Given an input x, for each layer i the referee chooses a random parametric curve $\varphi_i(t)$ and a random point z_i. ($\gamma_i(z_i)$ corresponds to the point u_i of [GKR08].) The referee sends $\varphi_i(z_i), \varphi_i(t)$ to P_1 and P_2, respectively, and asks the servers for the values of $\widetilde{V}_i(\varphi_i(z_i))$ and $\widetilde{V}_i(\varphi_i(t))$. Next, he checks whether those answers agree on z_i. If they agree, then he assumes both answers are correct and continues to checking the next layer, $i - 1$. Otherwise, he executes a one-round sum-check protocol *a la.* [FK97] to determine the correct value of $\widetilde{V}_i(\varphi_i(z_i))$. As we said, a subtle issue here is how the referee checks the correctness of the sum-checks without being able to compute $f_{\varphi_i(z_i)}^{(i)}$ by himself. Specifically, in the protocol of [FK97] the referee needs to compute $f_{\varphi_i(z_i)}^{(i)}$ on a point that is not known to P_1. In order to solve this problem we use the polynomial $\widetilde{V}_i(\varphi_i(t))$ to get this value "implicitly" from the servers themselves. When the referee believes that the answer on $\widetilde{V}_{i+1}(\varphi_{i+1}(t))$ for layer $i + 1$ is correct, he takes few random points on $\widetilde{V}_{i+1}(\varphi_{i+1}(t))$ and uses that to compute the value of $f_{\varphi_i(z_i)}^{(i)}$ on the required point. The solution requires increasing by one the degrees of the polynomials of the protocol of [FK97] in order to keep the added point secret (see Appendix A). Note that P_2 can easily win if it knows the intersection point z_i, thus, we ask P_2 to answer the sum-check challenges for *all* the points on $\varphi_i(t)$, including the value at z_i. Then, our referee calls the referee of the one-round sum-check protocol of [FK97] to determine who is the honest server.

The detailed protocol (P_1, P_2, R) is presented in Fig. 1 and Fig. 2. Since some of the polynomials conceal secret intersection points, when the referee sends some polynomial to the servers, we require that he sends the canonical representation of that polynomial.

The referee's running time is $poly(|F|, m, d, |H|) + n \cdot poly(|H|, m) = n \cdot poly(d, log(S))$, the servers running time is $poly(S, |F|, m, d) = poly(S)$ and the communication complexity is $poly(|F|, m, d) = poly(d, log(S))$.

Theorem 2. *Let L be a language in $\mathcal{NC}$ and let C_L be the circuit that decides on L. For any input x and for any constant error probability ε, given a circuit specification oracle for C_L, the protocol $(P_1(x), P_2(x), R(x))$ is ε-RDoC with two servers for the circuit C_L.*

The crucial point of the proof is that a server can cheat with high probability only if he knows the curves' intersection points. Let's see what information each server has about the other server's curves.

Lemma 1. *Let V_1 be the view of P_1 and let i be a round in the protocol. For all $\alpha, \alpha', \beta, \beta' \in F$ and $j \in [1 \ldots 3m]$*

$$Pr[a_j = \alpha | V_1] = Pr[a_j = \alpha' | V_1] \tag{1}$$
$$Pr[r = \beta | V_1] = Pr[r = \beta' | V_1]. \tag{2}$$

Let V_2 be the view of P_2 and let i be a round in the protocol. For all $\alpha, \alpha', \beta, \beta', \gamma, \gamma' \in F$ and $j \in [1 \ldots 3m]$

$$Pr[z_i = \alpha | V_2] = Pr[z_i = \alpha' | V_2] \tag{3}$$
$$Pr[a_j = \beta | V_2] = Pr[a_j = \beta' | V_2] \tag{4}$$
$$Pr[b_j = \gamma | V_2] = Pr[b_j = \gamma' | V_2] \tag{5}$$

Proof. The lemma follows from inspecting the protocol.

1. $D_j(t)$ is of degree at least 1. Even if we give P_1 the value of b_j, he does not have enough information to recover $D_j(t)$, so any $(a_j, C_j(a_j))$ is a possible intersection point.
2. Since P_1 has no information on w, w' besides from the curve C_{3m}, and, $\varphi_i(t)$ is of degree 2, r is simply a random point on that curve from his point of view.
3. $C_j(t)$ is of degree at least $|H|$. Even if we give P_2 the value of b_j, he does not have enough information to recover $C_j(t)$, so any $(a_j, D_j(a_j))$ is a possible intersection point. Similar argument is true for b_j. □

Proof (Theorem 2). Using Lemma 1, let's see how much a malicious server can cheat without knowing the intersection points z_i, a_j and b_j. For a fixed input x and a fixed circuit C, let S_2 be the event that although P_2 is the malicious server the referee outputs a wrong result (i.e., $Q_0(0)$ that is not equal to $C(x)$).

Publicly known parameters

H, F, m, d, S, n, δ as in Sect. 2.

Initialization

For $i = 1, \ldots d$, R randomly picks $z_i \in F$ and a random degree-2 parametric curve $\varphi_i(t) \in F[t]^m$.

He also sets $\varphi_0 \equiv 0$ and $z_0 = 0$, and computes $Q_d(t) = \tilde{V}_d(\varphi_d(t))$ and $M_d = \tilde{V}_d(\varphi_d(z_d))$.

For $i = d, \ldots, 1$

R's computations :

R sets $w = \varphi_i(0), w' = \varphi_i(1)$ and randomly chooses $p, r \in F$.

For $1 \leq j \leq 3m$, R chooses random vectors $A_j, B_j \in F^j$ and random elements $a_j, b_j \in F$.

For $1 \leq j \leq 3m - 1$ let $C_j(t) \in F[t]^j$ be the unique degree-$|H|$ parametric curve going through

$$(0, A_{j-1} \circ 0), \ldots, (|H| - 1, A_{j-1} \circ (|H| - 1)), (|H|, B_j)$$

and let $C_{3m}(t) \in F[t]^{3m}$ be the unique degree-$(|H|+1)$ parametric curve going through

$$(0, A_{3m-1} \circ 0), \ldots, (|H| - 1, A_{3m-1} \circ (|H| - 1)), (|H|, B_{3m}), (r, p \circ w \circ w').$$

For $1 \leq j \leq 3m$, let $D_j(t) \in F[t]^j$ be the unique degree-1 parametric curve going through
$$(a_j, C_j(a_j)), (b_j, A_j).$$

We define

$$\Phi_{j,q}(x_1, \ldots, x_j) = \sum_{x_{j+1}, \ldots, x_{3m} \in H} f_q^{(i-1)}(x_1, \ldots, x_j, x_{j+1}, \ldots, x_{3m}).$$

R sends to P_1 :

$C_j(t)$, for $1 \leq j \leq 3m$, and the point m_{i-1} where $m_{i-1} = \varphi_{i-1}(z_{i-1})$.

P_1 sends to R :

Define $F_j(t) = \Phi_{j,m_{i-1}}(C_j(t))$.

P_1 sends $F_j(t)$ for $1 \leq j \leq 3m$, and, M_{i-1} where $M_{i-1} = \tilde{V}_{i-1}(m_{i-1})$.

R sends to P_2 :

$D_j(t)$ for $1 \leq j \leq 3m$, and the curve $\varphi_{i-1}(t)$.

P_2 sends to R :

For all $q \in F$ define $G_{j,q}(t) = \Phi_{j,\varphi_{i-1}(q)}(D_j(t))$.

P_2 sends $G_{j,q}(t)$ for $1 \leq j \leq 3m$ and all $q \in F$, and, $Q_{i-1}(t)$ where $Q_{i-1}(t) = \tilde{V}_{i-1}(\varphi_{i-1}(t))$.

Fig. 1. One-round RDoC protocol: initialization and interactive phase

Let E_i be the event that $Q_i(t)$ is indeed $\tilde{V}_i(\varphi_i(t))$, and let T_i be the event that $Q_i(z_i)$ is indeed $\tilde{V}_i(\varphi_i(z_i))$. Then,

$$Pr[S_2] \leq Pr[\exists i \in [d-1] \text{ s.t. } \neg T_i \wedge T_{i+1}] \leq \sum_{i=0}^{d-1} Pr[\neg T_i \wedge T_{i+1}].$$

Checking layer i for $i = d, \ldots, 1$

P_1 is declared as the cheater if for some j, $F_j(t)$ has degree greater than $\deg(C_j) \cdot j \cdot 2\delta$. P_2 is declared as the cheater if $Q_{i-1}(t)$ has degree bigger than $2m \cdot (|H| - 1)$ or if for some j, $G_{j,z_{i-1}}(t)$ has degree greater than $\deg(D_j) \cdot j \cdot 2\delta$.

If $M_{i-1} = Q_{i-1}(z_{i-1})$ the referee continues to the proof of layer $i - 1$. Otherwise, he continues as follows.

R computes $f_{z_{i-1}}^{(i-1)}(p \circ w \circ w')$ using $Q_i(0), Q_i(1)$ (and the oracle).

Now, R verifies the sum-check of $M_{i-1} = \displaystyle\sum_{\hat{p},\hat{w},\hat{w}' \in H^m} f_{m_{i-1}}^{(i-1)}(\hat{p}, \hat{w}, \hat{w}')$ using the referee from [FK97]. Concretely:

- In case for all j, $G_{j,z_{i-1}}(a_j) = F_j(a_j)$, if $\displaystyle\sum_{h=0}^{|H|-1} F_1(h) = M_{i-1}$ then P_1 wins.

  Otherwise, P_2 wins.
- Denote by j the largest number such that $G_{j,z_{i-1}}(a_j) \neq F_j(a_j)$:
  - In case $1 \leq j < 3m$, if $\displaystyle\sum_{h=0}^{|H|-1} F_{j+1}(h) \neq G_{j,z_{i-1}}(b_j)$ then P_1 wins. Otherwise, P_2 wins.
  - In case $j = 3m$, if $F_{3m}(r) = f_{z_{i-1}}^{(i-1)}(p \circ w \circ w')$ then P_1 wins. Otherwise, P_2 wins.

Outputting the result

If P_1 was declared as the honest server or P_2 was declared as the cheater, R outputs M_0, otherwise he outputs $Q_0(0)$. (Recall that M_0 is the claimed result of P_1 and $Q_0(0)$ is the claimed result of P_2.)

Fig. 2. One-round RDoC protocol: verification of answers

For every $i \in [d - 1]$,

$$Pr[\neg T_i \wedge T_{i+1}] = Pr[\neg T_i \wedge T_{i+1} \wedge E_{i+1}] + Pr[\neg T_i \wedge T_{i+1} \wedge \neg E_{i+1}].$$

By the soundness property of the protocol from [FK97] (see Appendix A), we have that

$$Pr[\neg T_i \wedge T_{i+1} \wedge E_{i+1}] \leq Pr[\neg T_i \wedge E_{i+1}] \leq \frac{(|H| + 1) \cdot 2(3m)^2 \cdot 2\delta}{|F|} = \frac{(|H| + 1) \cdot 36m^2 \cdot \delta}{|F|}.$$

By the fact that two distinct univariate degree-t polynomials agree on at most t points we get that

$$Pr[\neg T_i \wedge T_{i+1} \wedge \neg E_{i+1}] \leq Pr[T_{i+1} \wedge \neg E_{i+1}] \leq \frac{2m \cdot (|H| - 1)}{|F|}.$$

Therefore, we get that (assuming $2 \leq m$)

$$Pr[\neg T_i \wedge T_{i+1}] \leq \frac{(|H| + 1) \cdot 36m^2 \cdot \delta}{|F|} + \frac{2m \cdot (|H| - 1)}{|F|} \leq \frac{(|H| + 1) \cdot 37m^2 \cdot \delta}{|F|}.$$

Thus, summing the error probabilities for all layers, we get

$$Pr[S_2] \leq d \cdot \frac{(|H|+1) \cdot 37m^2 \cdot \delta}{|F|}.$$

Let S_1 be the event that although P_1 is the malicious server, the referee outputs a wrong result (i.e., M_0 that is not equal to $C(x)$). The only step P_1 can cheat is in some of the executions of the [FK97] protocol. Thus, by union bound we get that $Pr[S_1]$ is also bounded by the same probability.

Thus, for any constant soundness ε we can take F to be of size $\geq \frac{d \cdot (|H|+1) \cdot 37m^2 \cdot \delta}{\varepsilon}$ which is $poly(|H|)$. $\square$

Realizing the Oracle for $\mathcal{L}$-Uniform $\mathcal{NC}$ Circuits. For any language $L \in \mathcal{L}$-uniform $\mathcal{NC}$ there exists a circuit C_L of poly-size and polylogarithmic-depth that computes L. Furthermore, the polynomials $\widetilde{\text{spec}}_{c(i)}$ of C_L can be computed by a log-space TM, which means that $\widetilde{\text{spec}}_{c(i)}$ can be computed by an $\mathcal{NL}$ circuit, $C_{\text{spec}(L)}$. As shown in [GKR08], the circuit specification function $\widetilde{\text{spec}}_{c(i)}$ of circuits in $\mathcal{NL}$ can be computed in poly-logarithmic time. This means that the referee can compute $\widetilde{\text{spec}}_{c(i)}$ of $C_{\text{spec}(L)}$ by himself, and execute the protocol from Sect. 3.2 without an oracle assistance.

Recall the idea of [GKR08] for extending the *bare-bones* protocol to $\mathcal{L}$-uniform $\mathcal{NC}$ circuits. In order to verify the computation of the circuit C_L, the referee runs the bare-bones protocol for verifying C_L, and asks the server for the required values of the circuit specification function $\widetilde{\text{spec}}_{c(i)}$ (i.e. the server acts as the oracle). Then, the referee checks each of those claimed values by executing the bare-bones protocol for the circuit $C_{\text{spec}(L)}$ (for which he can compute the oracle answers by himself).

Now, if we try to follow this idea for extending the protocol from Sect. 3.2 to work with $\mathcal{L}$-uniform $\mathcal{NC}$ circuits, and try to run in parallel the protocol also for verification of $C_{\text{spec}(L)}$, we get contradicting requirements. On the one hand, for verification of $C_{\text{spec}(L)}$, both servers have to know p, w, w' as those are the *inputs* for the specification circuit (and the protocol assumes those inputs are known to both servers). But on the other hand, for verification of C_L, the soundness of the protocol requires that those values will not be known to P_1.

In order to tackle this problem, we use a similar idea to the one used in the previous protocol. The referee asks P_1 to answer on many points, without revealing the actual p, w, w'. Note that p, w, w' is implicitly known to P_1 from $C_{3m}(t)$. P_2 already knows w, w' and we can send him also the value p without ruining the soundness of the previous protocol.

Using those two observations, we construct a protocol (P_1', P_2', R') for any language in $\mathcal{L}$-uniform $\mathcal{NC}$. For verification of the output of C_L, the referee executes the protocol from Sect. 3.2, where P_1' runs P_1 and P_2' runs P_2, with two modifications: 1) The referee sends to P_2' also the values of p for all layers, and, 2) P_2' sends the (claimed) values of $\widetilde{\text{spec}}_{c(i)}(b, p, w, w')$ for all layers.

For each of the answers $\widetilde{\text{spec}}_{c(i)}(b, p, w, w')$, the referee executes the protocol from Sect. 3.2 for verification of those claimed values using the circuit $C_{\text{spec}(L)}$

(for which he can compute the circuit specification by himself). As we mentioned before, p, w, w' is not explicitly known to P_1'. So instead we ask it to answer on many points instead of the specific p, w, w'. Specifically, for verification of $\widetilde{spec}_{c(i)}(b, p, w, w')$ of layer i of C_L, we execute the protocol from Sect. 3.2, where P_2' plays the role of P_2 and knows p, w, w', and P_1' plays the role of P_1 for *all the points* on the curve $C_{3m}(t)$ as the possible inputs for $C_{spec(L)}$. (There are at most $|F|$ points on this curve). This means that P_1' does not know the specific p, w, w'. However, since $C_{3m}(t)$ passes through p, w, w', one of those answers will be the needed P_1''s answer for the input p, w, w'.

When the referee receives the messages from both servers (for verification of $C_{spec(L)}$ and of C_L), he checks if they agree on all the values of $\widetilde{spec}_{c(i)}(b, p, w, w')$. If they disagree on some of the values, then the referee checks one of those disagreements using the referee R from Sect. 3.2 and outputs according to his answer. If the servers agree on all the values of $\widetilde{spec}_{c(i)}$, then by the assumption that one of them is honest, those values are correct. Then, the referee verifies the computation of the circuit C_L given the values of $\widetilde{spec}_{c(i)}$ he got before. He runs the checking phase of the referee from Sect. 3.2 and outputs according to his answer.

The overhead of this solution is only polynomial in all parameters since for each layer we have two invocations of the protocol form Sect. 3.2 where P_1' executes the protocol for $|F|$ points. Summing over all layers, the running time is increased by a factor of $2d \cdot |F|$ which is still poly-logarithmic in the size of the input.

Theorem 3. *Let L be a language in $\mathcal{L}$-uniform $\mathcal{NC}$. For any input x and for any constant error probability ε, the protocol $(P_1'(x), P_2'(x), R'(x))$ is ε-RDoC with two servers for the circuit C_L.*

Proof. Note that the information that the referee sends for the verification of $C_{spec(L)}$ is independent of the messages for the verification of C_L. Those proofs share only one piece of information, the values of p, w, w' as the inputs for the circuit $C_{spec(L)}$.

Let's assume P_1' is the cheater. He can cheat either on some value of $\widetilde{spec}_{c(i)}$ or on the computation of C_L. In the first case, he will be caught with high probability by the soundness of the protocol from Sect. 3.2. For the second case, if P_1' cheats on the computation of C_L (while the values of $\widetilde{spec}_{c(i)}$ are correct), then it means he can cheat in the protocol from Sect. 3.2 in the case where he has an oracle access to $\widetilde{spec}_{c(i)}$.

By a union bound of the cheating probabilities of the $2d+1$ invocations of the protocol, we can bound the probability of cheating by $(2d+1) \cdot d \cdot \frac{(|H|+1) \cdot 37m^2 \cdot \delta}{|F|}$. Thus, for any constant soundness ε we can take F to be of size $\geq (2d+1) \cdot d \cdot \frac{(|H|+1) \cdot 37m^2 \cdot \delta}{\varepsilon}$ which is $poly(|H|)$. $\square$

By Theorem 1 the error probability can be reduced exponentially using parallel repetition.

4   Offline/Online Verifiable Delegation of Computation with a Public Offline Stage

Previous constructions and definitions (e.g., [GGP10, CKV10, AIK10, CKLR11], [BGV11]) allow the client to work longer in the offline stage, and compute some secret key which he could later use in the online stage. This assumes that at some point in time, the client *can* work harder or has access to a trusted third-party. Furthermore, the server must not learn any information about this key, so if the client uses the assistance of a trusted third-party he has to get a unique secret key, for his use only.

A natural extension of this model is where instead of generating a secret key in the offline stage, the computing party outputs a public key that can be used by anyone. In addition, any (powerful enough) player can verify that key. An example for a real-world scenario is the following:

- Google publishes a (singed) set of public keys that corresponds to a set of functions.
- Google's competitors (or anyone powerful enough in that matter) can verify these keys and in particular publish an accusation proof in case some of the keys are invalid.
- A weak client can delegate his computation to *any* server, using the published public keys. He does not have to run the offline stage by himself.
- In case the proof of the server is invalid, the client can publish the transcript and its own coins, and prove that the server is a cheater. We stress that by publishing his coins, the client does not loss privacy of any other key (as happens with some of the previous constructions).

4.1   Splitting the [GKR08] Protocol

Given a circuit specification oracle, the bare-bones protocol from Sect. 2.2 requires the client to run in time proportional to $n \cdot \mathrm{poly}(d, \log(S))$. However, it remains to see how to realize the oracle. As discussed above, [GKR08] shows a way to realize the oracle for $\mathcal{L}$-uniform $\mathcal{NC}$ languages.

If we are interested in a larger class of languages, we can use an efficient computationally-sound protocol for realizing the oracle, and use the bare-bones protocol only for the verification of the computation itself. Specifically, given a circuit C, the client (or some other third party) computes in the offline stage the polynomials $\widetilde{\mathrm{spec}}_{c(i)}$ and the evaluation of these polynomials on all their domains. Then, the client computes the root of the Merkle Hash Tree on these values (i.e., the tree leaves are the values of the polynomials). The total running time for computing this root is $\mathrm{poly}(S)$. Later on, in the (possibly many) online stages, the client and the server run the bare-bones protocol. When the client needs a value of the circuit specification predicate, he asks this value from the server, which returns it along with a proof of consistency with the root of the Merkle Hash Tree.

A useful property of this protocol is that the information computed in the offline stage can be used by *any* interested client, and, as such, the protocol is secure also against adaptive adversaries. Also, since the computation of the offline stage is deterministic, this computation can be done by the server and be verified by any interested third party (following the above example).

The combined protocol is similar to the one presented next, thus we omit further details.

4.2   One-Round OVDoC with Public Offline Stage

Using a similar split and by utilizing the transformation of [KR09] we can construct a 1-round computationally-sound protocol with public offline stage for more than $\mathcal{L}$-uniform $\mathcal{NC}$ circuits. (Note that the [KR09] transformation of the [GKR08] protocol requires only a single round, without an offline stage. However, it works only with $\mathcal{L}$-uniform $\mathcal{NC}$ circuits.) The idea follows the transformation of [KR09]: Execute the bare-bones protocol under cPIR queries for verifying the computation of $C(x)$, and, query the values of the circuit specification predicate also under cPIR queries.

The Model. A One-Round Offline/Online Verifiable Delegation of Computation with Public Offline Stage scheme (denoted by 1RPDoC) consists of offline and online stages. The offline stage is executed only once before the online stage whereas the online stage can be executed many times. The algorithms are as following:

- KeyGen(F, λ) $\rightarrow PK$: Based on the security parameter λ, the deterministic key generation algorithm generates a public key that encodes the function F, which is used by a client to verify delegations of F.
  Let $T(F)$ be the time bound required to compute F on any input. We require that the running time of the algorithm will be $\leq \text{poly}(T(F), \lambda)$.
- ProbGen(x, PK, λ) $\rightarrow (k_x, c_x)$: The problem generation algorithm uses the public key and the input x to generate a challenge c_x that is given to the server, and a secret key k_x that is kept private by the client.
- Compute(x, PK, c_x) $\rightarrow (y, \pi_y)$: Using the public key and the input, the server computes the function's output $y = F(x)$ along with a proof of correctness π_y given the challenge c_x.
  We require that the running time of the algorithm will be $\leq \text{poly}(T(F), \lambda)$.
- VerifyResult(PK, k_x, y, π_y) $\rightarrow y \cup \bot$: Using the secret key k_x, the verification algorithm verifies the server's proof π_y and if succussed outputs y. Otherwise it outputs $\bot$.
  We require that the sum of the running times of this algorithm and ProbGen() for the same input, will be $o(T(F), \lambda)$.

Note that since KeyGen() is deterministic, anyone can verify (in $\text{poly}(T(F), \lambda)$ time) whether PK is a valid encoding of the target function F.

As for completeness and soundness, we require the following:

Definition 2 (ε-secure 1RPDoC). *We say that a scheme is a ε-secure 1RP-DoC for a circuit C if after the offline stage (and given a valid PK) the following holds for any input x and $(k_x, c_x) = $ ProbGen(x, PK, λ):*

- *(Completeness) If $(y, \pi_y) = $ Compute(x, PK, c_x) then VerifyResult$(PK, k_x, y, \pi_y) = y$.*
- *(Soundness) For any $y^* \neq C(x)$ and π_{y^*}, Pr[VerifyResult$(PK, k_x, y^*, \pi_{y^*}) = \perp] \geq 1 - \varepsilon$.*

In concurrent work, Parno, Raykova and Vaikuntanathan [PRV12] propose two notions, *public delegatability* and *public verifiability*, and show a construction based on attribute-based encryption. The first notion is similar to ours except that in their definition the player that generates the public key (in the offline stage) is trusted. Their second notion allows *any* player to verify the computation, instead of just the player that delegated it. We note that in our definition the client uses fresh coins for each delegation, and therefore, in case he want to prove the server is cheating, he can publish his coins along with the server's answer. Thus, we can get the stronger notion by adding another message to our protocol. We remark that in the definition (and the construction) of [PRV12], a malicious client can frame the server by simply generating an invalid verification key, whereas in the above extension of our protocol, which can be applied also to the [PRV12] protocol, a malicious client cannot do that.

The Protocol. The protocol is presented in Fig. 3.

Theorem 4. *For any circuit C and for any constant error probability ε, the protocol from Fig. 3 is ε-secure 1RPDoC for the circuit C. In the online stage, the client runs in $n \cdot$ poly(depth(C), log$(|C|)$) time and the server in poly$(|C|)$ time.*

Proof. Completeness follows from inspecting the protocol.

As for soundness, we look on the protocol as a composition of two different protocols. The first is the protocol of GKR-KR where the verification of $C(x)$ is reduced to the correctness of a random point on the low degree extension of the input x, given a circuit specification oracle. We denote by s_1 the soundness of GKR-KR (can be arbitrarily small, see [GKR08, KR09]). The second protocol is the cPIR queries on a database which includes the circuit specification truth table augmented with proofs of consistency. The soundness of this protocol s_2 is negligible from the collision resistance of the hash function

Since we hide the queries using cPIR queries, the requested b^i, w_1^i, w_2^i, w_3^i in the second protocol are computationally indistinguishable, and therefore, the server in the first protocol does not get useful information about it (otherwise, we can break the security of the cPIR).

We claim that the soundness of the composition is bounded by $s_1 + s_2 + neg(\lambda)$. Suppose there is an adversary A that breaks the protocol with probability $p \geq$

KeyGen(F, λ):

This algorithm is called in the offline stage. Let C be the circuit that computes the function F, and let H be a collision resistant hash function given the security parameter λ. Also, define the GKR-KR protocol parameters as in Sect. 2.2.

- Compute the polynomials $\widetilde{\mathrm{spec}}_{c(i)}$ and the values of $\widetilde{\mathrm{spec}}_{c(i)}(b, w_1, w_2, w_3)$ for all $b \in \{0, 1\}$ and $w_1, w_2, w_3 \in F^m$.
- Construct a Merkle Hash Tree where the leaves of the tree are the values $\mathsf{H}(\widetilde{\mathrm{spec}}_{c(i)}(b, w_1, w_2, w_3))$.
- Return $PK = [ID_F, \mathrm{size}(C), \mathrm{depth}(C), \lambda, h, root)]$ where ID_F is a short string that identifies the function F, and $root$ is the root of the merkle hash tree.

Note that any player can compute all the above values. In particular, once PK is published, other players can verify it. However, this computation requires polynomial time (in the size of C).

ProbGen(x, PK):

When the client wants to delegate a computation (in the online stage), he computes the following:

- Let $m_1 = \mathsf{GKR\text{-}KR_v}(\mathrm{size}(C), \mathrm{depth}(C), \lambda)$ be the first message sent by the client in the GKR-KR protocol for the bare-bones protocol only (i.e., for verification of the computation of C only), and let $(b^{(i)}, w_1^{(i)}, w_2^{(i)}, w_3^{(i)})$ (for $i = 0 \ldots \mathrm{depth}(C)$) be the quadruplets that the protocol queries for their $\widetilde{\mathrm{spec}}_{c(i)}$ values.
- Compute cPIR queries for each quadruplet $(b^{(i)}, w_1^{(i)}, w_2^{(i)}, w_3^{(i)})$. Denote the resulting set of queries by m_2.
- Let k_x be the random coins used for the computation of $\mathsf{GKR\text{-}KR_v}$ and the cPIR queries. Return $c_x = [m_1, m_2]$ and k_x.

Note that the above steps do not depend on the input x.

Compute(x, PK, c_x):

The server receives the input x, the public key and the challenge, and does the following:

- Evaluate $y = C(x)$.
- Prepare two databases. The first is a database with the answers to the GKR-KR protocol, and the second is a database that includes the values of $\widetilde{\mathrm{spec}}_{c(i)}(b, w_1, w_2, w_3)$ augmented with the Merkle Hash Tree proofs of consistency. I.e., the database consists of $2|F|^{3m} = \mathrm{poly}(\mathrm{size}(C))$ entries, where in the (a, b, c, d) entry there is the value of $\widetilde{\mathrm{spec}}_{c(i)}(a, b, c, d)$ and the path in Merkle Hash Tree from $\mathsf{H}(\widetilde{\mathrm{spec}}_{c(i)}(a, b, c, d))$ to the root.
- Let $(m_1, m_2) = c_x$. Compute $m_1' = \mathsf{GKR\text{-}KR_p}(C, x, m_1)$ (i.e. the answers according to the GKR-KR protocol and the first database).
- Compute the cPIR answers for the queries m_2 and the second database. Denote the results by m_2'.
- Return $y, [m_1', m_2']$.

Fig. 3. 1RPDoC protocol

VerifyResult(PK, k_x, y, π_y):

Given the claimed output y, the proof $(m_1', m_2') = \pi_y$ and his secret key k_x, the client does the following:

- Verify that the answers in m_2' are consistent with the root from PK.
- Run the verifier of the GKR-KR protocol on m_1' where each time a value of $\widetilde{spec}_{c(i)}$ is needed, use the answers from m_2'.

If both checks succussed, output y. Otherwise, output $\perp$.

Fig. 3. *(Continued)*

$s_1 + s_2 + neg(\lambda) + c$ where $c > 0$ is a constant. In order to cheat, the adversary has to cheat (at least) in either the first or the second protocol. Let A_1 be an adversary for the GKR-KR protocol that simulates the second protocol and executes A on both the GKR-KR messages and the simulated ones and let p_1 be the probability it cheats. Similarly, let A_2 be an adversary for the second protocol where it simulates the GKR-KR messages, and let p_2 be its cheating probability. Since $Pr[A$ cheats$] \leq Pr[A_1$ cheats$] + Pr[A_2$ cheats$]$ we get that $p_1 + p_2 \geq p \geq s_1 + s_2 + neg(\lambda) + c$. Hence, one of p_i is at least $s_i + c/2 + neg(\lambda)$, which contradicts the assumption about the soundness of the original protocols.

By carefully picking the parameters of the GKR-KR protocol and the hash function we use, it is possible to get any constant soundness. □

By parallel repetition the error probability can be reduced exponentially (using the results of Bellare *et al.* [BIN97] and Canetti *et al.* [CHS05]).

To the best of our knowledge, the resulting protocol is the only delegation protocol with a public offline stage and a single round in the online stage for more than $\mathcal{L}$-uniform $\mathcal{NC}$ circuits (based on standard assumptions). We note that the same technique can be applied to the protocols of [CKLR11] for memory and streaming delegation that are based on the protocol of [GKR08].

References

[AIK10] Applebaum, B., Ishai, Y., Kushilevitz, E.: From Secrecy to Soundness: Efficient Verification via Secure Computation. In: Abramsky, S., Gavoille, C., Kirchner, C., Meyer auf der Heide, F., Spirakis, P.G. (eds.) ICALP 2010. LNCS, vol. 6198, pp. 152–163. Springer, Heidelberg (2010)

[BCCR12] Bitansky, N., Canetti, R., Chiesa, A., Tromer, E.: From extractable collision resistance to succinct non-interactive arguments of knowledge, and back again. In: Proceedings of the 3rd Innovations in Theoretical Computer Science Conference, pp. 326–349. ACM (2012)

[BG02] Barak, B., Goldreich, O.: Universal arguments and their applications. SIAM J. Comput. 38, 1661–1694 (2008)

[BGKW88] Ben-Or, M., Goldwasser, S., Kilian, J., Wigderson, A.: Multi-prover interactive proofs: how to remove intractability assumptions. In: Proceedings of the
Twentieth Annual ACM Symposium on Theory of Computing, pp. 113–131. ACM
(1988)

[BGV11] Benabbas, S., Gennaro, R., Vahlis, Y.: Verifiable Delegation of Computation
over Large Datasets. In: Rogaway, P. (ed.) CRYPTO 2011. LNCS, vol. 6841, pp.
111–131. Springer, Heidelberg (2011)

[BIN97] Bellare, M., Impagliazzo, R., Naor, M.: Does parallel repetition lower the
error in computationally sound protocols? In: Proceedings of the 38th Annual
Symposium on Foundations of Computer Science, pp. 374–383. IEEE Computer
Society (1997)

[CHS05] Canetti, R., Halevi, S., Steiner, M.: Hardness Amplification of Weakly Verifiable Puzzles. In: Kilian, J. (ed.) TCC 2005. LNCS, vol. 3378, pp. 17–33. Springer,
Heidelberg (2005)

[CKLR11] Chung, K.-M., Kalai, Y.T., Liu, F.-H., Raz, R.: Memory Delegation. In:
Rogaway, P. (ed.) CRYPTO 2011. LNCS, vol. 6841, pp. 151–168. Springer, Heidelberg (2011)

[CKV10] Chung, K.-M., Kalai, Y., Vadhan, S.: Improved Delegation of Computation
Using Fully Homomorphic Encryption. In: Rabin, T. (ed.) CRYPTO 2010. LNCS,
vol. 6223, pp. 483–501. Springer, Heidelberg (2010)

[CL08] Di Crescenzo, G., Lipmaa, H.: Succinct NP Proofs from an Extractability Assumption. In: Beckmann, A., Dimitracopoulos, C., Löwe, B. (eds.) CiE 2008.
LNCS, vol. 5028, pp. 175–185. Springer, Heidelberg (2008)

[CMT12] Cormode, G., Mitzenmacher, M., Thaler, J.: Practical verified computation
with streaming interactive proofs. In: Proceedings of the 3rd Innovations in Theoretical Computer Science Conference, pp. 90–112. ACM (2012)

[CRR11] Canetti, R., Riva, B., Rothblum, G.N.: Practical delegation of computation
using multiple servers. In: Proceedings of the 18th ACM Conference on Computer
and Communications Security, pp. 445–454. ACM (2011)

[DFH12] Damgård, I., Faust, S., Hazay, C.: Secure Two-Party Computation with Low
Communication. In: Cramer, R. (ed.) TCC 2012. LNCS, vol. 7194, pp. 54–74.
Springer, Heidelberg (2012)

[FK97] Feige, U., Kilian, J.: Making games short (extended abstract). In: Proceedings
of the Twenty-Ninth Annual ACM Symposium on Theory of Computing, pp.
506–516. ACM (1997)

[GGP10] Gennaro, R., Gentry, C., Parno, B.: Non-Interactive Verifiable Computing:
Outsourcing Computation to Untrusted Workers. In: Rabin, T. (ed.) CRYPTO
2010. LNCS, vol. 6223, pp. 465–482. Springer, Heidelberg (2010)

[GKR08] Goldwasser, S., Kalai, Y.T., Rothblum, G.N.: Delegating computation: interactive proofs for muggles. In: Proceedings of the 40th Annual ACM Symposium
on Theory of Computing, pp. 113–122. ACM (2008)

[GLR11] Goldwasser, S., Lin, H., Rubinstein, A.: Delegation of computation without
rejection problem from designated verifier cs-proofs. Cryptology ePrint Archive,
Report 2011/456 (2011), http://eprint.iacr.org/

[K92] Kilian, J.: A note on efficient zero-knowledge proofs and arguments (extended
abstract). In: Proceedings of the Twenty-Fourth Annual ACM Symposium on
Theory of Computing, pp. 723–732. ACM (1992)

[KR09] Kalai, Y.T., Raz, R.: Probabilistically Checkable Arguments. In: Halevi, S.
(ed.) CRYPTO 2009. LNCS, vol. 5677, pp. 143–159. Springer, Heidelberg (2009)

[KR11] Kol, G., Raz, R.: Competing provers protocols for circuit evaluation. Technical Report TR11-122, Electronic Colloquium on Computational Complexity (September 14, 2011), http://eccc.hpi-web.de/

[LFKN92] Lund, C., Fortnow, L., Karloff, H., Nisan, N.: Algebraic methods for interactive proof systems. J. ACM 39, 859–868 (1992)

[M00] Micali, S.: Computationally sound proofs. SIAM J. Comput. 30, 1253–1298 (2000)

[PRV12] Parno, B., Raykova, M., Vaikuntanathan, V.: How to Delegate and Verify in Public: Verifiable Computation from Attribute-Based Encryption. In: Cramer, R. (ed.) TCC 2012. LNCS, vol. 7194, pp. 422–439. Springer, Heidelberg (2012)

[R09] Rothblum, G.N.: Delegating computation reliably: paradigms and constructions. Ph.D. Thesis. Massachusetts Institute of Technology (2009)

A   The Protocol of [FK97]

Intuition. We present a variant of the one-round refereed game from [FK97] for the sum-check task. In this task we have a finite field F, a subset of F denoted by H, a fixed number k and a multivariate polynomial $f : F^k \to F$ of degree $\leq d$ in each variable.[3] The referee can evaluate f by himself in polynomial time in the size of f. Server 1 claims that

$$\sum_{x_1, x_2, \ldots, x_k \in H} f(x_1, x_2, \ldots, x_k) = N_0$$

for some value N_0 and Server 2 claims otherwise (denote this value by N_0').

Lund *et al.* [LFKN92] show an interactive proof with one server for the sum-check task. Their protocol requires k rounds. In the first round, the server sends to the client the univariate polynomial $g_1(x) = \sum_{x_2, \ldots, x_k \in H} f(x, x_2, \ldots, x_k)$ and the client checks if $\sum_{x \in H} g_1(x) = N_0$. Then, the client chooses a random element $c_1 \in F$ and sends it to the server. The protocol continues to the next rounds, where in round i (for $i \in [2..k]$) the server sends to the client $g_i(x) = \sum_{x_i, \ldots, x_k \in H} f(c_1, \ldots, c_{i-1}, x, x_{i+1} \ldots, x_k)$ and client checks if $\sum_{x \in H} g_i(x) = g_{i-1}(c_{i-1})$. Then, the client chooses another random element $c_i \in F$ and sends it to the server. In the last round, the client does not send c_k to the server. Instead, he computes $f(c_1, \ldots, c_k)$ by himself, and checks whether it equals to $g_k(c_k)$. Note that the correctness of the protocol requires that the server cannot guess the c_i-s in advance as they are randomly chosen by the client. Actually, this is why the protocol requires k rounds. If the client would have send all the c_i-s in one round, the server could easily cheat.

---

[3] The [FK97] protocol considers $f : \{0,1\}^k \to F$. We extend it to $f : F^k \to F$. Furthermore, the last stage of the protocol was simplified following a suggestion from an anonymous reviewer.

In order to reduce the number of rounds, the protocol of [FK97] uses information from both servers. Intuitively, instead of asking the server for a fixed prefix along the rounds (i.e., $c_1, c_2, \ldots c_{i-1}$ is the prefix for round i), for each $i \in [1..k]$ the referee asks on many random prefixes of length i. This allows the referee to send all those prefixes in a single round. However now, since the prefixes are not fixed, the referee cannot efficiently do the *consistency check* between $g_i(x)$ and $g_{i-1}(x)$ (i.e., checking that $\sum_{x \in H} g_i(x) = g_{i-1}(c_{i-1})$). So, the referee uses the second server for that. The consistency check is done by asking both servers for the polynomials g_i-s for random prefixes, such that for each length i there is one prefix that both servers receive from the referee. If both servers answer the same for that specific prefix, then by the assumption that one of the servers is honest, this answer is correct.

The Protocol. Following the intuition behind the protocol, we now describe the protocol in detail. For simplicity, we use the shorthand $a \circ b$ for a vector that is a concatenation of a and b (where a, b are vectors or single elements). We assume the elements of H are $0, 1, \ldots, |H| - 1$. Instead of working with prefixes, all computations are done using low degree parametric curves, which is a more compact representation. (A parametric curve of degree d in $F[t]^j$ is a tuple of j one-parameter polynomials over the field F, each one of degree $\leq d$.)

The protocol is as presented in Fig. 4.

Theorem 5. *Let F be a finite field and H subset of F. Let $f : F^k \to F$ be a multivariate polynomial of degree $\leq d$ in each variable and let*

$$N = \sum_{x_1, x_2, \ldots, x_k \in H} f(x_1, x_2, \ldots, x_k).$$

The above protocol is a refereed game with the following properties:

- *If P_1 claims that $N_0 = N$, then he will be declared as the winner with probability $\geq 1 - \frac{|H| \cdot 2k^2 \cdot d}{|F|}$.*
- *If P_1 claims that $N_0 \neq N$, then he will be declared as the winner with probability $\leq \frac{|H| \cdot 2k^2 \cdot d}{|F|}$*

The referee is polynomial in $|H|$ and k, the (honest) servers are polynomial in $|F|^k$ and the communication complexity is polynomial in $|F|$ and k.

Proof (sketch). Let S_1 be the event that

$$\sum_{x_1, x_2, \ldots, x_k \in H} f(x_1, x_2, \ldots, x_k) \neq N_0$$

but P_1 is declared as the winner (i.e., P_2 is the honest server). Let U_i be the event that $F_i(t)$ is indeed $\Phi_i(C_i(t))$, let E_i be the event that $F_i(a_i)$ is indeed $\Phi_i(C_i(a_i))$ and let E' be the event that $F_k(r)$ is indeed $f(C_k(r))$

R's computations: For $1 \leq j \leq k$, R chooses random vectors $A_j, B_j \in F^j$ and random elements $a_j, b_j \in F$. Let $C_j(t) \in F[t]^j$ be the unique degree-$|H|$ parametric curve going through

$$(0, A_{j-1} \circ 0), \ldots, (|H| - 1, A_{j-1} \circ (|H| - 1)), (|H|, B_j)$$

and let $D_j(t) \in F[t]^j$ be the canonical representation of the unique degree-1 parametric curve going though

$$(a_j, C_j(a_j)), (b_j, A_j).$$

For $j = 1 \ldots k$ we define the functions

$$\Phi_j(x_1, \ldots, x_j) = \sum_{x_{j+1}, \ldots, x_k \in H} f(x_1, \ldots, x_j, x_{j+1} \ldots, x_k).$$

Note that

$$\Phi_j(x_1, \ldots, x_j) = \sum_{x_{j+1} \in H} \Phi_{j+1}(x_1, \ldots, x_{j+1}).$$

R sends to P_1: $C_1(t), \ldots, C_k(t)$.
P_1 sends to R: $N_0, F_1(t), \ldots, F_k(t)$, where $F_j(t) = \Phi_j(C_j(t))$.
R sends to P_2: $D_1(t), \ldots, D_k(t)$.
P_2 sends to R: $N_0', G_1(t), \ldots, G_k(t)$, where $G_j(t) = \Phi_j(D_j(t))$.
R declares the winner: P_1 loses immediately if for some j, $F_j(t)$ has degree greater than $|H| \cdot j \cdot d$. P_2 loses immediately if for some j, $G_j(t)$ has degree greater than $j \cdot d$.
In case for all j, $G_j(a_j) = F_j(a_j)$, if $\sum_{i=0}^{|H|-1} F_1(i) = N_0$ then P_1 wins. Otherwise, P_2 wins.
Denote by j the largest number such that $G_j(a_j) \neq F_j(a_j)$:

- In case $1 \leq j < k$, if $\sum_{i=0}^{|H|-1} F_{j+1}(i) \neq G_j(b_j)$ then P_1 wins. Otherwise, P_2 wins.
- In case $j = k$, if $F_k(r) = f(C_k(r))$ for a randomly chosen $r \in F$, then P_1 wins. Otherwise, P_2 wins.

Fig. 4. One-round refereed game for the sum-check task

$$Pr[S_1] \leq Pr[E' \wedge \neg U_k] + Pr[\exists i \in [1..k] \ s.t. \ E_i \wedge \neg U_i] \leq Pr[E' \wedge \neg U_k] + \sum_{i=1}^{k} Pr[E_i \wedge \neg U_i].$$

By the fact that two distinct univariate degree-t polynomials agree on at most t points we get that

$$Pr[E' \wedge \neg U_k] \leq \frac{|H| \cdot k \cdot d}{|F|},$$

and that

$$Pr[E_i \wedge \neg U_i] \leq \frac{|H| \cdot i \cdot d}{|F|} \leq \frac{|H| \cdot k \cdot d}{|F|}.$$

Thus,

$$Pr[S_1] \leq \frac{|H| \cdot k \cdot d}{|F|} + k \cdot \frac{|H| \cdot k \cdot d}{|F|} \leq (k+1) \cdot \frac{|H| \cdot k \cdot d}{|F|}.$$

Let S_2 be the event that P_1 is the honest server but P_2 is declared to be the winner. Using a similar calculation, we have that

$$Pr[S_2] \leq k \cdot \frac{k \cdot d}{|F|}.$$

The only differences are that in this case the degrees of $G_j(t)$ are smaller than the degrees of $F_j(t)$ by a factor of $|H|$, and, that we do not check $G_k(t)$ on a random point r. Therefore, the soundness of the protocol is bounded by $\frac{|H| \cdot 2k^2 \cdot d}{|F|}$.   □

We remark that our protocol from Sect. 3.2 has another difference compared to the above protocol. We increase by one the degree of the curve C_k. Using a similar argument to the above it can be shown that the soundness of that protocol is bounded by $\frac{(|H|+1) \cdot 2k^2 \cdot d}{|F|}$.

On the Amortized Complexity of Zero Knowledge Protocols for Multiplicative Relations

Ronald Cramer, Ivan Damgård, and Valerio Pastro

CWI Amsterdam and Dept. of Computer Science, Aarhus University

Abstract. We present a protocol that allows to prove in zero-knowledge that committed values x_i, y_i, z_i, $i = 1, \ldots, l$ satisfy $x_i y_i = z_i$, where the values are taken from a finite field. For error probability 2^{-u} the size of the proof is linear in u and only logarithmic in l. Therefore, for any fixed error probability, the amortized complexity vanishes as we increase l. In particular, when the committed values are from a field of small constant size, we improve complexity of previous solutions by a factor of l. Assuming preprocessing, we can make the commitments (and hence the protocol itself) be information theoretically secure. Using this type of commitments we obtain, in the preprocessing model, a perfect zero-knowledge interactive proof for circuit satisfiability of circuit C where the proof has size $O(|C|)$. We then generalize our basic scheme to a protocol that verifies l instances of an algebraic circuit D over K with v inputs, in the following sense: given committed values $x_{i,j}$ and z_i, with $i = 1, \ldots, l$ and $j = 1, \ldots, v$, the prover shows that $D(x_{i,1}, \ldots, x_{i,v}) = z_i$ for $i = 1, \ldots, l$. The interesting property is that the amortized complexity of verifying one circuit only depends on the multiplicative depth of the circuit and not the size. So for circuits with small multiplicative depth, the amortized cost can be asymptotically smaller than the number of multiplications in D. Finally we look at commitments to integers, and we show how to implement information theoretically secure homomorphic commitments to integer values, based on preprocessing. After preprocessing, they require only a constant number of multiplications per commitment. We also show a variant of our basic protocol, which can verify l integer multiplications with low amortized complexity. This protocol also works for standard computationally secure commitments and in this case we improve on security: whereas previous solutions with similar efficiency require the strong RSA assumption, we only need the assumption required by the commitment scheme itself, namely factoring.

1   Introduction

The notions of commitment schemes and zero-knowledge proofs are among the most fundamental in the theory and practice of cryptographic protocols. Intuitively, a commitment scheme provides a way for a prover to put a value x in a locked box and commit to x by giving this box $[x]$ to a verifier. Later the prover can choose to open the box by giving away the key to the box.

A. Smith (Ed.): ICITS 2012, LNCS 7412, pp. 62–79, 2012.

In a zero-knowledge protocol, a prover wants to convince a verifier that some statement is true, such that the verifier learns nothing except the validity of the assertion. Typically, the prover claims that an input string u is in a language L, and after the interaction, the verifier accepts or rejects. We assume the reader is familiar with the basic theory of zero-knowledge protocols and just recall the most important notions informally: the protocol is an interactive zero-knowledge proof system for L if it is *complete*, i.e., if $u \in L$, then the verifier accepts – and *sound*, i.e., if $u \notin L$ then no matter what the prover does, the verifier accepts with at most probability ϵ, where ϵ is called the soundness error of the protocol. Finally, zero-knowledge means that given only that $u \in L$, conversations between the honest prover and an arbitrary poly-time verifier can be efficiently simulated and are indistinguishable from real conversations.

In this paper we concentrate on commitments to elements in a finite field K, or to integers and we assume that commitments are also homomorphic, i.e., both commitments and randomness are chosen from (finite) groups, and $[x] \cdot [y] = [x + y]$ (we will describe this property more in detail in section 2.1 and 7). For $K = \mathbb{F}_q$ for a prime q, such commitments can, for instance, be constructed from any q-invertible group homomorphism [CD98] that exists, if factoring or discrete log are hard problems. It is also easy based on known techniques – but perhaps less well known – that homomorphic commitments with unconditional hiding *and* binding can be built if we assume preprocessing, e.g., the committer gets random field elements and information theoretic MACs and the receiver gets corresponding keys. We give more details on this later (see Section 2.1). Finally, Homomorphic commitments to integers based on factoring were proposed in [FO97, DF02].

In typical applications of these commitment schemes, the prover needs to convince the verifier that the values he commits to satisfy a certain algebraic relation. A general way to state this is that the prover commits to $x_1, \ldots, x_v$, and the verifier wants to know that $D(x_1, \ldots, x_v) = 0$ for an algebraic circuit D defined over K or over the integers. If D uses only linear operations, the verifier can himself compute a commitment to $D(x_1, \ldots, x_v)$ (using the homomorphic properties of the commitment scheme) and the prover opens this to reveal 0. However, if D uses multiplication, we need a zero-knowledge protocol where the prover convinces the verifier that three committed values x, y, z satisfy $xy = z$.

In [CDD+99], such a multiplication protocol was proposed for homomorphic commitments over any finite field K. The soundness error for that protocol is $1/|K|$, which is too large if K is a field with small size (constant or logarithmic in the security parameter). The only known way to have a smaller error is to repeat the protocol. This solution leads to a protocol with communication complexity $\Theta(\kappa l)$ for soundness error 2^{-l} and where commitments have size κ bits.

Likewise, a multiplication protocol for integer commitments was proposed in [FO97, DF02]. This protocol has essentially optimal communication complexity $\Theta(\kappa + l + k)$, where k is size in bits of the prover's secret integers, but it requires an extra assumption, namely the strong RSA assumption. If we only want to assume

what the commitment scheme requires (factoring), the best known complexity
is $\Theta((\kappa + k)l)$.

An approach to improving this state of affairs was proposed in [CD09], where
it was suggested to take advantage of the fact that many applications require
the prover to make many ZK proofs of similar statements. The idea is to make
the amortized complexity per proof be small by combining all the proofs into
one protocol. In our case, this would mean that the prover commits to x_i, y_i, z_i
for $i = 1, \ldots, l$ and wants to convince the verifier that $x_i y_i = z_i$ for all i. The
technique from [CD09] yields a protocol with amortized complexity $\Theta(\kappa + l)$ but,
unfortunately, requires that all x_i's are equal (or all y_i's are equal), and in most
applications, this condition is not satisfied.

1.1   Our Contribution

In this paper, we construct a new zero-knowledge protocol that works for arbitrary x_i, y_i, z_i, and uses black-box access to any homomorphic commitment
scheme. If we instantiate the commitments by a standard unconditionally binding and computationally hiding scheme, the amortized complexity is $O(\frac{u}{l}(\kappa +
\log(l + u)))$ bits for error probability 2^{-u}. In particular, for $l = u$, we get
$O(\kappa + \log l)$. Therefore, when the committed values are from a field of small
constant size, we improve the complexity of previous solutions by a factor of l.
We also propose (based on standard techniques) a way to implement unconditionally secure homomorphic commitments assuming preprocessing. Using this
implementation, the amortized complexity is $O(\frac{u}{l}(u + \log(l + u)))$. In particular,
for for both types of commitments and any fixed error probability, the amortized
overhead vanishes as we increase l.

We generalize our approach to obtain a protocol that verifies l instances of
an algebraic circuit D over K with v inputs, in the following sense: given committed values $x_{i,j}$ and z_i, with $i = 1, \ldots, l$ and $j = 1, \ldots, v$, the prover shows
that $D(x_{i,1}, \ldots, x_{i,v}) = z_i$ for $i = 1, \ldots, l$ (the protocol easily generalizes to circuits with more than one output). The amortized cost to verify one circuit with
multiplicative depth δ is $O(2^\delta \kappa + v\kappa + \delta \log l)$ bits for an error probability of 2^{-l}
and so does not depend on the circuit size. For circuits with small multiplicative
depth (sometimes known as the classes $K\text{-}SAC^0$ or $K\text{-}SAC^1$), this approach is
better than using our first protocol, in fact the amortized communication cost
can be asymptotically smaller than the number of multiplications in D.

Another interesting feature of this protocol is that prover and verifier can
execute it given only black-box access to an algorithm computing the function
implemented by D. This is in contrast to standard protocols where the parties
work their way through the circuit and must therefore agree on the layout. Our
protocol would, for instance, allow the verifier to outsource computation of the
function to a third party. As long as the verifier chooses the random challenge in
the protocol, this would be secure if the prover is malicious and the third party
is semi-honest.

Our final result is a zero-knowledge protocol using black-box access to homomorphic commitments to k-bit integers. For checking l integer multiplications

and error probability 2^{-l}, the amortized complexity is $O(\kappa + k + l \log(l))$. When instantiating the commitments using a standard computationally secure scheme, this improves security of previous solutions that needed the strong RSA assumption, while we need no assumption, other than what the underlying commitment scheme requires (typically factoring). We also show a new technique for implementing unconditionally secure homomorphic commitments to integers based on preprocessing. This makes the protocol be much more efficient, as only a constant number of multiplications per commitment is required.

When using information theoretically secure commitments based on preprocessing, our protocols are perfect zero-knowledge against general verifiers. When using standard computationally secure commitments, they are only honest verifier zero-knowledge, but can be made zero-knowledge in general using standard techniques.

Our technique is somewhat related to the "MPC-in-the-head" technique from [IKOS09], but with an important difference: both strategies make use of "virtual players", that is, the prover in his head imagines n players that receive shares of his secret values and he must later reveal information to the verifier relating to these shares. The protocol from [IKOS09] has complexity linear in n, because the prover must commit to the view of each virtual player. We use a different approach, exploiting the homomorphic property of the commitment scheme to get a protocol with complexity logarithmic in n. This is the reason our amortized overhead vanishes instead of being constant, as one would get using MPC-in-the-head. On the other hand, we show that a combination of "multiparty computation in the head" and our protocol for verifying algebraic circuits can actually improve the communication complexity for some parameter values. In concurrent and independent work, Ben-Sasson et al. [BSFO11] show a multiparty protocol for honest majority that checks several multiplicative relations on secret-shared values with low amortized complexity. The technique is somewhat related in that it is based on secret sharing, but the checking works in a different way since in that setting there is no single prover who knows all values.

1.2 Applications

One obvious application of our protocol is to give ZK proofs for satisfiability of a Boolean circuit C: the prover commits to the bits on each wire in the circuit, opens the output as a 1 and shows that, for each AND-gate, the corresponding multiplicative relation holds for the committed bits. To explain how this compares to previous work, we define the (computational or communication) overhead of a protocol to be its (computational or communication) complexity divided by $|C|$. One can think of this as the overhead factor one has to pay to get security, compared to an insecure implementation. Now, in the ideal commitment model (i.e., assuming access to a ideal commitment functionality) [IKOS09] obtained constant communication overhead and polynomial computation overhead, as a function of the security parameter u, for error probability 2^{-u}. Later, [DIK10] showed how to make both overheads poly-logarithmic. For both protocols, the ideal commitments can be implemented by doing preprocessing, and the resulting "on-line" protocol will still have the same complexity.

As mentioned, our protocol can be thought of as working in the ideal *homomorphic* commitment model where the commitment functionality can do linear operations on committed bits (but where we of course charge for the cost of these operations). In this model our protocol achieves constant computational and communication overhead.

We may then instantiate the commitments using the information theoretically secure homomorphic scheme. This incurs an extra cost for local computing, so as a result we obtain a ZK-protocol with constant communication overhead and polynomial computation overhead (essentially $O(u \log u)$). Asymptotically, the overheads match those of [IKOS09], but the involved constants are smaller in our case because we do not need the "detour" via a multiparty protocol. Finally, we pay no communication for linear operations, while this seems hard to achieve in the protocol from [IKOS09].

Another application area where our result can improve state of the art is the following: as shown in [CDN01], general multiparty computation can be based on additively homomorphic encryption schemes. Many such schemes are known, and in several cases, the plaintext space is a small field. One example is the Goldwasser-Micali (GM)-scheme [GM84], where the plaintext space is $\mathbb{F}_2$. Supplying inputs to such a protocol amounts to sending them in encrypted form to all players and proving knowledge of the corresponding plaintexts. However, in many applications one would want to check that inputs satisfy certain conditions, e.g., an auction may require that bids are numbers in a certain interval. Since ciphertexts in such an additively homomorphic scheme can be thought of as homomorphic commitments over the field, our protocol can be used by a player to prove that his input satisfy a given condition much more efficiently that by previous techniques.

A final type of application is in the area of anonymous credentials and group signatures. Such constructions are often based on zero-knowledge proofs that are made non-interactive using the Fiat-Shamir heuristic. If the proof requires showing that a committed number is in a given interval, the standard solution is to "transfer" the values to an integer commitment scheme and use the proof technique of Boudot [Bou00]. This in turn requires multiplication proofs, so if sufficiently many proofs are to be given in parallel, one can use our technique for integer commitments. Assuming preprocessing and our information theoretically secure commitments this can be very efficient, requiring only a constant number of multiplications per commitment.

2   Preliminaries

2.1   Information Theoretic Commitments

In this section we assume a setup that allows commitments to be unconditionally secure. We use $[v]$ as shorthand for a commitment to v in the following. Operations on committments are supposed to be multiplicative, while values that are committed lie in an additive group. Therefore a commitment scheme is homomorphic if $[v] \cdot [v'] = [v + v']$ for all v, v' in the proper domain (either a finite field K or the integers). Also, if $\mathbf{v} = (v_1, \ldots, v_m)$ is a vector with entries in K (or in the integers), $[\mathbf{v}]$ denotes a vector of commitments, one to each coordinate in $\mathbf{v}$. If $\mathbf{u} = (u_1, \ldots, u_m)$ is a vector of the same length as $\mathbf{v}$, then $[\mathbf{v}]^{\mathbf{u}}$ means $[\mathbf{v}]^{\mathbf{u}} = \prod_i [v_i]^{u_i}$, which is a commitment containing the inner product of $\mathbf{u}$ and $\mathbf{v}$. Moreover $[\mathbf{u}] * [\mathbf{v}]$ refers to the component-wise product.

Field Scenario. Let K be a finite field and L be an extension of K. Although the set-up is general, we will think of K as a small constant size field in the following. Let $a \in L$ be a private value held by the verifier. We suppose that the prover has a list A of uniform values $u_1, \ldots, u_i, \ldots \in K$ and for each u_i he also has a value $m_{u_i} = a \cdot u_i + b_{u_i}$, where b_{u_i} is uniform in L and privately held by the verifier. One can think of m_{u_i} as an information theoretic message authentication code on u_i, and of (a, b_{u_i}) as the key to open such a MAC on u_i. It is possible to achieve this situation assuming a functionality for the preprocessing phase of a multiparty computation protocol, such as in the ones in [BDOZ11, DPSZ12].

With this setup, commitments can be done as follows: In order for the prover to commit to $v \in K$, the prover sends $u - v$ to the verifier and sets $m_v = m_u = a \cdot u + b_u$, where u is the first unused value in the list A; the verifier then updates the corresponding key b_u into $b_v = b_u + a \cdot (u - v)$. A commitment to v can therefore expressed as the following data (where P denotes the prover, and V denotes the verifier);

$$[v] = \begin{cases} P : v, \ u, \ m_v = a \cdot u + b_u \\ V : u - v, \ a, \ b_v = b_u + a \cdot (u - v) \end{cases}$$

In order to open commitment $[v]$, the prover sends v, m_v to the verifier, who checks if $a \cdot v + b_v$ equals m_v.

Commitments of this form are unconditionally binding: A prover committing to v can send an opening $\tilde{v}, \tilde{m}$ with $\tilde{v} \neq v$ if and only if $a \cdot \tilde{v} + b_v = \tilde{m}$. This is equivalent for the prover to be able to sample two distinct points $(P_x, P_y) = (v, m_v), (Q_x, Q_y) = (\tilde{v}, \tilde{m})$ from the line $Y = a \cdot u + b_v$; which is equivalent for the prover to know the key (a, b_v) privately held by the verifier. This shows that the probability of a prover succeeding in opening to a different value is bounded by the probability of guessing a random element in a line over L; such a probability equals $1/|L|$. Since we want to have a negligible probability of breaking the binding property of the commitment scheme, we require $|L| = 2^{\Theta(\kappa)}$, where κ is the security parameter. In particular, this means that in (the unfortunate) case where K is a field with constant size, then L is an extension of K of degree linear in κ.

These commitments are also unconditionally hiding: A verifier receiving a commitment $u - v$ only knows a and $b_{u_1}, \ldots, b_{u_i}, \ldots$, which are all independent from v.

Moreover, the above commitments are homomorphic (meaning: $[v] \cdot [v'] = [v + v']$), where $[v] \cdot [v']$ is defined as follows:

$$[v] \cdot [v'] := \begin{cases} P : v + v', \ u + u', \ m_{v+v'} = m_u + m_{u'} \\ V : (u - v) + (u' - v'), \ a, \ b_{v+v'} = b_u + b_{u'} + a \cdot (u - v + u' - v') \end{cases}$$

Integers Scenario. We here give a construction of unconditionally secure commitments on k-bits integers. Contrary to the previous construction, this one is new, to the best of our knowledge. Let a be a prime in the interval $[-2^\kappa, \ldots, 2^\kappa]$ privately held by the verifier. We assume the prover has a list A of integer values $u_1, \ldots, u_i, \ldots$ uniform in $[-2^{k+\kappa}, \ldots, 2^{k+\kappa}]$ and for each u_i he also has an integer $m_{u_i} = a \cdot u_i + b_{u_i}$, where b_{u_i} is a uniform integer in $[-2^{k+3\kappa}, \ldots, 2^{k+3\kappa}]$ and privately held by the verifier.

With this setup, commitments can be done as follows: In order for the prover to commit to the integer $v \in [-2^k, \ldots, 2^k]$, the prover sends $u - v$ to the verifier and sets $m_v = m_u = a \cdot u + b_u$, where u is the first unused value in the list A; the verifier then updates the corresponding key b_u into $b_v = b_u + a \cdot (u - v)$. A commitment to v can therefore expressed as the following data (where P denotes the prover, and V denotes the verifier);

$$[v] = \begin{cases} P : v, \ u, \ m_v = a \cdot u + b_u \\ V : u - v, \ a, \ b_v = b_u + a \cdot (u - v) \end{cases}$$

In order to open commitment $[v]$, the prover sends v, m_v to the verifier, who checks if $a \cdot v + b_v$ equals m_v.

Commitments of this form are homomorphic, unconditionally hiding (same arguments as above) and unconditionally binding: A prover committing to v can send an opening $\tilde{v}, \tilde{m}$ with $\tilde{v} \neq v$ if and only if $a \cdot \tilde{v} + b_v = \tilde{m}$. Subtracting the latter equation to the relation $m_v = a \cdot v + b_v$, we obtain $\tilde{m} - m_v = a \cdot (\tilde{v} - v)$, so the prover must know a multiple of a of length $k + \kappa$ bits. Any $(k + \kappa)$-bits integer can be thought of its factorization, and the prover can break the binding property if he knows a $(k + \kappa)$-bits integer where a appears in its factorization. Since a $(k + \kappa)$-bits integer contains at most $(k + \kappa)/\kappa$ prime factors of length κ and the number of κ-bits primes is $\Theta(2^\kappa/\kappa)$, then the error probability of the scheme is equal to $\Theta(((k + \kappa)/\kappa) \cdot (\kappa/2^\kappa)) = \Theta((k + \kappa)/2^\kappa)$. If $k = O(\kappa)$, the error probability is $O(\kappa/2^\kappa)$.

2.2   Linear Secret Sharing Schemes

The model of linear secret sharing schemes we consider here is essentially equivalent to both the monotone span program formalism [KW93, CDM00] and the linear code based formalism [CCG+07]. However, we generalize to schemes where several values from the underlying field can be shared simultaneously. The model is designed to allow us to describe our protocol to follow as easily as possible.

Let K be a finite field and let m be a positive integer. Consider the m-dimensional K-vector space K^m. Consider the index set $I = \{1, 2, \ldots, m\}$, and write $\mathbf{x} = (x_i)_{i \in I}$ for the coordinates of $\mathbf{x} \in K^m$. In the following, linear functions between finite spaces are considered. It is useful to recall that because such functions are (additive) group homomorphisms, they are always regular; that is, each element in the image has the same number of pre-images, namely the cardinality of the kernel.

For a non-empty set $A \subseteq I$, the **restriction** to A is the K-linear function

$$\pi_A : K^m \longrightarrow K^{|A|}$$
$$\mathbf{x} \longmapsto (x_i)_{i \in A}.$$

Let $C \subseteq K^m$ be a K-linear subspace which we keep fixed throughout this section. Let $A, S \in I$ be non-empty sets. We say that S **offers uniformity** if $\pi_S(C) = K^{|S|}$. Note that by regularity of π_S, if $\mathbf{c}$ is uniform in C, then $\pi_S(\mathbf{c})$ is uniform in $K^{|S|}$.

Jumping ahead, we will use the subspace C for secret sharing by choosing a random vector $\mathbf{c} \in C$ such that $\pi_S(\mathbf{c}) = \mathbf{s}$ where S is a set offering uniformity and $\mathbf{s}$ is the vector of secret values to be shared. The shares are then the coordinates of $\mathbf{c}$ that are not in S.

We say that A **determines** S if there is a function $f : K^{|A|} \to K^{|S|}$ such that, for all $\mathbf{c} \in C$, $(f \circ \pi_A)(\mathbf{c}) = \pi_S(\mathbf{c})$. Note that such f is K-linear if it exists. Note that if $\mathbf{c}$ is uniformly chosen from C and if A determines S, then $\pi_A(\mathbf{c})$ determines $\pi_S(\mathbf{c})$ with probability 1.

We say that A and S are **mutually independent** if the K-linear function

$$\phi_{A,S} : C \longrightarrow \pi_A(C) \times \pi_S(C)$$
$$\mathbf{c} \longmapsto (\pi_A(\mathbf{c}), \pi_S(\mathbf{c}))$$

is surjective. Note that $\pi_S(C) = \{\mathbf{0}\}$ is the only condition under which it occurs that both A and S are independent and A determines S. In particular, if $\mathbf{c}$ is uniformly chosen from C, then $\pi_S(C) \neq \{\mathbf{0}\}$ and if A and S are independent, then $\pi_A(\mathbf{c})$ and $\pi_S(\mathbf{c})$ are distributed independently.

Suppose S offers uniformity. Let e be a positive integer and let

$$g : K^{|S|+e} \longrightarrow C$$

be a surjective K-linear function. Define $\pi_g : K^{|S|+e} \to K^{|S|}$ as the projection to the first $|S|$ coordinates. We say that g is an **S-generator** for C if $\pi_g = \pi_S \circ g$, that is, if the first $|S|$ coordinates of $\rho \in K^{|S|+e}$ are the same as the coordinates of $g(\rho)$ designated by S. Such an S-generator always exists, by elementary linear algebra, with $|B| + \rho = \dim_K(C)$.

For any S-generator g we have that if $\mathbf{s} \in K^{|S|}$ is fixed and if $\rho_{\mathbf{s}}$ is uniformly chosen in $K^{|S|+e}$ subject to $\pi_g(\rho_{\mathbf{s}}) = \mathbf{s}$, then $g(\rho_{\mathbf{s}})$ has the uniform distribution on the subset of C consisting of those $\mathbf{c} \in C$ with $\pi_S(\mathbf{c}) = \mathbf{s}$.

We are now ready to define linear secret sharing schemes in our model: Let $S \subset I$ be non-empty and proper. Write $S^* = I \setminus S$. The tuple (C, S) is a **linear secret sharing scheme** if S offers uniformity and if S^* determines S.

If that is the case, S^* is called the **player set**, $\pi_S(C)$ is the **secret-space**, and $\pi_{S^*}(C)$ is the **share-space**. If $j \in S^*$, then $\pi_j(C)$ is called the **share-space** for the j-th player. If $l = |S|$, the scheme is said to be l-**multi-secret**. For $A \subseteq S^*$, we say that the scheme has A-**privacy** (or A is an unqualified set) if $A = \varnothing$ or if A and S are independent. There is A-**reconstruction** (or A is qualified) if A is non-empty and if A determines S. The scheme offers t-**privacy** if, for all A in the player set with $|A| = t$, there is A-privacy. The scheme offers r-**reconstruction** if, for all A in the player set with $|A| = r$, there is A-reconstruction.

Note that $0 \leq t < r \leq |S^*|$ if there is t-privacy and r-reconstruction. A **generator** for (C, S) is an S-generator for C.

Let (C, S) be a secret sharing scheme, and let g be a generator. If $\mathbf{s} \in K^{|S|}$ is the secret, shares for the players in S^* are computed as follows. Select a vector $\rho_{\mathbf{s}}$ according to the uniform probability distribution on $K^{|S|+e}$, subject to $\pi_g(\rho_{\mathbf{s}}) = \mathbf{s}$ and compute $\mathbf{c} = g(\rho_{\mathbf{s}})$. The "full vector of shares" is the vector $\pi_{S^*}(\mathbf{c})$.

In the following, where we write $\rho_{\mathbf{s}}$, it will usually be understood that it holds that $\pi_g(\rho_{\mathbf{s}}) = \mathbf{s}$, and we say that such a vector is consistent with the secret $\mathbf{s}$.

Multiplication Properties. For any $\mathbf{x}, \mathbf{y} \in K^m$, the **Schur-product** (or component-wise product) between them is the element $(\mathbf{x} * \mathbf{y}) \in K^m$ defined as $(\mathbf{x} * \mathbf{y}) = (x_j \cdot y_j)_{j \in I}$. If $C \subset K^m$ is a K-linear subspace, then its **Schur-product transform** is the subspace $\widehat{C} \subset K^m$ defined as the K-linear subspace generated by all elements of the form $\mathbf{c} * \mathbf{c}'$, where $\mathbf{c}, \mathbf{c}' \in C$.

Note that if (C, S) is a linear secret sharing scheme, then S offers uniformity in $\widehat{C}$ as well. But in general it does not hold that S^* determines S in $\widehat{C}$. However, suppose that it does (so $(\widehat{C}, S)$ is a linear secret sharing scheme). Then (C, S) is said to offer $\widehat{r}$-**product reconstruction** if $(\widehat{C}, S)$ offers $\widehat{r}$-reconstruction.

Sweeping Vectors. Let (C, S) be a linear secret sharing scheme, let g be a generator for it and let A be an unqualified set. Since A and S are mutually independent so that $\phi_{A,S}$ is surjective, it follows that for any index $j \in S$, there exists $\mathbf{c}_{A,j} \in C$ such that $\phi_{A,S}(\mathbf{c}_{A,j}) = (\mathbf{0}, \mathbf{e}_j)$ where $\mathbf{e}_j$ is the vector with a 1 in position j and zeros elsewhere. Note that since the generator g is surjective on C we can choose $\mathbf{w}_{A,j}$ such that $g(\mathbf{w}_{A,j}) = \mathbf{c}_{A,j}$, and $\pi_g(\mathbf{w}_{A,j}) = \mathbf{e}_j$. The vector $\mathbf{w}_{A,j}$ is called a jth **sweeping vector**.

To see the purpose of these vectors, suppose we have shared a vector of $|S|$ zeros, so we have $\mathbf{c}_0 = g(\rho_0)$. It is now easy to see that the vector

$$\rho_0 + \sum_{j=1}^{|S|} x_j \mathbf{w}_{A,j}$$

is consistent with the secret $(x_1, \ldots, x_{|S|})$. Moreover, if we apply g to this vector, the player set A gets the same shares as when 0's were shared.

3   Our Protocol

We are now ready to solve the problem mention in the introduction, namely the prover holds values $\mathbf{x} = (x_1, \ldots, x_l), \mathbf{y} = (y_1, \ldots, y_l), \mathbf{z} = (z_1, \ldots, z_l)$, has sent commitments $[\mathbf{x}], [\mathbf{y}], [\mathbf{z}]$ to the verifier and now wants to convince the verifier that $x_i y_i = z_i$ for $i = 1, \ldots, l$, i.e., that $\mathbf{x} * \mathbf{y} = \mathbf{z}$.

We suppose that both the prover and the verifier agreed on using an l-multisecret linear secret sharing scheme (C, S), for d players, offering $\widehat{r}$-product reconstruction, and with privacy threshold t. We fix a generator $g : K^{l+e} \to C$. Moreover, we suppose that $\widehat{g} : K^{l+\widehat{e}} \to \widehat{C}$ is a generator for $(\widehat{C}, S)$ and that a public basis for K^{l+e} (respectively for $K^{l+\widehat{e}}$) has been chosen such that the linear mapping g (resp. $\widehat{g}$) can be computed as the action of a matrix M (resp. $\widehat{M}$).

The idea of the protocol is as follows: the prover secret shares $\mathbf{x}$ and $\mathbf{y}$ using (C, S) and $\mathbf{z}$ using $(\widehat{C}, S)$, in such a way that the resulting vectors of shares $\mathbf{c_x}, \mathbf{c_y}, \widehat{\mathbf{c_z}}$ satisfy $\mathbf{c_x} * \mathbf{c_y} = \widehat{\mathbf{c_z}}$, which is possible since (C, S) offers product reconstruction. The prover commits to the randomness used in all sharings, which, by the homomorphic property, allows the verifier to compute commitments to any desired share. The verifier now chooses t coordinate positions randomly and asks the prover to open the commitments to the shares in those positions. The verifier can then check that the shares in $\mathbf{x}, \mathbf{y}$ multiply to the shares in $\mathbf{z}$. This is secure for the prover since any t shares reveal no information, but on the other hand, if the prover's claim is false, thus $\mathbf{x} * \mathbf{y} \neq \mathbf{z}$, then $\mathbf{c_x} * \mathbf{c_y}$ and $\widehat{\mathbf{c_z}}$ can be equal in at most $\widehat{r}$ positions, so the verifier has a good chance of finding a position that reveals the cheat. More formally, the protocol goes as follows:

Protocol Verify Multiplication

1. The prover chooses two vectors $\mathbf{r_x}, \mathbf{r_y} \in K^e$, and sets $\rho_{\mathbf{x}} = (\mathbf{x}, \mathbf{r_x}), \rho_{\mathbf{y}} = (\mathbf{y}, \mathbf{r_y})$. Define $\mathbf{c_x} = M\rho_{\mathbf{x}}, \mathbf{c_y} = M\rho_{\mathbf{y}}$. Now, the prover computes $\widehat{\rho}_{\mathbf{z}} \in K^{l+\widehat{e}}$ such that $\widehat{\rho}_{\mathbf{z}}$ is consistent with secret $\mathbf{z}$ and such that $\widehat{M}\widehat{\rho}_{\mathbf{z}} = \mathbf{c_x} * \mathbf{c_y}$.
   Note that this is possible by solving a system of linear equations, exactly because $\mathbf{x} * \mathbf{y} = \mathbf{z}$. We then write $\widehat{\rho}_{\mathbf{z}} = (\mathbf{z}, \widehat{\mathbf{r_z}})$ for some $\widehat{\mathbf{r_z}} \in K^{\widehat{e}}$. Set $\widehat{\mathbf{c_z}} = \widehat{M}\widehat{\rho}_{\mathbf{z}}$.
2. The prover sends vectors of commitments $[\mathbf{r_x}], [\mathbf{r_y}], [\widehat{\mathbf{r_z}}]$ to the verifier. Together with the commitments to $\mathbf{x}, \mathbf{y}$ and $\mathbf{z}$, the verifier now holds vectors of commitments $[\rho_{\mathbf{x}}], [\rho_{\mathbf{y}}], [\widehat{\rho}_{\mathbf{z}}]$.
3. The verifier chooses t uniform indices $O \subset S^*$ and sends them to the prover.
4. Let $\mathbf{m}_i$ be the i'th row of M and $\widehat{\mathbf{m}}_i$ the i'th row of $\widehat{M}$. For each $i \in O$, using the homomorphic property of the commitments, both prover and verifier compute commitments

$$[(\mathbf{c_x})_i] = [\rho_{\mathbf{x}}]^{\mathbf{m}_i}, \qquad [(\mathbf{c_y})_i] = [\rho_{\mathbf{y}}]^{\mathbf{m}_i}, \qquad [(\widehat{\mathbf{c_z}})_i] = [\widehat{\rho}_{\mathbf{x}}]^{\widehat{\mathbf{m}}_i}.$$

   The prover opens these commitments to the verifier.
5. The verifier accepts if and only if the opened values satisfy $(\mathbf{c_x})_i \cdot (\mathbf{c_y})_i = (\widehat{\mathbf{c_z}})_i$ for all $i \in O$.

Theorem 1. *Assume the commitment scheme used is the one described in section 2.1. Then protocol Verify Multiplication is perfect zero-knowledge, and if for some i, $x_i y_i \neq z_i$, the verifier accepts with probability at most $((\widehat{r}-1)/d)^t + 1/|L|$.*

In the appendix we give a proof for the above theorem [1]. Theorem 4 given later covers the case where we use standard computationally based commitments.

Demands to the Secret Sharing Schemes. Above, we have described the protocol for a fixed secret sharing scheme, but what we really want to look at is the asymptotic behavior as a function of l, the number of secrets we handle in one execution, and u, where we want error probability 2^{-u}. For this, we need a family of secret sharing schemes, parametrized by l, u, which will make t, d, e, $\widehat{r}$ and $\widehat{e}$ be functions of l, u.

Say that committing requires sending κ_c bits while opening requires κ_o bits. For standard computationally secure commitments, it is usually the case that κ_c is $\Theta(\kappa_o)$, but this is not the case for the information theoretically secure commitments, where κ_c can be much smaller than κ_o. Using this notation, the communication complexity of the protocol is $O(\kappa_c(e + \widehat{e}) + \kappa_o t + t \log d)$ bits.

Now, suppose we can build a family of secret sharing schemes, where $e, \widehat{e}$ are $O(u)$ and $\widehat{r}$ is $O(l + u)$, t is $\Theta(u)$ and $(\widehat{r} - 1)/d$ is $O(1)$. This allows d to be $O(l + u)$ and so we can achieve the complexities we promised earlier: For standard computationally hiding commitments, we get we get soundness error $2^{-\alpha u}$ for some constant $\alpha > 0$ for one instance of the protocol. For the information theoretically secure commitments, we get the same if we set $|L| = 2^{\Theta(u)}$. In any case, if necessary, we can achieve 2^{-u} by repeating in parallel a constant number of times. Inserting in the above expression, and dividing by l, we get the complexity per multiplicative relation: $O(\frac{u}{l}(\kappa_c + \kappa_o + \log(l + u)))$. For standard commitments we will have $\kappa_c = \kappa_o = \kappa$, and for information theoretically secure commitments we have κ_c is $O(1)$ and κ_o is $O(u)$. So this gives us the complexities we promised in the Introduction.

We show in Section 4 how to construct a secret sharing scheme with the right properties.

Application to Zero-Knowledge Proofs for Circuit Satisfiability. An obvious application of our protocol is to give ZK proofs for Boolean circuit satisfiability: the prover commits to the bits on each wire in the circuit C, opens the output as a 1 and shows that, for each AND-gate, the corresponding multiplicative relation holds for the committed bits.

We can apply the Verify Multiplication protocol to do this. Then we have that l is $O(|C|)$. If we run the protocol with error probability 2^{-u}, our expression for

---

[1] We note already now that since we assume preprocessing for this type of commitment, the simulator constructed for zero-knowledge emulates the verifier's output from the preprocessing as well as his view of the proof (as is standard for set-up models).

the total communication complexity becomes $O(|C|\kappa_c + u(\kappa_c + \kappa_o + \log(|C|+u)))$, note that we have to add the cost of committing to the bits in the circuit.

Now we note that if we use the information-theoretic commitments as described above, then $\kappa_c = 1$ and κ_o is $O(u)$. Therefore the complexity is actually $O(|C|+u(u+\log(|C|+u)))$ bits, and when dividing by $|C|$ we get communication overhead $O(1)$, as promised in the introduction.

4 A Concrete Example

In this section we explain how to design a secret-sharing scheme meeting the demands we stated earlier. For simplicity we first show the details for the case of $u = l$.

As a stepping stone, we consider the following scheme based on Shamir's scheme. Suppose $2(t + l - 1) < d$ and $d + l \leq |K|$. Choose pairwise distinct elements $q_1, \ldots, q_l, p_1, \ldots, p_d \in K$, and define

$$C = \{(f(q_1), \ldots, f(q_l), f(p_1), \ldots, f(p_d)) \mid f \in K[X]_{\leq t+l-1}\} \subset K^{l+d},$$

where $K[X]_{\leq t+l-1}$ denotes the K-vector space of polynomials with coefficients in K and of degree at most $t + l - 1$. Let S correspond to the first l coordinates. Then, by Lagrange Interpolation, it is straightforward to verify that (C, S) is an l-multi-secret K-linear secret sharing scheme of length d, with t-privacy and $(2t + 2l - 1)$-product reconstruction. So if we set $t = l$ (and hence the degrees are at most $2l - 1$), $d = 8l$, and $|K| \geq 9l$, then $2(t + l - 1) = 4l - 2 < 8l = d$, $d + l = 9l \leq |K|$, and $\hat{r} = 2t + 2l - 1 = 4l - 1 < 4l = d/2$. In particular, $\frac{\hat{r}-1}{d} < \frac{1}{2}$. Moreover, $e = 2l$, and $\hat{e} = 4l - 1$. So all requirements are satisfied, except for the fact that in this approach $|K| = \Omega(\log l)$.

Before we present a scheme which works over a *constant size field*, yet asymptotically it meets all requirements, we describe simple, useful lifting technique. Suppose the finite field of interest K, i.e., the field over which our zero-knowledge problem is defined, does not readily admit the required secret sharing scheme, but that some degree-u extension L of K does. Then we may choose a K-basis of L of the form $1, x, \ldots, x^{u-1}$ for some $x \in L$. It is then easy to "lift" the commitment scheme and to obtain one that is L-homomorphic instead: simply consider the elements of L as coordinate-vectors over K, according to the basis selected above, and commit to such a vector by committing separately to each coordinate. This scheme is clearly homomorphic with respect to addition in L. Multiplication by (publicly known) scalars from L is easily seen to correspond to applying an appropriate (publicly known) K-linear form to the vector of K-homomorphic commitments. Furthermore, K is embedded into L by mapping $a \in K$ to $a + 0 \cdot x + \ldots + 0 \cdot x^{u-1}$. When committing to $a \in K$, simply commit to a in the original commitment scheme, and append $u - 1$ "default commitments to 0." This way, the protocol problem can be solved over K, with a secret sharing scheme over L. However, communication-wise, even though all further parameters may be satisfied, there are now $O(ul)$ commitments, instead of $O(l)$ as required.

For example, if the above secret sharing scheme is implemented, then since the field K of interest is of constant size, the field L over which the secret sharing is defined must grow proportionally to $\log l$. Hence, the total communication is a logarithmic factor off of what we promised. This is resolved as follows, by using a technique that allows passing to an extension whose degree u is *constant* instead of logarithmic.

Let F be an algebraic function field over the finite field $\mathbb{F}_q$ with q elements. Write g for its genus and n for its number of rational points. Suppose $2g + 2(t + l - 1) < d$ and $d + l \leq n$. Choose pairwise distinct rational points $Q_1, \ldots, Q_l, P_1, \ldots, P_d \in F$, and define

$$C = \{(f(Q_1), \ldots, f(Q_l), f(P_1), \ldots, f(P_d)) \mid f \in \mathcal{L}(G)\} \subset \mathbb{F}_q^{l+d},$$

where G is a divisor of degree $2g + t + l - 1$ whose support does not contain any of the Q_j's nor any of the P_i's, and where $\mathcal{L}(G)$ is the Riemann-Roch space of G. As before, let S correspond to the first l coordinates. Using a similar result as in [CC06], one proves, using the Riemann-Roch Theorem that (C, S) is an l-multi-secret $\mathbb{F}_q$-linear secret sharing scheme of length d, with t-privacy and $(2g + 2t + 2l - 1)$-product reconstruction. Moreover, $e = g + t + l$ and $\hat{e} \leq 3g + 2t + 2l - 1$. Asymptotically, using this result in combination with optimal towers over the *fixed* finite field $\mathbb{F}_q$ where $q \geq 49$ is a square, we get $g/n = \frac{1}{\sqrt{q}-1} < 1/6$. Hence, if we set, for example, $t = l = n/20$ and $d = 19/20n$, then there is $\Omega(l)$-privacy, $\frac{\hat{r}-1}{d} < c < 1$ for some constant c, and $e = \Omega(l)$, $\hat{e} = \Omega(l)$. Therefore, at most a degree 6 extension of the field of interest is required, as the maximum is attained for $K = \mathbb{F}_2$ with the extension being $\mathbb{F}_{64}$. Finally, these schemes can be implemented efficiently.

The more general case where u and l are independent parameters follows easily from the above and we leave the details to the reader. The basic reason why it works is that the number of required random field elements for a sharing $(e, \hat{e})$ is linear in the required privacy threshold which we want to be $\Theta(u)$ and furthermore the reconstruction threshold $(\hat{r})$ is linear in the sum of the length of the secret vector and the privacy threshold, which here is $l + \Theta(u)$.

5   A More General Approach

In this section we define linear secret sharing with a more general multiplicative property, and we use the notation from Section 2.2. Let D be an arithmetic circuit over K with v inputs and one output. Then for $\mathbf{c}_1, \ldots, \mathbf{c}_v \in K^m$, we define $D(\mathbf{c}_1, \ldots, \mathbf{c}_v) \in K^m$ as the vector whose j'th coordinate is $D((\mathbf{c}_1)_j, \ldots, (\mathbf{c}_v)_j)$, i.e., we simply apply D to the j'th coordinate of all input vectors.

If $C \subset K^m$ is a linear subspace, then C^D is defined as the K-linear subspace generated by all vectors of form $D(\mathbf{c}_1, \ldots, \mathbf{c}_v)$ where $\mathbf{c}_1, \ldots, \mathbf{c}_v \in C$. Just as for the standard multiplication property, if (C, S) is a secret sharing scheme, then S offers uniformity in C^D, but in general it does not necessarily hold that S^* determines S in C^D. If it does, however, so that (C^D, S) is a linear secret sharing scheme, then we say that (C, S) offers $(\tilde{r}, D)$-**product reconstruction** if (C^D, S) offers $\tilde{r}$-product reconstruction.

As a concrete example of this, one may think of Shamir secret sharing. Here, each c_i is a sequence of evaluations of a polynomial f_i at a fixed set of points. Then $D(c_1, \ldots, c_v)$ denotes the vector having coordinates of the form $D(f_1(j), \ldots, f_v(j))$ for j in the set of evaluation points. These coordinates can be thought as the evaluations of the polynomial $D(f_1, \ldots, f_v)$ (defined in the natural way), and sufficiently many of those will determine $D(f_1, \ldots, f_v)$ uniquely.

Based on this more general notion, we can design a protocol where a prover commits to vectors $x_1, \ldots, x_v, z$ and wants to prove that $D(x_1, \ldots, x_v) = z$.

Similarly to what we assumed in the first protocol, we suppose that both the prover and the verifier agreed on using an l-multisecret linear secret sharing scheme (C, S), for d players, with $(\tilde{r}, D)$-product reconstruction, and t-privacy. We fix a generator $g : K^{l+e} \to C$. Moreover, we suppose that $\tilde{g} : K^{l+\tilde{e}} \to C^D$ is a generator for (C^D, S) and that a public basis for K^{l+e} (respectively for $K^{l+\tilde{e}}$) has been chosen such that the linear mapping g (resp. $\tilde{g}$) can be computed as the action of a matrix M (resp. $\widetilde{M}$). The protocol goes as follows:

Protocol. Verify Circuit

1. The prover chooses v vectors $r_1, \ldots, r_v \in K^e$, and sets $\rho_j = (x_j, r_j)$ for $j = 1, \ldots, v$. Define $c_j = M\rho_j$. Now, the prover computes $\tilde{\rho}_z \in K^{l+\tilde{e}}$ such that $\tilde{\rho}_z$ is consistent with secret z and such that $\widetilde{M}\tilde{\rho}_z = D(x_1, \ldots, x_v)$. Note that this is possible by solving a system of linear equations, because $D(x_1, \ldots, x_v) = z$. We then write $\tilde{\rho}_z = (z, \tilde{r}_z)$ for some $\tilde{r}_z \in K^{\tilde{e}}$. Set $\tilde{c}_z = \widetilde{M}\tilde{\rho}_z$.

2. The prover sends vectors of commitments $[r_j]$, $j = 1, \ldots, v$ and $[\tilde{r}_z]$ to the verifier. Together with the commitments to x_j and z, the verifier now holds vectors of commitments $[\rho_j]$, $j = 1, \ldots, v$, and $[\tilde{\rho}_z]$.

3. The verifier chooses t uniform indices $O \subset S^*$ and sends them to the prover.

4. Let m_i be the i'th row of M and let $\tilde{m}_i$ be the i'th row of $\widetilde{M}$. For each $i \in O$, using the homomorphic property of the commitments, both prover and verifier compute commitments

$$[(c_j)_i] = [\rho_j]^{m_i}, \text{ for } j = 1, \ldots, v, \qquad [(\tilde{c}_z)_i] = [\tilde{\rho}_z]^{\tilde{m}_i}.$$

The prover opens these commitments to the verifier.

5. The verifier accepts if and only if the opened values satisfy $D((c_1)_i, \ldots, (c_v)_i) = (\tilde{c}_z)_i$ for all $i \in O$.

Using a similar proof as for theorem 1, one easily shows

Theorem 2. *Assume the commitment scheme used is the one described in section 2.1. Then the protocol Verify Circuit is perfect honest-verifier zero-knowledge and if $D(x_1, \ldots, x_v) \neq z$, the verifier accepts with probability at most $((\tilde{r} - 1)/d)^t + 1/|L|$.*

The interesting question is whether we can build secret sharing schemes with this type of D-reconstruction and whether the resulting more general protocol offers advantages over the first one.

The answer to the first question is positive, the construction was already hinted at above: we can base a scheme on Shamir secret sharing extended à la Franklin and Yung [FY92] to share blocks of l secrets. This requires polynomials of degree $e = l + t - 1$. Since each multiplication in D doubles the degree of the polynomials, the degree after applying D will be $2^\delta t$ where δ is the multiplicative depth of D. This means that $\widetilde{e} = \widetilde{r} = 2^\delta t$ for this construction, and d should be a constant factor larger than $\widetilde{r}$ to get exponentially small error probability.

We assume for simplicity that the cardinality of K is larger than $d + l$, in order to have the required number of evaluation points. If this is not the case, we can pass to an extension field at cost a logarithmic factor, as explained in the previous section. Note that the algebraic geometric approach presented in Section 2.2 does not give any non-constant improvement over the Shamir-based approach in the setting of D-reconstruction. However, it appears that the algebraic geometric approach can be extended to get a non-trivial improvement here as well, using more advanced techniques. A detailed analysis is given in the full version.

We can now compare two natural approaches to verifying that committed vectors $\mathbf{x}_1, \ldots, \mathbf{x}_v, \mathbf{z}$ satisfy $D(\mathbf{x}_1, \ldots, \mathbf{x}_v) = \mathbf{z}$:

The first approach is to perform the Verify Circuit protocol using the secret sharing scheme we sketched. If we go for error probability 2^{-l} and therefore choose t to be $\Theta(l)$, simple inspection of the protocol shows:

Lemma 1. *Using the Verify Circuit Protocol, the amortized communication complexity to verify one instance of a circuit with multiplicative depth δ and v inputs is $O(2^\delta \kappa + v\kappa + \delta \log l)$ bits for an error probability of 2^{-l}.*

Note that, except for the cost of committing to the inputs the communication complexity only depends on the depth of the circuit.

The second approach is to use the Verify Multiplication protocol. The prover will, for every multiplication gate T in D, commit to a vector $\mathbf{z}_T$ where $(\mathbf{z}_T)_i$ is the output from T in the instance of D where the inputs are $(\mathbf{x}_1)_i, \ldots, (\mathbf{x}_v)_i$. Now, for every multiplication gate T the verifier can compute vectors of commitments $[\mathbf{x}_T], [\mathbf{y}_T]$ to the inputs to T (since any linear operations in D "between multiplication gates" can be done by the verifier alone). We then use the Verify Multiplication protocol to check that $\mathbf{x}_T * \mathbf{y}_T = \mathbf{z}_T$. Using this protocol verifying a multiplication has communication cost $O(\kappa + \log l)$ bits, so the total cost to verify one instance of the circuit corresponds to $O(\mu(\kappa + \log l) + v\kappa)$ bits, where μ is the number of multiplication gates in D.

Notice that large fan-out comes at no cost in our model, and that linear operations with large fan-in are also for free. Moreover, both approaches generalize easily to circuits with several outputs. Therefore, there is no fixed relation between μ and δ, in particular, we could consider families of circuits where δ is constant or logarithmic in the input size, but μ grows faster than 2^δ. In such a case, using the Verify Circuit protocol is better; it has the interesting property that the amortized cost of verifying a single instance of D can be asymptotically smaller than the number of multiplication gates in D.

In the appendix, we sketch a final variant of the Verify Circuit Protocol using the "MPC in the head approach" [IKOS09] where we try to limit the dominating cost of committing to the $\tilde{e}$ entries of $\tilde{\mathbf{r}}_\mathbf{z}$. The idea is as follows: instead of committing to the values in $\tilde{\mathbf{r}}_\mathbf{z}$ in the usual way, the prover will simply send the required commitments to shares $[(\tilde{\mathbf{c}}_\mathbf{z})_i]$ and use the "MPC in the head" approach to prove to the verifier that the commitments contain the correct shares.

The cost of this approach to generate the required commitments to shares is $O(l^2\kappa + \tilde{e}l^2 k)$.

This should be compared to the normal Verify Circuit protocol where the cost of this same step is $O((\tilde{e} + l)\kappa)$. We see that if $\kappa > l^2 k$ and $\tilde{e} > l^2$ - which may well be the case in practice - then this solution has smaller cost.

6   Proving Integer Multiplication

In the full version, we show a protocol designed for the case where the prover's secret values are integers. We use a specific integer linear secret sharing scheme based on polynomials and the commitment scheme described in section 2.1. The idea of the protocol is otherwise similar to the one for finite fields. Due to space limitation we only give an informal result here, details can be found in the full version.

Theorem 3 (Informal). *Assume the commitment scheme used is the one described in section 2.1. There exists a perfect zero-knowledge proof for showing that committed l-vectors $\mathbf{x}, \mathbf{y}, \mathbf{z}$ satisfy $\mathbf{x} \cdot \mathbf{y} = \mathbf{z}$, and if for some i, $x_i y_i \neq z_i$, the verifier accepts with probability at most $(2(t + l)/d)^t + O(\kappa/2^\kappa)$.*

7   Commitment Schemes Based on Computational Assumptions

We consider two kinds of commitment schemes: The first one is over a finite field K and can be seen as a function $com_{pk} : K \times H \to G$ where H, G are finite groups and pk is a public key (this includes the examples suggested in [CD98]). The second one is over the integers, and $com_{pk} : \mathbb{Z} \times \mathbb{Z} \to G$.

The public key pk is generated by a PPT algorithm $\mathcal{G}$ on input a security parameter κ. To commit to value $x \in K$ or an integer x, the prover chooses r uniformly in H (or, in case of integer commitments, in some appropriate interval) and sends $C = com_{pk}(x, r)$ to the verifier. A commitment is opened by sending x, r. We assume that the scheme is homomorphic, i.e. $com_{pk}(x, r) \cdot com_{pk}(y, s) = com_{pk}(x + y, rs)$. For simplicity, we assume throughout that K is a prime field. Then, by repeated addition, that we also have $com_{pk}(x, r)^y = com_{pk}(xy, r^y)$ for any $y \in K$. We also use $[x]$ as shorthand for a commitment to x in the following, and hence suppress the randomness from the notation.

We consider *computationally hiding* schemes: for any two values x, x' the distributions of $pk, com_{pk}(x, r)$ and $pk, com_{pk}(x', s)$ must be computationally indistinguishable, where pk is generated by $\mathcal{G}$ on input security parameter κ. Such schemes are usually *unconditionally binding*, meaning that for any pk that can be output from $\mathcal{G}$, there does not exist x, r, x', s with $x \neq x'$ such that $com_{pk}(x, r) = com_{pk}(x', s)$. For such schemes, the prover usually runs $\mathcal{G}$, sends pk to the verifier and may have to convince him that pk was correctly generated before the scheme is used.

One may also consider *unconditionally hiding and computationally binding* schemes, where $pk, com_{pk}(x, r)$ and $pk, com_{pk}(x', s)$ must be statistically indistinguishable, and where it must be infeasible to find x, r, x', s with $x \neq x'$ such that $com_{pk}(x, r) = com_{pk}(x', s)$.

8 Results with Standard Commitments

Theorem 4. *Assume the commitment scheme used is unconditionally binding and computationally hiding. Then the Verify Multiplication protocol is a computationally honest-verifier zero-knowledge interactive proof system for the language*

$$\left\{ ([x_i], [y_i], [z_i])_{i=1}^{l} \mid x_i y_i = z_i, \text{ for } i = 1, \ldots, l \right\}$$

with soundness error $((\hat{r} - 1)/d)^t$.

In the appendix, we give a proof for the above theorem and explain how to modify the protocol to work for an unconditionally hiding commitment scheme. Using a similar proof as for theorem 4, one easily shows

Theorem 5. *Assume the commitment scheme used is unconditionally binding and computationally hiding. Then the protocol Verify Circuit is a computationally honest-verifier zero-knowledge interactive proof system for the language*

$$\{([\mathbf{x}_1], \ldots, [\mathbf{x}_v], [\mathbf{z}]) \mid D(\mathbf{x}_1, \ldots, \mathbf{x}_v) = \mathbf{z}\}$$

with soundness error $((\tilde{r} - 1)/d)^t$.

Theorem 6 (Informal). *Given a commitment scheme for integers in the interval* $[-2^k, \ldots, 2^k]$ *that is computationally binding and unconditionally hiding. There exists an statistical honest-verifier zero-knowledge argument of knowledge for showing that committed l-vectors* $\mathbf{x}, \mathbf{y}, \mathbf{z}$ *satisfy* $\mathbf{x} \cdot \mathbf{y} = \mathbf{z}$. *The protocol has amortized complexity* $O(\kappa + l \log l + k)$ *bits and knowledge error* 2^{-l}.

References

[BDOZ11] Bendlin, R., Damgård, I., Orlandi, C., Zakarias, S.: Semi-Homomorphic Encryption and Multiparty Computation. In: Paterson, K.G. (ed.) EUROCRYPT 2011. LNCS, vol. 6632, pp. 169–188. Springer, Heidelberg (2011)

[Bou00]   Boudot, F.: Efficient Proofs that a Committed Number Lies in an Interval. In: Preneel, B. (ed.) EUROCRYPT 2000. LNCS, vol. 1807, pp. 431–444. Springer, Heidelberg (2000)

[BSFO11]   Ben-Sasson, E., Fehr, S., Ostrovsky, R.: Near-linear unconditionally-secure multiparty computation with a dishonest minority. Cryptology ePrint Archive, Report 2011/629 (2011), http://eprint.iacr.org/

[CC06]   Chen, H., Cramer, R.: Algebraic Geometric Secret Sharing Schemes and Secure Multi-Party Computations over Small Fields. In: Dwork, C. (ed.) CRYPTO 2006. LNCS, vol. 4117, pp. 521–536. Springer, Heidelberg (2006)

[CCG+07]   Chen, H., Cramer, R., Goldwasser, S., de Haan, R., Vaikuntanathan, V.: Secure Computation from Random Error Correcting Codes. In: Naor, M. (ed.) EUROCRYPT 2007. LNCS, vol. 4515, pp. 291–310. Springer, Heidelberg (2007)

[CD98]   Cramer, R., Damgård, I.: Zero-Knowledge Proofs for Finite Field Arithmetic or: Can Zero-Knowledge Be for Free? In: Krawczyk, H. (ed.) CRYPTO 1998. LNCS, vol. 1462, pp. 424–441. Springer, Heidelberg (1998)

[CD09]   Cramer, R., Damgård, I.: On the Amortized Complexity of Zero-Knowledge Protocols. In: Halevi, S. (ed.) CRYPTO 2009. LNCS, vol. 5677, pp. 177–191. Springer, Heidelberg (2009)

[CDD+99]   Cramer, R., Damgård, I., Dziembowski, S., Hirt, M., Rabin, T.: Efficient Multiparty Computations Secure Against an Adaptive Adversary. In: Stern, J. (ed.) EUROCRYPT 1999. LNCS, vol. 1592, pp. 311–326. Springer, Heidelberg (1999)

[CDM00]   Cramer, R., Damgård, I., Maurer, U.M.: General Secure Multi-party Computation from any Linear Secret-Sharing Scheme. In: Preneel, B. (ed.) EUROCRYPT 2000. LNCS, vol. 1807, pp. 316–334. Springer, Heidelberg (2000)

[CDN01]   Cramer, R., Damgård, I., Nielsen, J.B.: Multiparty Computation from Threshold Homomorphic Encryption. In: Pfitzmann, B. (ed.) EUROCRYPT 2001. LNCS, vol. 2045, pp. 280–299. Springer, Heidelberg (2001)

[DF02]   Damgård, I., Fujisaki, E.: A Statistically-Hiding Integer Commitment Scheme Based on Groups with Hidden Order. In: Zheng, Y. (ed.) ASIACRYPT 2002. LNCS, vol. 2501, pp. 125–142. Springer, Heidelberg (2002)

[DIK10]   Damgård, I., Ishai, Y., Krøigaard, M.: Perfectly Secure Multiparty Computation and the Computational Overhead of Cryptography. In: Gilbert, H. (ed.) EUROCRYPT 2010. LNCS, vol. 6110, pp. 445–465. Springer, Heidelberg (2010)

[DPSZ12]   Damgård, I., Pastro, V., Smart, N.P., Zakarias, S.: Multiparty Computation from Somewhat Homomorphic Encryption. In: Safavi-Naini, R. (ed.) CRYPTO 2012. LNCS, vol. 7417, pp. 643–662. Springer, Heidelberg (2012)

[FO97]   Fujisaki, E., Okamoto, T.: Statistical Zero Knowledge Protocols to Prove Modular Polynomial Relations. In: Kaliski Jr., B.S. (ed.) CRYPTO 1997. LNCS, vol. 1294, pp. 16–30. Springer, Heidelberg (1997)

[FY92]   Franklin, M.K., Yung, M.: Communication complexity of secure computation (extended abstract). In: STOC, pp. 699–710. ACM (1992)

[GM84]   Goldwasser, S., Micali, S.: Probabilistic encryption. J. Comput. Syst. Sci. 28(2), 270–299 (1984)

[IKOS09]   Ishai, Y., Kushilevitz, E., Ostrovsky, R., Sahai, A.: Zero-knowledge proofs from secure multiparty computation. SIAM J. Comput. 39(3), 1121–1152 (2009)

[KW93]   Karchmer, M., Wigderson, A.: On Span Programs. In: Structure in Complexity Theory Conference, pp. 102–111 (1993)

Universally Composable Oblivious Transfer from Lossy Encryption and the McEliece Assumptions

Bernardo Machado David[1],
Anderson C. A. Nascimento[1], and Jörn Müller-Quade[2]

[1] Department of Electrical Engineering, University of Brasilia, Brazil
bernardo.david@aluno.unb.br, andclay@ene.unb.br
[2] Institute of Cryptography and Security, Faculty of Informatics,
Karlsruhe Institute of Technology, Germany
mueller-quade@kit.edu

Abstract. Oblivious transfer (OT) is a primitive of great importance in two-party and multi-party computation. We introduce a general construction of universally composable (UC) oblivious transfer protocols based on lossy cryptosystems in the common reference string (CRS) model, yielding protocols under several assumptions. In order to achieve this, we show that for most known lossy encryption constructions it is possible to distinguish between lossy and injective public keys given the corresponding secret key, similarly to dual-mode encryption in messy mode.

Furthermore, we adapt the techniques of our general construction to obtain the first UC secure OT protocol based on the McEliece assumptions, which are coding theory based assumptions that until now have resisted quantum attacks, thus introducing the first UC secure OT protocol based on coding assumptions.

However, differently from previous results based on dual-mode encryption, our scheme does not require a trapdoor for opening lossy ciphertexts, relying instead on CRS manipulation and cut-and-choose techniques to construct the simulators. In both constructions we circumvent the need for universally composable string commitment schemes, which are required by previous black-box compilers.

1 Introduction

Oblivious Transfer [34,17] is an important cryptographic primitive which implies secure two-party computation [27,20] as well as multi-party computation [12] (in the presence of a broadcast channel). Although different types of oblivious transfer exist, they were all proven to be equivalent. In the present work, we focus on one-out-of-two oblivious transfer (OT_1^2). This is a two-party primitive where a *sender* (Alice) inputs two messages b_0, b_1 and a *receiver* (Bob) inputs a bit c, referred to as the *choice bit*. Bob learns b_c but not b_{1-c} and Alice learns nothing about Bob's choice (the value of c).

A. Smith (Ed.): ICITS 2012, LNCS 7412, pp. 80–99, 2012.

In current literature there are several constructions of OT under different assumptions, such as enhanced trapdoor permutations [17], hardness of factoring [34], Diffie-Hellman [4], Decisional Diffie-Hellman (DDH) [30,2] (both round optimal protocols), Quadratic or Higher-Order Residuosity and the Extended Riemman Hypothesis [26]. The McEliece assumptions are coding theory based and until now have resisted quantum attacks. Furthermore, a recent result in CRYPTO 2011 [1] shows that quantum Fourier sampling attacks (which are used to brak RSA and El Gamal encryption) are useless against these assumptions. Thus, the Mceliece assumptions are a good candidate for the post quantum scenario. The first protocol for oblivious transfer based on the McEliece assumptions without random oracles was proposed in [16]. This protocol was proven to be fully secure in a stand-alone setting, offering computational security for both the sender and the receiver, whereas most constructions offer statistical security for at least one of the parties.

Even though many classical OT protocols have been proved secure in a standalone setting, it is important to analyse the security of cryptographic protocols under different kinds of composition. Among the techniques employed for this analysis, the real/ideal simulation paradigm and universal composability (UC) [6] provide widely accepted security notions for analysing protocols under sequential and arbitrarty composition, respectively. Universal composability stands as one of the most meaningful frameworks for proving the security of cryptographic protocols, since it yields security guarantees for real world deployment of protocols under arbitrary composition. Furthermore, UC secure protocols and constructions can be used as building blocks for more complex applications and other cryptographic protocols, *e.g.* universally composable two-party and multi-party secure computation [8].

Related Works: Obtaining UC secure OT without trusted setup assumptions is known to be impossible [7], thus several protocols have been proposed based on different computational and setup assumptions. A general framework for efficient (round optimal) and composable 1-out-of-2 oblivious transfer in the common reference string (CRS) model was introduced in [32], yielding constructions based on DDH, QR and LWE. Another efficient construction based on the Decisional Linear (DLIN) assumption over bilinear groups and assuming the existence of a key registration authority was proposed in [14]. Protocols for universally composable committed oblivious transfer were introduced in [25,19], both in the common reference string model. While the construction in [25] is based on DCR, the result on [19] relies on multiple assumptions, including DCR, strong RSA and DDH. Adaptive OT is considered in [21], where a universally composable construction is given under the q-hidden LRSW assumption in the CRS model.

The current construction that most resembles our constructions is the framework proposed by Peikert *et al.* in CRYPTO 2008 [32]. This framework is based on dual-mode encryption and is also constructed in the common reference string model. Besides being round-optimal, this framework has the interesting property of yielding OT protocols statistically secure for the sender or the receiver depending on the setup procedure used to generate the CRS. Dual-mode cryptosystems operate in either *messy* mode or *decryption* mode, having public keys divided into a messy branch and a decryptable branch. Both modes and public key branches are computationally indistinguishable. The messy mode behaves similarly to a lossy cryptosystem [23] in that any information encrypted with the public key's messy branch is statistically lost, but it is possible to distinguish the messy branch from the decryptable branch using a trapdoor. In decryption mode, ciphertexts generated by the messy branch cannot be decrypted using the corresponding secret key, but are decryptable under a trapdoor. Moreover, the definition states that each public key has exactly one messy branch and one decryptable branch.

Building on those characteristics, it is straightforward to derive an oblivious transfer protocol. First, the receiver generates a public key where the branch corresponding to his chosen message is decryptable while the branch corresponding to the other message is messy. The sender then uses this key to encrypt both messages and sends the ciphertexts to the reciever, who can only obtain the message he had previously chosen. Notice that the sender cannot obtain any information about the receiver's choice bit (since the key branches are indistinguishable), and that the receiver can only obtain one of the messages (since one of the branches is always messy). In order to prove UC security, the simulator sets up the dual-mode cryptosystem instance in the appropriate mode and simply uses the appropriate trapdoor to find the messy branch (*i.e.* the choice bit inverse) or decrypt ciphertexts generated under both branches (*i.e.* retrieve both of sender's messages). Indistinguishability between ideal and real executions then follows from the fact that modes are computationally indistinguishable. However, even though there exist known constructions of dual-mode encryption under LWE, DDH and Quadratic Residuosity (QR) assumptions [32], until now there is no such construction based on coding assumptions. Hence, this framework cannot be employed to obtain universally composable oblivious transfer based on the McEliece assumptions.

Lossy encryption was defined in [23,3] as a flavor of public key encryption with "lossy" public keys that generate ciphertexts independently from the inputted plaintext, statistically losing information as in dual-mode encryption in messy mode. In contrast to dual-mode encryption, lossy cryptosystems do not enjoy explicitly defined trapdoors that allow a simulator to distinguish between lossy and injective keys (corresponding to messy and decryptable public key branches, respectively) or to recover messages encrypted under a lossy key. Besides being unfit for obtaining a McEliece based protocol, the framework in [32] also leaves open the question of whether it is possible to obtain a general construction for universally composable OT based on black-box or non-black-box access to lossy encryption as defined in [23,3]. However, it may be possible to obtain similar properties building on internal details of specific lossy encryption constructions. This poses new interesting challenges for constructing universally composable oblivious transfer protocols. Since it is already proved in [23] that round optimal oblivious transfer is equivalent to lossy encryption, such a construction would provide interesting insight into the relation between both primitives.

Yet another powerful approach for achieving UC secure OT protocols from various assumptions is the use of compilers that obtain such protocols given black-box access to an instance of stand-alone static semi-honest OT, such as Haitner's [22], or defensible OT, such as Ishai's *et al.* [24]. Choi *et al.* [10] build on these previous constructions to obtain a compiler that yields universally composable OT protocol secure against adaptive adversaries. The protocols constructed via these compilers have a general structure similar to our construction, relying on multiple copies of a semi-honest OT protocol running in parallel and cut-and-choose techniques to achieve UC security. However, in order to achieve universal composability, these reductions require access to universally composable string commitment schemes, which have not been constructed from lossy encryption or the McEliece assumptions yet. Nevertheless, the general protocol presented in [10,22] provides a solid starting point for obtaining our results.

Our Contributions: In this work we introduce a general construction of universally composable oblivious transfer based on lossy encryption, a primitive that can be obtained from a number of assumptions [32](*i.e.* LWE, DDH and QR) and from other primitives [23] (*i.e.* re-randomizable cryptosystems and smooth projective hashing [11]). Furthermore, we use similar techniques to obtain a UC secure protocol based on the McEliece assumptions [29]. The following contributions are presented:

- Theorem 1, Section 3.4 : A general efficient construction for universally composable oblivious transfer based on lossy encryption schemes for which it is possible to distinguish lossy public keys from injective public keys given the corresponding secret key.
- Theorem 2, Section 4.1: The first efficient universally composable oblivious transfer protocol solely based on coding assumptions, *i.e.* the McEliece assumptions.
- Appendix B: We observe that, given the corresponding secret key, it is possible to distinguish lossy public keys from injective public keys of many current lossy encryption construction. This property yields a trapdoor lossy key distinguishing algorithm.

In order to obtain these results we build on a fully simulatable protocol first introduced by Lindell [28] and on key scrambling techniques employed in the stand alone McEliece based OT protocol proposed by Dowsley *et al.* [16] to obtain protocols similar to the black-box transformation of [10] but without requiring universally composable string commitment schemes. Similarly to [10], our protocols consist of several copies of a semi-honest stand alone OT protocol running in parallel with an intermediate cut-and-choose phase to bound the probability of the receiver cheating. In contrast to [10], our constructions do not start with bit OT protocol and then apply a combiner to achieve string OT, using instead string OT constructions that arise naturally from lossy encryption [33] and the McEliece assumptions [15]. Furthermore, we use non-black-box access to lossy encryption and McEliece based encryption to obtain an algorithm for distinguishing between lossy and injective keys given the corresponding secret key and constructing extractable string commitment schemes, which are crucial tools for constructing the simulators.

Since lossy encryption was constructed in [23] from re-randomizable cryptosystems, smooth projective hashing, round optimal oblivious transfer (and thus dual-mode encryption [32]), our general construction yields protocols based on broader range of number theoretical and lattice based assumptions than the framework of [32]. Our lossy encryption based protocol provides statistical security for the sender. On the other hand, differently from all the other constructions of universally composable OT in current literature, the protocol based on the McEliece assumptions provides computational security for both parties, similarly to the stand alone construction in [16]. This curious fact may shed light on the nature of the McEliece assumptions, which until now have only yielded OT protocols with computational security for both parties.

Our approach cannot be trivially obtained from the protocols in [28] or from the dual-mode encryption approach of [32], since we base it solely on lossy encryption without requiring all the properties of a dual-mode cryptosystem. Our protocols are at least as efficient as the protocol of [28]. As in the framework of [32], the common reference string (CRS) can be reused for an unbounded number of protocol executions and, depending on the underlying assumption, be obtained from general uniform randomness sources. Our protocols largely differ from [32] in that we trade round optimality and statistical security for the receiver for a broader range of instantiations that spans many computational assumptions, including coding based assumptions that until now did not yield any universally composable oblivious transfer protocols. Our non-black-box approach also circumvents the need for universally composable string commitment schemes of the black-box compiler in [10] and obtains similar results specifically for lossy encryption and the McEliece assumptions.

Organization: In Section 2, we establish notation and introduce the security definitions and assumptions used throughout the paper. In Section 3, we describe our lossy encryption based OT protocol and prove its security. In Section 4, we construct the McEliece based protocol and prove its security. In Section 5, we conclude with a summary of our results and directions for future research.

2   Preliminaries

Hereupon, we will denote by $x \in_R D$ an uniformly random choice of element x over its domain D; by $\oplus$ a bit-wise exclusive OR of strings; and by $a \mid b$ the concatenation of string a with string b. All logarithms are to the base 2. For a probabilistic polynomial-time (PPT) machine A, we use $coins(A)$ to denote the distribution of the internal randomness of A and $a \leftarrow A$ to denote running the machine A and obtaining an output, where a is distributed according to the internal randomness of A.

If X and Y are families of distributions indexed by a security parameter λ, we use $X \overset{s}{\approx} Y$ to mean the distributions X and Y are *statistically close*, i.e., for all polynomials p and sufficiently large λ, we have $\sum_x |Pr[X = x] - Pr[Y = x]| < 1$. Two sequences $X_n, n \in \mathbb{N}$ and $Y_n, n \in \mathbb{N}$ of random variables are said to be *computationally indistinguishable*, denoted by $X \overset{c}{\approx} Y$, if for every non-uniform *PPT* distinguisher D there exists a negligible function $\epsilon(\cdot)$ such that for every $n \in \mathbb{N}$, $| Pr[D(X_n) = 1] - Pr[D(Y_n) = 1] | < \epsilon(n)$.

2.1 Universal Composability

The Universal Composability framework was introduced by Canetti in [6] to analyse the security of cryptographic protocols and primitives under arbitrary composition. In this framework, protocol security is analysed by comparing an ideal world execution and a real world execution under the supervision of an *environment* $\mathcal{Z}$, which is represented by a *PPT* machine and has direct access to all inputs and outputs of the individual parties and an adversary. In the ideal world execution, dummy parties (possibly controlled by a *PPT simulator*) interact directly with the ideal functionality $\mathcal{F}$, which works as a fully secure third party that computes the desired function or primitive. In the real world execution, several *PPT* parties (possibly corrupted by a real world adversary $\mathcal{A}$) interact with each other by means of a protocol π that realizes the ideal functionality. The real world execution is represented by the ensemble $EXEC_{\pi,\mathcal{A},\mathcal{Z}}$, while the ideal execution is represented by the $IDEAL_{\mathcal{F},\mathcal{S},\mathcal{Z}}$. The rationale behind this framework lies in showing that the environment $\mathcal{Z}$ is not able to efficiently distinguish between $EXEC_{\pi,\mathcal{A},\mathcal{Z}}$ and $IDEAL_{\mathcal{F},\mathcal{S},\mathcal{Z}}$, thus implying that the real world protocol is as secure as the ideal functionality. See Appendix A.1 for formal definitions of UC security and the OT and CRS ideal functionalities.

2.2 Lossy Encryption

A lossy cryptosystem [23,3] is informally defined as a type of cryptosystem with two types of public keys, *injective* and *lossy* keys, which specify different results of encryption. If injective keys are used, the cryptosystem behaves regularly (correctly decrypting ciphertexts with the right secret key) while if the *lossy* public keys are used, the ciphertexts generated by the encryption algorithm are independent from the plaintext messages,causing information to be statistically lost. It is also required that lossy keys be computationally indistinguishable from injective keys.

It has been shown that it is possible to obtain lossy cryptosystems from round optimal oblivious transfer, re-randomization and smooth projective hashing [23]. It is also possible to obtain lossy encryption from dual-mode encryption in messy mode, which yields lossy cryptosystems based on DDH, QR and LWE [32].

2.3   McEliece Assumptions and Public-Key Cryptosystem

The McEliece cryptosystem [29] consists of a triplet of probabilistic algorithms $ME = (Gen_{ME}, Enc_{ME}, Dec_{ME})$ over a message space $M = \{0,1\}^k$. A semantically secure variant of the McEliece cryptosystem in the standard model was proposed by Nojime *et al.* in [31] and its full description is given in Appendix A.2. This cryptosystem is secure under the McEliece assumptions, which are formally stated as follows:

Assumption 1. *There is no PPT algorithm that can distinguish the public-key matrix G of the McEliece cryptosystem from a random matrix of the same size with non-negligible probability.*

Assumption 2. *The Syndrome Decoding Problem is hard for every PPT algorithm.*

The syndrome decoding problem was proved to be equivalent to the Learning Parity with Noise (LPN) problem [35] and also NP-complete [5]. Notice that a recent attack introduced in [18] breaks the McEliece assumptions for the case where a high rate Goppa code is used. Therefore, a low rate Goppa code should be used in the McEliece cryptosystem instantiation in order to guarantee that the assumptions above hold.

3   Oblivious Transfer from Lossy Encryption

In this section, we describe our protocol for universally composable oblivious transfer based on lossy encryption. This protocol is based on a combination of the DDH based fully simulatable OT protocol of [28], which yields a construction conceptually similar to [32] and [10]. Intuitively, we construct a stand-alone semi-honest OT protocol where the receiver generates a lossy and an injective public keys and sends them to the sender in such an order that the injective key corresponds to the choice bit. The sender then encrypts its first message with the first key received and its second message with the second key, sending the ciphertexts back to the receiver. We then run several copies of this basic protocol in parallel, using the cut-and-choose methods presented in [28] to construct the overall protocol and bound the probability that the receiver successfully cheats.

3.1   Distinguishing Lossy and Injective Keys

In this construction we will use the fact that it is possible to efficiently distinguish between the lossy and injective keys of several lossy encryption constructions given a trapdoor t, which is simply the corresponding secret key for most cases. The algorithm that determines whether a public key pk is lossy given a trapdoor t is formally denoted as:

- $KD(t, pk)$ is a PPT algorithm that receives as input a public key pk and a trapdoor t, and outputs 0 if pk is lossy. Otherwise, it outputs 1.

This property is similar to trapdoor identification of a messy branch in dual mode encryption [32] and is intrinsic to many flavors of lossy encryption such as the general constructions based on re-randomization and smooth projective hashing [23], for which such an algorithm can be built by simply using the secret key corresponding to pk as a trapdoor. We construct a KD algorithm for several flavors of lossy encryption in Appendix B.

3.2   Extractable String Commitment Schemes

A string commitment scheme is said to be *extractable* if there exists a polynomial time simulator that is able to obtain the the committed value m before the Open phase. In the CRS model, such a scheme can be trivially constructed from any IND-CPA secure public key cryptosystem (Gen, Enc, Dec) with a deterministic decryption algorithm. Consider the following generic construction, which is computationally hiding and statistically binding:

Extractable String Commitment. A common reference string $crs = pk$, $(pk, sk) \leftarrow Gen(1^n)$ containing a random public key is given to the sender and the receiver. The sender inputs a bit-string m.

- $\mathsf{Com}_{crs}(m)$ The sender encrypts m under the key crs with randomness r and sends the corresponding ciphertext $y = Enc(crs, m, r)$ to the receiver.
- $\mathsf{Open}_{crs}(m)$ The receiver sends the bit-string m and the randomness r to the receiver. The receiver encrypts m under the key in crs with randomness r and accepts the commitment if the result $Enc_{ME}(crs, m, r)$ is equal to y (received in the *Commit* stage). Otherwise, the receiver detects that the sender is cheating.

Notice that the computational hiding and statistical binding properties of this commitment are implied by the semantic security and correctness property of the cryptosystem, respectively. In order to extract the bit-string m, the simulator begins by generating a key pair (pk, sk), setting $crs = pk$ and storing sk. It then runs the commitment protocol as an honest receiver, but it can obtain m from y by computing $Dec_{ME}(sk, c)$, since it has the secret key sk corresponding to the public key pk contained in crs (and used by the sender to encrypt m). Thus, this string commitment scheme is considered extractable.

3.3   The Protocol

We consider a lossy cryptosystem for which it is possible to distinguish between lossy and injective public keys given a trapdoor (in this case the corresponding secret key) denoted by $LO = (Gen, Enc, Dec, KD)$[1] and the commitment scheme described in Section 3.2. Both parties are also assumed to share a security parameter s, which is implicitly embedded into the CRS.

---

[1] Here KD is the lossy key distinguishing algorithm, constructed for several flavors of lossy encryption in Appendix B.

Protocol OT_{LO}

Inputs: The receiver (**R**) has a choice bit $(sid, ssid, c)$ and the sender (**S**) has a pair of messages $(sid, ssid, b_0, b_1)$ that belong to LO's message space.

Common reference string: Three random LO public keys $pk_0, pk_1, pk_2 \leftarrow Gen(1^n)$.

1. After being activated with their inputs, the parties query $\mathcal{F}_{CRS}$ with $(sid, \mathbf{S}, \mathbf{R})$ and receive (sid, crs) as response.

2. For $i = 1, \ldots, s$, **R** chooses a random bit $c_i \in_R \{0, 1\}$, generates an injective key pair $(sk_{inj,i}, pk_{inj,i})$ and generates a lossy key pair $(sk_{lossy,i}, pk_{lossy,i})$. It stores
$(sid, ssid, sk_{inj,0}, \ldots, sk_{inj,s})$, sets $P_{i,c_i} = pk_{i,inj}, P_{i,0} = pk_{i,lossy}$ and sends the public key pairs $(sid, ssid, (P_{1,0}, P_{1,1}), \ldots, (P_{s,0}, P_{s,1}))$ to **S** . Additionally, **R** commits to the secret key pairs $(sk_{i,0}, sk_{i,1})$ using pk_0 in the crs sending $(sid, ssid, \mathsf{Com}_{crs}(sk_{1,0}, sk_{1,1}), \ldots, \mathsf{Com}_{crs}(sk_{s,0}, sk_{s,1}))$ to **S** , where $sk_{i,0}$ and $sk_{i,1}$ correspond to $P_{i,0}$ and $P_{i,1}$, respectively.

3. **S** stores the pairs $(sid, ssid, (P_{1,0}, P_{1,1}), \ldots, (P_{s,0}, P_{s,1}))$.

4. **S** and **R** now run a coin tossing protocol to obtain a common random string r:

   (a) **S** chooses a random bit string $v \in_R \{0, 1\}^s$ and sends $(sid, ssid, \mathsf{Com}_{crs}(v))$ to **R** using pk_1 in the crs for the commitment.

   (b) **R** chooses a random bit string $v' \in_R \{0, 1\}^s$ and sends $(sid, ssid, \mathsf{Com}_{crs}(v'))$ to **S** using pk_2 in the crs for the commitment.

   (c) **S** sends $(sid, ssid, \mathsf{Open}_{crs}(v))$ to **R** and **R** sends $(sid, ssid, \mathsf{Open}_{crs}(v'))$ to **S** , opening their commitments to v and v' respectively. **S** and **R** store $(sid, ssid, r)$, which they obtain by computing $r = v \oplus v'$. Denote $r = r_1, \ldots, r_s$.

5. Let $i_1, \ldots, i_{\hat{s}}$ be the indices i where $r_i = 1$. For every $i_1, \ldots, i_{\hat{s}}$, **R** opens its commitment to $(sk_{i,0}, sk_{i,1})$, sending $(sid, ssid, \mathsf{Open}_{crs}(sk_{i_1,0}, sk_{i_1,1}), \ldots, \mathsf{Open}_{crs}(sk_{i_{\hat{s}},0}, sk_{i_{\hat{s}},1}))$ to **S** .

6. Let $j_1, \ldots, j_{s'}$ be the indices j where $r_j = 0$. For $j_1, \ldots, j_{s'}$, **R** sends a "reordering" of $P_{j,0}$ and $P_{j,1}$ such that, in the resulting pairs $(P_{j,0}, P_{j,1})$, $P_{j,c}$ is an injective public key and $P_{j,1-c}$ is a lossy public key. This reordering is a bit m_j such that if it equals 0 then the pairs are left as is, and if it equals 1 then $P_{j,0}$ and $P_{j,1}$ are interchanged. **R** sends $(sid, ssid, m_{j_1}, \ldots, m_{j_{s'}})$ to **S** .

7. For every i where $r_i = 1$, **S** uses the secret keys obtained from the opened commitment to verify that P_{i,c_i} is an injective public key while $P_{i,1-c_i}$ is a lossy public key, otherwise it halts and outputs $(sid, ssid, \bot)$.

8. Employing a reduction given in [13], **S** chooses s' random bits $b_{0,1}, \ldots, b_{0,s'}$ and s' random bits $b_{1,1}, \ldots, b_{1,s'}$ such that $b_0 = b_{0,1} \oplus \ldots \oplus b_{0,s'}$ and $b_1 = b_{1,1} \oplus \ldots \oplus b_{1,s'}$. For $t = 1, \ldots, s'$, **S** encrypts each bit $b_{0,t}$ and $b_{1,t}$ with the corresponding public key, computing $\hat{b}_{0,t} = Enc(P_{j_t,0}, b_{0,t})$ and $\hat{b}_{1,t} = Enc(P_{j_t,1}, b_{1,t})$. **S** sends the pairs $(sid, ssid, (\hat{b}_{0,1}, \hat{b}_{1,1}), \ldots, (\hat{b}_{0,s'}, \hat{b}_{1,s'}))$ to **R**

9. For each pair of ciphertexts $(\hat{b}_{0,t}, \hat{b}_{1,t})$ received, **R** computes $b_{c,t} = Dec(sk_{in_{j,j_t}}, \hat{b}_{c,s'})$. Finally, **R** computes $b_c = b_{c,1} \oplus \ldots \oplus b_{c,t}$, obtaining b_c. **R** outputs $(sid, ssid, b_c)$. If Dec yields an error for any $\hat{b}_{c,t}$, it outputs $(sid, ssid, 0)$.

Correctness: Before constructing the simulators and presenting the security proof, we show that Protocol OT_{LO} is correct, in the sense that, given that both parties are honest, the correct output is obtained. First of all, it is clear that the protocol runs in polynomial time.

Notice that, after the reordering, all the pairs $(sid, ssid, (P_{j,0}, P_{j,1}))$ are such that $P_{j,c}$ is an injective public key and $P_{j,1-c}$ is a lossy public key. Thus, **R** is able to decrypt all of the ciphertexts $\hat{b}_{c,t}$ for $t = 1, \ldots, s'$, obtaining all of the $b_{c,t}$ bits necessary to compute the bit $b_c = b_{c,1} \oplus \ldots \oplus b_{c,s'}$.

3.4   Security

Theorem 1. *For every lossy cryptosystem LO for which it is possible to distinguish lossy and injective public keys given the corresponding secret key, Protocol OT_{LO} securely realizes the functionality $\hat{\mathcal{F}}_{OT}$ in the $\mathcal{F}_{CRS}$-hybrid model with statistical security for the sender.*

Intuitivelly, in the case that both parties are honest, security for **S** follows from the fact that **R** is not able to decrypt the ciphertexts $\hat{b}_{1-c,t}$, since they are created under a lossy public key. If **R** cheats by constructing injective keys $P_{j_t,1-c}$, he will be detected by **S** with high probability. On the other hand, security for **R** follows from the fact that, if the commitment scheme is secure, **S** is unable to learn **R**'s choice bit c, since it can't distinguish between $P_{j_t,c}$ and $P_{j_t,1-c}$, which follows from indistinguishability of lossy keys. Also, if **S** sends a invalid ciphertext in order to force **R** to complain and reveal c, **R** simply outputs 0 as if **S** had input $b_c = 0$.

Now we analyse security under corruption. Let $\mathcal{A}$ be a static adversary that interacts with parties **S** and **R** running protocol OT_{LO}. We now construct a simulator $\mathcal{S}$ that interacts with $\hat{\mathcal{F}}_{OT}$ such that no environment $\mathcal{Z}$ can distinguish between interactions with $\mathcal{A}$ in the real world and interactions with $\mathcal{S}$ in the ideal world. $\mathcal{S}$ invokes an internal copy of $\mathcal{A}$ and simulates the interactions of $\mathcal{A}$ with $\mathcal{Z}$ and with the parties **S** and **R** . We partly base the simulators for the cases when **S** and **R** are individually corrupted on the techniques of [28], which mainly consist in manipulating the coin tossing result to obtain arbitrary results in the cut-and-choose phase. For each corruption scenario, $\mathcal{S}$ works as follows:

Simulating Communication with $\mathcal{Z}$: $\mathcal{S}$ writes every message received from $\mathcal{Z}$ in $\mathcal{A}$'s input tape, simulating $\mathcal{A}$'s environment. Also, $\mathcal{S}$ forwards every message written on $\mathcal{A}$'s output tape to $\mathcal{Z}$ by copying to its own output tape.

Simulating Trivial Cases: If both **S** and **R** are corrupted, $\mathcal{S}$ simply runs $\mathcal{A}$ internally. Notice that $\mathcal{A}$ will generate the messages from both corrupted **S** and **R** .

If both **S** and **R** are honest, $\mathcal{S}$ runs the protocol between honest **S** and **R** internally on inputs $(sid, ssid, c = 0)$ and $(sid, ssid, b_0 = 0, b_1 = 1)$, respectively. All messages are delivered to $\mathcal{A}$.

Simulating When only S Is Corrupted: $\mathcal{S}$ runs Gen three times, obtaining three key pairs $(pk_0, sk_0), (pk_1, sk_1), (pk_2, sk_2)$. It sets $crs = pk_0, pk_1, pk_2$ and stores (sid, sk_0, sk_1, sk_2) in order to extract subsequent commitments. When the parties query $\mathcal{F}_{CRS}$, $\mathcal{S}$ hands them (sid, crs). When the dummy **S** is activated, $\mathcal{S}$ proceeds as follows:

1. $\mathcal{S}$ generates a random string $r \in_R \{0,1\}^s$, denoted by $r = r_1, \ldots, r_s$. For $i = 1, \ldots, s$, $\mathcal{S}$ chooses a random bit $c_i \in_R \{0,1\}$, generates an injective key pair $(sk_{inj,i}, pk_{inj,i})$ and sets $P_{i,c_i} = pk_{inj,i}$. For $i = 1, \ldots, s$, if $r_i = 0$, $\mathcal{S}$ generates a lossy key pair $(sk_{lossy,i}, pk_{lossy,i})$ and sets $P_{i,1-c_i} = pk_{lossy,i}$, if $r_i = 0$, $\mathcal{S}$ generates another injective key pair $(\hat{sk}_{inj,i}, \hat{pk}_{inj,i})$ and sets $P_{i,1-c_i} = \hat{pk}_{inj,i}$. $\mathcal{S}$ stores
   $(sid, ssid, sk_{inj,0}, \hat{sk}_{inj,0} \ldots, sk_{inj,\hat{s}}, \hat{sk}_{inj,\hat{s}})$, and sends commitments
   $(sid, ssid, \mathsf{Com}_{crs}(sk_{0,0}, sk_{0,1}), \ldots, \mathsf{Com}_{crs}(sk_{s,0}, sk_{s,1}))$ using pk_0 in the crs and the public key pairs
   $(sid, ssid, (P_{0,0}, P_{0,1}), \ldots, (P_{s,0}, P_{s,1}))$ to **S** , where $sk_{0,0}$ and $sk_{0,1}$ correspond to $P_{0,0}$ and $P_{0,1}$, respectively.
2. Coin tossing phase: $\mathcal{S}$ simulates the coin tossing in order to obtain r as output:
   (a) $\mathcal{S}$ receives the commitment $(sid, ssid, \mathsf{Com}_{crs}(v))$ from $\mathcal{A}$ and extracts the bit string v using (sid, sk_1).
   (b) $\mathcal{S}$ computes $v' = r \oplus v$ and commits to this value using pk_2, sending $(sid, ssid, \mathsf{Com}_{crs}(v'))$ to $\mathcal{A}$.
   (c) If $\mathcal{A}$ does not correctly open its commitment $(sid, ssid, \mathsf{Com}_{crs}(v))$, then $\mathcal{S}$ sends $\perp$ to $\hat{\mathcal{F}}_{OT}$, simulating **R** aborting and halts. However, if $\mathcal{A}$ correctly opens its commitment, $\mathcal{S}$ proceeds to the next step. Hence, the result of the coin tossing is the arbitrary $(sid, ssid, r)$ chosen by $\mathcal{S}$.
3. For every i where $r_i = 1$, $\mathcal{S}$ opens its commitment to $(sk_{i,0}, sk_{i,1})$, sending $(sid, ssid, \mathsf{Open}_{crs}(sk_{i_1,0}, sk_{i_1,1}), \ldots, \mathsf{Open}_{crs}(sk_{i_s,0}, sk_{i_s,1}))$ to **S** . Then it hands a random reordering of $P_{j,0}$ and $P_{j,1}$ for every j for which $r_j = 0$ by computing
   $m_{j_1}, \ldots, m_{j_{s'}} \in \{0,1\}$ and sending $(sid, ssid, m_{j_1}, \ldots, m_{j_{s'}})$ to $\mathcal{A}$.
4. If $\mathcal{A}$ does not reply with a valid message, then $\mathcal{S}$ sends $\perp$ to $\hat{\mathcal{F}}_{OT}$ and halts. Otherwise, it receives the pairs of ciphertexts $\langle(\hat{b}_{0,1}, \hat{b}_{1,1}), \ldots, (\hat{b}_{0,s'}, \hat{b}_{1,s'})\rangle$. $\mathcal{S}$ then obtains both b_0 and b_1 using the same method as a honest **R** . However, it is able to decrypt both $\hat{b}_{0,t}$ and $\hat{b}_{1,t}$ with the injective secret keys sk_{inj,j_t} and $\hat{sk}_{inj,j_t}$, obtaining a series of pairs $(b_{0,t}, b_{1,t})$, for $t = 1, \ldots, s'$. It then computes $b_0 = b_{0,1} \oplus \ldots \oplus b_{0,s'}$ and $b_1 = b_{1,1} \oplus \ldots \oplus b_{1,s'}$. $\mathcal{S}$ sends the pair $(sid, ssid, b_0, b_1)$ to $\hat{\mathcal{F}}_{OT}$ as **S** 's input and halts.

Simulating When only R Is Corrupted: S runs Gen three times, obtaining three key pairs $(pk_0, sk_0), (pk_1, sk_1), (pk_2, sk_2)$. It sets $crs = pk_0, pk_1, pk_2$ and stores (sid, sk_0, sk_1, sk_2) in order to extract subsequent commitments. When the parties query $\mathcal{F}_{CRS}$, S hands them (sid, crs). When the dummy R is activated, S proceeds as follows:

1. S receives the commitments $(sid, ssid, \mathsf{Com_{crs}}(sk_{0,0}, sk_{0,1}), \ldots, \mathsf{Com_{crs}}(sk_{s,0}, sk_{s,1}))$ from $\mathcal{A}$ and then extracts the secret keys using (sid, sk_0), storing $(sid, ssid, sk_{0,0}, sk_{0,1}, \ldots, sk_{s,0}, sk_{s,1})$.

2. Coin tossing phase: S commits to a random $v \in_R \{0,1\}^s$ using pk_1, sending $(sid, ssid, \mathsf{Com_{crs}}(v))$ to $\mathcal{A}$. After receiving $\mathcal{A}$'s commitment $(sid, ssid, \mathsf{Com_{crs}}(v'))$, S sends $(sid, ssid, \mathsf{Open_{crs}}(v))$ to $\mathcal{A}$ and receives $(sid, ssid, \mathsf{Open_{crs}}(v'))$ from $\mathcal{A}$. The final result is $r = v \oplus v'$.

3. S receives the decommitments $(sid, ssid, \mathsf{Open_{crs}}(P_{i_1}), \ldots, \mathsf{Open_{crs}}(P_{i_s}))$ and the pair reorderings $(sid, ssid, m_{j_1}, \ldots, m_{j_{s'}})$ from $\mathcal{A}$. S then verifies that the pair $(P_{i,0}, P_{i,1})$ is valid by checking that P_{i,c_i} is an injective key and P_{i,c_i} is a lossy key, for i where $r_i = 1$. If these pairs are not valid or $\mathcal{A}$ did not send valid openings, S halts and outputs $(sid, ssid, \perp)$. If the pairs are valid, S continues to the next step.

4. S searches the pairs $(P_{j,0}, P_{j,1})$ for at least one valid pair $(P_{t,0}, P_{t,1})$ (*i.e.* a pair containing an injective and a lossy key), for j where $r_j = 0$. It uses the secret keys $(sid, ssid, sk_{0,0}, sk_{0,1}, \ldots, sk_{s,0}, sk_{s,1})$, obtained by extracting $\mathcal{A}$'s commitment in step 1, to test whether the pairs are valid. If no such pair is found, S halts, outputting fail. Otherwise, it sets $c = 0$ if, after the reordering, $P_{t,c_t} = P_{t,0}$. Conversely, it sets $c = 1$ if, after the reordering, $P_{t,c_t} = P_{t,1}$.

5. In order to complete the protocol, S sends $(sid, ssid, c)$ to $\hat{\mathcal{F}}_{OT}$, receiving $(sid, ssid, b)$ in response. S then computes the last message from S to R honestly, setting $b_c = b$, $b_{1-c} \in_R \{0,1\}$ and running the instructions of an honest S to compute this last message. S sends $(sid, ssid, (\hat{b}_{0,1}, \hat{b}_{1,1}), \ldots, (\hat{b}_{0,s'}, \hat{b}_{1,s'}))$ to $\mathcal{A}$ and halts.

In order to prove Theorem 1 we will use the following lemmas:

Lemma 1. *(Computational security for* R *) When* $\mathcal{A}$ *corrupts only* S *, for any lossy cryptosystems LO for which it is possible to distinguish lossy and injective public keys given the corresponding secret key, the following holds:*

$$EXEC_{OT_{LO}, \mathcal{A}, \mathcal{Z}} \overset{c}{\approx} IDEAL_{\hat{\mathcal{F}}_{OT}, S, \mathcal{Z}}$$

Lemma 2 *(Statistical security for* S *) When* $\mathcal{A}$ *corrupts only* R *, for any lossy cryptosystems LO for which it is possible to distinguish lossy and injective public keys given the corresponding secret key, the following holds:*

$$EXEC_{OT_{LO}, \mathcal{A}, \mathcal{Z}} \overset{s}{\approx} IDEAL_{\hat{\mathcal{F}}_{OT}, S, \mathcal{Z}}$$

The proofs for both lemmas are left for the full version of this paper. Notice that security for S depends on the lossiness of keys while security for R depends on the indistinguishability of lossy and injective keys.

4   Oblivious Transfer from the McEliece Assumptions

Although we are not able to obtain lossy encryption from the McEliece assumptions, it is possible to use the same approach of Protocol OT_{LO} to construct a new UC secure OT protocol that is secure under these assumptions. Intuitively, we use a "interactive key generation" procedure to obtain a pair of matrices of size $k \times n$ such that one is a valid McEliece public key and the other is a random matrix, along with trapdoor information that allows **S** or the simulators to test whether a given matrix is a valid public key or not later on during protocol execution. The valid McEliece public key works as an injective key and the random matrix works as a "lossy" key, since the receiver cannot decrypt messages generated under it. This method was introduced in [16] and substitutes the properties of lossy encryption that were used in the previous protocol. The rest of the protocol has the same structure as before, being based on several copies of a semi-honest string OT protocol running in parallel with an intermediate cut-and-choose phase to bound the probability that the receiver successfully cheats.

In the following protocol we consider the semantically secure McEliece public key cryptosystem $ME = (Gen_{ME}, Enc_{ME}, Dec_{ME})$ defined in Appendix A.2 and an instance of the extractable commitment scheme defined in Section 3.2 constructed from ME. Both parties also have access to a security parameter s, which is implicitly embedded in the CRS.

Protocol OT_{ME}
Inputs: The receiver (**R**) has a choice bit $(sid, ssid, c)$ and the sender (**S**) has a pair of messages $(sid, ssid, b_0, b_1)$ that belong to ME's message space.
Common reference string: Three random $k \times n$ matrices $pk_0, pk_1, pk_2 \leftarrow Gen_{ME}(1^n)$ used as a public keys in the extractable commitment scheme.

1. After being activated with their inputs, the parties query $\mathcal{F}_{CRS}$ with $(sid, \mathbf{S}, \mathbf{R})$ and receive (sid, crs) as response.
2. Public Key Pair Generation:
   (a) For $i = 1, \ldots, s$, **R** chooses a random bit $c_i \in_R \{0,1\}$ and generates a McEliece secret key $sk_i = (S_i, G_i, P_i)$. For each bit c_i, Bob computes a public key $P_{i,c_i} = S_i G_i P_i$. It stores $(sid, ssid, sk_0, \ldots, sk_s)$ and $(sid, ssid, P_{0,c_0}, \ldots, P_{s,c_s})$, and sends
   $(sid, ssid, \mathsf{Com_{crs}}(sk_1), \ldots, \mathsf{Com_{crs}}(sk_s))$ to **S**, using pk_0 for the commitment.
   (b) **S** generates s random matrices $(Q_1, \ldots, Q_s)$ and sends $(sid, ssid, Q_1, \ldots, Q_s)$ to **R**.
   (c) **R** generates computationally lossy keys by computing $P_{i,1-c_i} = P_{i,c_i} \oplus Q_i$ for $i = 1, \ldots, s$. **R** sends $(sid, ssid, P_{1,0}, \ldots, P_{s,0})$ to **S** and stores $(sid, ssid, P_{1,1-c_1}, \ldots, P_{s,1-c_s})$.
   (d) For $i = 1, \ldots, s$, **S** computes $P_{i,1} = P_{i,0} \oplus Q_i$ and stores $(sid, ssid, P_{1,1}, \ldots, P_{s,1})$.
3. **S** and **R** now run a coin tossing protocol to obtain a common random string r:

(a) **S** chooses a random bit string $v \in_R \{0,1\}^s$ and sends $(sid, ssid, \mathsf{Com}_{\mathsf{crs}}(v))$ to **R** , using pk_1 for the commitment.

(b) **R** chooses a random bit string $v' \in_R \{0,1\}^s$ and sends $(sid, ssid, \mathsf{Com}_{\mathsf{crs}}(v'))$ to **S** , using pk_2 for the commitment.

(c) **S** sends $(sid, ssid, \mathsf{Open}_{\mathsf{crs}}(v))$ to **R** and **R** sends $(sid, ssid, \mathsf{Open}_{\mathsf{crs}}(v'))$ to **S** , opening their commitments to v and v' respectively. **S** and **R** store $(sid, ssid, r)$, which they obtain by computing $r = v \oplus v'$. Denote $r = r_1, \ldots, r_s$.

4. Let $i_1, \ldots, i_{\hat{s}}$ be the indices i where $r_i = 1$. For every $i_1, \ldots, i_{\hat{s}}$, **R** opens its commitment to sk_i, sending $(sid, ssid, \mathsf{Open}_{\mathsf{crs}}(sk_{i_1}), \ldots, \mathsf{Open}_{\mathsf{crs}}(sk_{i_{\hat{s}}}))$ to **S** .

5. Let $j_1, \ldots, j_{s'}$ be the indices j where $r_j = 0$. For $j_1, \ldots, j_{s'}$, **R** sends a "re-ordering" of $P_{j,0}$ and $P_{j,1}$ such that, in the resulting pairs $(P_{j,0}, P_{j,1})$, $P_{j,c}$ is a valid McEliece public key and $P_{j,1-c}$ is a random matrix. This reordering is a bit m_j such that if it equals 0 then the pairs are left as is, and if it equals 1 then $P_{j,0}$ and $P_{j,1}$ are interchanged. **R** sends $(sid, ssid, m_{j_1}, \ldots, m_{j_{s'}})$ to **S** .

6. For every i where $r_i = 1$, **S** verifies that P_{i,c_i} obtained from the opened commitment is equal to $P_{i,0}$ or $P_{i,1}$, otherwise it halts and outputs $(sid, ssid, \bot)$.

7. Employing a reduction given in [13], **S** chooses s' random bits $b_{0,1}, \ldots, b_{0,s'}$ and s' random bits $b_{1,1}, \ldots, b_{1,s'}$ such that $b_0 = b_{0,1} \oplus \ldots \oplus b_{0,s'}$ and $b_1 = b_{1,1} \oplus \ldots \oplus b_{1,s'}$. For $t = 1, \ldots, s'$, **S** encrypts each bit $b_{0,t}$ and $b_{1,t}$ with the corresponding public key, computing $\hat{b}_{0,t} = Enc(P_{j_t,0}, b_{0,t})$ and $\hat{b}_{1,t} = Enc(P_{j_t,1}, b_{1,t})$. **S** sends the pairs $(sid, ssid, (\hat{b}_{0,1}, \hat{b}_{1,1}), \ldots, (\hat{b}_{0,s'}, \hat{b}_{1,s'}))$ to **R** .

8. For each pair of ciphertexts $(\hat{b}_{0,t}, \hat{b}_{1,t})$ received, **R** computes $b_{c,t} = Dec_{ME}(sk_{j_t}, \hat{b}_{c,s'})$. Finally, **R** computes $b_c = b_{c,1} \oplus \ldots \oplus b_{c,t}$, and outputs b_c. If Dec_{ME} yields a decoding error for any $\hat{b}_{c,t}$, it outputs 0.

The same correctness analysis of protocol OT_{LO} applies here.

4.1   Security

Theorem 2. *Protocol OT_{ME} securely realizes the functionality $\hat{\mathcal{F}}_{OT}$ in the $\mathcal{F}_{CRS}$-hybrid model under the McEliece assumptions with computational security for both parties.*

The proof of Theorem 2 is very similar to that of Theorem 1. The main difference lies in that this protocol provides computational security for both parties. Despite this difference, similar simulators are constructed with added trivial steps for handling interactive key generation. The simulators and security proofs are left for the full version of this paper.

5   Conclusion

We introduce a general non-black-box construction of universally composable oblivious transfer from lossy encryption and another construction based on the

McEliece assumptions. The lossy encryption based protocol sheds light on previous results by Peikert *et al.* [32], showing that it is possible to construct universally composable oblivious transfer with statistical security for the sender with a primitive that is weaker than dual-mode encryption. Our construction based on the McEliece assumptions yields the first universally composable oblivious transfer protocol based on coding assumptions, which are also resistant to current quantum attacks. Although both assumptions are apparently unrelated, the protocol structure and the proofs in both cases are similar. Therefore, it raises the question of whether lossy encryption definitions may be generalized to include constructions based on the McEliece assumptions.

References

1. Dinh, H., Moore, C., Russell, A.: McEliece and Niederreiter Cryptosystems that Resist Quantum Fourier Sampling Attacks. In: Rogaway, P. (ed.) CRYPTO 2011. LNCS, vol. 6841, pp. 761–779. Springer, Heidelberg (2011)
2. Aiello, W., Ishai, Y., Reingold, O.: Priced Oblivious Transfer: How to Sell Digital Goods. In: Pfitzmann, B. (ed.) EUROCRYPT 2001. LNCS, vol. 2045, pp. 119–135. Springer, Heidelberg (2001)
3. Bellare, M., Hofheinz, D., Yilek, S.: Possibility and Impossibility Results for Encryption and Commitment Secure under Selective Opening. In: Joux, A. (ed.) EUROCRYPT 2009. LNCS, vol. 5479, pp. 1–35. Springer, Heidelberg (2009)
4. Bellare, M., Micali, S.: Non-interactive Oblivious Transfer and Applications. In: Brassard, G. (ed.) CRYPTO 1989. LNCS, vol. 435, pp. 547–557. Springer, Heidelberg (1990)
5. Berlekamp, E.R., McEliece, R., van Tilborg, H.C.A.: On the inherent intractability of certain coding problems (corresp). IEEE Transactions on Information Theory (24) (1978)
6. Canetti, R.: Universally composable security: A new paradigm for cryptographic protocols. In: Proceedings of the 42nd IEEE symposium on Foundations of Computer Science, FOCS 2001, pp. 136–145. IEEE Computer Society, Washington, DC (2001)
7. Canetti, R., Fischlin, M.: Universally Composable Commitments. In: Kilian, J. (ed.) CRYPTO 2001. LNCS, vol. 2139, pp. 19–40. Springer, Heidelberg (2001)
8. Canetti, R., Lindell, Y., Ostrovsky, R., Sahai, A.: Universally composable two-party and multi-party secure computation. In: Proceedings of the Thiry-Fourth Annual ACM Symposium on Theory of Computing, STOC 2002, pp. 494–503. ACM, New York (2002)
9. Canetti, R., Rabin, T.: Universal Composition with Joint State. In: Boneh, D. (ed.) CRYPTO 2003. LNCS, vol. 2729, pp. 265–281. Springer, Heidelberg (2003)
10. Choi, S.G., Dachman-Soled, D., Malkin, T., Wee, H.: Simple, Black-Box Constructions of Adaptively Secure Protocols. In: Reingold, O. (ed.) TCC 2009. LNCS, vol. 5444, pp. 387–402. Springer, Heidelberg (2009)
11. Cramer, R., Shoup, V.: Universal Hash Proofs and a Paradigm for Adaptive Chosen Ciphertext Secure Public-Key Encryption. In: Knudsen, L.R. (ed.) EUROCRYPT 2002. LNCS, vol. 2332, pp. 45–64. Springer, Heidelberg (2002)
12. Crépeau, C., van de Graaf, J., Tapp, A.: Committed Oblivious Transfer and Private Multi-Party Computation. In: Coppersmith, D. (ed.) CRYPTO 1995. LNCS, vol. 963, pp. 110–123. Springer, Heidelberg (1995)

13. Damgård, I., Kilian, J., Salvail, L.: On the (im)possibility of Basing Oblivious Transfer and Bit Commitment on Weakened Security Assumptions. In: Stern, J. (ed.) EUROCRYPT 1999. LNCS, vol. 1592, pp. 56–73. Springer, Heidelberg (1999)

14. Damgård, I., Nielsen, J.B., Orlandi, C.: Essentially Optimal Universally Composable Oblivious Transfer. In: Lee, P.J., Cheon, J.H. (eds.) ICISC 2008. LNCS, vol. 5461, pp. 318–335. Springer, Heidelberg (2009)

15. David, B.M., Nascimento, A.C.A.: Efficient fully simulatable oblivious transfer from the mceliece assumptions. In: Information Theory Workshop (ITW), pp. 638–642. IEEE (October 2011)

16. Dowsley, R., van de Graaf, J., Müller-Quade, J., Nascimento, A.C.A.: Oblivious Transfer Based on the Mceliece Assumptions. In: Safavi-Naini, R. (ed.) ICITS 2008. LNCS, vol. 5155, pp. 107–117. Springer, Heidelberg (2008)

17. Even, S., Goldreich, O., Lempel, A.: A randomized protocol for signing contracts. In: CRYPTO 1982, pp. 205–210 (1982)

18. Faugère, J.C., Gauthier, V., Otmani, A., Perret, L., Tillich, J.P.: A distinguisher for high rate mceliece cryptosystems. Cryptology ePrint Archive. Report 2010/331 (2010)

19. Garay, J.A., Mackenzie, P., Yang, K.: Efficient and Universally Composable Committed Oblivious Transfer and Applications. In: Naor, M. (ed.) TCC 2004. LNCS, vol. 2951, pp. 297–316. Springer, Heidelberg (2004)

20. Goldreich, O., Micali, S., Wigderson, A.: How to play any mental game. In: STOC 1987: Proceedings of the Nineteenth Annual ACM Symposium on Theory of Computing, pp. 218–229. ACM, New York (1987)

21. Green, M., Hohenberger, S.: Universally Composable Adaptive Oblivious Transfer. In: Pieprzyk, J. (ed.) ASIACRYPT 2008. LNCS, vol. 5350, pp. 179–197. Springer, Heidelberg (2008)

22. Haitner, I.: Semi-Honest to Malicious Oblivious Transfer—the Black-Box Way. In: Canetti, R. (ed.) TCC 2008. LNCS, vol. 4948, pp. 412–426. Springer, Heidelberg (2008)

23. Hemenway, B., Libert, B., Ostrovsky, R., Vergnaud, D.: Lossy Encryption: Constructions from General Assumptions and Efficient Selective Opening Chosen Ciphertext Security. In: Lee, D.H. (ed.) ASIACRYPT 2011. LNCS, vol. 7073, pp. 70–88. Springer, Heidelberg (2011)

24. Ishai, Y., Kushilevitz, E., Lindell, Y., Petrank, E.: Black-box constructions for secure computation. In: Proceedings of the Thirty-Eighth Annual ACM Symposium on Theory of Computing, STOC 2006, pp. 99–108. ACM, New York (2006), http://doi.acm.org/10.1145/1132516.1132531

25. Jarecki, S., Shmatikov, V.: Efficient Two-Party Secure Computation on Committed Inputs. In: Naor, M. (ed.) EUROCRYPT 2007. LNCS, vol. 4515, pp. 97–114. Springer, Heidelberg (2007)

26. Kalai, Y.T.: Smooth Projective Hashing and Two-Message Oblivious Transfer. In: Cramer, R. (ed.) EUROCRYPT 2005. LNCS, vol. 3494, pp. 78–95. Springer, Heidelberg (2005)

27. Kilian, J.: Founding crytpography on oblivious transfer. In: STOC 1988: Proceedings of the Twentieth Annual ACM Symposium on Theory of Computing, pp. 20–31. ACM, New York (1988)

28. Lindell, A.Y.: Efficient Fully-Simulatable Oblivious Transfer. In: Malkin, T. (ed.) CT-RSA 2008. LNCS, vol. 4964, pp. 52–70. Springer, Heidelberg (2008)

29. McEliece, R.J.: A public-key cryptosystem based on algebraic coding theory. dsn progress report. In: Jet Propulsion Laboratories, CALTECH, pp. 42–44 (1978)

30. Naor, M., Pinkas, B.: Efficient oblivious transfer protocols. In: Proceedings of the Twelfth Annual ACM-SIAM Symposium on Discrete Algorithms, SODA 2001, Society for Industrial and Applied Mathematics, Philadelphia, PA, USA, pp. 448–457 (2001)
31. Nojima, R., Imai, H., Kobara, K., Morozov, K.: Semantic security for the mceliece cryptosystem without random oracles. Des. Codes Cryptography 49(1-3), 289–305 (2008)
32. Peikert, C., Vaikuntanathan, V., Waters, B.: A Framework for Efficient and Composable Oblivious Transfer. In: Wagner, D. (ed.) CRYPTO 2008. LNCS, vol. 5157, pp. 554–571. Springer, Heidelberg (2008)
33. Peikert, C., Waters, B.: Lossy trapdoor functions and their applications. In: Proceedings of the 40th Annual ACM Symposium on Theory of Computing, STOC 2008, pp. 187–196. ACM, New York (2008)
34. Rabin, M.O.: How to exchange secrets by oblivious transfer. Technical Memo TR-81. Aiken Computation Laboratory, Harvard University (1981)
35. Regev, O.: On lattices, learning with errors, random linear codes, and cryptography. In: STOC 2005: Proceedings of the Thirty-Seventh Annual ACM Symposium on Theory of Computing, pp. 84–93. ACM, New York (2005)

A   Definitions and Basic Constructions

In this section we present further formal definitions of functionalities and a rerandomization lossy encryption construction with a corresponding trapdoor lossy key distinguishing algorithm.

A.1   Universal Composability

Security in the UC framework is formally defined as:[2]

Definition 1. *A protocol π is said to UC-realize an ideal functionality $\mathcal{F}$ if, for every adversary $\mathcal{A}$, there exists a simulator $\mathcal{S}$ such that, for every environment $\mathcal{Z}$, the following holds:*

$$EXEC_{\pi,\mathcal{A},\mathcal{Z}} \overset{c}{\approx} IDEAL_{\mathcal{F},\mathcal{S},\mathcal{Z}}$$

In this work we consider security against static adversaries, *i.e.* once a party is corrupted it remains so during the whole execution. The security of our protocol is proved in the Common Reference String (CRS) model (referred to as the $\mathcal{F}_{CRS} - hybrid$ model in [6]), where all parties are assumed to have access to a common string generated in a setup phase before protocol execution. $\mathcal{F}_{CRS}$ is formally presented in Appendix A.1.

---

[2] For the sake of brevity, we refer the reader to Canetti's work [6] for further details and definitions regarding the UC framework.

Oblivious Transfer Ideal Functionality. The basic 1-out-of-2 oblivious transfer functionality $\mathcal{F}_{OT}$ as defined in [8] is presented bellow.

Functionality $\mathcal{F}_{OT}$

$\mathcal{F}_{OT}$ interacts with a sender **S** and a receiver **R**.

• Upon receiving a message $(\mathtt{sid}, \mathtt{sender}, b_0, b_1)$ from **S**, where each $b_i \in \{0,1\}^\ell$, store (b_0, b_1) (The length of the strings is fixed and known to all parties).

• Upon receiving a message $(\mathtt{sid}, \mathtt{receiver}, c)$ from **R**, check if a $(\mathtt{sid}, \mathtt{sender}, \cdots)$ message was previously sent. If yes, send $(\mathtt{sid}, b_c)$ to **R** and $(\mathtt{sid})$ to the adversary S and halt. If not, send nothing to **R** (but continue running).

Similarly to the framework of [32], our protocols reuse the same CRS for multiple oblivious transfer invocations. In order to achieve this, we employ the same techniques of [32]. Namely, we "wrap" each single execution of $\mathcal{F}_{OT}$ with a multi session extension $\hat{\mathcal{F}}_{OT}$ of the OT functionality, which handles the multiple independent execution of the OT protocol and coordinates the interaction with parties. The security of the resulting protocol is implied by the UC theorem with joint state (JUC) [9], which states that any protocol π operating in the $\mathcal{F}_{OT} - hybrid$ model can be securely emulated in the real world by appropriately composing π with a single execution of a protocol ρ that implements $\hat{\mathcal{F}}_{OT}$.

Common Reference String Ideal Functionality. The following formal definition of the ideal functionality $\mathcal{F}^{\mathcal{D}}_{CRS}$ is taken from [9].

Functionality $\mathcal{F}^{\mathcal{D}}_{CRS}$

$\mathcal{F}^{\mathcal{D}}_{CRS}$ runs with parties $(P_1, ..., P_n)$ and is parametrized by an algorithm $\mathcal{D}$.

• When receiving a message (sid, P_i, P_j) from P_i , let $crs \leftarrow \mathcal{D}(1^n)$, send (sid, crs) to P_i and send (crs, P_i, P_j) to the adversary. Next, when receiving (sid, P_i, P_j) from P_j (and only P_j), send (sid, crs) to P_j and to the adversary, and halt.

A.2   Semantically Secure McEliece Cryptosystem

The semantically secure McEliece cryptosystem [31] consists of a triplet of probabilistic algorithms $ME = (Gen_{ME}, Enc_{ME}, Dec_{ME})$ over a message space $M = \{0,1\}^k$. The following definition has been taken from [31]:

- Key generation algorithm: The PPT key generation algorithm $Gen_{ME}(1^n)$ works as follows:

1. Generate a $k \times n$ generator matrix $\mathbf{G}'$ of a binary Goppa code, where we assume that there is an efficient error-correction algorithm Correct which can always correct up to w errors.
2. Generate a $k \times k$ random non-singular matrix $\mathbf{S}$.
3. Generate a $n \times n$ random permutation matrix $\mathbf{P}$.
4. Set $\mathbf{G} = \mathbf{S}\mathbf{G}'\mathbf{P}$, and outputs $pk = (\mathbf{G}, w)$ and $sk = (\mathbf{S}, \mathbf{G}', \mathbf{P})$.

- The encryption algorithm: The PPT encryption algorithm $Enc_{ME}(pk, m, r)$ takes a public-key pk, a plaintext $m \in \{0, 1\}^\ell$ and randomness $r \in \{0, 1\}^{k-\ell}$ as input and outputs ciphertext $c = [r|m]\mathbf{G} \oplus e$, where $e \in \{0, 1\}^n$ is a random vector of hamming weight w.
- The decryption algorithm: The polynomial-time algorithm $Dec_{ME}(sk, c)$ works as follows:
  1. Compute $c\mathbf{P}^{-1} = (([r|m]\mathbf{S})\mathbf{G}' \oplus e\mathbf{P}^{-1})$, where $\mathbf{P}^{-1}$ denotes the inverse matrix of $\mathbf{P}$.
  2. Compute $[r|m]\mathbf{S} = \text{Correct}(c\mathbf{P}^{-1})$.
  3. Compute $[r|m] = ([r|m]\mathbf{S})\mathbf{S}^{-1}$.
  4. Output m.

A.3   Lossy Encryption Constructions

First we present a formal definition of Lossy Encryption similar to the definition given in [23]:

Definition 2. *A lossy public-key encryption scheme is a tuple* (Gen, Enc, Dec) *of efficient algorithms such that*

- $Gen(1^\lambda, \text{inj})$ *outputs keys* (pk^{inj}, sk^{inj}), *keys generated by* $Gen(1^\lambda, \text{inj})$ *are called injective keys.*
- $Gen(1^\lambda, \text{lossy})$ *outputs keys* (pk^{lossy}, sk^{lossy}), *keys generated by* $Gen(1^\lambda, \text{lossy})$ *are called lossy keys.*
- $Enc(pk, m, r)$ *is an encryption algorithm that takes as input a public key, a plain-text message and randomness, outputting a ciphertext.*
- $Dec(sk, c)$ *is a decryption algorithm that takes as input a secret key and ciphertext, outputting a plain-text message.*

Additionally, the algorithms must satisfy the following properties:

- **Correctness on injective keys.** *For all plaintexts* $x \in X$,

$$Pr\left[(pk^{inj}, sk^{inj}) \xleftarrow{\$} Gen(1^\lambda, \text{inj}); r \xleftarrow{\$} coins(Enc) : Dec(sk^{inj}, Enc(pk^{inj}, x, r)) = x\right] = 1$$

- **Indistinguishability of keys.** *In lossy mode, public keys are computationally indistinguishable from those in the injective mode given no previous information. Specifically, if* $proj : (pk, sk) \to pk$ *is the projection map, then*

$$\{proj(Gen(1^\lambda, \text{inj}))\} \stackrel{c}{\approx} \{proj(Gen(1^\lambda, \text{lossy}))\}$$

- **Lossiness of lossy keys.** If $(pk^{lossy}, sk^{lossy}) \overset{\$}{\leftarrow} Gen(1^\lambda, \text{lossy})$, then for all $x_0, x_1 \in X$, the statistical distance between the distributions $Enc(pk^{lossy}, x_0, R)$ and $Enc(pk^{lossy}, x_1, R)$ is negligible in λ.

This definition differs from the one given in [23] in that we do not require openability property. Moreover, note that this definition implies semantic security as shown in [23].

B   Distinguishing Lossy and Injective Keys: Constructions

In this section we construct efficient algorithms that distinguish lossy and injective public keys given the corresponding secret key.

Lossy Encryption from Re-Randomization. Here we consider the rerandomization based lossy cryptosystem presented in [23].

- $KD(sk, pk)$: First compute test ciphertext $c = Enc(pk, 1)$. Then output whatever $Dec(sk, c)$ outputs.

It is clear that, if the public key pk is injective, this algorithm will output 1, which is the information encrypted into the ciphertext. Otherwise, if the public key is lossy, this algorithm will output 0, since the ciphertext generated by Enc is always an encryption of 0 if the public key pk is lossy.

Lossy Encryption from DDH, QR and LWE. In this case we build on the general construction from dual-mode encryption to simply utilize the algorithm $FindMessy$ to distinguish a lossy public key from an injective public key. Algorithm KD is constructed as follows:

- $KD(sk, pk)$: First, parse pk as (crs, pk_{dm}, ρ) and sk as (t, sk_{dm}). Run $FindMessy(t, pk_{dm})$ obtaining b, output 0 if $b = \rho$ and output 1 if $b \neq \rho$.

Since ρ indicates the branch of pk_{dm} that is used in encryption, if $FindMessy(t, pk_{dm})$ outputs ρ, then the public key $pk = (crs, pk_{dm}, \rho)$ is lossy.

Shannon Impossibility, Revisited

Yevgeniy Dodis

New York University
dodis@cs.nyu.edu

In this note we revisit the famous result of Shannon [Sha49] stating that any encryption scheme with perfect security against computationally unbounded attackers must have a secret key as long as the message. This result motivated the introduction of modern encryption schemes, which are secure only against a computationally bounded attacker, and allow some small (negligible) advantage to such an attacker. It is a well known folklore that both such relaxations — limiting the power of the attacker and allowing for some small advantage — are necessary to overcome Shannon's result. To our surprise, we could not find a clean and well documented proof of this folklore belief. (In fact, two proofs are required, each showing that only one of the two relaxations above is not sufficient.) Most proofs we saw either made some limiting assumptions (e.g., encryption is deterministic), or proved a much more complicated statement (e.g., beating Shannon's bound implies the existence of one-way functions [IL89].)

In this note we rectify this situation, by presenting two clean, elementary extensions of Shannon's impossibility result, showing that, in order to beat the famous Shannon lower bound [Sha49] on key length for one-time-secure encryption, one must *simultaneously* restrict the attacker to be efficient, and also allow the attacker to break the system with some non-zero (i.e., negligible) probability. Unlike most prior proofs we have seen, our proof seamlessly handles *probabilistic* encryption, small decryption error, and can be taught without any extra background (e.g., notions of entropy, etc.) in a first lecture of an introductory cryptography class.

For intellectual curiosity, we also discuss some "entropy extensions" of our proof, and the relation between our "indistinguishability-based" proof and Shannon's original "mutual-information-based" proof.

ORGANIZATION. The main results are presented in Sections 1 and 2, giving the main definitions and impossibility results. These are presented in a completely elementary way (e.g., no notion of entropy is used). In Section 3 we give some simple "entropy-based" extensions of our "indistinguishability-based" definition, and in Section 4 we also present the "mutual-information-based" definitions, and discuss their relation to "indistinguishability-based" notions.

1 Definitions

SOME NOTATION. In general, we use capital letters for random variables, and lower case letters for specific values; e.g., M, C, S denote appropriately defined random messages, ciphertexts and keys, while m, c, s denote some specific value

A. Smith (Ed.): ICITS 2012, LNCS 7412, pp. 100–110, 2012.
© Springer-Verlag Berlin Heidelberg 2012

of those. When A is a probabilistic algorithm taking input x, we write $Y \leftarrow A(x)$ to denote the random variable $A(x; R)$ for uniformly random R. When X itself it a random variable, we write $Y \leftarrow A(X)$. Finally, we use calligraphic letters for message spaces; e.g., key space $\mathcal{S}$ and message space $\mathcal{M}$.

ENCRYPTION. Let (Gen, Enc, Dec) be any encryption scheme with key space $\mathcal{S}$ and message space $\mathcal{M}$. The key generation algorithm Gen outputs a secret key s chosen according to some key distribution S over $\mathcal{S}$. In most common schemes S is simply uniform over $\mathcal{S}$, but our results hold for any key distribution S, so we will not assume that S must be uniform.

The encryption algorithm Enc takes a key $s \in \mathcal{S}$, a message $m \in \mathcal{M}$, and outputs ciphertext $C \leftarrow \mathsf{Enc}_s(m)$. We stress that we allow the encryption algorithm Enc to be *probabilistic*, so C is really $\mathsf{Enc}_s(m; R)$ for random coins R. Luckily, we structure our proofs in a way which will easily handle this case, without explicitly talking about the random coins R. In particular, to simplify the notation, when some encryption is computed inside some probability, we do not explicitly put the choice or R under Pr; for example, $\Pr_S[\mathsf{Enc}_S(m) = c]$ really means $\Pr_{S,R}[\mathsf{Enc}_S(m; R) = c]$. We will assume that the message m is chosen from some distribution M over $\mathcal{M}$ which is independent of the key distribution $S \leftarrow \mathsf{Gen}()$.

The (possibly probabilistic) decryption algorithm Dec takes a ciphertext c and a key s and outputs the decryption $\tilde{M} \leftarrow \mathsf{Dec}_s(c)$. Ordinarily, we require *perfect correctness* stating that for any $m \in \mathcal{M}$ and $s \in \mathcal{S}$ we have $\mathsf{Dec}_s(\mathsf{Enc}_s(m)) = m$. However, since we are proving a lower bound, we relax the correctness guarantee to allow for some small decryption error γ.

Definition 1. *An encryption scheme* (Gen, Enc, Dec) *is called* $(1 - \gamma)$*-correct on* M *if*

$$\Pr_{S,M}[\mathsf{Dec}_S(\mathsf{Enc}_S(M)) = M] \geq 1 - \gamma \tag{1}$$

We say that (Gen, Enc, Dec) *is* $(1 - \gamma)$*-correct (in general) if it is* $(1 - \gamma)$*-correct on every message distribution M; equivalently, for any $m \in \mathcal{M}$, $\Pr_S[\mathsf{Dec}_S(\mathsf{Enc}_S(m)) = m] \geq 1 - \gamma$.*

SECURITY. There are many equivalent formulations of "perfect" Shannon's security, when the attacker *Eve* is allowed to be computationally unbounded, and the "advantage" of any such *Eve* must be 0. Roughly, these definitions can be partitioned into two types. Some, including Shannon's original notion [Sha49], use the notions of Shannon's entropy and mutual information (see Section 4). While elegant and easy to state, it is not obvious to relax such notions to *computationally bounded* attackers.[1] Other definitions, inspired by the Goldwasser-Micali [GM84] notions of semantic security and indistinguishability, are based on statistical distance. Such definitions have a clean and natural extensions to both computationally bounded attackers and non-zero advantage. Therefore, our

---

[1] However, in Section 4 we will propose a natural relaxation to small non-zero advantage.

definition below will be of this type. Since we are proving a lower bound, we will state what we feel is the *weakest* such definition. Of course, since our lower bound will be so strong even for such "weak-looking" definition, it will imply lower bounds for other, stronger definitions.

Definition 2. *An encryption scheme* $(\mathsf{Gen}, \mathsf{Enc}, \mathsf{Dec})$ *is called* (t, ε)-*secure on message distribution* M *if for there exists a random variable* Y *(independent of* M*) such that for any (possibly probabilistic) adversary Eve running in time at most* t*, it holds*

$$| \Pr_{S,M}[Eve(M, \mathsf{Enc}_S(M)) = 1] - \Pr_{S,Y}[Eve(M, Y) = 1] | \le \varepsilon \qquad (2)$$

An encryption scheme $(\mathsf{Gen}, \mathsf{Enc}, \mathsf{Dec})$ *is called* (t, ε)-*secure if it is* (t, ε)-*secure on all message distributions* M*. When Eve is allowed to be computationally unbounded (e.g.,* $t = \infty$*), we say that* $(\mathsf{Gen}, \mathsf{Enc}, \mathsf{Dec})$ *is* ε-*secure.*

1.1   Few Remarks on the Definition

We make a few remarks on our definition. These remarks can be skipped by readers who already find the definition to be natural (and such readers can directly move to Section 2).

Intuitively, our definition states that whatever bit of information about M Eve could derive from the actual ciphertext C, she could have also derived from some random variable Y which is independent of M. Thus, Eve did not learn any new information from the ciphertext which she could not have learned from simply knowing the a-priori message distribution M (and some side information Y *independent* of M). However, while restricting Eve to run in time at most t, we do not make any restrictions on the complexity of sampling this independent distribution Y, and do not "charge" Eve for sampling Y. In particular, we do not insist on setting $Y \leftarrow \mathsf{Enc}_S(M')$, where M' is a fresh independent sample of M. Similarly, for general (t, ε)-security, we allow different Y's for different M's. Once again, such relaxations are done to make our lower bound stronger.

Also notice that the above definition is trivially true for any "singleton" distribution $M \leftarrow m$, for any $m \in \mathcal{M}$, and seems getting harder and harder as M becomes more and more "well-spread" (see Theorem 2 how this intuition translates to our lower bound). Still, even for the most "well-spread" uniform distribution M over $\mathcal{M}$, although we will see that our definition implies a strong bound on the size of the key space (Theorem 1), the definition is still noticeably weaker than general (t, ε)-security for *all* message distributions. For example, modifying a secure encryption (such as one-time pad) to be identity on some fixed $m \in \mathcal{M}$, still leaves the encryption very secure on the uniform distribution, while making the encryption of m easily distinguishable from encryptions of all other messages m'. In contrast, the general definition of security against all distributions is easily seen to be equivalent (ignoring factor of 2 in ε) to security against all distributions $M_{m,m'}$, for all $m, m' \in \mathcal{M}$, where each $M_{m,m'}$ is uniform over a pair of messages $\{m, m'\}$. In turn, the latter definition is simply the classical definition of (t, ε)-*indistinguishability* of Goldwasser-Micali [GM84], which states that for any messages $m, m' \in \mathcal{M}$, and any adversary *Eve* running in time at most t, it holds

$$|\Pr_S[Eve(\mathsf{Enc}_S(m)) = 1] - \Pr_S[Eve(\mathsf{Enc}_S(m')) = 1]| \leq \varepsilon \tag{3}$$

We refer to [IO11] for discussions of several other nearly equivalent forms of "indistinguishability-based" security (such as semantic security) for one-time symmetric-key encryption, and stress that our lower bound easily holds for all such notions. We also discuss a natural "mutual-information-based" definition in Section 4.

2 Main Result

Recall the classical Shannon lower bound [Sha49] states that $(\infty, 0)$-security implies $|\mathcal{S}| \geq |\mathcal{M}|$. In fact, this conclusion holds even if M is restricted to be the uniform distribution over $\mathcal{M}$. Here we show an elegant extension of this result confirming that, in order to beat the Shannon bound in a non-trivial way, one must *simultaneously* restrict *Eve* to be efficient, as well as allow for some non-zero (but possibly negligible) probability ε of security failure. Just like the Shannon's original bound, our bounds will already follow by restricting M to be the uniform distribution. Our proof also handles decryption error γ.

Theorem 1. *Let M be the uniform distribution over $\mathcal{M}$, and assume* (Gen, Enc, Dec) *is $(1 - \gamma)$-correct on M. Then:*

- **Small error needed.** *Let v denote maximum bit length of a plaintext plus ciphertext.*
  If (Gen, Enc, Dec) *is $(v, 0)$-secure on M, then $|\mathcal{S}| \geq |\mathcal{M}|(1 - \gamma)$.*
- **Small time needed.** *Let d denote maximum decryption time.*
  If (Gen, Enc, Dec) *is $(|\mathcal{S}|d, \varepsilon)$-secure on M, then $|\mathcal{S}| \geq |\mathcal{M}|(1 - \varepsilon - \gamma)$.*

Proof of First Part. Let Y be the distribution on ciphertexts guaranteed by Definition 2, so that Equation (2) holds with $\varepsilon = 0$ for any *Eve* running in time at most v. We claim that this implies that the joint distribution $(M, \mathsf{Enc}_S(M))$ is *identical* to (M, Y), where Y is independent from M:

$$(M, \mathsf{Enc}_S(M)) \equiv (M, Y) \tag{4}$$

To show this formally, for any fixed message $m \in \mathcal{M}$ and ciphertext c, consider the following $Eve_{m,c}(m', c')$ running in time $t = v$:

$Eve_{m,c}(m', c')$: *output 1 if and only if $m' = m$ and $c' = c$.*

Applying Equation (2) with $\varepsilon = 0$ to $Eve_{m,c}$, we get

$$\Pr_{S,M}[M = m \text{ and } \mathsf{Enc}_S(M)) = c] = \Pr_{M,Y}[M = m \text{ and } Y = c]$$

Using the fact that M is uniform and independent from Y, the above is equivalent to

$$\Pr_S[\mathsf{Enc}_S(m)) = c] = \Pr_Y[Y = c]$$

Since the above holds for all m and c, the distribution $\mathsf{Enc}_S(m) \equiv Y$ for all $m \in \mathcal{M}$, which means that the ciphertext distribution is the same for all messages. In particular, going back to the uniform distribution M, we have $(M, \mathsf{Enc}_S(M)) \equiv (M, Y)$, as claimed in Equation (4).[2]

Now, pick a fresh uniformly random key S' and look at[3]

$$\Delta \stackrel{\text{def}}{=} \Pr_{M,S',Y}[\mathsf{Dec}_{S'}(Y) = M] \tag{5}$$

On the one hand, it is clear that

$$\Delta \leq \frac{1}{|\mathcal{M}|} \tag{6}$$

since M is uniform and $\mathsf{Dec}_{S'}(Y)$ is independent of M. On the other hand, we know that the distribution (M, Y) is identical to $(M, \mathsf{Enc}_S(M))$. Hence, we can rewrite Equation (5) as

$$\Delta = \Pr_{S,M,S'}[\mathsf{Dec}_{S'}(\mathsf{Enc}_S(M)) = M]$$

$$\geq \Pr[S = S'] \cdot \Pr_{M,S}[\mathsf{Dec}_S(\mathsf{Enc}_S(M)) = M] \tag{7}$$

$$\geq \frac{1}{|\mathcal{S}|} \cdot (1 - \gamma) \tag{8}$$

Here Equation (7) followed from the fact that the distribution of S conditioned on the event $S = S'$ is *the same* as the original distribution S, since S' is uniform. On the other hand, Equation (8) followed from Equation (1) and, again, the fact that S' is uniform, so $\Pr[S = S'] = 1/|\mathcal{S}|$.

Comparing the resulting inequality above with Equation (6), we get $\frac{1}{|\mathcal{S}|} \cdot (1 - \gamma) \leq \Delta \leq \frac{1}{|\mathcal{M}|}$, which implies $|\mathcal{S}| \geq (1 - \gamma)|\mathcal{M}|$. $\qquad\square$

Proof of Second Part. We show that $(|\mathcal{S}|d, \varepsilon)$-security implies $|\mathcal{S}| \geq |\mathcal{M}|(1 - \varepsilon - \gamma)$. As before, let Y be the ciphertext distribution guaranteed by Definition 2. Consider the following attacker *Eve* of complexity $t = |\mathcal{S}|d$:

Eve(m, c): Run $\mathsf{Dec}_s(c)$ for all $s \in \mathcal{S}$. Output 1 if and only if at least one answer was m.

---

[2] In essence, we showed a more general fact: to conclude that two distributions A and B are identical, it is sufficient to show that they are $(t, 0)$-indistinguishable, for t equal to the maximum description length of any element in the support of A and B.

[3] Note, if $S \leftarrow \mathsf{Gen}()$ is not uniform, S' has a different distribution than S.

Now, let us compute both probabilities when we apply Equation (2) to this Eve. First,

$$\Pr_{S,M}[Eve(M, \mathsf{Enc}_S(M)) = 1] = \Pr_{S,M}[\exists s \text{ s.t. } \mathsf{Dec}_s(\mathsf{Enc}_S(M)) = M]$$

$$\geq \Pr_{S,M}[\mathsf{Dec}_S(\mathsf{Enc}_S(M)) = M]$$

$$\geq 1 - \gamma$$

where the last inequality used Equation (1). By Equation (2), we get

$$\Pr_{M,Y}[Eve(M, Y) = 1] \geq \Pr_{S,M}[Eve(M, \mathsf{Enc}_S(M)) = 1] - \varepsilon \geq 1 - \varepsilon - \gamma \quad (9)$$

On the other hand,

$$\Pr_{M,Y}[Eve(M, Y) = 1] = \Pr_{M,Y}[\exists s \text{ s.t. } \mathsf{Dec}_s(Y) = M]$$

$$\leq \sum_s \Pr_{M,Y}[\mathsf{Dec}_s(Y) = M]$$

However, M is uniform over $\mathcal{M}$ and, for any $s \in \mathcal{S}$, $\mathsf{Dec}_s(Y)$ is independent of M. Thus, $\Pr[M = \mathsf{Dec}_s(Y)] \leq \frac{1}{|\mathcal{M}|}$, which means that

$$\Pr_{M,Y}[Eve(M, Y)) = 1] \leq \sum_s \frac{1}{|\mathcal{M}|} = \frac{|\mathcal{S}|}{|\mathcal{M}|} \quad (10)$$

Combining Equation (9) and Equation (10), we get $1 - \varepsilon - \gamma \leq \frac{|\mathcal{S}|}{|\mathcal{M}|}$ or $|\mathcal{S}| \geq |\mathcal{M}|(1 - \varepsilon - \gamma)$. $\square$

TIGHTNESS. Both bounds are nearly tight, which can be shown by tweaking the generalization of the one-time pad (OTP) encryption for general cardinality N message spaces (not just the power of 2, which can be accomplished by addition modulo N). For simplicity, we only do it for two special cases $\varepsilon = 0$ and $\gamma = 0$, leaving the common generalization as a (tedious) exercise. For both cases we will actually satisfy the stronger (t, ε)-indistinguishability given by Equation (3).

First, assume $\varepsilon = 0$. Take any $|\mathcal{M}|$ of cardinality N, and any subset $\mathcal{M}_0 \subseteq \mathcal{M}$ of cardinality $N(1 - \gamma)$. Start with the OTP scheme over $\mathcal{M}_0$ (so that $|\mathcal{S}| = N(1 - \gamma)$ as well), and enlarge it to all of $\mathcal{M}$ by taking any fixed $m_0 \in \mathcal{M}_0$ and defining $\mathsf{Enc}_s(m_1) = \mathsf{Enc}_s(m_0)$, for $m_1 \in \mathcal{M} \backslash \mathcal{M}_0$. The addition of these γN messages (which decrypt incorrectly) to our OTP does not affect the security of the scheme (since $\mathsf{Enc}(m_0)$ is perfectly secure), but creates a decryption error with probability γ, and with $|\mathcal{S}| = |\mathcal{M}|(1 - \gamma)$.

Second, assume $\gamma = 0$. Now, for any $\mathcal{M}$ of cardinality N, take the OTP for $\mathcal{M}$ (so that $|\mathcal{S}| = N$), and simply remove $\varepsilon N/2$ keys from $\mathcal{S}$, defining the actual set $\mathcal{S}_0$ of $N(1 - \varepsilon/2)$ keys, and sampling a random key s from $\mathcal{S}_0$. To argue the $\Omega(\varepsilon)$-security of this scheme, one can imagine sampling a key $s \leftarrow \mathcal{S}_0$ by first sampling the key $s \leftarrow \mathcal{S}$ and claiming that Eve unconditionally won the game if

$s \in \mathcal{S} \backslash \mathcal{S}_0$. Equivalently, we can always actually run Eve on a fully uniform key s from $\mathcal{S}$, but then declare Eve victorious anyway if $s \in \mathcal{S} \backslash \mathcal{S}_0$. Clearly, when s is fully uniform, Eve has probability exactly $1/2$ telling apart encryptions of m_0 from m_1, so now her probability is at most $1/2 + \varepsilon/2$, creating distinguishing advantage at most ε with $|\mathcal{S}_0| = |\mathcal{M}|(1 - \varepsilon/2)$.

3   Some Extensions

The result of the previous section was completely elementary, did not explicitly use any technical notions such as entropy, statistical distance, etc., and could be easily taught in the first lecture of an undergraduate class (especially for the case of perfect correctness $\gamma = 0$). In this section we make several elementary "entropy-extensions" of our main result.

3.1   Extension to General M

We observe that Theorem 1 easily generalizes to arbitrary message distributions M (as opposed to the uniform distribution), as follows. We define the *min-entropy* of M to be $\mathbf{H}_\infty(M) \stackrel{\text{def}}{=} -\log(\max_m \Pr[M = m])$. In particular, for any random variable M' independent of M, we have $\Pr[M' = M] \leq 2^{-\mathbf{H}_\infty(M)}$. Examining now the proofs of both parts of Theorem 1, we see that the only places where the uniformity of M was used were Equation (6) and Equation (10). In both cases, we needed to upped bound $\Pr[M' = M]$ for some probability distribution M' which was independent of M (e.g., $M' = \mathsf{Dec}_{S'}(Y)$ for Equation (6) and $M' = \mathsf{Dec}_s(Y)$ for Equation (10)). Hence, we get the following analog of Theorem 1 where $|\mathcal{M}|$ is replaced by $2^{\mathbf{H}_\infty(M)}$.

Theorem 2. *Let M be the any distribution over $\mathcal{M}$, and assume* (Gen, Enc, Dec) *is $(1 - \gamma)$-correct on M. Then:*

- **Small error needed.** *Let v denote maximum bit length of a plaintext plus ciphertext.*
  If (Gen, Enc, Dec) *is $(v, 0)$-secure on M, then $|\mathcal{S}| \geq 2^{\mathbf{H}_\infty(M)} \cdot (1 - \gamma)$.*
- **Small time needed.** *Let d denote maximum decryption time.*
  If (Gen, Enc, Dec) *is $(|\mathcal{S}|d, \varepsilon)$-secure on M, then $|\mathcal{S}| \geq 2^{\mathbf{H}_\infty(M)} \cdot (1 - \varepsilon - \gamma)$.*

Notice, this bound is tight, in general, by taking M to be uniform over some subset $\mathcal{M}'$ of $\mathcal{M}$ of cardinality $2^{\mathbf{H}_\infty(M)}$, and then doing the OTP scheme over $\mathcal{M}'$.

3.2   Slightly Stronger Bound for Perfect Completeness and Perfect Security

Recall, the bounds of Theorem 1 (and more general Theorem 2) held for any key distribution $S \leftarrow$ Gen(), but only gave lower bounds of the cardinality of $\mathcal{S}$ (or, more generally, on cardinality of the support set of S). In contrast, as we recap in Section 4 below, Shannon's original bound [Sha49] gave the lower bound on the Shannon entropy $\mathbf{H}_1(S)$ of S, which could be stronger for sufficiently non-uniform S. Here we observe that our proof for the first part of Theorem 1 can be strengthened to give the lower bound on the min-entropy $\mathbf{H}_\infty(S)$ for the case of perfect correctness $\gamma = 0$. For elegance, we right away state the improved bound for general message distribution M as well.

Theorem 3. *Let M be the any distribution over $\mathcal{M}$, and assume* (Gen, Enc, Dec) *is 1-correct on M. Let v denote maximum bit length of a plaintext plus ciphertext. Then, if* (Gen, Enc, Dec) *is $(v, 0)$-secure on M, then $\mathbf{H}_\infty(S) \geq \mathbf{H}_\infty(M)$. In particular, if* (Gen, Enc, Dec) *is $(v, 0)$-secure on uniform M, we have $\mathbf{H}_\infty(S) \geq \log|\mathcal{M}|$.*

Proof: We follow the same proof as in Theorem 1 (and its extension to general M in Theorem 2), except we define the value S' to be the most likely value s of the key S, instead of being uniform. Namely, we set $S' = s$ satisfying $\Pr[S = s] = 2^{-\mathbf{H}_\infty(S)}$. Then, the value Δ becomes

$$\Delta \overset{\text{def}}{=} \Pr_{M,Y}[\mathsf{Dec}_s(Y) = M]$$

We can argue, as before, that $\Delta \leq 2^{-\mathbf{H}_\infty(M)}$, since M is independent of $\mathsf{Dec}_s(Y)$. On the other hand, since the distribution (M, Y) is identical to $(M, \mathsf{Enc}_S(M))$ and we have perfect completeness, we get

$$\Delta = \Pr_{S,M}[\mathsf{Dec}_s(\mathsf{Enc}_S(M)) = M]$$
$$\geq \Pr[S = s] \cdot \Pr_M[\mathsf{Dec}_s(\mathsf{Enc}_s(M)) = M]$$
$$\geq 2^{-\mathbf{H}_\infty(S)} \cdot 1 \tag{11}$$

where Equation (11) used the definition of s and the perfect correctness of the encryption. Combining the two bounds on Δ, we get $2^{-\mathbf{H}_\infty(S)} \leq \Delta \leq 2^{-\mathbf{H}_\infty(M)}$, which implies $\mathbf{H}_\infty(S) \geq \mathbf{H}_\infty(M)$.   □

As we recap in Section 4 below, when $\varepsilon = 0$ our definition is equivalent to the original definition of Shannon [Sha49], who showed the bound $\mathbf{H}_1(S) \geq \log|\mathcal{M}|$, where $\mathbf{H}_1$ is Shannon's entropy. Since $\log|\mathcal{S}| \geq \mathbf{H}_1(S) \geq \mathbf{H}_\infty(S)$, we can view the last bound of Theorem 3 as a nice strengthening of Shannon's original bound for perfect security (and perfect correctness):[4] not only $\mathbf{H}_1(S) \geq \log|\mathcal{M}|$, but also $\mathbf{H}_\infty(S) \geq \log|\mathcal{M}|$.

4   Bounds for Mutual Information Based Definition

The *Shannon entropy* of X is defined as $\mathbf{H}_1(X) \overset{\text{def}}{=} \mathbb{E}_{x \leftarrow X}[-\log \Pr[X = x]]$. We also define *conditional Shannon entropy* of a random variable X conditioned on another random variable Z by

---

[4] Actually, our proof above extends to imperfect correctness, as long as we require that $\Pr_M[\mathsf{Dec}_s(\mathsf{Enc}_s(M)) = M] \geq 1 - \gamma$, for all $s \in \mathcal{S}$, instead of only on average over $s \leftarrow S$.

$$\mathbf{H}_1(X|Z) \overset{\text{def}}{=} \mathbb{E}_{(x,z)\leftarrow(X,Z)}\left[-\log\Pr[X=x|Z=z]\right]$$

where $\mathbb{E}_{z\leftarrow Z}$ denotes the expected value over $z \leftarrow Z$. It is well known that $\mathbf{H}_1(X) \geq \mathbf{H}_1(X|Z) \geq 0$. The *mutual information* between X and Y is $\mathbf{I}(X;Y) \overset{\text{def}}{=} \mathbf{H}_1(X)-\mathbf{H}_1(X|Y)$. It is well known that $\mathbf{I}(X;Y) = \mathbf{I}(Y;X) \geq 0$. The conditional mutual information of X and Y given Z is defined analogously. We assume the reader is familiar with other elementary facts about Shannon entropy and mutual information (such as the chain rule used below); see [CT06].

Let (Gen, Enc, Dec) be encryption scheme, S be it key distribution Gen(), M be some message distribution and $C \leftarrow \mathsf{Enc}_S(M)$. We now give the following natural definitions generalizing the original definitions of [Sha49] to imperfect correctness and security.

Definition 3. *An encryption scheme* (Gen, Enc, Dec) *is called* $(1-\gamma')$*-Shannon correct on* M *if*

$$\mathbf{H}_1(M|\mathsf{Dec}_S(C)) \leq \gamma'$$

(Gen, Enc, Dec) *is* $(1-\gamma')$*-Shannon correct (in general) if it is* $(1-\gamma')$*-Shannon correct on all message distributions* M.

An encryption scheme (Gen, Enc, Dec) *is called* ε'*-Shannon secure on* M *if*

$$\mathbf{I}(M;C) \leq \varepsilon'$$

(Gen, Enc, Dec) *is* ε'*-Shannon secure (in general) if it is* ε'*-Shannon secure on all message distributions* M.

We start with the following Lemma, translating the elegant "proof-by-picture" exposition of Shannon's bound by Wolf [Wol98] (for $\varepsilon' = 0$) into a concrete inequality. (We suspect the Lemma is well-known, but we could not locate an explicit reference.)

Lemma 1. *For any (possibly correlated) distributions* M, S, C, *we have*

$$\mathbf{H}_1(S) \geq \mathbf{H}_1(M) - \mathbf{H}_1(M|(S,C)) - \mathbf{I}(M;C) \tag{12}$$

Proof:

$$
\begin{aligned}
\mathbf{H}_1(M) &= \mathbf{H}_1(M|(S,C)) + \mathbf{I}(M;(S,C)) \\
&= \mathbf{H}_1(M|(S,C)) + \mathbf{I}(M;C) + \mathbf{I}(M;S|C) \\
&= \mathbf{H}_1(M|(S,C)) + \mathbf{I}(M;C) + \mathbf{H}_1(S|C) - \mathbf{H}_1(S|(M,C)) \\
&\leq \mathbf{H}_1(M|(S,C)) + \mathbf{I}(M;C) + \mathbf{H}_1(S)
\end{aligned}
$$

where the equalities used the definitions and the chain rule, and the last inequality used the facts that $\mathbf{H}_1(S|C) \leq \mathbf{H}_1(S)$ and $\mathbf{H}_1(S|(M,C)) \geq 0$. $\qquad\square$

As a corollary, we get the following straightforward extension of Shannon's result:

Theorem 4. *If* $(\mathsf{Gen}, \mathsf{Enc}, \mathsf{Dec})$ *is* ε'-*Shannon secure and* $(1 - \gamma')$-*Shannon correct on* M, *then*

$$\mathbf{H}_1(S) \geq \mathbf{H}_1(M) - \gamma' - \varepsilon' \tag{13}$$

In particular, if M *is the uniform distribution over* $\mathcal{M}$, *then* $\mathbf{H}_1(S) \geq \log |\mathcal{M}| - \gamma' - \varepsilon'$.

Proof: Follows from Equation (12) and $\mathbf{H}_1(M|(S, C)) \leq \mathbf{H}_1(M|\mathsf{Dec}_S(C)) \leq \gamma'$.

$\square$

RELATION TO INDISTINGUISHABILITY NOTIONS. Here we relate the $(1 - \gamma')$-Shannon correctness and ε'-Shannon security to the "indistinguishability-based" notions of $(1 - \gamma)$-correctness and ε-security[5] from Section 1. Using Fano's inequality (see [CT06]), we can relate γ' to γ as follows:

$$\gamma' \leq h(\gamma) + \gamma \cdot (\log |\mathcal{M}| - 1) \tag{14}$$

where h is binary entropy function $h(x) = -x \log_2 x - (1 - x) \log_2(1 - x)$. Unfortunately, no meaningful converse relation can be made, since changing $\mathsf{Dec}_S(C)$ to return $M + 1$ instead of M has 0-correctness and 1-Shannon correctness.[6]

More interestingly, to relate Shannon security on M with indistinguishability security on M, we use the following result (implicitly) proven by Bellare et al. [BTV12] using Pinsker's inequality (see [CT06]).

Lemma 2 ([BTV12]). *For any (possibly correlated) distributions* M, C *over some spaces* $\mathcal{M}$ *and* $\mathcal{C}$, *let*[7]

$$\varepsilon = \mathbf{SD}((M, C); M \times C)$$

where $M \times C$ *is the product distribution of the independent marginal distributions* M *and* C. *Then,*

$$2\varepsilon^2 \leq \mathbf{I}(M; C) \leq 2\varepsilon \cdot \log(|\mathcal{M}|/\varepsilon) \tag{15}$$

In particular, notice that our notion of ε-security on M from Definition 2 is essentially equivalent to $\mathbf{SD}((M, C); M \times C) \leq \varepsilon$.[8] Thus, ε'-Shannon security

---

[5] Here we set $t = \infty$, as it is not clear what is the analog of time for Shannon's security.

[6] Because of this, in contrast to standard correctness, the notion of "Shannon-correctness" is not a very useful notion, and we defined it only because the quantity $\mathbf{H}_1(M|\mathsf{Dec}_S(C))$ naturally came up in the proof. Luckily, Equation (14) shows that $(1 - \gamma)$-correctness implies a decent bound on γ' as well.

[7] The *statistical distance* $\mathbf{SD}(X; Y)$ between two random variables X, Y is defined by:

$$\mathbf{SD}(X, Y) \stackrel{\text{def}}{=} \frac{1}{2} \sum_x |\Pr[X = x] - \Pr[Y = x]| = \max_{Eve} |\Pr[Eve(X) = 1] - \Pr[Eve(Y) = 1]|$$

[8] Up to a factor of 2 in ε since Y might not be equal to C. I.e., ε-security implies 2ε bound on the statistical distance above, and is implied by the ε bound on that distance.

on M implies $\sqrt{2\varepsilon'}$-security on M. Conversely, ε-security on M implies $(2\varepsilon \cdot \log(|\mathcal{M}|/\varepsilon))$-Shannon security on M. Hence, ignoring efficiency issues for Eve and the square root degradation on ε', Shannon starts with stronger security assumption than we do, but also gets slightly stronger conclusion: bound on $\mathbf{H}_1(S)$, not just $|\mathcal{S}|$. However, for perfect security $\varepsilon = 0$ we are still slightly stronger by Theorem 3, getting a bound on $\mathbf{H}_\infty(S)$, and not just $\mathbf{H}_1(S)$.

Acknowledgments. The author would like to thank Dario Fiore, Stefano Tessaro and Daniel Wichs for useful discussions.

References

[BTV12] Bellare, M., Tessaro, S., Vardy, A.: Semantic Security for the Wiretap Channel. In: Safavi-Naini, R. (ed.) CRYPTO 2012. LNCS, vol. 7417, pp. 294–311. Springer, Heidelberg (2012); Earlier version available at Cryptology ePrint Archive: Report 2012/015

[CT06] Cover, T.M., Thomas, J.A.: Elements of information theory, 2nd edn. Wiley (2006)

[GM84] Goldwasser, S., Micali, S.: Probabilistic encryption. In: JCSS, vol. 28(2), pp. 270–299 (1984)

[IL89] Impagliazzo, R., Luby, M.: One-way Functions are Essential for Complexity Based Cryptography. In: FOCS 1989, pp. 230–235 (1989)

[IO11] Iwamoto, M., Ohta, K.: Security Notions for Information Theoretically Secure Encryptions. In: ISIT 2011 (2011), http://arxiv.org/abs/1106.1731

[Sha49] Shannon, C.: Communication Theory of Secrecy systems. Bell Systems Technical J. 28, 656–715 (1949); Note: The material in this paper appeared originally in a confidential report 'A Mathematical Theory of Cryptography', which has now been declassified (September 1, 1945)

[Wol98] Wolf, S.: Unconditional Security in Cryptography. In: Damgård, I. (ed.) EEF School 1998. LNCS, vol. 1561, pp. 217–250. Springer, Heidelberg (1999)

Statistically Secure Linear-Rate Dimension Extension for Oblivious Affine Function Evaluation

Nico Döttling[*], Daniel Kraschewski, and Jörn Müller-Quade

Institute of Cryptography and Security, Department of Informatics,
Karlsruhe Institute of Technology, Germany
{doettling,kraschewski,mueller-quade}@kit.edu

Abstract. Consider the following natural generalization of the well-known Oblivious Transfer (OT) primitive, which we call *Oblivious Affine Function Evaluation (OAFE)*: Given some finite vector space $\mathbb{F}_q^k$, a designated sender party can specify an arbitrary affine function $f : \mathbb{F}_q \to \mathbb{F}_q^k$, such that a designated receiver party learns $f(x)$ for a single argument $x \in \mathbb{F}_q$ of its choice. This primitive is of particular interest, since analogously to the construction of garbled boolean circuits based on OT one can construct garbled arithmetic circuits based on OAFE.

In this work we treat the quite natural question, if general $\mathbb{F}_q^k$-OAFE can be efficiently reduced to $\mathbb{F}_q$-OAFE (i.e. the sender only inputs an affine function $f : \mathbb{F}_q \to \mathbb{F}_q$). The analogous question for OT has previously been answered positively, but the respective construction turns out to be not applicable to OAFE due to an unobvious, yet non-artificial security problem. Nonetheless, we are able to provide an efficient, information-theoretically secure reduction along with a formal security proof based on some specific algebraic properties of random $\mathbb{F}_q$-matrices.

Keywords: secure function evaluation, information-theoretic reductions, oblivious transfer, universal composability, garbled arithmetic circuits.

1 Introduction

Secure Multi-Party Computation is a cryptographic research area, whose origins go back to Yao's Millionaire's Problem [Yao82]. Since then, an increasing research community has found numerous constructions for cryptographically secure computations, e.g. [Yao86, GMW87, Kil88, GL91, CvdGT95, CLOS02, IPS08, GIS+10] to name only a few. The Oblivious Transfer (OT) primitive introduced by [Rab81] has gained special interest in this context, since it turned out to be complete, i.e. taking OT for granted one can securely implement any multi-party computation [Yao86, Kil88, CvdGT95, IPS08]. OT in its currently most used variant allows a designated sender party to provide an input tuple (s_0, s_1), such that a designated receiver party can arbitrarily choose to learn one

---
[*] Supported by IBM Research & Development Germany within the HomER project.

A. Smith (Ed.): ICITS 2012, LNCS 7412, pp. 111–128, 2012.
© Springer-Verlag Berlin Heidelberg 2012

of them, say s_c. The crucial security features are that the sender does not learn c and the receiver stays oblivious of s_{1-c}. To make the bit length of s_0 and s_1 explicit, we write k-bit-OT.

In this paper we deal with a natural generalization of OT, which we call *Oblivious Affine Function Evaluation (OAFE)*. This primitive allows the sender party to specify an affine function f, such that the receiver party can evaluate f obliviously on a single argument x. More specifically, OAFE is parametrized by a finite vector space $\mathbb{F}_q^k$, so that the sender chooses $a, b \in \mathbb{F}_q^k$ and the receiver learns $ax + b$ for a single $x \in \mathbb{F}_q$ of his choice. To make the input domains explicit, we write $\mathbb{F}_q^k$-OAFE. The $\mathbb{F}_q$-OAFE primitive, i.e. $k = 1$, can also be considered a special case of Oblivious Polynomial Evaluation [NP99]. In this context, $\mathbb{F}_q$-OAFE is occasionally referred to as *Oblivious Linear Function Evaluation (OLFE)* in the literature.

Though way less present in the literature than OT, the OAFE primitive can be considered similarly important. Not only can $\mathbb{F}_2^k$-OAFE and k-bit-OT be transformed into each other without any overhead (cf. Section 3.1), but $\mathbb{F}_q^k$-OAFE also allows for a very interesting alternative to the standard construction of Yao's Garbled Circuits. The latter transforms any given boolean circuit into a set of tables (one for each gate) with bit values replaced by random labels, so that OT can be used to transfer the keys needed for a single evaluation on a circuit input selected by the receiver [Yao86]. The OAFE based alternative are so-called *garbled arithmetic circuits* [CFIK03, AIK11], that amongst other issues exhibit the following differences to the construction of [Yao86]:

- The circuit to be garbled is not consisting of boolean gates (AND, OR, XOR, ...), but arithmetic operations (specifically, additions and multiplications) over some finite field $\mathbb{F}_q$.
- The concept of tables with random labels standing for bit values is replaced by affine functions that map circuit inputs to randomly looking matrices. (Here, OAFE comes into play.)

1.1   Our Contribution

Yao's Garbled Circuits are based on k-bit-OT with k increasing polynomially in the security parameter. Analogously, the general construction of garbled arithmetic circuits builds on $\mathbb{F}_q^k$-OAFE, where k and/or $\log q$ may increase polynomially in the security parameter. This raises the natural question, whether one can efficiently reduce k-bit-OT and $\mathbb{F}_q^k$-OAFE to the respective weaker variants 1-bit-OT and $\mathbb{F}_q$-OAFE. For OT this question was answered positively by [BCS96].

Our contribution is a similar result for OAFE. The interesting part of our contribution is not so much the protocol construction itself, but the security proof. The high level protocol idea resembles well-known standard techniques, but for the security proof we need some completely new technical tools. We also show that known standard tools do not work. In particular, we show that directly applying the construction of [BCS96] to $\mathbb{F}_q$-OAFE with large filed size q is inherently insecure in an unobvious way and we argue that the only other known information-theoretic standard approach, namely 2-universal hashing [ILL89], does not help either.

Thus our contribution is twofold. Firstly, we investigate what goes wrong when one tries to reduce $\mathbb{F}_q^k$-OAFE to $\mathbb{F}_q$-OAFE by known techniques. Interestingly, the occurring problems are neither obvious nor artificial. Secondly, we develop some novel algebraic/combinatorial tools (in particular, we verify several handy properties of random $\mathbb{F}_q$-matrices) by that one can easily prove that a slight modification of the construction of [BCS96] yields a secure reduction approach for $\mathbb{F}_q^k$-OAFE to $O(k)$ instances of $\mathbb{F}_q$-OAFE. Though the protocol itself is rather self-suggesting, we have to employ for the security proof some tricky use of linear algebra.

Certainly, it was already known before, that using general completeness results [Kil91, Kil00, KMQ11] one can reduce $\mathbb{F}_q^k$-OAFE to $\mathbb{F}_q$-OAFE. However, such an approach would first implement OT on top of $\mathbb{F}_q$-OAFE and then exploit completeness of OT, resulting in some polynomial reduction rate. In contrast, our approach is direct and to the best of our knowledge we provide the first construction with reduction rate linear in the dimension k regardless of the field size q.

1.2 Related Work

We see our work closely related to the literature on information-theoretic tools and reduction results. Most notably, our work is inspired by [BCS96], where k-bit-OT is securely reduced to $O(k)$ instances of 1-bit-OT using a non-interactive protocol based on intersecting codes. The most appealing feature of this construction is its non-interactiveness, due to that it is also applicable to non-interactive OT variants, e.g. implemented by hardware tokens [GKR08, GIS+10]. We also make use of the results of [WW06], where techniques for storing and/or reversing OT and $\mathbb{F}_q$-OAFE (there called OLFE) are provided as well as reductions to randomized variants of these primitives.

Similar in mind but not concretely related to our work are other information-theoretic reduction results, like [CMW05, IKO+11] or [DKMQ11], and the classic literature on privacy amplification and randomness extraction, e.g. [BBR88, ILL89, BBCM95].

2 Framework

2.1 Notion of Security

We state and prove our results in the Universal-Composability (UC) framework [Can01]. In this framework security is defined by comparison of an *ideal model* and a *real model*. The protocol of interest is running in the latter, where an adversary $\mathcal{A}$ coordinates the behavior of all corrupted parties. In the ideal model, which is secure by definition, an ideal functionality $\mathcal{F}$ implements the desired protocol task and a simulator $\mathcal{S}$ tries to mimic the actions of $\mathcal{A}$. An environment $\mathcal{Z}$ is plugged either to the ideal or the real model and has to guess, which model it is actually plugged to. When $\mathcal{Z}$ cannot distinguish between ideal and real

---

Functionality $\mathcal{F}_{\text{OAFE}}^{(q,k)}$

Parametrized by a finite field size q and a dimension k, which may each depend on the security parameter.

- Upon receiving input $(a, b) \in \mathbb{F}_q^k \times \mathbb{F}_q^k$ from Alice, verify that there is no stored input tuple from Alice, yet; else ignore that input. Next, record (a, b) and send (`processing, Alice`) to the adversary.
- Upon receiving input $x \in \mathbb{F}_q$ from Bob, verify that there is no stored input from Bob, yet; else ignore that input. Next, record x and send (`processing, Bob`) to the adversary.
- Upon receiving a message (`delivery, Alice`) from the adversary, verify that Alice and Bob have both already provided some input; else ignore that message. Next, send an empty message to Alice. Henceforth, never again send any message to Alice.
- Upon receiving a message (`delivery, Bob`) from the adversary, verify that Alice and Bob have both already provided some input; else ignore that message. Next, compute $y \leftarrow ax + b$ and send y to Bob. Henceforth, never again send any message to Bob.

When a party is corrupted, the adversary is granted unrestricted access to the channel between $\mathcal{F}_{\text{OAFE}}^{(q,k)}$ and the corrupted party, including the ability of deleting and/or forging arbitrary messages.

Fig. 1. The ideal $\mathbb{F}_q^k$-OAFE functionality

model, the protocol is considered *UC-secure*. Since our results are of information-theoretic nature, the adversarial entities $\mathcal{A}$ and $\mathcal{S}$ and the environment $\mathcal{Z}$ are computationally unbounded. For further details we refer to [Can01].

2.2   The $\mathbb{F}_q^k$-OAFE Primitive in the UC Framework

Security in the UC framework is only defined relatively to some ideal functionality $\mathcal{F}$. Thus, we need to define some ideal functionality $\mathcal{F}_{\text{OAFE}}^{(q,k)}$ that represents the $\mathbb{F}_q^k$-OAFE primitive. We present the formal definition in Figure 1, but throughout the rest of this paper we will prefer the more graphic description given by Figure 2. Moreover, for better readability we will henceforth mostly omit the grayed parts of Figure 2.

Fig. 2. Graphical representation of the $\mathbb{F}_q^k$-OAFE primitive

3 Satistically UC-secure $\mathbb{F}_q^k$-OAFE from $O(k)$ Instances of $\mathbb{F}_q$-OAFE

3.1 The Basic Protocol Idea and Why It Does Not Work

In [BCS96] a very handy construction for 2-bit-OT from three instances of 1-bit-OT was proposed, which we briefly recap for the sake of self-containedness. Given its 2-bit-OT inputs $s_0, s_1 \in \mathbb{F}_2^2$, the sender party picks six random bits $\sigma_1, \bar{\sigma}_1, \sigma_2, \bar{\sigma}_2, \sigma_3, \bar{\sigma}_3 \in \mathbb{F}_2$ subject to the following condition:

$$\begin{pmatrix} 1 & 1 & 0 \\ 0 & 1 & 1 \end{pmatrix} \cdot \begin{pmatrix} \sigma_1 & \bar{\sigma}_1 \\ \sigma_2 & \bar{\sigma}_2 \\ \sigma_3 & \bar{\sigma}_3 \end{pmatrix} = \begin{pmatrix} s_0 & s_1 \end{pmatrix}$$

Then he sends the tuples $(\sigma_i, \bar{\sigma}_i)$ to the receiver party via 1-bit-OT. The receiver party always inputs its choice bit c into the underlying 1-bit-OT instances, thus learning some τ_1, τ_2, τ_3, and computes and outputs:

$$s_c = \begin{pmatrix} 1 & 1 & 0 \\ 0 & 1 & 1 \end{pmatrix} \cdot \begin{pmatrix} \tau_1 \\ \tau_2 \\ \tau_3 \end{pmatrix}$$

It is pretty obvious that this protocol is perfectly secure: A corrupted sender in fact cannot deviate from the protocol other than just changing his input tuple (s_0, s_1), and even a corrupted receiver has to query at least two of the three underlying 1-bit-OT instances with the same choice bit c, whereby he learns information-theoretically nothing about s_{1-c}. Furthermore, this protocol can be directly adapted for construction of k-bit-OT from three instances of $\frac{k}{2}$-bit-OT, and last not least in [BCS96] analogous constructions are presented for k-bit-OT from $O(k)$ instances of 1-bit-OT.

Noting that k-bit-OT and $\mathbb{F}_2^k$-OAFE can be reduced to each other just by local computation (q.v. Figure 3), it might seem a good idea to adapt the techniques of [BCS96] for constructing $\mathbb{F}_q^k$-OAFE from some given $\mathbb{F}_q$-OAFE instances. The resulting protocol scheme is depicted in Figure 4. Indeed, this approach works correctly, if only the matrix H has full rank. Further, it is perfectly secure against any corrupted sender. Moreover, if $q = 2$, the results of [BCS96] do directly carry over and we can choose H appropriately, so that we get also perfect security against corrupted receivers. Surprisingly, if q grows super-polynomially

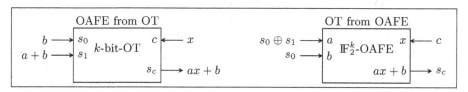

Fig. 3. Reductions between k-bit-OT and $\mathbb{F}_2^k$-OAFE; protocols taken from [WW06]

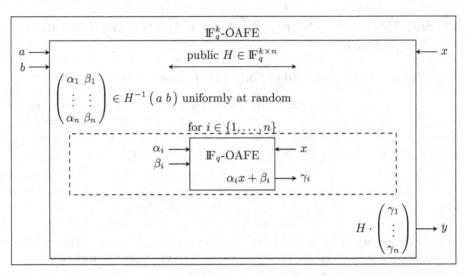

Fig. 4. Straightforward adaption of the protocol scheme from [BCS96] for reduction of $\mathbb{F}_q^k$-OAFE to n instances of $\mathbb{F}_q$-OAFE; protocol parametrized by a public matrix $H \in \mathbb{F}_q^{k \times n}$ that may depend on the security parameter. If $q \geq n + 2$, this protocol cannot be secure (q.v. Lemma 1).

in the security parameter (what is the interesting case), a rather unobvious problem occurs, which renders the protocol scheme inherently insecure against a corrupted receiver. We address this by the following lemma.

Lemma 1. *The protocol in Figure 4 is insecure against a corrupted receiver, if $k \geq 2$ and $q \geq n + 2$.*

Proof. First note that the ideal $\mathbb{F}_q^k$-OAFE functionality upon uniformly random sender input $a, b \in \mathbb{F}_q^k$ lets the receiver not learn any value of the following form with linearly independent $d, e \in \mathbb{F}_q^{1 \times k}$:

$$(d\ e) \cdot \begin{pmatrix} a \\ b \end{pmatrix}$$

We show now that in the protocol of Figure 4, with parameters $k \geq 2$ and $q \geq n + 2$, a corrupted receiver can always choose his $\mathbb{F}_q$-OAFE inputs appropriately, so that he can compute such a value (and the corresponding vectors d and e) from his $\mathbb{F}_q$-OAFE outputs γ_i and the public matrix H.

Let $X \in \mathbb{F}_q^{n \times n}$ be the diagonal matrix whose diagonal elements are the corrupted receiver's inputs for the underlying $\mathbb{F}_q$-OAFE instances, and let $I \in \mathbb{F}_q^{n \times n}$ be the identity matrix. By construction it always holds:

$$\underbrace{\begin{pmatrix} X & I \\ H & \\ & H \end{pmatrix}}_{=:M} \cdot \begin{pmatrix} \alpha_1 \\ \vdots \\ \alpha_n \\ \beta_1 \\ \vdots \\ \beta_n \end{pmatrix} = \begin{pmatrix} \gamma_1 \\ \vdots \\ \gamma_n \\ a \\ b \end{pmatrix}$$

Thus, we have to find some $(c,d,e) \in \mathbb{F}_q^{1\times n} \times \mathbb{F}_q^{1\times k} \times \mathbb{F}_q^{1\times k}$ and a diagonal matrix $X \in \mathbb{F}_q^{n\times n}$, such that d and e are linearly independent and $(c,d,e) \cdot M = 0$. In other words, we are looking for $(c,d,e) \in \mathbb{F}_q^{1\times n} \times \mathbb{F}_q^{1\times k} \times \mathbb{F}_q^{1\times k}$ with linearly independent $\{d,e\}$ and a diagonal matrix $X \in \mathbb{F}_q^{n\times n}$, such that $cX + dH = c + eH = 0$. Obviously, it suffices to find some linearly independent $d,e \in \mathbb{F}_q^{1\times k}$ and a diagonal matrix $X \in \mathbb{F}_q^{n\times n}$, such that $eHX = dH$, because then we can just set $c := -eH$. However, we can always choose X appropriately, if only every index of a zero-coefficient of eH is also an index of a zero-coefficient of dH, i.e. for every $i \in \{1,\ldots,n\}$ the following implication must hold true:

$$(eH)[i] = 0 \quad \Rightarrow \quad (dH)[i] = 0$$

Now, let h_1 and h_2 denote the first and second row of H respectively. Further, let $r \in \mathbb{F}_q \setminus \{0\}$, such that $h_1[i] \neq r \cdot h_2[i]$ for every index i with $h_2[i] \neq 0$. Such an r does exist, since $q \geq n+2$ by assumption. Finally, we set $d := (1,0,\ldots,0)$ and $e := (1,-r,0,\ldots,0)$—here we need that $k \geq 2$. Thereby we get that d and e are linearly independent and every index of a zero-coefficient of the vector eH is also an index of a zero-coefficient of the vector dH. $\qquad\square$

3.2 Why Universal Hashing Does Not Help

Another standard approach for implementing k-bit-OT from 1-bit-OT is 2-universal hashing. The high level idea is that the sender party transfers $(2+2\varepsilon)k$ random tuples $(\sigma_i, \bar{\sigma}_i) \in \mathbb{F}_2 \times \mathbb{F}_2$ via 1-bit-OT, then announces a random 2-universal hash function $h : \mathbb{F}_2^{(2+2\varepsilon)k} \to \mathbb{F}_2^k$ and computes and outputs $s_0 := h(\sigma_1, \sigma_2, \ldots)$ and $s_1 := h(\bar{\sigma}_1, \bar{\sigma}_2, \ldots)$. The receiver always inputs his choice bit c into the underlying 1-bit-OT instances, thus learning some τ_i, and computes and outputs $s_c = h(\tau_1, \tau_2, \ldots)$. Obviously, this only implements k-bit-OT with randomized sender input, but derandomization is possible by standard techniques (e.g., see [WW06]).

It is straightforward to see that this protocol is perfectly secure against a corrupted sender. Security against a corrupted receiver can be shown by the well-known Leftover Hash Lemma [BBR88, ILL89]. The main argument is that from the view of a corrupted receiver either the string $(\sigma_1, \sigma_2, \ldots)$ or the string $(\bar{\sigma}_1, \bar{\sigma}_2, \ldots)$ has min-entropy lower bounded by $(1+\varepsilon)k$ and hence either s_0 or s_1 is $\sqrt{2^{-\varepsilon k}}$-close to uniform randomness. However, this technique is not applicable in our case, what we will argue for next.

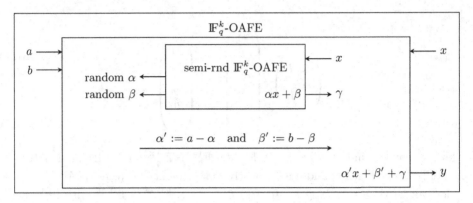

Fig. 5. Straightforward reduction of $\mathbb{F}_q^k$-OAFE to semi-random $\mathbb{F}_q^k$-OAFE. Note that the protocol is perfectly secure even against a corrupted sender that can arbitrarily change α and β.

In our case, it just does not suffice that from a (possibly corrupted) receiver's view the vector $ax + b$ is negligibly close to uniform randomness for all but one $x \in \mathbb{F}_q$. We also must rule out that a corrupted receiver may learn some non-trivial relation between $ax + b$ and $ax' + b$ with distinct $x, x' \in \mathbb{F}_q$. Moreover for *any* subset $\{x_1, \ldots, x_m\} \subseteq \mathbb{F}_q$, relations on $(ax_1 + b, \ldots, ax_m + b)$ that neither can be derived from $a\tilde{x} + b$ with some specific $\tilde{x} \in \mathbb{F}_q$ nor hold regardless of a and b, must be hidden from the receiver. At least if the field size q increases exponentially in the security parameter, it is completely unclear how this could be achieved using 2-universal hashing. Direct application of the classic tool set of privacy amplification and randomness extraction helps generating full-entropy bit-strings, but it does not necessarily disguise relations on *exponentially large* vectors.

3.3   Our Solution

In this section we present our information-theoretically UC-secure construction of $\mathbb{F}_q^k$-OAFE from $O(k)$ instances of $\mathbb{F}_q$-OAFE. Our construction consists of two steps. First, we implement a randomized variant of the ideal $\mathbb{F}_q^k$-OAFE functionality that differs from the original definition (q.v. Figure 1 in Section 2.2) in the following way:

- An honest sender does not provide arbitrarily selectable input (a, b), but the primitive chooses for him uniformly at random.
- A *corrupted* sender can still select (a, b) arbitrarily.

Then, by the protocol given in Figure 5 we transform this randomized $\mathbb{F}_q^k$-OAFE primitive into an ideal $\mathbb{F}_q^k$-OAFE instance as defined in Section 2.2.

Since it is straightforward to see that the second step of our construction (the reduction in Figure 5) is perfectly UC-secure, we just have to show how one

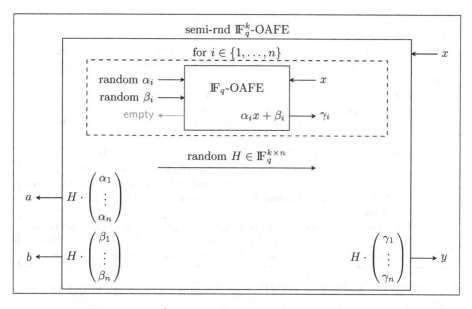

Fig. 6. Implementation of $\mathbb{F}_q^k$-OAFE with randomized sender input from n instances of $\mathbb{F}_q$-OAFE; protocol idea adapted from [BCS96]. Note that a corrupted sender can arbitrarily fix his otherwise random output (a, b). Further, we stress that H must not be announced before the receiver did provide some input to all n underlying $\mathbb{F}_q$-OAFE instances in the dashed box, i.e. the sender has to await all n empty messages. The protocol is UC-secure, if $k \log q$ increases polynomially in the security parameter and $n \geq (2 + \varepsilon)k$ for some constant $\varepsilon > 0$ (cf. Theorem 1).

can reduce the randomized $\mathbb{F}_q^k$-OAFE variant to $O(k)$ instances of $\mathbb{F}_q$-OAFE. The respective protocol is given in Figure 6. The high level idea is identical to the techniques discussed in Section 3.1, but compared to the insecure protocol of Figure 4 there is a crucial difference in the details: The matrix H is now chosen uniformly at random and only announced *after* all the receiver's choices are fixed[1]. This obviously renders the general attack strategy discussed in Section 3.1 impossible. However, giving a formal security proof still turns out pretty challenging, since standard techniques do not apply.

Our overall proof strategy is as follows. Since correctness of the protocol and perfect UC-security against a corrupted sender party can be shown straightforwardly, it suffices to focus on the case of a corrupted receiver. We first show that with overwhelming probability the random matrix H and the corrupted receiver's inputs for the underlying $\mathbb{F}_q$-OAFE instances have some specific algebraic properties. This is the difficult part and can be considered a major technical contribution. Then, based on that properties we are able to show that

---

[1] In fact, this *is* a way of 2-universal hashing. However, for the security proof we need some more sophisticated properties of random $\mathbb{F}_q$-matrices than just being 2-universal hash functions.

Simulator $\mathcal{S}_{\mathrm{rec}}(\mathcal{A})$

- Set up a simulated version of the given adversary $\mathcal{A}$ (which especially imperson-ates the corrupted receiver party) and wire it to the environment right the way they would be wired in the real model.
- Pick $H \in \mathbb{F}_q^{k \times n}$ and $\gamma_1, \ldots, \gamma_n \in \mathbb{F}_q$ uniformly at random.
- Answer on $\mathcal{A}$'s j-th $\mathbb{F}_q$-OAFE query x_j as follows:
  - If $j \leq \frac{n}{2}$ or no $\lfloor \frac{n}{2} \rfloor$ previous $\mathbb{F}_q$-OAFE queries are equal to x_j, then just return γ_j.
  - If exactly $\lfloor \frac{n}{2} \rfloor$ previous $\mathbb{F}_q$-OAFE queries are equal to x_j, then
    1. send x_j to the ideal functionality, thus receiving some $y \in \mathbb{F}_q^k$,
    2. pick randomly $\tilde{\gamma}_1, \ldots, \tilde{\gamma}_n \in \mathbb{F}_q$ subject to the condition that $H \cdot (\tilde{\gamma}_1, \ldots, \tilde{\gamma}_n)^{\mathrm{T}} = y$ and $\tilde{\gamma}_i = \gamma_i$ for every $i < j$ with $x_i = x_j$, and
    3. return $\tilde{\gamma}_j$ to $\mathcal{A}$.
    If it is impossible to find any such $\tilde{\gamma}_1, \ldots, \tilde{\gamma}_n$, just give up and terminate.
  - If more than $\lfloor \frac{n}{2} \rfloor$ previous $\mathbb{F}_q$-OAFE queries are equal to x_j, then return $\tilde{\gamma}_j$.
- If $\mathcal{A}$ has queried all n underlying $\mathbb{F}_q$-OAFE instances, announce H to him.

Fig. 7. Sketch of the simulator program $\mathcal{S}_{\mathrm{rec}}(\mathcal{A})$, given an adversary $\mathcal{A}$ that corrupts the receiver.

a straightforward simulation approach does work well. More specifically, our line of argument is as follows:

1. We show that any fixed $\frac{n}{2}$-subset of columns of H with overwhelming prob-ability contains a basis of the linear space $\mathbb{F}_q^k$.
2. We show that, given a receiver that queries more than half of the n un-derlying $\mathbb{F}_q$-OAFE instances on the same input x and given that the corre-sponding columns of H contain a basis of $\mathbb{F}_q^k$, all other $\mathbb{F}_q$-OAFE outputs γ_i (that correspond to inputs distinct from x) are just completely independent randomness.
3. We show that, given a receiver that queries at most half of the underlying $\mathbb{F}_q$-OAFE instances on the same input x, the set union of the rows of H and HX is linearly independent with overwhelming probability, where X denotes the diagonal matrix consisting of the receiver's $\mathbb{F}_q$-OAFE inputs.
4. We show that, conditioned to the abovementioned property of H and the corrupted receiver's $\mathbb{F}_q$-OAFE inputs, the honest sender's random output (a, b) is statistically independent from the receiver's complete view.

Once these facts are proven, it is pretty straightforward to see that the simulator for a corrupted receiver party can just work as described in Figure 7. We conclude our work with our main theorem.

Theorem 1. *Our* $\mathbb{F}_q^k$*-OAFE construction, given by the combination of Figure 5 and Figure 6, is perfectly UC-secure against a corrupted sender and statistically UC-secure against a corrupted receiver, if* $k \log q$ *increases polynomially in the security parameter and* $n \geq (2 + \varepsilon)k$ *with constant* $\varepsilon > 0$. *More particularly, for every real model adversary* $\mathcal{A}$ *that corrupts the receiver party, there exists a* *simulator $\mathcal{S}$, such that for every environment $\mathcal{Z}$ the statistical distance between $\mathcal{Z}$'s view in the real model (with protocol given by Figure 5 and Figure 6 and adversary $\mathcal{A}$) and $\mathcal{Z}$'s view in the ideal model (with ideal functionality given by Figure 2 and simulator $\mathcal{S}$) is upper bounded by:*

$$m := \max\left(2q^{k-\frac{n}{2}}, \; \frac{q^{2k-n} + 2q^{k-\frac{n}{2}}}{1 - q^{-k}} + q^{k-n}\right) \qquad \text{i.e.,} \quad m = O\!\left(q^{k-\frac{n}{2}}\right)$$

Proof (Sketch). We just have to show that the protocol in Figure 6, given an adversary $\mathcal{A}$ that corrupts the receiver party, is successfully simulated by $\mathcal{S}_{\mathrm{rec}}(\mathcal{A})$ at least with probability $1 - m$; everything else then follows straightforwardly.

Our proof is based on four technical lemmata, whose proofs can be found in the appendix. We start with the case that more than $\frac{n}{2}$ of the underlying $\mathbb{F}_q$-OAFE instances in Figure 6 are queried on the same input. In this case, we first of all need that only with negligible probability the simulator $\mathcal{S}_{\mathrm{rec}}(\mathcal{A})$ may give up (i.e. terminate unsuccessfully) in his search for $\tilde{\gamma}_1, \ldots, \tilde{\gamma}_n$. Thereto, we employ the following lemma.

Lemma 2. *Given $G \in \mathbb{F}_q^{m \times l}$ uniformly at random, it holds that $\Pr[\mathrm{rank}(G) = \min(m, l)] > 1 - q^{-|m-l|}$. In other words, there exist more than $q^{ml}\left(1 - q^{-|m-l|}\right)$ matrices $M \in \mathbb{F}_q^{m \times l}$ with full rank $\min(m, l)$.*

For the very moment when $\mathcal{S}_{\mathrm{rec}}(\mathcal{A})$ tries to generate $\tilde{\gamma}_1, \ldots, \tilde{\gamma}_n$ we fix the $\lfloor \frac{n}{2} \rfloor$ indices corresponding to $\mathbb{F}_q$-OAFE instances that were previously queried on the same value x_j which is now sent to the ideal functionality. By Lemma 2, the remaining $n - \lfloor \frac{n}{2} \rfloor$ columns of H do contain a basis of $\mathbb{F}_q^k$ with some probability greater than $1 - q^{k-\frac{n}{2}}$. However, under this condition one can always find the desired $\tilde{\gamma}_1, \ldots, \tilde{\gamma}_n$. Thus, $\mathcal{S}_{\mathrm{rec}}(\mathcal{A})$ will give up with some probability less than $q^{k-\frac{n}{2}}$.

Next, still considering the case that more than $\frac{n}{2}$ of the $\mathbb{F}_q$-OAFE inputs are equal, we need to show that all other values γ_i returned to $\mathcal{A}$ are distributed as in the real model. Note that by Lemma 2 with probability greater than $1 - q^{k-\frac{n}{2}}$ the columns of H corresponding to the most frequent $\mathbb{F}_q$-OAFE input x contain a basis of $\mathbb{F}_q^k$. Now, by the following lemma we get exactly what we need, namely that under this condition in the real model all remaining $\mathbb{F}_q$-OAFE outputs are just completely independent randomness.

Lemma 3. *In the protocol of Figure 6, given a receiver that queries at least k of the n underlying $\mathbb{F}_q$-OAFE instances on the same input x and given that the corresponding columns of H contain a basis of $\mathbb{F}_q^k$, all other $\mathbb{F}_q$-OAFE outputs γ_i (that correspond to inputs distinct from x) are statistically independent from $(a, b, H, x_1, \ldots, x_n)$, where x_i denotes the receiver's i-th $\mathbb{F}_q$-OAFE input.*

Further, note that by construction the $\mathbb{F}_q$-OAFE outputs $\tilde{\gamma}_i$ corresponding to the most frequent $\mathbb{F}_q$-OAFE input x always are identically distributed as in the real model. Thus, we have already shown: Conditioned to the event that more than $\frac{n}{2}$ of the corrupted receiver's $\mathbb{F}_q$-OAFE inputs are equal, the statistical distance between the environment's views in the ideal and the real model is upper bounded by $2q^{k-\frac{n}{2}}$.

So, finally we have to consider the case that no more than $\frac{n}{2}$ of the underlying $\mathbb{F}_q$-OAFE instances are queried on the same input. In this case, $\mathcal{S}_{\text{rec}}(\mathcal{A})$ just solely returns random $\mathbb{F}_q$-OAFE outputs γ_i to $\mathcal{A}$ that are completely unrelated to the ideal sender's output (a, b). By the following two lemmata we find a random event $\mathcal{E}$, such that conditioned to $\mathcal{E}$ the same does happen in the real model, and $\mathcal{E}$ has overwhelming probabilty.

Lemma 4. *In the protocol of Figure 6 let X denote the diagonal matrix whose diagonal elements are the (corrupted) receiver's inputs for the n underlying $\mathbb{F}_q$-OAFE instances. Then, conditioned to the event that the set union consisting of the rows of H and HX is linearly independent, the honest sender's random output tuple (a, b) is statistically independent from $(X, \gamma_1, \ldots, \gamma_n, H)$.*

Lemma 5. *Let any diagonal matrix $X \in \mathbb{F}_q^{n \times n}$ be given, such that at most half of the diagonal elements are equal, and let H be uniformly random over $\mathbb{F}_q^{k \times n}$. Further, let p denote the probability that the set union consisting of the rows of H and HX is linearly independent. Then we have:*

$$p > 1 - \frac{q^{2k-n} + 2q^{k-\frac{n}{2}}}{1 - q^{-k}} - q^{k-n}$$

In particular, Lemma 4 and Lemma 5 yield: Conditioned to the event that no more than $\frac{n}{2}$ of the corrupted receiver's $\mathbb{F}_q$-OAFE inputs are equal, the statistical distance between the environment's views in the ideal and the real model is upper bounded by $\left(q^{2k-n} + 2q^{k-\frac{n}{2}}\right) / \left(1 - q^{-k}\right) + q^{k-n}$. This concludes our proof of Theorem 1. $\square$

References

[AIK11]   Applebaum, B., Ishai, Y., Kushilevitz, E.: How to garble arithmetic circuits. In: Ostrovsky, R. (ed.) Proceedings of FOCS 2011, pp. 120–129. IEEE (2011)

[BBCM95] Bennett, C.H., Brassard, G., Crépeau, C., Maurer, U.M.: Generalized privacy amplification. IEEE Transactions on Information Theory 41(6), 1915–1923 (1995)

[BBR88]   Bennett, C.H., Brassard, G., Robert, J.-M.: Privacy amplification by public discussion. SIAM J. Comput. 17(2), 210–229 (1988)

[BCS96]   Brassard, G., Crépeau, C., Santha, M.: Oblivious transfers and intersecting codes. IEEE Transactions on Information Theory 42(6), 1769–1780 (1996)

[Can01]   Canetti, R.: Universally composable security: A new paradigm for cryptographic protocols. In: Proceedings of FOCS 2001, pp. 136–145 (2001), http://eprint.iacr.org/2000/067

[CFIK03]   Cramer, R., Fehr, S., Ishai, Y., Kushilevitz, E.: Efficient Multi-party Computation Over Rings. In: Biham, E. (ed.) EUROCRYPT 2003. LNCS, vol. 2656, pp. 596–613. Springer, Heidelberg (2003)

[CLOS02] Canetti, R., Lindell, Y., Ostrovsky, R., Sahai, A.: Universally composable two-party and multi-party secure computation. In: Reif, J.H. (ed.) Proceedings of STOC 2002, pp. 494–503. ACM (2002)

[CMW05] Crépeau, C., Morozov, K., Wolf, S.: Efficient Unconditional Oblivious Transfer from Almost any Noisy Channel. In: Blundo, C., Cimato, S. (eds.) SCN 2004. LNCS, vol. 3352, pp. 47–59. Springer, Heidelberg (2005)

[CvdGT95] Crépeau, C., van de Graaf, J., Tapp, A.: Committed Oblivious Transfer and Private Multi-party Computation. In: Coppersmith, D. (ed.) CRYPTO 1995. LNCS, vol. 963, pp. 110–123. Springer, Heidelberg (1995)

[DKMQ11] Döttling, N., Kraschewski, D., Müller-Quade, J.: Efficient Reductions for Non-Signaling Cryptographic Primitives. In: Fehr, S. (ed.) ICITS 2011. LNCS, vol. 6673, pp. 120–137. Springer, Heidelberg (2011)

[GIS+10] Goyal, V., Ishai, Y., Sahai, A., Venkatesan, R., Wadia, A.: Founding Cryptography on Tamper-Proof Hardware Tokens. In: Micciancio, D. (ed.) TCC 2010. LNCS, vol. 5978, pp. 308–326. Springer, Heidelberg (2010)

[GKR08] Goldwasser, S., Kalai, Y.T., Rothblum, G.N.: One-Time Programs. In: Micciancio, D. (ed.) CRYPTO 2008. LNCS, vol. 5157, pp. 39–56. Springer, Heidelberg (2008)

[GL91] Goldwasser, S., Levin, L.A.: Fair Computation of General Functions in Presence of Immoral Majority. In: Menezes, A., Vanstone, S.A. (eds.) CRYPTO 1990. LNCS, vol. 537, pp. 77–93. Springer, Heidelberg (1991)

[GMW87] Goldreich, O., Micali, S., Wigderson, A.: How to play any mental game or a completeness theorem for protocols with honest majority. In: Aho, A.V. (ed.) Proceedings of STOC 1987, pp. 218–229. ACM (1987)

[IKO+11] Ishai, Y., Kushilevitz, E., Ostrovsky, R., Prabhakaran, M., Sahai, A., Wullschleger, J.: Constant-Rate Oblivious Transfer from Noisy Channels. In: Rogaway, P. (ed.) CRYPTO 2011. LNCS, vol. 6841, pp. 667–684. Springer, Heidelberg (2011)

[ILL89] Impagliazzo, R., Levin, L.A., Luby, M.: Pseudo-random generation from one-way functions (extended abstracts). In: Proceedings of STOC 1989, pp. 12–24. ACM (1989)

[IPS08] Ishai, Y., Prabhakaran, M., Sahai, A.: Founding Cryptography on Oblivious Transfer – Efficiently. In: Wagner, D. (ed.) CRYPTO 2008. LNCS, vol. 5157, pp. 572–591. Springer, Heidelberg (2008)

[Kil88] Kilian, J.: Founding cryptography on oblivious transfer. In: Proceedings of STOC 1988, pp. 20–31. ACM (1988)

[Kil91] Kilian, J.: A general completeness theorem for two-party games. In: Koutsougeras, C., Vitter, J.S. (eds.) Proceedings of STOC 1991, pp. 553–560. ACM (1991)

[Kil00] Kilian, J.: More general completeness theorems for secure two-party computation. In: Frances, F.Y., Luks, E.M. (eds.) Proceedings of STOC 2000, pp. 316–324. ACM (2000)

[KMQ11] Kraschewski, D., Müller-Quade, J.: Completeness Theorems with Constructive Proofs for Finite Deterministic 2-Party Functions. In: Ishai, Y. (ed.) TCC 2011. LNCS, vol. 6597, pp. 364–381. Springer, Heidelberg (2011)

[NP99] Naor, M., Pinkas, B.: Oblivious transfer and polynomial evaluation. In: Vitter, J.S., Larmore, L.L., Leighton, F.T. (eds.) Proceedings of STOC 1999, pp. 245–254. ACM (1999)

[Rab81] Michael, O., Rabin, M.O.: How to exchange secrets by oblivious transfer. Technical report, Aiken Computation Laboratory. Harvard University (1981)

[WW06]   Wolf, S., Wullschleger, J.: Oblivious Transfer is Symmetric. In: Vaude-nay, S. (ed.) EUROCRYPT 2006. LNCS, vol. 4004, pp. 222–232. Springer, Heidelberg (2006)

[Yao82]   Yao, A.C.-C.: Protocols for secure computations (extended abstract). In: Proceedings of FOCS 1982, pp. 160–164. IEEE Computer Society Press (1982)

[Yao86]   Yao, A.C.-C.: How to generate and exchange secrets (extended abstract). In: Proceedings of FOCS 1986, pp. 162–167. IEEE Computer Society Press (1986)

A   Proof of Lemma 2

Claim. Let $G \in \mathbb{F}_q^{m \times l}$ be uniformly random. Then, $\Pr\left[\text{rank}(G) = \min(m, l)\right] > 1 - q^{-|m-l|}$. In other words, there exist more than $q^{ml}\left(1 - q^{-|m-l|}\right)$ matrices $M \in \mathbb{F}_q^{m \times l}$ with full rank $\min(m, l)$.

Proof. W.l.o.g. let $m \leq l$. Note that, given any full-rank matrix $M \in \mathbb{F}_q^{i \times l}$ with $i < l$, there exist exactly $q^l - q^i$ rows (only the linear combinations of the rows of M are excluded) by that one can extend M to a full-rank matrix of dimension $(i+1) \times l$. Thus it holds:

$$\#\{M \in \mathbb{F}_q^{m \times l} \mid \text{rank}(M) = m\} = \prod_{i=0}^{m-1} q^l - q^i$$

Hence we can estimate:

$$\Pr\left[\text{rank}(G) = m\right] = \prod_{i=0}^{m-1} 1 - q^{i-l} \geq 1 - \sum_{i=0}^{m-1} q^{i-l} = 1 - \frac{q^m - 1}{q^l(q-1)} > 1 - q^{m-l}$$

This is what we had to show.   □

B   Proof of Lemma 3

Claim. In the protocol of Figure 6, given a receiver that queries at least k of the n underlying $\mathbb{F}_q$-OAFE instances on the same input x and given that the corresponding columns of H contain a basis of $\mathbb{F}_q^k$, all other $\mathbb{F}_q$-OAFE outputs γ_i (that correspond to inputs distinct from x) are statistically independent from $(a, b, H, x_1, \ldots, x_n)$, where x_i denotes the receiver's i-th $\mathbb{F}_q$-OAFE input.

Proof. Fix a, b, H, x and $x_1, \ldots, x_n$, such that at least k of the x_i are equal to x and the corresponding columns of H contain a basis of $\mathbb{F}_q^k$; also fix the corresponding γ_i. We have to show that, when one uniformly resamples $\alpha_1, \ldots, \alpha_n$ and $\beta_1, \ldots, \beta_n$ conditioned to the fixed values $a, b, H, x_1, \ldots, x_n$ and the fixed γ_i, then the remaining γ_i are uniformly random.

W.l.o.g. we may rearrange the index set $\{1, \ldots, n\}$, such that $x_1 = \ldots = x_l = x$ for some $l \geq k$ and all other x_i are different from x. Note that such a rearrangement in particular includes a corresponding permutation of the columns of H. Now, we define the following vectors:

$$\boldsymbol{\alpha} := \begin{pmatrix} \alpha_1 \\ \vdots \\ \alpha_l \end{pmatrix} \qquad \boldsymbol{\beta} := \begin{pmatrix} \beta_1 \\ \vdots \\ \beta_l \end{pmatrix} \qquad \boldsymbol{\gamma} := \begin{pmatrix} \gamma_1 \\ \vdots \\ \gamma_l \end{pmatrix}$$

$$\boldsymbol{\alpha}' := \begin{pmatrix} \alpha_{l+1} \\ \vdots \\ \alpha_n \end{pmatrix} \qquad \boldsymbol{\beta}' := \begin{pmatrix} \beta_{l+1} \\ \vdots \\ \beta_n \end{pmatrix} \qquad \boldsymbol{\gamma}' := \begin{pmatrix} \gamma_{l+1} \\ \vdots \\ \gamma_n \end{pmatrix}$$

Further,

- let $\tilde{X}'$ denote the diagonal matrix with diagonal elements $x_{l+1}, \ldots, x_n$,
- let $\tilde{H}$ denote the matrix consisting of the first l columns of H, and
- let $\tilde{H}'$ denote the matrix consisting of the remaining $n - l$ columns of H.

Note that $\tilde{H}$ has full rank k by assumption. Now, resampling $\alpha_1, \ldots, \alpha_n$ and $\beta_1, \ldots, \beta_n$ corresponds to uniformly sampling $(\boldsymbol{\alpha}, \boldsymbol{\alpha}', \boldsymbol{\beta}, \boldsymbol{\beta}')$ subject to the following conditions:

$$a \;=\; \tilde{H}\boldsymbol{\alpha} + \tilde{H}'\boldsymbol{\alpha}' \qquad b \;=\; \tilde{H}\boldsymbol{\beta} + \tilde{H}'\boldsymbol{\beta}' \qquad \boldsymbol{\alpha} \cdot x + \boldsymbol{\beta} \;=\; \boldsymbol{\gamma}$$

Equivalently, we can uniformly sample $(\boldsymbol{\alpha}, \boldsymbol{\alpha}', \boldsymbol{\beta}, \boldsymbol{\beta}', \boldsymbol{\gamma}')$ subject to the following conditions:

$$\begin{aligned} a &= \tilde{H}\boldsymbol{\alpha} + \tilde{H}'\boldsymbol{\alpha}' & \boldsymbol{\alpha} \cdot x + \boldsymbol{\beta} &= \boldsymbol{\gamma} \\ b &= \tilde{H}\boldsymbol{\beta} + \tilde{H}'\boldsymbol{\beta}' & \tilde{X}'\boldsymbol{\alpha}' + \boldsymbol{\beta}' &= \boldsymbol{\gamma}' \end{aligned}$$

Note that the set of all valid samples $(\boldsymbol{\alpha}, \boldsymbol{\alpha}', \boldsymbol{\beta}, \boldsymbol{\beta}', \boldsymbol{\gamma}')$, since being the solution space of a linear equation system, is an affine subspace of $\mathbb{F}_q^l \times \mathbb{F}_q^{n-l} \times \mathbb{F}_q^l \times \mathbb{F}_q^{n-l} \times \mathbb{F}_q^{n-l}$ and each valid $\boldsymbol{\gamma}'$ corresponds to a solution subspace of the same dimension. Thus, each valid $\boldsymbol{\gamma}'$ is equally likely and we have just to show that $\boldsymbol{\gamma}'$ may take *every* value in $\mathbb{F}_q^{n-l}$.

However, for our upcoming argumentation we first need to show that $a \cdot x + b - \tilde{H}\boldsymbol{\gamma}$ is an image of $\tilde{H}'$. Thereto, we reformulate the resampling conditions as follows:

$$\begin{aligned} \tilde{H}\boldsymbol{\alpha} &= a - \tilde{H}'\boldsymbol{\alpha}' & \boldsymbol{\beta} &= \boldsymbol{\gamma} - \boldsymbol{\alpha} \cdot x \\ b &= \tilde{H}\boldsymbol{\beta} + \tilde{H}'\boldsymbol{\beta}' & \boldsymbol{\beta}' &= \boldsymbol{\gamma}' - \tilde{X}'\boldsymbol{\alpha}' \end{aligned}$$

Plugging the identities for $\boldsymbol{\beta}$ and $\boldsymbol{\beta}'$ into the identity for b yields:

$$\tilde{H}\boldsymbol{\alpha} = a - \tilde{H}'\boldsymbol{\alpha}' \qquad b = \tilde{H}\boldsymbol{\gamma} - \tilde{H}\boldsymbol{\alpha} \cdot x + \tilde{H}'\boldsymbol{\gamma}' - \tilde{H}'\tilde{X}'\boldsymbol{\alpha}'$$

Plugging the identity for $\tilde{H}\boldsymbol{\alpha}$ into the identity for b and some rearrangement yield:

$$a \cdot x + b - \tilde{H}\boldsymbol{\gamma} = \tilde{H}'(\boldsymbol{\gamma}' + \boldsymbol{\alpha}' \cdot x - \tilde{X}'\boldsymbol{\alpha}')$$

Thus, $a \cdot x + b - \tilde{H}\gamma$ must be an image of $\tilde{H}'$, as otherwise there would not exist *any* valid sample $(\alpha, \alpha', \beta, \beta', \gamma')$.

Now, let some arbitrary $\gamma' \in \mathbb{F}_q^{n-l}$ be given. By the following construction we find some $\alpha, \alpha', \beta, \beta'$, such that $(\alpha, \alpha', \beta, \beta', \gamma')$ is a valid sample, what will conclude our proof. Let I denote the identity matrix in $\mathbb{F}_q^{(n-l) \times (n-l)}$ and let ζ be some $\tilde{H}'$-preimage of $a \cdot x + b - \tilde{H}\gamma$. Firstly, since $\tilde{X}'$ is a diagonal matrix with diagonal elements distinct from x, the matrix $(\tilde{X}' - x \cdot I)$ is invertible and we find some α', such that $\gamma' - (\tilde{X}' - x \cdot I)\alpha' = \zeta$ and hence $\tilde{H}'(\gamma' - (\tilde{X}' - x \cdot I)\alpha') = a \cdot x + b - \tilde{H}\gamma$. Secondly, since $\tilde{H}$ has full rank, we find some α, such that $\tilde{H}\alpha = a - \tilde{H}'\alpha'$. Thirdly, we set $\beta' := \gamma' - \tilde{X}'\alpha'$ and $\beta := \gamma - \alpha \cdot x$. Thus, by construction we have:

$$b = \tilde{H}'(\gamma' - (\tilde{X}' - x \cdot I)\alpha') - a \cdot x + \tilde{H}\gamma \qquad \gamma' = \beta' + \tilde{X}'\alpha'$$
$$a = \tilde{H}\alpha + \tilde{H}'\alpha' \qquad\qquad\qquad \gamma = \beta + \alpha \cdot x$$

Plugging the other three identities into the identity for b yields that $b = \tilde{H}\beta + \tilde{H}'\beta'$ and thus the tuple $(\alpha, \alpha', \beta, \beta', \gamma')$ meets all four conditions for a valid sample. □

C   Proof of Lemma 4

Claim. In the protocol of Figure 6 let X denote the diagonal matrix whose diagonal elements are the (corrupted) receiver's inputs for the n underlying $\mathbb{F}_q$-OAFE instances. Then, conditioned to the event that the set union consisting of the rows of H and HX is linearly independent, the honest sender's random output tuple (a, b) is statistically independent from $(X, \gamma_1, \ldots, \gamma_n, H)$.

Proof. Fix $(X, \gamma_1, \ldots, \gamma_n, H)$, such that the set union consisting of the rows of H and HX is linearly independent. We show that under this condition the honest sender's output (a, b) is still uniformly random over $\mathbb{F}_q^k \times \mathbb{F}_q^k$. Note that conditioned to these parameters, we still have that $(\alpha_1, \ldots, \alpha_n)$ is uniformly random and $(\beta_1, \ldots, \beta_n)$ can be computed from $(\alpha_1, \ldots, \alpha_n)$ by the following equality:

$$X \cdot \begin{pmatrix} \alpha_1 \\ \vdots \\ \alpha_n \end{pmatrix} + \begin{pmatrix} \beta_1 \\ \vdots \\ \beta_n \end{pmatrix} = \begin{pmatrix} \gamma_1 \\ \vdots \\ \gamma_n \end{pmatrix} \quad \text{i.e.,} \quad \begin{pmatrix} \beta_1 \\ \vdots \\ \beta_n \end{pmatrix} = \begin{pmatrix} \gamma_1 \\ \vdots \\ \gamma_n \end{pmatrix} - X \cdot \begin{pmatrix} \alpha_1 \\ \vdots \\ \alpha_n \end{pmatrix}$$

Hence, noting that a and b are generated from the α_i-vector and β_i-vector respectively by multiplication with the matrix H, it follows:

$$\begin{pmatrix} H \\ -HX \end{pmatrix} \cdot \begin{pmatrix} \alpha_1 \\ \vdots \\ \alpha_n \end{pmatrix} + \begin{pmatrix} 0 \\ H \end{pmatrix} \cdot \begin{pmatrix} \gamma_1 \\ \vdots \\ \gamma_n \end{pmatrix} = \begin{pmatrix} a \\ b \end{pmatrix}$$

Note that on the left side of this equation everything but the α_i-vector is fixed, and the leftmost matrix has full rank by assumption. Thus, since the α_i-vector is uniformly random, we must have that (a, b) is uniformly random, too. □

D   Proof of Lemma 5

Claim. Let any diagonal matrix $X \in \mathbb{F}_q^{n \times n}$ be given, such that at most half of the diagonal elements are equal, and let H be uniformly random over $\mathbb{F}_q^{k \times n}$. Further, let p denote the probability that the set union consisting of the rows of H and HX is linearly independent. Then we have:

$$p > 1 - \frac{q^{2k-n} + 2q^{k-\frac{n}{2}}}{1 - q^{-k}} - q^{k-n}$$

Proof. We have to show:

$$\Pr\left[\exists v, w \in \mathbb{F}_q^{1 \times k} : (v,w) \neq (0,0) \wedge vH + wHX = 0\right] < \frac{q^{2k-n} + 2q^{k-\frac{n}{2}}}{1 - q^{-k}} + q^{k-n}$$

Equivalently, we will upper bound the following probability:

$$\Pr\left[\exists u \in \mathbb{F}_q^{1 \times n}, v, w \in \mathbb{F}_q^{1 \times k} : (v,w) \neq (0,0) \wedge vH + uX = 0 \wedge wH - u = 0\right] \quad (1)$$

Thus, we have to upper bound the probability that some u and uX can be linearly combined from the rows of H and at least one of the linear combinations is non-trivial. Note that by Lemma 2 it holds:

$$\Pr\left[\text{rank}(H) = k\right] > 1 - q^{k-n}$$

So, we can henceforth condition the event that $\text{rank}(H) = k$ and will thereby make an error of at most q^{k-n}. Now, we define the random matrix $G \in \mathbb{F}_q^{n \times (n-k)}$ whose columns are a random basis of the kernel of H. By construction, the following implication always holds true:

$$vH + uX = 0 \wedge wH - u = 0 \quad \Rightarrow \quad uXG = 0 \wedge uG = 0$$

Thus, instead of (1) we can now upper bound the following probability—note that $u \neq 0$, because we conditioned to the event that H has full rank:

$$\Pr\left[\exists u \in \mathbb{F}_q^{1 \times n} \setminus \{0\} : uXG = 0 \wedge uG = 0\right] \quad (2)$$

Note that G is a uniformly random full-rank matrix, since due to the condition that $\text{rank}(H) = k$ the kernel of H is a uniformly random $(n - k)$-dimensional subspace of $\mathbb{F}_q^n$.

We estimate (2) by differentiating between the cases that $\{u, uX\}$ is linearly independent or not. For every $u \in \mathbb{F}_q^{1 \times n}$ with $uX \notin \text{span}(u)$ we can estimate:

$$\Pr\left[uXG = uG = 0\right] \leq \frac{\#\{M \in \mathbb{F}_q^{n \times (n-k)} \mid uXM = uM = 0\}}{\#\{M \in \mathbb{F}_q^{n \times (n-k)} \mid \text{rank}(M) = n - k\}}$$

By Lemma 2 follows:

$$\Pr\left[uXG = uG = 0\right] < \frac{q^{(n-2)(n-k)}}{q^{n(n-k)}(1 - q^{-k})} = \frac{q^{-2(n-k)}}{1 - q^{-k}}$$

Applying the Union Bound yields:

$$\Pr\left[\exists u \in \mathbb{F}_q^{1 \times n} \setminus \{0\} : uX \notin \text{span}(u) \wedge uXG = uG = 0\right] < \frac{q^{2k-n}}{1 - q^{-k}}$$

Yet, there is only the case left that $uX = \lambda u$ for some $\lambda \in \mathbb{F}_q$. However, for each $i \in \{1, \ldots, n\}$ this means that the i-th coefficient of u is zero or the i-th diagonal element of X is λ. In other words, with d_λ denoting the dimension of the eigenspace for the eigenvalue λ of X, it holds:

$$\#\{u \in \mathbb{F}_q^{1 \times n} \setminus \{0\} \mid uX \in \text{span}(u)\} = \sum_\lambda (q^{d_\lambda} - 1)$$

Since by assumption at most half of the diagonal elements of X may be equal, this leaves at most $2(q^{\frac{n}{2}} - 1)$ possible vectors u with $uX \in \text{span}(u)$. For every such u we can estimate:

$$\Pr\left[uXG = uG = 0\right] = \Pr\left[uG = 0\right] \leq \frac{\#\{M \in \mathbb{F}_q^{n \times (n-k)} \mid uM = 0\}}{\#\{M \in \mathbb{F}_q^{n \times (n-k)} \mid \text{rank}(M) = n - k\}}$$

By Lemma 2 follows:

$$\Pr\left[uXG = uG = 0\right] < \frac{q^{(n-1)(n-k)}}{q^{n(n-k)}(1 - q^{-k})} = \frac{q^{-(n-k)}}{1 - q^{-k}}$$

Applying the Union Bound yields:

$$\Pr\left[\exists u \in \mathbb{F}_q^{1 \times n} \setminus \{0\} : uX \in \text{span}(u) \wedge uXG = uG = 0\right] < \frac{2q^{\frac{n}{2} - (n-k)}}{1 - q^{-k}}$$

Putting things together, we have shown:

$$\Pr\left[\exists u \in \mathbb{F}_q^{1 \times n} \setminus \{0\} : uXG = 0 \wedge uG = 0\right] < \frac{q^{2k-n} + 2q^{k-\frac{n}{2}}}{1 - q^{-k}}$$

Thus, if we take into account the error introduced by the condition that the random matrix H has full rank k, we finally get:

$$\Pr\left[\exists v, w \in \mathbb{F}_q^{1 \times k} : (v, w) \neq (0, 0) \wedge vH + wHX = 0\right] < \frac{q^{2k-n} + 2q^{k-\frac{n}{2}}}{1 - q^{-k}} + q^{k-n}$$

This is what we had to show.   □

Passive Corruption
in Statistical Multi-Party Computation
(Extended Abstract)*

Martin Hirt[1], Christoph Lucas[1], Ueli Maurer[1], and Dominik Raub[2]

[1] Department of Computer Science, ETH Zurich, Switzerland
{hirt,clucas,maurer}@inf.ethz.ch
[2] Department of Computer Science, University of Århus, Denmark
raub@cs.au.dk

Abstract. The goal of *Multi-Party Computation* (MPC) is to perform an arbitrary computation in a distributed, private, and fault-tolerant way. For this purpose, a fixed set of n parties runs a protocol that tolerates an adversary corrupting a subset of the parties, preserving certain security guarantees like correctness, secrecy, robustness, and fairness. Corruptions can be either *passive* or *active*: A passively corrupted party follows the protocol correctly, but the adversary learns the entire internal state of this party. An actively corrupted party is completely controlled by the adversary, and may deviate arbitrarily from the protocol. A *mixed adversary* may at the same time corrupt some parties actively and some additional parties passively.

In this work, we consider the statistical setting with mixed adversaries and study the exact consequences of active and passive corruptions on secrecy, correctness, robustness, and fairness separately (i.e., hybrid security). Clearly, the number of passive corruptions affects the thresholds for secrecy, while the number of active corruptions affects all thresholds. It turns out that in the statistical setting, the number of passive corruptions in particular also affects the threshold for correctness, i.e., in all protocols there are (tolerated) adversaries for which a single additional passive corruption is sufficient to break correctness. This is in contrast to both the perfect and the computational setting, where such an influence cannot be observed. Apparently, this effect arises from the use of information-theoretic signatures, which are part of most (if not all) statistical protocols.

Keywords: Multi-party computation, passive corruption, statistical security, hybrid security, mixed adversaries.

* The full version of this paper is available at the *Cryptology ePrint Archive*: http://eprint.iacr.org/2012/272. This work was partially supported by the Zurich Information Security Center.

A. Smith (Ed.): ICITS 2012, LNCS 7412, pp. 129–146, 2012.

1   Introduction

1.1   Secure Multi-Party Computation

Multi-Party Computation (MPC) allows a set of n parties to securely perform an arbitrary computation in a distributed manner, where security means that secrecy of the inputs and correctness of the output are maintained even when some of the parties are dishonest. The dishonesty of parties is modeled with a central adversary who corrupts parties. The adversary can be *passive*, i.e. can read the internal state of the corrupted parties, or *active*, i.e., can make the corrupted parties deviate arbitrarily from the protocol.

MPC was originally proposed by Yao [Yao82]. The first general solution was provided in [GMW87], where, based on computational intractability assumptions, security against a passive adversary was achieved for $t < n$ corruptions, and security against an active adversary was achieved for $t < \frac{n}{2}$. Information-theoretic security was achieved in [BGW88, CCD88] at the price of lower corruption thresholds, namely $t < \frac{n}{2}$ for passive and $t < \frac{n}{3}$ for active adversaries. The latter bound can be improved to $t < \frac{n}{2}$ if both broadcast channels are assumed and a small error probability is tolerated [RB89, Bea89]. These results were generalized to the non-threshold setting, where the corruption capability of the adversary is not specified by a threshold t, but rather by a so called adversary structure $\mathcal{Z}$, a monotone collection of subsets of the player set, where the adversary can corrupt the players in one of these subsets [HM97].

All mentioned protocols achieve full security, i.e. secrecy, correctness, and robustness. *Secrecy* means that the adversary learns nothing about the honest parties' inputs and outputs (except, of course, for what can be derived from the corrupted parties' inputs and outputs). *Correctness* means that all parties either output the right value or no value at all. *Robustness* means that the adversary cannot prevent the honest parties from learning their respective outputs. This last requirement turns out to be very demanding. Therefore, relaxations of full security have been proposed, where robustness is replaced by weaker output guarantees: *Fairness* means that the adversary can possibly prevent the honest parties from learning their outputs, but then also the corrupted parties do not learn their outputs. *Agreement on abort* means that the adversary can possibly prevent honest parties from learning their output, even while corrupted parties learn their outputs, but then the honest parties at least reach agreement on this fact (and typically make no output). In our constructions, all abort decisions are based on publicly known values. Hence, we have agreement on abort for free.[1]

The traditional setting of MPC has been generalized in two directions. On the one hand, the notion of *hybrid security* was introduced to allow for protocols with different security guarantees depending on the number of corruptions [Cha89, FHHW03, FHW04, IKLP06, Kat07, LRM10, HLMR11]. Intuitively, the more corrupted parties, the less security is guaranteed. This model also allows to analyze each security guarantee separately and independent of other guarantees. On the other hand, protocols were presented that do not restrict the adversary to

---
[1] The impossibility proof holds even when agreement on abort is not required.

a single corruption type [Cha89, DDWY93, FHM98, FHM99, BFH$^+$08, HMZ08, HLMR11]. The *mixed adversaries* considered there can perform each corruption with one out of several corruption types. This allows to consider e.g. active and passive corruption in the same protocol execution.

1.2 Contributions

In this work, we consider a setting with mixed adversaries and hybrid security. This allows, for the first time, to separately analyze the relation between passive corruption and the various security guarantees. It turns out that, in the statistical model, passive corruption does not only affect secrecy, but in particular also correctness. In most statistically secure protocols, some kind of information-theoretic signature is used. When combining active and passive corruptions, one inherent problem of any kind of information-theoretic signature is that passively corrupted parties cannot reliably verify signed values. Existing protocols for the statistical setting assume an honest majority. Therefore, a simple majority vote on the signature guarantees reliable verification even for passively corrupted parties. In this work, we show that this assumption is too strong, and that signatures can be used even without an honest majority. As the main technical contribution, we provide optimal protocols for both general and threshold adversaries that cope with this issue. As a new technique for the setting with general adversaries, we introduce *group commitments*, a non-trivial extension of IC-Signatures, which might be of independent interest.

Furthermore, we introduce the notion of *multi-thresholds*. To the best of our knowledge, all known protocols for threshold mixed adversaries (e.g. [FHM98]) characterize the tolerable adversaries with a single pair of thresholds (one threshold for the number of actively, and one for the number of passively corrupted parties). This pair represents the single maximal adversary that can be tolerated. We generalize this basic characterization to allow for several incomparable maximal adversaries. It turns out that, in our setting, multi-thresholds allow to construct protocols that tolerate strictly more adversaries than a single pair of thresholds, without losing efficiency.

1.3 Model

We consider n parties $p_1, \ldots, p_n$, connected by pairwise synchronous secure channels and authenticated broadcast channels[2], who want to compute some probabilistic function over a finite field $\mathbb{F}$, represented as circuit with input, addition, multiplication, random, and output gates. This function can be reactive, where parties can provide further inputs after having received some intermediate outputs.

There is a central adversary with unlimited computing power who corrupts some parties passively (and reads their internal state) or even actively (and

---

[2] In [PW92] it is shown how broadcast can be implemented given a setup.

makes them misbehave arbitrarily). We denote the actual sets of actively (passively) corrupted parties by $\mathcal{D}^*$ ($\mathcal{E}^*$), where $\mathcal{D}^* \subseteq \mathcal{E}^*$. Uncorrupted parties are called *honest*, non-actively corrupted parties are called *correct*. The security of our protocols is statistical, i.e. information-theoretic with a small error probability. We say a security guarantee holds *statistically* if it holds with overwhelming probability. The guaranteed security properties (secrecy, correctness, fairness, robustness, agreement on abort) depend on $(\mathcal{D}^*, \mathcal{E}^*)$.

For ease of notation, we assume that if a party does not receive an expected message (or receives an invalid message), a default message is used instead. Furthermore, we use subprotocols that might abort. Such an abort is always global, i.e., if any subprotocol aborts, the whole protocol execution halts.

In the analysis of our protocols, we assume "instant randomness", i.e. parties generate their randomness on the fly when needed in the protocol run. This allows even passively corrupted parties to e.g. choose challenges in zero-knowledge proofs that are unpredictable to the adversary. Note that in a setting without secrecy, we have no input independence[3]. Hence, standard techniques (e.g. Blum coin-toss) to jointly generate these challenges are insecure.

1.4 Outline of the Paper

The paper is organized as follows: In Sec. 2, we present information checking, which is used as a basic primitive in our protocols. As a main technical contribution, in Sections 3 and 4, we present protocols for the model with mixed adversaries and hybrid security for both general and threshold adversaries, together with optimal bounds. In Sec. 5, we provide conclusions of our results.

2 Information Checking

Information checking (IC) [RB89, CDD+99] is a primitive that allows a sender to send a value to an intermediary, such that when the receiver obtains this value from the intermediary, he can check that this is indeed the value from the sender. When all parties act as receivers, this primitive is called *IC signature*, and the sender is called signer. IC signatures are realized using a pair of protocols IC-SIGN and IC-REVEAL. IC-SIGN allows a signer to sign a value for a particular intermediary (while providing secrecy with respect to the remaining parties), and IC-REVEAL allows this intermediary to verifiably forward this value to all other parties.

More precisely, let $\langle v \rangle_{i,j}$ denote the state of all players where a value v is *IC-signed* (or simply *signed*) by signer p_i for intermediary p_j. In analogy to traditional signatures, we equivalently say that the intermediary p_j *holds* the signature $\langle v \rangle_{i,j}$. We require that a default signature $\langle v \rangle_{i,j}$ can always be generated given that all parties know the value v, and that signatures are linear, i.e., the

---

[3] That means, the adversary can choose the inputs of actively corrupted parties after learning the inputs of correct parties.

sum of two signatures $\langle v \rangle_{i,j}$ and $\langle v' \rangle_{i,j}$ from signer p_i to intermediary p_j for values v and v', respectively, is a signature from p_i to p_j for the sum $v + v'$. IC-SIGN is a protocol that, given a signer p_i and an intermediary p_j that both know the same value v, provides the following guarantees: If p_i and p_j are correct, IC-SIGN correctly computes a valid signature $\langle v \rangle_{i,j}$ on v without leaking any information about v to the remaining parties. Otherwise, IC-SIGN either correctly computes a valid signature $\langle v \rangle_{i,j}$ on v, or all (correct) parties output $\perp$, with overwhelming probability. Given a signature $\langle v \rangle_{i,j}$, IC-REVEAL robustly computes the output $x_k \in \{(\text{"accept"}, v'), \text{"reject"}\}$ for each p_k. We make the following correctness requirements: If p_j is correct, all correct parties p_k output $x_k = (\text{"accept"}, v)$. Else, if both p_i and p_k are honest, then $x_k \in \{(\text{"accept"}, v), \text{"reject"}\}$ (with overwhelming probability, even when p_j is active). Note that we do not require agreement on the output of correct parties in IC-REVEAL. Furthermore, if p_j is active and p_i or p_k is not honest, then p_k might output $x_k = (\text{"accept"}, v')$ for $v' \neq v$.

In the full version of this paper, we provide an instantiation of IC signatures.

3 MPC with General Adversaries

Traditionally, protocols for general adversaries are characterized by an adversary structure $\mathcal{Z}$ that specifies the tolerated subsets of the player set [HM97]. For our setting, we have to extend this basic representation: On the one hand, we consider mixed adversaries, which are characterized by adversary structures consisting of tuples $(\mathcal{D}, \mathcal{E})$ of subsets of $\mathcal{P}$, where the adversary may corrupt the parties in $\mathcal{E}$ passively, and the parties in $\mathcal{D} \subseteq \mathcal{E}$ even actively. On the other hand, each security guarantee depends on the sets of *actually* corrupted parties $(\mathcal{D}^*, \mathcal{E}^*)$. We consider four security guarantees, namely correctness, secrecy, robustness, and fairness. This is modeled with four adversary structures $\mathcal{Z}^c$, $\mathcal{Z}^s$, $\mathcal{Z}^r$, and $\mathcal{Z}^f$, one for each security requirement[4]: Correctness is guaranteed for $(\mathcal{D}^*, \mathcal{E}^*) \in \mathcal{Z}^c$, secrecy is guaranteed for $(\mathcal{D}^*, \mathcal{E}^*) \in \mathcal{Z}^s$, robustness is guaranteed for $(\mathcal{D}^*, \mathcal{E}^*) \in \mathcal{Z}^r$, and fairness is guaranteed for $(\mathcal{D}^*, \mathcal{E}^*) \in \mathcal{Z}^f$. We have the assumption that $\mathcal{Z}^r \subseteq \mathcal{Z}^c$ and $\mathcal{Z}^f \subseteq \mathcal{Z}^s \subseteq \mathcal{Z}^c$, as secrecy and robustness are not well defined without correctness, and as fairness cannot be achieved without secrecy.

Our protocol for general adversaries is based on [HMZ08], which is an adaptation of the perfectly secure protocol of [Mau02] to the statistical case. For a generic protocol construction, it is sufficient to consider two parameters [HLMR11]: First, the state that is held in the protocol is defined in terms of a parameter that influences the secrecy. This parameter is the sharing parameter $\mathcal{S}$, a collection of subsets of $\mathcal{P}$ that defines which party obtains which values. Second, the reconstruct protocol is expressed in terms of an additional parameter determining the amount of error correction taking place. This parameter is the reconstruction parameter $\mathcal{R}$. In contrast to the perfect case, here we need to

---

[4] Since all our protocols achieve agreement on abort for free, we do not introduce a separate structure for this security property.

consider both active and passive corruption. Therefore, the reconstruction parameter is a monotone collection of pairs $(\mathcal{D}, \mathcal{E})$ of subsets of $\mathcal{P}$ where $\mathcal{D} \subseteq \mathcal{E}$: If all errors can be explained with an adversary $(\mathcal{D}, \mathcal{E}) \in \mathcal{R}$, the errors are corrected and the protocol continues; otherwise it aborts. This implies that the protocol aborts only if the actual adversary is not in $\mathcal{R}$. Such aborts are global, i.e., if some subprotocol aborts, the entire protocol execution halts.

3.1   A Parametrized Protocol for General Adversaries

In the following, we present the parametrized subprotocols for general adversaries and analyze them with respect to correctness, secrecy, and robustness. The main result (including fairness) is discussed in Sec. 3.2. As a first step, we introduce *group commitments* which are a generalization of IC signatures that allow even passively-corrupted parties to reliably verify signatures even without an honest majority. We then use these group commitments to construct a verifiable secret-sharing scheme, and describe how to perform computations on shared values.

Group Commitments. As a first step, we introduce the notion of *group commitments*, which is a pair of protocols GROUPCOMMIT and GROUPREVEAL. GROUPCOMMIT allows a group $\mathcal{G}$ to commit to a value v on which they agree (while providing secrecy with respect to the remaining parties $\mathcal{P} \setminus \mathcal{G}$), and GROUPREVEAL allows them to reveal this value to the remaining parties. Our definitions and protocols for group commitments are based on the IC signatures introduced in Sec. 2.

Definition 1 (IC Group Commitment). *A group $\mathcal{G}$ is IC group committed (or simply committed) to a value v, denoted by $\langle\!\langle v \rangle\!\rangle_\mathcal{G}$, if for all pairs $(p_i, p_j) \in \mathcal{G} \times \mathcal{G}$, v is IC-signed with $\langle v \rangle_{i,j}$.*

Note that a default group commitment $\langle\!\langle v \rangle\!\rangle_\mathcal{G}$ can be generated given that all parties in $\mathcal{P}$ know the value v. Furthermore, if all parties in $\mathcal{G}$ are actively corrupted, then any values held by correct parties constitute a valid group commitment. Additionally, group commitments inherit linearity from the underlying IC signature scheme.

Protocol GROUPCOMMIT: Given a set $\mathcal{G}$ of parties that agree on a value v, compute a valid group commitment $\langle\!\langle v \rangle\!\rangle_\mathcal{G}$ on v.

1. For each pair $(p_i, p_j) \in \mathcal{G} \times \mathcal{G}$ invoke IC-SIGN on v with signer p_i and intermediary p_j.
2. If any invocation of IC-SIGN outputs $\perp$, all parties output $\perp$. Otherwise, each party outputs the concatenation of the outputs of the invocations of IC-SIGN.

Fig. 1. The group commit protocol for a group $\mathcal{G}$

Lemma 1. *Given a set $\mathcal{G}$ of parties that agree on a value v. If all parties in $\mathcal{G}$ are correct (i.e. $\mathcal{G} \cap \mathcal{D}^* = \emptyset$), GROUPCOMMIT correctly computes a valid group commitment $\langle\!\langle v \rangle\!\rangle_\mathcal{G}$ on v. Otherwise, GROUPCOMMIT either correctly computes a valid group commitment $\langle\!\langle v \rangle\!\rangle_\mathcal{G}$ on v, or all parties in $\mathcal{P}$ output $\bot$. GROUPCOMMIT is always secret and robust.*

Proof. SECRECY and ROBUSTNESS follow immediately by inspection. For CORRECTNESS, we first have to show that if the protocol outputs a group commitment, then all signatures held by correct parties p_j are for the value v. This follows from the fact that IC-SIGN always results either in a correct signature $\langle v \rangle_{i,j}$ or in $\bot$, even when the signer (or intermediary) is actively corrupted. Second, if all parties in $\mathcal{G}$ are correct, then it follows from the properties of IC-SIGN that it never outputs $\bot$. □

If a group $\mathcal{G}$ is committed to a value v (e.g. if the GROUPCOMMIT protocol resulted in a valid group commitment and did not output $\bot$), the GROUPREVEAL protocol reveals the value v to all parties in $\mathcal{P}$. During the protocol run, the adversary might be able to provoke conflicts that depend on the sets $\mathcal{D}^*$ and $\mathcal{E}^*$ of corrupted parties. Therefore, we introduce a parameter $\mathcal{R}$, which is a monotone collection of pairs $(\mathcal{D}, \mathcal{E})$ of subsets of the player set, where $\mathcal{D} \subseteq \mathcal{E}$: Whenever all conflicts in a given situation can be explained with an adversary $(\mathcal{D}, \mathcal{E}) \in \mathcal{R}$, the corresponding values are ignored (corrected), and the protocol proceeds; otherwise it aborts. Note that GROUPREVEAL is the only subprotocol that might abort. All other protocols abort only if they use GROUPREVEAL as a subprotocol. Therefore, it is sufficient to discuss agreement on abort only for this protocol.

We emphasize that the conflicts in GROUPREVEAL do not only depend on the set $\mathcal{D}^*$ of actively corrupted parties, but also on the set $\mathcal{E}^*$ of passively corrupted parties, due to their inability to reliably verify IC-signatures. That means, in this protocol, even passive corruptions have a strong impact on correctness (and robustness).

Lemma 2. *Given the reconstruction parameter $\mathcal{R}$, the commitment group $\mathcal{G}$, and a group commitment $\langle\!\langle v \rangle\!\rangle_\mathcal{G}$ for a value v, GROUPREVEAL reveals v to all parties. The protocol is statistically correct if $\mathcal{G} \not\subseteq \mathcal{D}^*$ and*
$$\forall(\mathcal{D}, \mathcal{E}) \in \mathcal{R}:$$
$$\mathcal{G} \setminus \mathcal{D} \not\subseteq \mathcal{D}^* \ \lor \ (\mathcal{G} \not\subseteq \mathcal{E} \ \land \ \mathcal{P} \setminus \mathcal{E} \not\subseteq \mathcal{D}^*) \ \lor \ (\mathcal{G} \not\subseteq \mathcal{E}^* \ \land \ \mathcal{P} \setminus \mathcal{E}^* \not\subseteq \mathcal{D}).$$
The protocol is statistically robust if additionally $(\mathcal{D}^*, \mathcal{E}^*) \in \mathcal{R}$, and always guarantees agreement on abort.

Proof. CORRECTNESS: Consider an actual protocol execution with correct value v and an adversary corrupting $(\mathcal{D}^*, \mathcal{E}^*)$. Denote with $\{\mathcal{V}_u\}$ the resulting collection of subsets of $\mathcal{P}$ in Step 3.

We first show that given the precondition $\mathcal{G} \not\subseteq \mathcal{D}^*$, we have
$$\left(\mathcal{P} \setminus (\mathcal{V}_\bot \cup \mathcal{V}_v) \subseteq \mathcal{D}^*\right) \ \land \ (\mathcal{G} \subseteq \mathcal{E}^* \ \lor \ \mathcal{P} \setminus \mathcal{V}_v \subseteq \mathcal{E}^*).$$
The precondition $\mathcal{G} \not\subseteq \mathcal{D}^*$ implies that there is at least one correct party $p_i \in \mathcal{G}$. In Step 1, this p_i broadcasts its value $u_i(= v)$ and invokes IC-REVEAL on the

---

Protocol GROUPREVEAL: Given the set $\mathcal{G}$ and a group commitment $\langle\!\langle v \rangle\!\rangle_{\mathcal{G}}$, reveal v to all parties.

1. For each party $p_i \in \mathcal{G}$:
   (a) p_i broadcasts v. Denote the broadcasted value with u_i.
   (b) For each party $p_j \in \mathcal{G}$: Invoke IC-REVEAL on $\langle v \rangle_{j,i}$.
   (c) A party $p_k \in \mathcal{P} \setminus \mathcal{G}$ accepts u_i if all invocations of IC-REVEAL output ("accept", u_i).
2. For each party $p_k \in \mathcal{P} \setminus \mathcal{G}$:
   (a) If p_k accepted at least one value in Step 1(c), and all accepted values are the same, then set u_k to this value. Else set $u_k := \bot$.
   (b) p_k broadcasts u_k.
3. Let $\mathcal{V}_u$ denote the set of parties that broadcasted u in Step 1(a) of 2(b), respectively. If $\exists (\mathcal{D}, \mathcal{E}) \in \mathcal{R}$ and a value v', such that
$$\mathcal{P} \setminus (\mathcal{V}_\bot \cup \mathcal{V}_{v'}) \subseteq \mathcal{D} \wedge (\mathcal{G} \subseteq \mathcal{E} \vee \mathcal{P} \setminus \mathcal{V}_{v'} \subseteq \mathcal{E})$$
then output v'. Else abort.

Fig. 2. The group reveal protocol for a group $\mathcal{G}$

signatures $\langle v \rangle_{j,i}$ for $p_j \in \mathcal{G}$. It follows from the properties of IC-REVEAL that all correct parties accept all these signatures. Hence, all correct parties in $\mathcal{P} \setminus \mathcal{G}$ accept the value $u_i (= v)$, and broadcast either v or $\bot$ in Step 2, but not a wrong value, i.e. $\mathcal{P} \setminus (\mathcal{V}_\bot \cup \mathcal{V}_v) \subseteq \mathcal{D}^*$. Furthermore, either $\mathcal{G} \subseteq \mathcal{E}^*$, or there is an honest party $p_j \in \mathcal{G}$. In the latter case, an actively corrupted $p_i \in \mathcal{G}$ can only forge the signatures $\langle v \rangle_{j,i}$ towards passively corrupted parties. Hence, it is guaranteed that all honest parties p_k broadcast the correct value $u_k = v$ in Step 2, and we have $\mathcal{P} \setminus \mathcal{V}_v \subseteq \mathcal{E}^*$.

Second, we show that given the precondition in the lemma, the protocol execution under consideration does not output an (incorrect) value $v' \neq v$, i.e., for all $v' \neq v$ and $(\mathcal{D}, \mathcal{E}) \in \mathcal{R}$ the condition in Step 3 is violated. To arrive at a contradiction, assume that for some $v' \neq v$ and $(\mathcal{D}, \mathcal{E}) \in \mathcal{R}$ it holds that $(\mathcal{P} \setminus (\mathcal{V}_\bot \cup \mathcal{V}_{v'}) \subseteq \mathcal{D}) \wedge (\mathcal{G} \subseteq \mathcal{E} \vee \mathcal{P} \setminus \mathcal{V}_{v'} \subseteq \mathcal{E})$. From above, we have that $(\mathcal{P} \setminus (\mathcal{V}_\bot \cup \mathcal{V}_v) \subseteq \mathcal{D}^*) \wedge (\mathcal{G} \subseteq \mathcal{E}^* \vee \mathcal{P} \setminus \mathcal{V}_v \subseteq \mathcal{E}^*)$. Furthermore, by assumption we have that the precondition in the lemma is fulfilled. We split the proof according to which or-term of the second part of this precondition is fulfilled for the given $(\mathcal{D}, \mathcal{E})$:

Case $\mathcal{G} \setminus \mathcal{D} \not\subseteq \mathcal{D}^*$: Since $\mathcal{P} \setminus (\mathcal{V}_\bot \cup \mathcal{V}_{v'}) \subseteq \mathcal{D}$ and $\mathcal{G} \subseteq \mathcal{P}$, we have $\mathcal{G} \setminus (\mathcal{V}_\bot \cup \mathcal{V}_{v'}) \subseteq \mathcal{D}$. It follows by inspection of the protocol that $\mathcal{G}$ and $\mathcal{V}_\bot$ are disjoint. Hence we have $\mathcal{G} \setminus \mathcal{V}_{v'} \subseteq \mathcal{D}$. Analogously, it follows from $\mathcal{P} \setminus (\mathcal{V}_\bot \cup \mathcal{V}_v) \subseteq \mathcal{D}^*$ that $\mathcal{G} \setminus \mathcal{V}_v \subseteq \mathcal{D}^*$. Therefore we have that $\mathcal{G} \subseteq \mathcal{D} \cup \mathcal{D}^*$, which is a contradiction to $\mathcal{G} \setminus \mathcal{D} \not\subseteq \mathcal{D}^*$.

Case $\mathcal{G} \not\subseteq \mathcal{E} \wedge \mathcal{P} \setminus \mathcal{E} \not\subseteq \mathcal{D}^*$: Since $\mathcal{G} \not\subseteq \mathcal{E}$, we have $\mathcal{P} \setminus \mathcal{V}_{v'} \subseteq \mathcal{E}$. Furthermore, we have that $\mathcal{P} \setminus (\mathcal{V}_\bot \cup \mathcal{V}_v) \subseteq \mathcal{D}^*$. It follows by inspection from the protocol that $\mathcal{V}_\bot, \mathcal{V}_{v'}$, and $\mathcal{V}_v$ are pairwise disjoint. Hence, we have that $\mathcal{P} \subseteq \mathcal{D}^* \cup \mathcal{E}$, which is a contradiction to $\mathcal{P} \setminus \mathcal{E} \not\subseteq \mathcal{D}^*$.

Case $\mathcal{G} \not\subseteq \mathcal{E}^* \wedge \mathcal{P} \setminus \mathcal{E}^* \not\subseteq \mathcal{D}$**:** This proof is identical to the previous case, with the only difference that $(\mathcal{D}^*, \mathcal{E}^*)$ is swapped with $(\mathcal{D}, \mathcal{E})$ and v with v'.

ROBUSTNESS: In the proof of correctness, we have shown that
$$(\mathcal{P} \setminus (\mathcal{V}_\perp \cup \mathcal{V}_v) \subseteq \mathcal{D}^*) \wedge (\mathcal{G} \subseteq \mathcal{E}^* \vee \mathcal{P} \setminus \mathcal{V}_v \subseteq \mathcal{E}^*).$$
Hence, given the correctness condition and $(\mathcal{D}^*, \mathcal{E}^*) \in \mathcal{R}$, it follows immediately that the condition in Step 3 is fulfilled for the correct value v and $(\mathcal{D}^*, \mathcal{E}^*)$, i.e., that the protocol terminates without abort.
AGREEMENT ON ABORT: Since the abort decision is based only on broadcasted values, we always have agreement on abort.   □

Given group commitments, protocols for sharing, reconstruction, addition, and multiplication can be constructed in a rather straightforward manner. Due to lack of space, the description of these protocols, as well as the proof of security of the parametrized protocol $\pi^{\mathcal{S},\mathcal{R}}$ (as stated in the following lemma) was moved to the full version of this paper.

Lemma 3. *Given the sharing specification $\mathcal{S}$ and the reconstruction parameter $\mathcal{R}$, the protocol $\pi^{\mathcal{S},\mathcal{R}}$ guarantees statistical correctness if*

$$\forall (\mathcal{D}, \mathcal{E}) \in \mathcal{R}, S, S' \in \mathcal{S} : \quad S \cap S' \neq \emptyset \quad \wedge \quad S \not\subseteq \mathcal{D}^* \quad \wedge$$
$$(S \setminus \mathcal{D} \not\subseteq \mathcal{D}^* \vee (S \not\subseteq \mathcal{E} \wedge \mathcal{P} \setminus \mathcal{E} \not\subseteq \mathcal{D}^*) \vee (S \not\subseteq \mathcal{E}^* \wedge \mathcal{P} \setminus \mathcal{E}^* \not\subseteq \mathcal{D}))$$

Furthermore, the protocol guarantees statistical secrecy *if additionally $\exists S \in \mathcal{S} :$ $S \cap \mathcal{E}^* = \emptyset$, and/or* statistical robustness *if additionally $(\mathcal{D}^*, \mathcal{E}^*) \in \mathcal{R}$.*

3.2 Main Result

The following theorem states the optimal bound for statistically secure MPC for general adversaries with both mixed adversaries and hybrid security. We show that the bound is sufficient for MPC by providing parameters for the generalized protocols described above. In the full version of this paper, we prove that the bound is also necessary.

Theorem 1. *In the secure channels model with broadcast and general adversaries, statistically secure (reactive) MPC among $n \geq 2$ parties with respect to $(\mathcal{Z}^c, \mathcal{Z}^s, \mathcal{Z}^r, \mathcal{Z}^f)$, where $\mathcal{Z}^r \subseteq \mathcal{Z}^c$ and $\mathcal{Z}^f \subseteq \mathcal{Z}^s \subseteq \mathcal{Z}^c$, is possible if $\mathcal{Z}^s = \{(\emptyset, \emptyset)\}$ or*

$$\forall (\cdot, \mathcal{E}^s), (\cdot, \mathcal{E}^{s'}) \in \mathcal{Z}^s, (\mathcal{D}^r, \mathcal{E}^r) \in \mathcal{Z}^r, (\mathcal{D}^c, \mathcal{E}^c) \in \mathcal{Z}^c :$$
$$\mathcal{E}^s \cup \mathcal{E}^{s'} \neq \mathcal{P} \quad \wedge \quad \mathcal{E}^s \cup \mathcal{D}^c \neq \mathcal{P} \quad \wedge$$
$$\left(\mathcal{D}^c \cup \mathcal{D}^r \cup \mathcal{E}^s \neq \mathcal{P} \vee (\mathcal{E}^s \cup \mathcal{E}^r \neq \mathcal{P} \wedge \mathcal{D}^c \cup \mathcal{E}^r \neq \mathcal{P}) \right.$$
$$\left. \vee (\mathcal{E}^s \cup \mathcal{E}^c \neq \mathcal{P} \wedge \mathcal{D}^r \cup \mathcal{E}^c \neq \mathcal{P}) \right)$$

This bound is tight: If violated, there are (reactive) functionalities that cannot be securely computed.

Proof (Sufficiency). If $\mathcal{Z}^s = \{(\emptyset, \emptyset)\}$, there is no secrecy requirement, and we can directly use the trivial non-secret protocol described in the Appendix of [HLMR11]. Otherwise, we employ the protocol $\pi^{\mathcal{S},\mathcal{R}}$ described in Sec. 3.1. We set $\mathcal{S} := \{\overline{\mathcal{E}^s} \mid (\cdot, \mathcal{E}^s) \in \mathcal{Z}^s\}$ and $\mathcal{R} = \mathcal{Z}^r \cup \mathcal{Z}^f$.

We apply Lemma 3 to derive correctness, secrecy and robustness: Given the bound in the theorem, the choice of the structures $\mathcal{S}$ and $\mathcal{R}$, and the fact that $(\mathcal{D}^*, \mathcal{E}^*)$ is an element of the corresponding adversary structure, it is easy to verify that the condition for each property is fulfilled. In particular, note that the correctness condition is also fulfilled for $(\mathcal{D}, \mathcal{E}) \in \mathcal{Z}^f$: Using that $\mathcal{Z}^f \subseteq \mathcal{Z}^s$, we have that $\mathcal{E}^s \cup \mathcal{E} \subseteq \mathcal{E}^s \cup \mathcal{E}^{s'} \neq \mathcal{P}$ (for some $\mathcal{E}^{s'}$) and $\mathcal{D}^c \cup \mathcal{E} \subseteq \mathcal{D}^c \cup \mathcal{E}^s \neq \mathcal{P}$ (where the inequalities follow from the second line of the condition in the theorem). This implies the condition for correctness.

Note that by our choice of $\mathcal{R}$, we have $\mathcal{Z}^f \subseteq \mathcal{R}$. Hence, for $(\mathcal{D}^*, \mathcal{E}^*) \in \mathcal{Z}^f$ the protocol is robust, and the adversary cannot abort. □

4   MPC with Threshold Adversaries

Trivially, the protocol for general adversaries can also be applied to the special case of threshold adversaries. Yet, protocols for general adversaries are super-polynomial in the number of parties for most adversary structures. Therefore, we present a protocol that exploits the symmetry of threshold adversaries, and is efficient in the number of parties.

The characterization for general adversaries (Sec. 3) can be adjusted for threshold adversaries: A mixed adversary is characterized by two thresholds (t_a, t_p), where he may corrupt up to t_p parties passively, and up to t_a of these parties even actively. The level of security (correctness, secrecy, robustness, and fairness) depends only on the number $(|\mathcal{D}^*|, |\mathcal{E}^*|)$ of actually corrupted parties. In the perfect setting [HLMR11], this is modeled with four pairs of thresholds, one for each security requirement, specifying the upper bound on the number of corruptions that the adversary may perform, such that the corresponding security requirement is still guaranteed. In the statistical setting, it follows from the bound for general adversaries that we need to consider multiple pairs of thresholds for each security guarantee. Consider the following example: Let $n = 6$ and $t_p^s = 2$. It is possible to obtain correctness for $(|\mathcal{D}^*|, |\mathcal{E}^*|) \leq (2,6)$ and $(|\mathcal{D}^*|, |\mathcal{E}^*|) \leq (3,3)$, and robustness for $(|\mathcal{D}^*|, |\mathcal{E}^*|) \leq (1,6)$ and $(|\mathcal{D}^*|, |\mathcal{E}^*|) \leq (2,3)$ in the same protocol. Yet, correctness and robustness cannot be guaranteed for $(|\mathcal{D}^*|, |\mathcal{E}^*|) \leq (3,6)$ and $(|\mathcal{D}^*|, |\mathcal{E}^*|) \leq (2,6)$, respectively. Hence, this situation cannot be captured using only a single pair of thresholds for each security guarantee. Therefore, we introduce multi-thresholds T, i.e. collections of pairs of thresholds (t_a, t_p).

We consider the four multi-thresholds T^c, T^s, T^r, and T^f:[5] Correctness is guaranteed for $(|\mathcal{D}^*|, |\mathcal{E}^*|) \leq T^c$,[6] secrecy is guaranteed for $(|\mathcal{D}^*|, |\mathcal{E}^*|) \leq T^s$,

---

[5] As in the setting with general adversaries, we do not introduce a separate multi-threshold for agreement on abort.

[6] We write $(t_a, t_p) \leq T$ if $\exists (t_a', t_p') \in T : (t_a, t_p) \leq (t_a', t_p')$, where $(t_a, t_p) \leq (t_a', t_p')$ is a shorthand for $t_a \leq t_a'$ and $t_p \leq t_p'$.

robustness is guaranteed for $(|\mathcal{D}^*|, |\mathcal{E}^*|) \leq T^r$, and fairness is guaranteed for $(|\mathcal{D}^*|, |\mathcal{E}^*|) \leq T^f$. Again, we have the assumption that $T^r \leq T^c$ and $T^f \leq T^s \leq T^r$,[7] as secrecy and robustness are not well defined without correctness, and as fairness cannot be achieved without secrecy.

For threshold adversaries, we proceed along the lines of the general adversary case: We generalize the protocol of [FHM98, CDD+99] and introduce the *sharing parameter* d (corresponding to $\mathcal{S}$), and the *reconstruction parameter* E (corresponding to $\mathcal{R}$). Since we consider multi-thresholds, the reconstruction parameter E is a list of pairs (e_a, e_p) where $e_a \leq e_p$. Since for secrecy the actively corrupted parties $\mathcal{D}^*$ are not relevant, there cannot be two incomparable maximal adversaries. Hence, a single threshold is sufficient.

In this section, we assume that each party p_i is assigned a unique and publicly known evaluation point $\alpha_i \in \mathbb{F} \setminus \{0\}$. This implies that the field $\mathbb{F}$ must have more than n elements.

4.1 A Parametrized Protocol for Threshold Adversaries

In the following, we present the parametrized subprotocols and analyze them with respect to correctness, secrecy, and robustness. The main result (including fairness) is discussed in Sec. 4.2. The protocol is based on IC signatures as introduced in Sec. 2.

Verifiable Secret Sharing. The state of the protocol is maintained with a Shamir sharing [Sha79] of each intermediate result.

Definition 2 (*d-Sharing*). *A value s is d-shared when (1) there is a polynomial $\hat{s}(x)$ of degree d with $\hat{s}(0) = s$, and every party p_i holds a share $s_i = \hat{s}(\alpha_i)$, (2) for each share s_i, p_i holds a share polynomial $\hat{s}_i(y)$ of degree d with $\hat{s}_i(0) = s_i$, and every party p_j holds a share share $s_{ij} = \hat{s}_i(\alpha_j)$, and (3) for each share share s_{ij}, party p_i holds a signature $\langle s_{ij} \rangle_{j,i}$, and p_j holds a signature $\langle s_{ij} \rangle_{i,j}$. We denote a d-sharing of s with $[s]$, and the share s_i with $[s]_i$. A sharing parameter d is t-permissive, if the shares of all but t parties uniquely define the secret, i.e., $n - t > d$.*

Note that it follows from the linearity of Shamir sharings (i.e. a polynomial $\hat{s}(x)$ with $\hat{s}(0) = s$ where each party $p_j \in \mathcal{P}$ holds $\hat{s}(\alpha_j)$) and IC signatures, that d-sharings are linear.

Lemma 4. *Let $d < n$ be the sharing parameter. A d-sharing is secret if $|\mathcal{E}^*| \leq d$, and uniquely defines a value if d is $|\mathcal{D}^*|$-permissive.*

Proof. It follows directly from the properties of a polynomial of degree d that secrecy is guaranteed if the number $|\mathcal{E}^*|$ of (actively or passively) corrupted parties is at most d. Furthermore, $n - |\mathcal{D}^*| > d$ implies that there are at least $d + 1$ correct parties whose shares uniquely define a share polynomial.   □

The share protocol takes as input a secret s from a dealer, and outputs a d-sharing $[s]$ (see Fig. 3).

---

[7] We write $T_1 \leq T_2$ if $\forall (t_a, t_p) \in T_1, \exists (t'_a, t'_p) \in T_2 : (t_a, t_p) \leq (t'_a, t'_p)$.

Protocol SHARE: Given input s from the dealer, compute a d-sharing $[s]$ of s.

1. The dealer chooses a random (bivariate) polynomial $g(x,y)$ with $g(0,0) = s$, of degree d in both variables, and sends to each party $p_i \in \mathcal{P}$ the (univariate) polynomials $k_i(y) = g(\alpha_i, y)$ and $h_i(x) = g(x, \alpha_i)$.

2. For each pair of parties (p_i, p_j): p_i sends $k_i(\alpha_j)$ to party p_j, and p_j checks whether $k_i(\alpha_j) = h_j(\alpha_i)$. If this check fails, it broadcasts a complaint.

3. For all $k_i(\alpha_j)$, for which no inconsistency was reported, IC-SIGN is invoked once with signer p_j and intermediary p_i to compute the signature $\langle k_i(\alpha_j) \rangle_{j,i}$, and once with signer p_i and intermediary p_j to compute the signature $\langle k_i(\alpha_j) \rangle_{i,j}$.

4. The dealer broadcasts each value for which either an inconsistency was reported (Step 2), or the output of IC-SIGN was $\perp$ (Step 3), and a default signature is used.

5. If some party p_i observes an inconsistency between the polynomials received in Step 1 and the broadcasted values in Step 4, it accuses the dealer. The dealer answers the accusation by broadcasting both $k_i(y)$ and $h_i(x)$. Now, if some other party p_j observes an inconsistency between the polynomial received in Step 1 and these broadcasted polynomials, it also accuses the dealer. This step is repeated until no additional party accuses the dealer. For all broadcasted values, default signatures are used.

6. If the dealer does not answer some complaint or accusation, or if the broadcasted values contradict each other, the parties output a default d-sharing of a default value (with default signatures). Otherwise, each party p_i outputs the share $s_i := k_i(0)$, the share polynomial $\hat{s}_i(y) := k_i(y)$ with signatures $\langle \hat{s}_i(\alpha_j) \rangle_{j,i}$ (for $j = 1, \ldots, n$), and the share shares $s_{ji} := h_i(\alpha_j)$ with signatures $\langle s_{ji} \rangle_{j,i}$ (for $j = 1, \ldots, n$). The dealer outputs $\hat{s}(x) := g(x, 0)$.

Fig. 3. The share protocol for threshold adversaries

Lemma 5. *Let $d < n$ be the sharing parameter. On input s from the dealer, SHARE correctly, secretly, and robustly computes a d-sharing. If d is $|\mathcal{D}^*|$-permissive, and if the dealer is correct, the sharing uniquely defines the secret s.*

Proof. SECRECY: It follows from the properties of a bivariate polynomial that $g(x,y)$ reveals no more information about s than the specified output. After Step 1, the adversary does not obtain any additional information: In Step 4, a value s_{ij} is broadcasted only if p_i, p_j or the dealer is actively corrupted, i.e., the adversary knew the value already beforehand. Hence, the protocol does not leak more information than the specified output, and thus always provides secrecy.

CORRECTNESS: First, we have to show that the protocol outputs a valid d-sharing. Due to the bilateral consistency checks, any inconsistency in the values held by correct parties is detected in Step 2 and resolved in Step 4. Therefore, the values held by correct parties uniquely define a polynomial $g'(x,y)$ of degree d, which implies that $g'(x,0)$ is of degree d. Furthermore, it follows from the properties of IC-SIGN that in Step 3, either a correct IC-signature is computed, or all parties output $\perp$. In the latter case, a default (and hence correct) IC-signature is used. Therefore, the output is a valid d-sharing. Second, we have to show that if d is $|\mathcal{D}^*|$-permissive and if the dealer is correct, then the shared value equals the input of the dealer. A correct dealer can always consistently answer all complains and accusations with the correct values. Hence, if d is $|\mathcal{D}^*|$-permissive, the unique value defined by the sharing is the secret s.

ROBUSTNESS: By inspection, the protocol does not abort.   □

The public reconstruction protocol (Fig. 4) proceeds sharewise: For each share s_i, first party p_i broadcasts the share s_i together with the sharing polynomial $\hat{s}_i(y)$, and opens the signatures on all share shares $\hat{s}_i(\alpha_j)$. Second, all parties broadcast their share shares s_{ij}, and open the corresponding signatures. If active corruption took place, these two steps might produce conflicts between certain parties. Note that these conflicts do not only depend on the actively, but also on the passively corrupted parties, due to their inability to reliably verify IC-signatures. If these conflicts can be explained with an adversary corrupting $(|\mathcal{D}^*|, |\mathcal{E}^*|) \leq E$, then the share is accepted. Otherwise it is ignored. This technique allows also passively-corrupted parties to reliably verify signatures and therefore reconstruct the correct value. Finally, the secret is reconstructed using the accepted shares. Note that PUBLIC RECONSTRUCTION is the only subprotocol that might abort. All other protocols abort only if they use PUBLIC RECONSTRUCTION as a subprotocol and the invocation thereof aborts. Therefore, it is sufficient to discuss agreement on abort only for this protocol.

Lemma 6. *Given the sharing parameter d, the reconstruction parameter E, and a d-sharing $[s]$ of some value s, PUBLIC RECONSTRUCTION reconstructs s to all parties. The protocol is statistically correct if $|\mathcal{D}^*| < n - d$ and*

$$\forall (e_a, e_p) \in E : \ |\mathcal{D}^*| < n - d - e_a \ \lor$$
$$(d + e_p < n \ \land \ |\mathcal{D}^*| < n - e_p) \ \lor \ (|\mathcal{E}^*| < n - d \ \land \ |\mathcal{E}^*| < n - e_a).$$

Furthermore, it is statistically robust if additionally $(|\mathcal{D}^*|, |\mathcal{E}^*|) \leq E$, and always guarantees agreement on abort.

Proof. CORRECTNESS: The protocol outputs a value only if at least $d+1$ shares are accepted. Trivially, the output is correct if all accepted shares are correct, i.e., when incorrect shares are not accepted. More precisely, we have to show that for any incorrect share $s_i' \neq s_i$ and for each $(e_a, e_p) \in E$, the condition in Step 1(d) is violated. In this proof, we distinguish three cases, depending on which or-term of the condition in the lemma is fulfilled:

i. *Case $|\mathcal{D}^*| < n - d - e_a$:*
   In order to broadcast a wrong share $s_i' \neq s_i$, an actively corrupted party p_i has to change the value of at least $n - d$ share shares. At least $n - d - |\mathcal{D}^*|$ of these share shares belong to correct parties that subsequently vote "no", i.e. $r \geq n - d - |\mathcal{D}^*|$. Since $|\mathcal{D}^*| < n - d - e_a$, this implies $r > e_a$, and the share is not accepted.

Protocol PUBLIC RECONSTRUCTION: Given a d-sharing $[s]$ of some value s, reconstruct s to all parties.

1. For each party p_i:
   (a) p_i broadcasts $\hat{s}_i(y)$ and invokes IC-REVEAL on the signatures $\langle \hat{s}_i(\alpha_j) \rangle_{j,i}$ ($j = 1, \ldots, n$) of all share shares.
   (b) Each p_j broadcasts its share share s_{ij} and invokes IC-REVEAL on the corresponding signature $\langle s_{ij} \rangle_{i,j}$.
   (c) **Voting:** Each p_k checks whether
      i. the polynomial $\hat{s}_i(y)$ broadcasted in Step 1(a) is consistent with its share share, i.e. $s_{ik} = \hat{s}_i(\alpha_k)$,
      ii. the output of all invocations of IC-REVEAL in Step 1(a) was "accept",
      iii. for all s_{ij} broadcasted in Step 1(b) either $s_{ij} = \hat{s}_i(\alpha_j)$ or the output of IC-REVEAL on the corresponding signature $\langle s_{ij} \rangle_{i,j}$ was "reject".
      p_k broadcasts "yes" if all checks succeed, "no" if check i. or ii. fails, and $\perp$ otherwise. Let a and r denote the number of parties broadcasting "yes" and "no", respectively.
   (d) **Decision:** Accept s_i if $\exists (e_a, e_p) \in E : r \leq e_a \ \wedge \ (e_p + d \geq n \ \vee \ a \geq n - e_p)$. Otherwise ignore s_i.
2. **Output:** If at least $d + 1$ shares are accepted, interpolate these shares with a polynomial $\hat{s}'(x)$ and output $\hat{s}'(0)$. Otherwise abort.

Fig. 4. The public reconstruction protocol for threshold adversaries

ii. *Case $d + e_p < n \ \wedge \ |\mathcal{D}^*| < n - e_p$:*
Since $|\mathcal{D}^*| < n - d$, there are at least $d + 1$ correct parties. Hence, in order to broadcast a wrong share $s'_i \neq s_i$, an actively corrupted party p_i has to change the value of at least one share share belonging to a correct party. In Step 1(b), this correct party broadcasts the correct share share with a valid signature, and no correct party accepts the wrong share s'_i, i.e. $a \leq |\mathcal{D}^*|$. Since $|\mathcal{D}^*| < n - e_p$, we have $a < n - e_p$. Since we also have $d + e_p < n$, the share is not accepted.

iii. *Case $|\mathcal{E}^*| < n - d \ \wedge \ |\mathcal{E}^*| < n - e_a$:*
Since $|\mathcal{E}^*| < n - d$, there are at least $d + 1$ honest parties. Hence, in order to broadcast a wrong share $s'_i \neq s_i$, an actively corrupted party has to change the value of at least one share share belonging to an honest party, and to create the signature on this (incorrect) share share. All honest parties notice that this signature is not valid and reject, i.e., $r \geq n - |\mathcal{E}^*|$. Since $|\mathcal{E}^*| < n - e_a$, we have $r > e_a$, and the share is not accepted.

ROBUSTNESS: Given that the correctness condition holds, the protocol guarantees robustness if enough (i.e. $d + 1$) shares are accepted. Let $(e_a, e_p) \in E$ such that $(|\mathcal{D}^*|, |\mathcal{E}^*|) \leq (e_a, e_p)$. First, observe that if party p_i is correct, then $r \leq e_a$: All share shares and signatures broadcasted in Step 1(a) are correct and valid. Therefore, no correct party votes "no". Furthermore, if party p_i is honest, then $a \geq n - e_p$: If some p_j broadcasts a contradicting (wrong) share share in Step 1(b), then the signature on this share share is invalid for all honest parties.

It follows from the two observations above that shares from honest parties are always accepted. If $e_p + d < n$, then there are at least $d + 1$ honest parties and the protocol does not abort. Otherwise, if $e_p + d \geq n$, then also shares from correct parties are accepted. Since $|\mathcal{D}^*| < n - d$ there are always at least $d + 1$ correct parties and the protocol does not abort.

AGREEMENT ON ABORT: Since the abort decision is based only on broadcasted values, we always have agreement on abort. □

Addition, Multiplication, and Random Values. Linear functions (and in particular additions) can be computed locally, since d-sharings are linear: Given sharings $[a]$ and $[b]$, and a constant c, one can easily compute the sharings $[a]+[b]$, $c[a]$, and $[a] + c$. Computing a shared random value can be achieved by letting each party p_i share a random value r_i, and computing $[r] = [r_1] + \ldots + [r_n]$.

For the multiplication of two shared values, we first provide a non-robust multiplication protocol, which we then make robust using *dispute control* [BH06] and *circuit randomization* [Bea91]. Due to lack of space, the full description of the multiplication protocol was moved to the full version of this paper.

The Security of the Parametrized Protocol. Considering the security of the subprotocols described above, we can derive the security of the parametrized protocol, denoted by $\pi^{d,E}$:

Lemma 7. *Let d be the sharing parameter, and E be the reconstruction parameter, the protocol $\pi^{d,E}$ guarantees statistical correctness if $d < n - |\mathcal{D}^*|$, $2d < n$, and*

$$\forall (e_a, e_p) \in E : \quad |\mathcal{D}^*| < n - d - e_a \ \vee$$
$$(d + e_p < n \ \wedge \ |\mathcal{D}^*| < n - e_p) \ \vee \ (|\mathcal{E}^*| < n - d \ \wedge \ |\mathcal{E}^*| < n - e_a).$$

Furthermore, the protocol guarantees statistical secrecy if additionally $|\mathcal{E}^*| \leq d$, and/or statistical robustness if additionally $(|\mathcal{D}^*|, |\mathcal{E}^*|) \leq E$.

Proof. $\pi^{d,E}$ provides a certain security guarantee against $(|\mathcal{D}^*|, |\mathcal{E}^*|)$ if all subprotocols and the sharing provide this guarantee against $(|\mathcal{D}^*|, |\mathcal{E}^*|)$. For each guarantee, it can easily be verified that the condition in the lemma implies the conditions in the corresponding lemmas. □

4.2 Main Result

The following theorem states the optimal bound for statistically secure MPC for threshold adversaries with both mixed adversaries and hybrid security. We show that the bound is sufficient for MPC by providing parameters for the generalized protocols described above. The necessity of the bound follows directly from the corresponding proof for general adversaries that can be found in the full version of this paper.

Theorem 2. *In the secure channels model with broadcast and threshold adversaries, statistically secure (reactive) MPC among $n \geq 2$ parties with multithresholds T^c, T^s, T^r, and T^f, where $T^f \leq T^s \leq T^c$ and $T^r \leq T^c$, is possible if $T^s = \{(0,0)\}$ or*

$$\forall (t_a^c, t_p^c) \in T^c, (t_a^r, t_p^r) \in T^r, (\cdot, t_p^s), (\cdot, t_p^{s\prime}) \in T^s :$$
$$t_p^s + t_p^{s\prime} < n \quad \wedge \quad t_p^s + t_a^c < n \quad \wedge$$
$$\left(t_a^c + t_a^r + t_p^s < n \quad \vee \quad (t_p^s + t_p^r < n \wedge t_a^c + t_a^r < n) \right.$$
$$\left. \vee \ (t_p^s + t_p^c < n \wedge t_a^r + t_p^c < n) \right)$$

This bound is tight: If violated, there are (reactive) functionalities that cannot be securely computed.

Proof (Sufficiency). If $T^s = \{(0,0)\}$, there is no secrecy requirement, and we can directly use the trivial non-secret protocol described in the Appendix of [HLMR11]. Otherwise, we employ the parametrized version $\pi^{d,E}$ of the protocol of [BGW88] described in Sec. 4.1 with $d := \tilde{t}_p^s$ and $E := T^r \cup T^f$, where $\tilde{t}_p^s = \max\{t_p^s \mid (\cdot, t_p^s) \in T^s\}$.

We apply Lemma 7 to derive correctness, secrecy and robustness: Given the bound in the theorem, the choice of the parameters d and E, and the fact that $(|\mathcal{D}^*|, |\mathcal{E}^*|)$ is below the corresponding threshold, it is easy to verify that the condition for each property is fulfilled. In particular, note that the correctness condition is also fulfilled for $(e_a, e_p) \in T^f$: Using that $T^f \leq T^s$, we have $d + e_p \leq 2\tilde{t}_p^s < n$ and $e_a + e_p \leq t_a^c + d < n$ (where the inequalities follow from the second line of the condition in the theorem with $t_p^s = t_p^{s\prime} = \tilde{t}_p^s$).

For fairness, note that $T^f \leq E$. Hence, for $(|\mathcal{D}^*|, |\mathcal{E}^*|) \leq (t_a^f, t_p^f)$ the protocol is robust, and the adversary cannot abort. $\qquad\Box$

5   Conclusion

Our results provide insights into the relations between passive corruption and different security requirements. The bounds presented in this work quantify the impact of passively corrupted parties on all security guarantees. We have shown that, in the statistical setting, passively corrupted parties play a significant role for all security guarantees, and not only for secrecy. Consider the following example: Let $n = 4$, $t_a^c = 2$, $t_p^c = 2$, $t_a^r = 1$, $t_p^r = 2$, and $t_p^s = 1$. For this choice of thresholds, the construction in this paper provides a protocol that is correct and robust (given that the adversary remains below the corresponding thresholds). Yet, we show that it is impossible to construct a protocol that tolerates a single additional passive corruption.

Furthermore, in addition to the known tradeoff between different security guarantees like robustness and correctness [HLMR11], we obtain a novel tradeoff between active and passive corruptions even when only considering a single security guarantee.

Solutions for the setting with general adversaries encompass all possible adversary structures. Yet, these protocols are usually superpolynomial in the number of parties. Therefore, protocols for the setting with threshold adversaries are of more practical relevance. In this work, we provide the first protocol allowing for multi-thresholds, a setting that is strictly more flexible than single-thresholds. This constitutes a substantial step towards general adversaries without losing efficiency.

References

[Bea89]   Beaver, D.: Multiparty Protocols Tolerating Half Faulty Processors. In: Brassard, G. (ed.) CRYPTO 1989. LNCS, vol. 435, pp. 560–572. Springer, Heidelberg (1990)

[Bea91]   Beaver, D.: Efficient Multiparty Protocols Using Circuit Randomization. In: Feigenbaum, J. (ed.) CRYPTO 1991. LNCS, vol. 576, pp. 420–432. Springer, Heidelberg (1992)

[BFH+08]   Beerliová-Trubíniová, Z., Fitzi, M., Hirt, M., Maurer, U., Zikas, V.: MPC vs. SFE: Perfect Security in a Unified Corruption Model. In: Canetti, R. (ed.) TCC 2008. LNCS, vol. 4948, pp. 231–250. Springer, Heidelberg (2008)

[BGW88]   Ben-Or, M., Goldwasser, S., Wigderson, A.: Completeness theorems for non-cryptographic fault-tolerant distributed computation. In: STOC 1988, pp. 1–10. ACM (1988)

[BH06]   Beerliová-Trubíniová, Z., Hirt, M.: Efficient Multi-party Computation with Dispute Control. In: Halevi, S., Rabin, T. (eds.) TCC 2006. LNCS, vol. 3876, pp. 305–328. Springer, Heidelberg (2006)

[CCD88]   Chaum, D., Crépeau, C., Damgård, I.: Multiparty unconditionally secure protocols. In: STOC 1988, pp. 11–19. ACM (1988)

[CDD+99]   Cramer, R., Damgård, I., Dziembowski, S., Hirt, M., Rabin, T.: Efficient Multiparty Computations Secure against an Adaptive Adversary. In: Stern, J. (ed.) EUROCRYPT 1999. LNCS, vol. 1592, pp. 311–326. Springer, Heidelberg (1999)

[Cha89]   Chaum, D.: The Spymasters Double-Agent Problem: Multiparty Computations Secure Unconditionally from Minorities and Cryptograhically from Majorities. In: Brassard, G. (ed.) CRYPTO 1989. LNCS, vol. 435, pp. 591–602. Springer, Heidelberg (1990)

[DDWY93]   Dolev, D., Dwork, C., Waarts, O., Yung, M.: Perfectly secure message transmission. Journal of the ACM 40(1), 17–47 (1993)

[FHHW03]   Fitzi, M., Hirt, M., Holenstein, T., Wullschleger, J.: Two-Threshold Broadcast and Detectable Multi-party Computation. In: Biham, E. (ed.) EUROCRYPT 2003. LNCS, vol. 2656, pp. 51–67. Springer, Heidelberg (2003)

[FHM98]   Fitzi, M., Hirt, M., Maurer, U.: Trading Correctness for Privacy in Unconditional Multi-party Computation (Extended Abstract). In: Krawczyk, H. (ed.) CRYPTO 1998. LNCS, vol. 1462, pp. 121–136. Springer, Heidelberg (1998)

[FHM99]   Fitzi, M., Hirt, M., Maurer, U.M.: General Adversaries in Unconditional Multi-party Computation. In: Lam, K.-Y., Okamoto, E., Xing, C. (eds.) ASIACRYPT 1999. LNCS, vol. 1716, pp. 232–246. Springer, Heidelberg (1999)

[FHW04]   Fitzi, M., Holenstein, T., Wullschleger, J.: Multi-party Computation with Hybrid Security. In: Cachin, C., Camenisch, J.L. (eds.) EUROCRYPT 2004. LNCS, vol. 3027, pp. 419–438. Springer, Heidelberg (2004)

[GMW87]   Goldreich, O., Micali, S., Wigderson, A.: How to play any mental game or a completeness theorem for protocols with honest majority. In: STOC 1987, pp. 218–229. ACM (1987)

[HLMR11] Hirt, M., Lucas, C., Maurer, U., Raub, D.: Graceful Degradation in Multi-Party Computation (Extended Abstract). In: Fehr, S. (ed.) ICITS 2011. LNCS, vol. 6673, pp. 163–180. Springer, Heidelberg (2011)

[HM97]   Hirt, M., Maurer, U.: Complete characterization of adversaries tolerable in secure multi-party computation. In: PODC 1997, pp. 25–34. ACM (1997)

[HMZ08]   Hirt, M., Maurer, U.M., Zikas, V.: MPC vs. SFE: Unconditional and Computational Security. In: Pieprzyk, J. (ed.) ASIACRYPT 2008. LNCS, vol. 5350, pp. 1–18. Springer, Heidelberg (2008)

[IKLP06] Ishai, Y., Kushilevitz, E., Lindell, Y., Petrank, E.: On Combining Privacy with Guaranteed Output Delivery in Secure Multiparty Computation. In: Dwork, C. (ed.) CRYPTO 2006. LNCS, vol. 4117, pp. 483–500. Springer, Heidelberg (2006)

[Kat07]   Katz, J.: On achieving the "best of both worlds" in secure multiparty computation. In: STOC 2007, pp. 11–20. ACM (2007)

[LRM10]   Lucas, C., Raub, D., Maurer, U.: Hybrid-secure MPC: Trading information-theoretic robustness for computational privacy. In: PODC 2010, pp. 219–228. ACM (2010)

[Mau02]   Maurer, U.M.: Secure Multi-party Computation Made Simple. In: Cimato, S., Galdi, C., Persiano, G. (eds.) SCN 2002. LNCS, vol. 2576, pp. 14–28. Springer, Heidelberg (2003)

[PW92]   Pfitzmann, B., Waidner, M.: Unconditional Byzantine Agreement for any Number of Faulty Processors. In: Finkel, A., Jantzen, M. (eds.) STACS 1992. LNCS, vol. 577, pp. 339–350. Springer, Heidelberg (1992)

[RB89]   Rabin, T., Ben-Or, M.: Verifiable secret sharing and multiparty protocols with honest majority. In: STOC 1989, pp. 73–85. ACM (1989)

[Sha79]   Shamir, A.: How to share a secret. Communications of the ACM 22(11), 612–613 (1979)

[Yao82]   Yao, A.C.: Protocols for secure computations (extended abstract). In: FOCS 1982, pp. 160–164. IEEE (1982)

Efficient Threshold Zero-Knowledge with Applications to User-Centric Protocols

Marcel Keller[1], Gert Læssøe Mikkelsen[2], and Andy Rupp[3]

[1] University of Bristol, UK
m.keller@bristol.ac.uk
[2] The Alexandra Institute, Denmark
gert.l.mikkelsen@alexandra.dk
[3] AGT Group (R&D) GmbH, Germany
arupp@agtinternational.com

Abstract. In this paper, we investigate on *threshold proofs*, a framework for distributing the prover's side of *interactive proofs of knowledge* over multiple parties. Interactive proofs of knowledge (PoK) are widely used primitives of cryptographic protocols, including important user-centric protocols, such as identification schemes, electronic cash (e-cash), and anonymous credentials.

We present a security model for threshold proofs of knowledge and develop threshold versions of well-known primitives such as range proofs, zero-knowledge proofs for preimages of homomorphisms (which generalizes PoKs of discrete logarithms, representations, p-th roots, etc.), as well as OR statements. These building blocks are proven secure in our model.

Furthermore, we apply the developed primitives and techniques in the context of user-centric protocols. In particular, we construct distributed-user variants of Brands' e-cash system and the bilinear anonymous credential scheme by Camenisch and Lysyanskaya. Distributing the user party in such protocols has several practical advantages: First, the security of a user can be increased by sharing secrets and computations over multiple devices owned by the user. In this way, losing control of a single device does not result in a security breach. Second, this approach also allows *groups of users* to jointly control an application (e.g., a joint e-cash account), not giving a single user full control.

The distributed versions of the protocols we propose in this paper are relatively efficient (when compared to a general MPC approach). In comparison to the original protocols only the prover's (or user's) side is modified while the other side stays untouched. In particular, it is oblivious to the other party whether it interacts with a distributed prover (or user) or one as defined in the original protocol.

Keywords: Multiparty computation, threshold cryptography, distributed provers, Σ-protocols, e-cash, anonymous credentials.

1   Introduction

The general idea of increasing the security of cryptographic primitives by distributing computations is not new. There is a large body of cryptographic literature dealing with threshold digital signatures [1, 15, 16, 19, 26, 35], where the security of a signature scheme is increased by splitting the signer player into several players. In this way one

A. Smith (Ed.): ICITS 2012, LNCS 7412, pp. 147–166, 2012.
© Springer-Verlag Berlin Heidelberg 2012

obtains schemes that stay secure even in case one or more (up to a certain threshold) of these players get corrupted.

We believe that in a world where people are expected to participate in more and more different and complex security protocols, there is a need for extending the idea of threshold schemes for users beyond signatures. In particular, the acceptance and deployment of user-centric cryptographic protocols including e-cash [8] and anonymous credentials [9] could profit from strengthening the security for the human user.

An important work in this vein (which however, still restricts to signatures) is due to Damgård and Mikkelsen [16]. They introduce a model where the human user in the context of a signature scheme is represented not by a single player, as often done in cryptographic literature, but by several players thereby decoupling the user and his actual equipment (e.g., a smart card and a PC). This leads to a more realistic model of the world, and, by using threshold signatures, it increases the security of the human user against identity theft: If only one of the user's devices gets corrupted, the adversary is still not able to make signatures on behalf of the user.

A major goal of the work at hand is to extend this approach to the more complex case of user-centric cryptographic protocols. Here, for instance, users need to be protected against loss of credentials, electronic coins, etc. due to corruption, theft, or loss of their devices. Another strongly related goal in this context is to protect a *group of users* who jointly own an e-cash account or hold a credential from misuse by an individual.

To achieve the above goals we need to distribute the user's part of these protocols in an appropriate way. From an implementation point of view, it is a very important objective for new protocols to work as seamlessly as possible together with existing solutions. If the other players in the protocol, e.g., the shop accepting electronic cash, are oblivious of the fact that the user is distributed, then a distributed-user variant of the protocol can be utilized in already working environments alongside other implementations, without requiring new standardizations and/or implementations of big and system-wide changes. In practice, we aim for distributing the user's private information between n players, and let these players communicate with some additional player C combining messages and acting with respect to the other party (e.g, the shop) as if it was a single user. For the purpose of implementing distributed-user protocols also on computationally weak devices like smart cards or phones, efficiency of the protocols is of great importance.

Related Work. Pedersen [33] considers *distributed provers* in the context of undeniable signatures. However, while our goal is to improve the security against theft of the user's identity, Pedersen's focus is on robustness. Desmedt et al. [18] propose a model similar to ours. While their model is based on zero-knowledge proofs of knowledge, our model extends the properties of Σ-protocols. This allows us to easily construct protocols that have arbitrary challenge spaces, which is more difficult to achieve with the general definition of zero-knowledge. In fact, they only present a protocol where the challenge is one bit. Furthermore, our model avoids interaction among the provers, and it preserves the communication pattern of the single-prover protocols. Desmedt [17] introduced the protocol presented in Figure 1. However, he does not give a security proof for his protocol, and he considers neither applications nor more intricate proofs as we do with OR proofs and range proofs.

Further examples of related work are [16] described earlier, and the work of Simoens et al. [38]. The latter work also utilizes threshold cryptography to enhance the security of users. The authors propose threshold signatures and threshold encryption schemes, focusing on very constrained devices. In contrast to our approach they design distributed schemes from scratch where the verifier is aware that it interacts with a distributed party.

Brands [5] considers a model called *wallet with observers*, where the user of an e-cash scheme is distributed into two different entities. The objective is to protect the bank against double spenders, and this is achieved by using tamper proof hardware. Our objective is to improve the security of the user without relying on tamper proof hardware.

Our Contribution. This work proposes a framework for threshold zero-knowledge proofs consisting of a security model as well as techniques and building blocks for constructing threshold user-centric protocols. In particular, we introduce threshold variants of numerous important Σ-protocols for proofs of knowledge which are frequently used as building blocks: This includes Schnorr's protocol [36] for discrete logarithms, Okamoto's [32] protocol for representations, Fiat-Shamir's [23] and Guillou-Quisquater's [27] protocols for modular roots, protocols for proving equalities, a protocol for proving correctness of DH keys, protocols for proving multiplicative relations of commitments, and many further protocols which are, e.g., used in e-cash and credential systems. To do so, we consider a generalization of the protocols above by Maurer [31] (PoK of a preimage of a homomorphism) instead of treating each protocol individually.

As a further contribution, we develop a threshold version of the OR construction for the generalized PoK mentioned above. While coming up with a distributed PoK for preimages is not too hard, this is not the case for the OR protocol. Here tricky modifications to the computation flow on the prover's side are required. The OR construction by Cramer et al. [11] is an important building block. For example, it is an efficient way to increase the security of proofs of knowledge: It can be used to obtain a *witness hiding* [21] Σ-protocol starting from one without this property. Moreover, by means of this construction one can turn a witness hiding Σ-protocol into a protocol providing zero-knowledge against dishonest verifiers. Furthermore, we develop threshold versions of the range proofs by Lipmaa [29] and Boudot [4] also used in various user-centric protocols. For all of our threshold variants of the above protocols we show zero-knowledge under passive as well as active corruption of the verifier and a number of provers.

As a case study to demonstrate the usefulness of our approach we apply it to obtain two distributed user-centric protocols. More precisely, we sketch distributed-user variants of Brands' e-cash system [5] and the pairing-based anonymous credential scheme by Camenisch and Lysyanskaya [7]. We note that our primary goal in the context of these applications is to improve the user's security rather than protecting its privacy (untraceability of transactions) in case the adversary gains control over a device. Nevertheless, in Section 4.3 we sketch how forward and backward untraceability of users could be achieved if a device becomes temporarily corrupted.

One may ask how our threshold protocols differ from a solution using full-fledged multi-party computation. The key difference is communication efficiency: Our protocols are highly efficient, most of them preserve the three move structure with respect to each prover, which is optimal for single-prover zero-knowledge proofs. We achieve this by avoiding full-featured multiparty computation, instead, we exploit the properties of linear and multiplicative secret sharing schemes. In particular, we use so-called pseudorandom secret sharing [10] to allow the provers to generate secret shared random numbers without communication. Moreover, we combine multiplicative secret sharing with pseudorandom zero-sharing to allow provers to carry out a multiplication of two secret shared numbers without communication. This approach differs from common multiparty computation [2] involving a resharing round after every local multiplication of shares.

Since the focus of this paper is on efficiency, we refrain from considering complex protocols such as the proof of knowledge of a Hamiltonian cycle [3]. Revealing the Hamiltonian cycle in the last step of this protocol involves branching, which is known to be relatively expensive in multiparty computation. For the same reason, we do not consider universally composable zero-knowledge or related notions like non-malleable zero-knowledge [25]. To the best of our knowledge, these imply the use of techniques that do not allow an efficient implementation as multiparty computation, like hash functions in [25] or converting secret values between different domains in [20].

Due to space constraints an extended version of this paper can be found in [28].

2   Security Model and Preliminaries

Contrary to the traditional model for user-centric protocols, where the user and his computing equipment is modeled as one player, this equipment can be represented as several players in the model we consider in this work. Computations done by a user are split up among several devices (each representing a player), which the user may carry with him. This could be for example a cell phone, smart cards, but a device might also be a server connected to the Internet.

The protocols we are going to consider in this model are *threshold proofs*, a distributed version of protocols for proofs of knowledge (PoK). While the model covers general zero-knowledge proofs of knowledge, this paper mainly considers Σ-protocols. Σ-protocols are a special class of PoK protocols, where the prover $\mathcal{P}$ starts the protocol by sending a message a to the verifier $\mathcal{V}$. $\mathcal{V}$ replies with an l-bit string e, called the challenge. From a, e and its private input $\mathcal{P}$ calculates a response z and sends z to $\mathcal{V}$. From a, e and z, $\mathcal{V}$ is able to verify the proof. Σ-protocols are an important primitive in many cryptographic protocols. For further details we refer to [13].

We study how the prover $\mathcal{P}$ of Σ-protocols can be distributed such that the private input is shared between n provers $\mathcal{P}_1, \ldots, \mathcal{P}_n$, representing the user's computing devices. Each of these provers communicates with a player, denoted combiner C, combining the messages in the proof and communicating with $\mathcal{V}$ as if C was $\mathcal{P}$ in the original protocol. The protocol view of $\mathcal{V}$ has to be indistinguishable from the single-prover protocol. C could represent one of the user's devices handling the communication with the verifier, or it could model a device not controlled by the user, e.g., a specially designed terminal for receiving e-cash in a threshold e-cash scheme. Because of this, we specify C in our protocols such that it does not store any user-specific data.

It should be noted that generally Σ-protocols do not achieve provable zero-knowledge against a malicious verifier, they only achieve what is known as *special honest-verifier zero-knowledge.* This translates in the threshold proofs to a lack of provable zero-knowledge against an actively corrupted combiner. However, the standard solutions against malicious verifiers also imply zero-knowledge against malicious combiners.

2.1 Security Model

We assume that up to t of the n provers can be corrupted either passively or actively by an adversary, with some additional control over the verifier $\mathcal{V}$ and the combiner C. The degree of control the adversary may have over $\mathcal{V}$ and C depends on the assumptions made in the original protocols regarding the corruption of $\mathcal{V}$. The security property we focus on is *zero-knowledge*, even in case of some corruptions, and *not correctness*, meaning the adversary is not allowed to gain information, but is allowed to prevent proofs from being accepted. It is, however, possible to construct robust protocols, which would lead to a lower threshold. We only consider static adversaries, although most of the protocols are secure against adaptive adversaries. We extend the properties of Σ-protocols as follows:

Definition 1 (Completeness). *If all provers and the combiner follow the protocol, the verifier accepts with overwhelming probability.*

Definition 2 (Special soundness). *From any two accepting conversations with the same initial message, the witness can be computed in polynomial time.*

Definition 2 is the same as in the single-prover case (e.g., see [13]). Informally speaking, we are not concerned with the question who actually "knows" the witness, e.g., it might be C interacting with $\mathcal{V}$ while ignoring the messages from the provers, or it might be just one prover.

Definition 3 (Special honest-verifier-combiner zero-knowledge with threshold t). *There exists a zero-knowledge simulator that, for any given challenge e, can simulate a protocol execution that is perfectly, statistically, or computationally indistinguishable from a real protocol execution with passive corruption of the verifier, the combiner, and up to t provers.*

Note that (single-prover) Σ-protocols in general cannot be proven to be zero-knowledge if the challenge is not independent of the initial message, and thus, the verifier and the combiner cannot be actively corrupted in our distributed Σ-protocols. However, in Definition 4 we allow the combiner to deviate partially, i.e., he is allowed to send differing challenges to the provers. This extension of adversary capabilities gives a model in between passive corruption and active corruption. This model is not so interesting by itself, however, we define it because a protocol that is *partial zero-knowledge* can by standard techniques be transformed into a protocol with full *zero-knowledge*.

Definition 4 (Partial zero-knowledge with threshold t). *There exists a zero-knowledge simulator that, for any set of challenges $\{e^{(i)}\}_{i\in[n]}$, can simulate a transcript that is perfectly, statistically, or computationally indistinguishable from a real execution with up to t actively corrupted provers and $e^{(i)}$ being sent to $\mathcal{P}_i$ for all $i \in [n]$. To do so, the simulator can interact with the corrupted provers in a black-box way.*

Definition 5 (Full zero-knowledge with threshold t**).** *Let an active adversary statically corrupt up to t provers, the combiner, and the verifier. Then there exists a zero-knowledge simulator that can simulate a transcript that is perfectly, statistically, or computationally indistinguishable from a real execution by rewindable black-box interaction with the corrupted parties.*

In [28], we show that any partial zero-knowledge protocol with threshold t can be extended to a protocol that implements a UC functionality corresponding to the notion of full zero-knowledge with threshold t. The extension essentially lets the provers commit the their first messages before they receive the challenge. An adversary computing a challenge dependent on a first message would then break the hiding property of the commitment scheme.

Definition 6 (Witness hiding with threshold t**).** *Let a computationally bounded, active adversary statically corrupt up to t provers, the combiner, and the verifier. Then the probability that the adversary can output the witness after a polynomial number of protocol runs is negligible.*

It is clear that computational full zero-knowledge with threshold t implies witness hiding with threshold t, however, the reverse is not known to hold.

2.2 Secret Sharing

To present our protocols in a general way, we briefly introduce here an abstract definition of linear and multiplicative secret sharing schemes. For more details we refer to [28].

Definition 7 (Linear secret sharing). *A linear secret sharing scheme for a ring consists of two algorithms:*

Share *Takes a secret value and some random values as input and outputs one or more shares for every player, using a linear operation on the inputs.*
Reconstr *Takes all shares given by* Share *to a qualified set of players as input and outputs the secret, using a linear operation on the inputs.*

The shares given to any unqualified set are perfectly or statistically indistinguishable from a sharing of zero.

Since Reconstr is linear, the sum of two share vectors output by Share is a sharing of the sum of the secrets. Therefore, computing a secret sharing of the output of any linear function from a secret sharing of the inputs can be done without communication. Desmedt et al. [18] describe how a linear secret sharing scheme for $\mathbb{Z}_m$ implies a secret sharing scheme for a group G of order m.

The simplest example of a linear secret sharing scheme is additive secret sharing, where the shares are simply random numbers adding up to the secret. It works for any ring, and can also be defined over a group, where the shares are reconstructed by applying the group operation on the shares. The only qualified set is the set of all players.

Definition 8 (Multiplicative secret sharing). *A multiplicative secret sharing scheme is a linear secret sharing scheme that in addition provides the following algorithm:*

Mult *Takes all shares of two secrets, given to a certain player, and outputs a value, using a bilinear operation on the two share vectors. The sum of the outputs of all players is the product of the two secrets.*

One of the first and most common linear secret sharing schemes is Shamir's secret sharing scheme [37] for finite fields. Shamir's secret sharing with threshold $t < n/2$ is multiplicative. Cramer et al. [12] show how to construct a multiplicative integer secret sharing scheme with threshold $t < n/2$.

The notion of multiplicative secret sharing schemes can be extended to cyclic groups $G = \langle g \rangle$, in the sense that the sum and the product of g^s and $g^{s'}$ are defined to be $g^{s+s'}$ and $g^{ss'}$, respectively. Since exponentiation with base g is homomorphic as well as Share and Reconstr are linear, those algorithms trivially can be applied in this setting. However, $g^{ss'}$ is in general not computable from g^s and $g^{s'}$ without knowing s or s'. Nevertheless, if the exponents of the second input vector are known, $\mathsf{Mult}'(g^{s_i}, s'_i) := g^{\mathsf{Mult}(s_i, s'_i)}$ can be computed because Mult is bilinear. Multiplicative integer secret sharing can be used with any cyclic group, whereas Shamir secret sharing over $\mathbb{Z}_{|G|}$ can be used if $|G|$ is prime.

Pseudorandom Secret Sharing (PRSS) and Zero Sharing (PRZS). Pseudorandom secret sharing was introduced by Cramer et al. [10]. It is a way for a number of players to generate a secret shared value without communication. PRSS is practical as long as the number of players is relatively small (as we can assume for our applications). We will refer to the sharing of a random number as pseudorandom secret sharing (PRSS) and to the additive sharing of 0 as pseudorandom zero sharing (PRZS). Furthermore, we denote by PRZS' an alternative version of the latter, which outputs a secret sharing of the neutral element 1 of a group. The full paper [28] provides details on the constructions used in this paper. For the sake of readability of the protocol descriptions, we omit that all the mentioned schemes are given a set of keys when used. We also omit that a variable changing from invocation to invocation (like a counter) is used internally so that, by every invocation of $\mathsf{PRSS}(i)$ or $\mathsf{PRZS}(i)$, $\mathcal{P}_i$ obtains its share of a new random number or its new share of 0, respectively.

3   Threshold Building Blocks

3.1   Proofs of Knowledge of Preimages of Homomorphisms

Let G and H be two finite Abelian groups both written multiplicatively and let $\psi : G \to H$ be a homomorphism. Furthermore, let $h \in H$ and q be a prime such that $u \in G$ with $\psi(u) = h^q$ is known. If H has prime order q (and thus is cyclic), this condition is fulfilled for $u = 1$ because $\psi(1) = 1 = h^q$. A proof of knowledge of a preimage $w \in G$ of h under ψ works as follows: The prover starts by sending $a := \psi(r)$ for a random $r \in G$, the verifier sends a random challenge $e \in \mathbb{Z}_q$, the prover responds with $z := rw^e$, and the verifier checks whether $\psi(z) = ah^e$. This protocol is due to Maurer [31] and generalizes

$\mathcal{P}_i$	C	$\mathcal{V}$
Input: $w^{(i)} \in G$, PRSS keys		Input: $h = \psi(w) \in H$
$r^{(i)} := \text{PRSS}(i)$		
$a^{(i)} := \psi(r^{(i)}) \in H$		
$\xrightarrow{\quad a^{(i)} \quad}$	$a := \text{Reconstr}(\{a^{(i)}\}_{i\in A}) = \psi(r) \xrightarrow{\quad a \quad}$	
$\xleftarrow{\quad e \quad}$	$\xleftarrow{\quad e \quad}$ $e \xleftarrow{\$} \mathbb{Z}_q$	
$z^{(i)} := r^{(i)}(w^{(i)})^e \in G$	$\xrightarrow{\quad z^{(i)} \quad}$ $z := \text{Reconstr}(\{z^{(i)}\}_{i\in A}) = rw^e \xrightarrow{\quad z \quad}$	$\psi(z) \stackrel{?}{=} ah^e \in H$

Fig. 1. Distributed proof of knowledge of a preimage $w \in G$ of an element $h \in H$ under a group homomorphism $\psi : G \to H$

proofs of knowledge of discrete logarithms, p-th roots, and many more. Using u of the form mentioned above, Maurer proves special soundness.

Desmedt [17] formulated a distributed version of this protocol (see Figure 1) using a linear secret sharing of the group elements r and w. Each prover executes the computations as in the original protocol with the only difference that it uses its shares $r^{(i)}$ and $w^{(i)}$ instead of r and w. The combiner C collects the messages $a^{(i)}$ and $z^{(i)}$ from the provers and computes a and z by reconstructing as soon as there are enough shares available. A denotes the qualified set of provers that are the first to send a share. If the linear scheme allows it, the provers are not required to be completely present.

Lemma 1. *The protocol in Figure 1 achieves completeness, special soundness, and computational partial zero-knowledge with the same threshold as the utilized secret sharing scheme.*

Proof. Completeness follows from the protocol description, and special soundness is proven in the same way as for the single-prover protocol. The partial zero-knowledge simulator implicitly runs the simulator of the original protocol, adapting to deviating provers and a partially deviating combiner. See [28] for details.

3.2   OR Construction for Proofs of Knowledge of Preimages

The OR construction is an important basic building block for Σ-protocols. It allows a prover to show that it knows a witness for one out of two given inputs *but without* revealing to which input the witness corresponds. The OR construction is itself a Σ-protocol. We consider the OR construction for proofs of preimages as described in the previous section. Figure 2 shows a protocol proving the knowledge of a ψ-preimage of one out of two given elements while hiding for which of the elements a preimage is known, i.e., the bit b is hidden.

To obtain a distributed version of this protocol where a prover $\mathcal{P}_i$ is not aware of the secret preimage w_b and the bit b, the first step is to make the computations on the prover's side uniform. That means the way one computes a_b, e_b, and z_b should not differ from the way to compute $a_{\bar{b}}$, $e_{\bar{b}}$, and $z_{\bar{b}}$, where $\bar{b} = 1 - b$. Figure 3 shows such an alternative version of the protocol but still for the case of a single prover. Secret sharing of the secrets of the prover finally leads to a distributed version of the protocol.

Figure 4 shows our threshold protocol for groups of prime order q. We use Shamir's secret sharing over $\mathbb{Z}_q$ with threshold $t < n/2$ and the abstract notion of multiplicative

$\mathcal{P}$	$\mathcal{V}$
Input: $b \in \{0,1\}, w_b \in G$	Input: $h_0 = \psi(w_0), h_1 = \psi(w_1) \in H$

$$r_b, z_{\bar{b}} \xleftarrow{\$} G, e_{\bar{b}} \xleftarrow{\$} \mathbb{Z}_q$$
$$a_b := \psi(r_b) \in H$$
$$a_{\bar{b}} := \psi(z_{\bar{b}}) h_{\bar{b}}^{-e_{\bar{b}}} \in H \qquad \xrightarrow{\quad a_0, a_1 \quad}$$

$$\xleftarrow{\quad e \quad} \qquad e \xleftarrow{\$} \mathbb{Z}_q$$

$$e_b := e - e_{\bar{b}} \in \mathbb{Z}_q$$
$$z_b := r_b w_b^{e_b} \in G \qquad \xrightarrow{\quad e_0, e_1, z_0, z_1 \quad} \quad e \overset{?}{=} e_0 + e_1 \in \mathbb{Z}_q$$
$$\psi(z_0) \overset{?}{=} a_0 h_0^{e_0} \in H$$
$$\psi(z_1) \overset{?}{=} a_1 h_1^{e_1} \in H$$

Fig. 2. Proof of knowledge of a ψ-preimage of h_b, given $h_0, h_1 \in H$

$\mathcal{P}$	$\mathcal{V}$
Input: $b \in \{0,1\}, w_b \in G$	Input: $h_0, h_1 \in H$
$h_b = \psi(w_b), h_{\bar{b}} \in H$	

$$r_0, r_1 \xleftarrow{\$} G, d_0, d_1 \xleftarrow{\$} \mathbb{Z}_q$$
$$a_0 := \psi(r_0) h_0^{-bd_0} \in H$$
$$a_1 := \psi(r_1) h_1^{-\bar{b}d_1} \in H \qquad \xrightarrow{\quad a_0, a_1 \quad}$$

$$e_0 := bd_0 + \bar{b}(e - d_1) \in \mathbb{Z}_q \xleftarrow{\quad e \quad} \qquad e \xleftarrow{\$} \mathbb{Z}_q$$
$$e_1 := b(e - d_0) + \bar{b}d_1 \in \mathbb{Z}_q$$
$$v_b := w_b \in G$$
$$v_{\bar{b}} := 1 \in G$$
$$z_0 := r_0 v_0^{e_0} \in G$$
$$z_1 := r_1 v_1^{e_1} \in G \qquad \xrightarrow{\quad e_0, e_1, z_0, z_1 \quad} \quad e \overset{?}{=} e_0 + e_1 \in \mathbb{Z}_q$$
$$\psi(z_0) \overset{?}{=} a_0 h_0^{e_0} \in H$$
$$\psi(z_1) \overset{?}{=} a_1 h_1^{e_1} \in H$$

Fig. 3. Alternative version of the proof of knowledge of a ψ-preimage of h_b, given $h_0, h_1 \in H$. Computations on prover's side have been unified, i.e., to compute a_0, a_1, e_0, e_1 and z_0, z_1 the same computations are performed.

secret sharing introduced in Section 2.2. $b^{(i)}$, $\bar{b}^{(i)}$, and $1^{(i)}$ denote a secret sharing of b, $\bar{b}$, and 1 over $\mathbb{Z}_q$, where $b \in \{0,1\}$ and $\bar{b} := 1 - b$. $1^{(i)}$ is only needed to convert shares into an additive secret sharing using Mult and can be computed using fixed randomness. Thus, $1^{(i)}$ can be seen as defined by the secret sharing scheme. $v_0^{(i)}$ and $v_1^{(i)}$ denote a secret sharing of v_0 and v_1 over G, where $v_b := w_b$ and $v_{\bar{b}} := 1$. We share these over G because the discrete logarithm of w_b might not be known in the setup phase. $r_0^{(i)}$ and $r_1^{(i)}$ can be understood as additive sharing of some random group elements r_0 and r_1.

PRSS refers to pseudorandom secret sharing for the multiplicative secret sharing scheme used, and PRZS and PRZS' refer to pseudorandom zero sharing for additive secret sharing. The reason for using PRZS is that the outputs of Mult and Mult' could reveal information about the inputs, i.e., the outputs do not form a random sharing of the product of the secrets. Therefore, we use PRZS to get a truly (pseudo)random additive secret sharing before sending outputs of Mult or Mult' to $\mathcal{C}$.

$\mathcal{P}_i$	C	$\mathcal{V}$
Input: $b^{(i)}, \bar{b}^{(i)}, 1^{(i)} \in \mathbb{Z}_q$, PRSS and PRZS keys,		Input: $h_0, h_1 \in H$
$v_0^{(i)}, v_1^{(i)} \in G, h_0, h_1 \in H$		

$r_0^{(i)}, r_1^{(i)} \xleftarrow{\$} G$

$d_0^{(i)} := \mathsf{PRSS}(i)$

$d_1^{(i)} := \mathsf{PRSS}(i)$

$a_0^{(i)} := \psi(r_0^{(i)}) \cdot h_0^{-\mathsf{Mult}(b^{(i)}, d_0^{(i)})} \cdot \mathsf{PRZS}'(i)$

$a_1^{(i)} := \psi(r_1^{(i)}) \cdot h_1^{-\mathsf{Mult}(\bar{b}^{(i)}, d_1^{(i)})} \cdot \mathsf{PRZS}'(i)$

$\xrightarrow{a_0^{(i)}, a_1^{(i)}}$ $a_0 := \prod_i a_0^{(i)}$

$a_1 := \prod_i a_1^{(i)}$ $\xrightarrow{a_0, a_1}$

$e_0^{(i)} := \mathsf{Mult}(b^{(i)}, d_0^{(i)}) + \mathsf{Mult}(\bar{b}^{(i)}, 1^{(i)})e$

$\xleftarrow{\quad e \quad}$ $\xleftarrow{\quad e \quad}$ $e \xleftarrow{\$} \mathbb{Z}_q$

$\quad - \mathsf{Mult}(\bar{b}^{(i)}, d_1^{(i)}) + \mathsf{PRZS}(i) \in \mathbb{Z}_q$

$e_1^{(i)} := \mathsf{Mult}(b^{(i)}, 1^{(i)})e - \mathsf{Mult}(b^{(i)}, d_0^{(i)})$

$\quad + \mathsf{Mult}(\bar{b}^{(i)}, d_1^{(i)}) + \mathsf{PRZS}(i) \in \mathbb{Z}_q$

$z_0^{(i)} := r_0^{(i)} \cdot \mathsf{Mult}'(v_0^{(i)}, 1^{(i)})^e / \mathsf{Mult}'(v_0^{(i)}, d_1^{(i)}) \cdot \mathsf{PRZS}'(i)$

$z_1^{(i)} := r_1^{(i)} \cdot \mathsf{Mult}'(v_1^{(i)}, 1^{(i)})^e / \mathsf{Mult}'(v_1^{(i)}, d_0^{(i)}) \cdot \mathsf{PRZS}'(i)$ $\xrightarrow{e_0^{(i)}, e_1^{(i)}, z_0^{(i)}, z_1^{(i)}}$ $e_0 := \sum_i e_0^{(i)}$

$e_1 := \sum_i e_1^{(i)}$

$z_0 := \prod_i z_0^{(i)}$

$z_1 := \prod_i z_1^{(i)}$ $\xrightarrow{e_0, e_1, z_0, z_1}$ $e \overset{?}{=} e_0 + e_1 \in \mathbb{Z}_q$

$\psi(z_0) \overset{?}{=} a_0 h_0^{e_0}$

$\psi(z_1) \overset{?}{=} a_1 h_1^{e_1}$

Fig. 4. Distributed version of the proof of knowledge of a ψ-preimage of h_b, given $h_0, h_1 \in H$. Assumption: G is of prime order q.

In the following, we show that the view of $\mathcal{V}$ is the same as in the protocol from Figure 2. e_0, e_1 are random numbers that sum up to e, and z_0 and z_1 pass the check by the verifier:

$$e_0 + e_1 = \sum_i e_0^{(i)} + e_1^{(i)} = (bd_0 + \bar{b}e - \bar{b}d_1) + (be - bd_0 + \bar{b}d_1) = \begin{cases} e & b = 0 \\ e & b = 1, \end{cases}$$

$$z_0 = \prod_i z_0^{(i)} = \prod_i r_0^{(i)} \cdot \mathsf{Mult}'(v_0^{(i)}, 1^{(i)})^e / \mathsf{Mult}'(v_0^{(i)}, d_1^{(i)}) \cdot \mathsf{PRZS}'(i) = r_0 v_0^{e-d_1}$$

$$= \begin{cases} r_0 v_0^{bd_0 + \bar{b}(e-d_1)} = r_0 v_0^{e_0} & b = 0 \\ r_0 v_{\bar{b}}^{e-d_1} = r_0 1^{e-d_1} = r_0 1^{e_0} = r_0 v_0^{e_0} & b = 1 \end{cases}$$

The same can be proven for z_1.

Applying standard multiparty computation secure against a passive adversary [2] would require one communication round among the provers per round of multiplication operations. Multiparty computation secure against an active adversary usually requires even more communication. This is what we save by directly publishing the output of Mult and Mult', re-randomized by PRZS and PRZS', respectively.

Lemma 2. *The protocol for prime order groups as described above achieves completeness, special soundness, and computational partial zero-knowledge with threshold $t < n/2$.*

$$
\begin{array}{ll}
\mathcal{P} & \mathcal{V} \\
\text{Input: } x \in [0, B], r & \text{Input: } g^{x^2} h^r
\end{array}
$$

$r_1 \in [0, 2^s N]$
$r_2 := r - r_1 x$
$C := g^x h^{r_1}$
$\omega \in_R [0, 2^{k+l} B]$
$v_1, v_2 \in_R [0, 2^{k+l+s} N]$
$a_1 := g^\omega h^{v_1}, a_2 := C^\omega h^{v_2}$ $\quad \xrightarrow{\;C, a_1, a_2\;}$

$\quad \xleftarrow{\qquad e \qquad} \quad e \in_R [0, 2^k]$

$z := \omega + xe$
$v_1 := v_1 + r_1 e, v_2 := v_2 + r_2 e \quad \xrightarrow{\;z, v_1, v_2\;} \quad g^z h^{v_1} \stackrel{?}{=} a_1 C^e$

$\quad\qquad\qquad\qquad\qquad\qquad\qquad C^z h^{v_2} \stackrel{?}{=} a_2 (g^{x^2} h^r)^e$

Fig. 5. Proof that a commitment hides a square

Proof. Completeness follows from the protocol description, and special soundness is proven in the same way as for the single-prover protocol. The partial zero-knowledge simulator implicitly runs the simulator of the original protocol, adapting to deviating provers and a partially deviating combiner. The essence of the proof is a smart combination of multiparty and zero-knowledge simulation techniques. See [28] for details.

Lemma 3. *The protocol described above is witness hiding with threshold t if the corresponding single-prover OR proof is witness hiding.*

Proof. The proof is done by reduction, i.e., we present a simulator that simulates the set of honest provers by accessing the honest prover of the single-prover protocol internally. See [28] for a complete proof.

3.3 Range Proofs

In this section, we will outline how to adapt the range proof by Lipmaa [29] to our distributed setting. All protocols in this section use the Fujisaki-Okamoto commitment scheme [14, 24] $\text{com}(x, r) := g^x h^r$ for $g, h \in \mathbb{Z}_N^*$ and $r \in_R [0, 2^s N]$ (s is a security parameter). Clearly, com is a homomorphic function from $\mathbb{Z} \times \mathbb{Z}$ to $\mathbb{Z}_N^*$. Therefore, one might want to construct a proof of knowledge of a preimage as in Section 3.1. However, $\mathbb{Z} \times \mathbb{Z}$ is not finite, and thus, the technique does not apply directly. Nevertheless, Damgård and Fujisaki [14] showed that a similar protocol achieves soundness if the strong RSA assumption holds for $\mathbb{Z}_N^*$. The protocol can efficiently be distributed like the protocol in Section 3.1 by using an additive secret sharing of x and r over the integers.

An essential building block of the range proof is the proof that a committed value is a square. However, $\text{com}(x^2, r)$ is not a homomorphic function in x and r, and therefore, the approach of the protocol in Section 3.1 cannot be used. The following construction solves the problem: $\mathcal{P}$ chooses a random r_1, and computes $r_2 := r - r_1 x$ and $C := \text{com}(x, r_1) = g^x h^{r_1}$. Then, $\text{com}(x^2, r) = g^{x^2} h^r = g^{x^2} h^{x r_1 + r_2} = C^x h^{r_2}$. The function $(x, r_1, r_2) \mapsto (g^x h^{r_1}, C^x h^{r_2})$ is a homomorphism; thus, a zero-knowledge proof can be constructed similarly to the proof of knowledge of a committed value if the strong RSA assumption holds for $\mathbb{Z}_N^*$ (see Figure 5 for details). Damgård and Fujisaki [14] prove

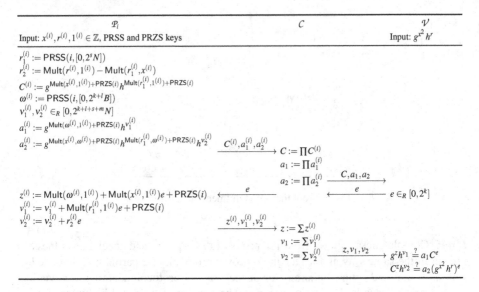

Fig. 6. Distributed proof that a commitment hides a square

that a more general version of the protocol achieves computational soundness and statistical honest-verifier zero-knowledge.

Since the protocol involves products of secret values, linear secret sharing does not suffice to get a distributed protocol. However, one can use the same techniques as for the OR proof, namely multiplicative secret sharing, PRSS, and PRZS. Again, this allows to minimize the communication. Figure 6 shows the details. $x^{(i)}$, $r^{(i)}$, and $1^{(i)}$ denote a multiplicative secret sharing of $x \in [0, B]$, r, and 1, respectively. s, k, l, and m are security parameters, e.g., m is the security parameter of the sharing scheme. As in the distributed OR proof, we use $\mathsf{Mult}(\cdot, 1^{(i)})$ to convert a multiplicative secret sharing into an additive one, and PRZS to randomize the output of Mult. Note that we use PRSS and PRZS with varying intervals here. $\mathsf{PRSS}(i, [0, b])$ denotes that $\mathcal{P}_i$ chooses pseudorandom inputs in the interval $[0, b]$. For any maximal unqualified set, the resulting secret shared number will then be computationally indistinguishable to a uniform number in some interval $[c, c+b]$. This reflects the indistinguishability property of the single-prover protocol. For $\mathsf{PRZS}(i)$, the pseudorandom inputs are chosen in an interval exponentially bigger than the maximal output of the adjacent Mult.

Now we describe how to prove that a committed number x lies in a certain range $[a, b]$. Clearly, proving $x \in [a, b]$ is equivalent to showing that $x - a$ and $b - x$ are non-negative. Furthermore, Lagrange's four-square theorem states that every non-negative integer can be written as the sum of four squares of integers. Together with the proof of a square, this directly allows to implement a range proof. First, the prover computes $\alpha_1, \ldots, \alpha_4, \beta_1, \ldots, \beta_4$ such that $\sum_{i=1}^{4} \alpha_i^2 = x - a$ and $\sum_{i=1}^{4} \beta_i^2 = b - x$, and the commitments $\mathsf{com}(\alpha_i^2, r_{1i})$, $\mathsf{com}(\beta_i^2, r_{2i})$ for all $i \in [1, 4]$ such that $\sum_{i=1}^{4} r_{1i} = r$ and $\sum_{i=1}^{4} r_{2i} = -r$. Then he sends the commitments to the verifier and uses the proof of square described above to prove that all these commitments hide a square. Finally, the verifier checks that $\mathrm{com}(x,r)/g^a = \sum_{i=1}^{4} \mathrm{com}(\alpha_i^2, r_{1i})$ and that $g^b/\mathrm{com}(x,r) = \sum_{i=1}^{4} \mathrm{com}(\alpha_i^2, r_{2i})$. Lipmaa [29] proposes an optimized proof based on the same ideas.

The proof can be adapted to our distributed setting if the provers hold a multiplicative secret sharing of $\alpha_1, \ldots, \alpha_4, \beta_1, \ldots, \beta_4$. The distributed generation of these shares using the algorithm in [29] requires very expensive MPC due to branching, but they can be generated in a setup phase because they only depend on the committed value and the range boundaries. Boudot's range proof [4] only requires the computation of integer square roots at that point, but has other drawbacks like not being exact.

4 Applications to User-Centric Protocols

4.1 E-Cash with Threshold Wallets

In this section we describe a threshold version of the e-cash scheme by Brands [5]. In the standard version, a user $\mathcal{U}$ opens an account in a bank $\mathcal{B}$. The user can then withdraw electronic money and later use it in a shop $\mathcal{S}$. $\mathcal{S}$ may then deposit the electronic money to his own bank account. Moreover, even if $\mathcal{B}$ and $\mathcal{S}$ cooperate they cannot link electronic coins to a specific user. In the threshold version the user $\mathcal{U}$ is split up into several entities $\mathcal{U}_1$ to $\mathcal{U}_n$ and a combiner $\mathcal{C}$ acting as the user with respect to $\mathcal{B}$ and $\mathcal{S}$. The global setup of the system and the protocol for $\mathcal{S}$ depositing the e-cash in $\mathcal{B}$ does not include the user and are therefore not changed.

Opening an account. The public key of $\mathcal{B}$ are three generators g, g_1, and $g_2 \in G_q$, where G_q is a cyclic group of prime order q. The private key of $\mathcal{B}$ is a random number $x \in \mathbb{Z}_q^*$. When $\mathcal{U}$ wants to open an e-cash account at $\mathcal{B}$, he samples $u_1 \xleftarrow{\$} \mathbb{Z}_q$ and uses u_1 as secret key. From u_1, $\mathcal{U}$ calculates $I := g_1^{u_1}$, sends I to $\mathcal{B}$ and proves knowledge of u_1 such that $I = g_1^{u_1}$. If the proof is accepted, $\mathcal{B}$ calculates $z := (Ig_2)^x$ and sends z to $\mathcal{U}$. The bank stores I as the account number of $\mathcal{U}$, and $\mathcal{U}$ stores u_1 and z. This protocol can easily be extended to a threshold protocol, where u_1 is generated distributedly as an additive secret shared value. From the shares of u_1, the players $\mathcal{U}_i$ and $\mathcal{C}$ can calculate I distributedly. The proof of knowledge of u_1 is distributed as in the protocol from Figure 1.

Withdrawing coins from the bank. This protocol can be viewed as a Σ-protocol, where $\mathcal{B}$ acts as prover, proving knowledge of its own secret key to $\mathcal{U}$. As a result $\mathcal{U}$ ends up with a blinded signature $sig(A,B)$ from $\mathcal{B}$ on a coin (A,B). This coin along with the signature can later be used for payment. Distributing a verifier might be straightforward, however, in this case the signature contains a hash value $\mathrm{H}(\cdot)$, and most hash functions are far from linear. They can therefore not be distributed easily. Nevertheless, we can still protect the user from theft of coins in case some $\mathcal{U}_i$ is corrupted, although this might jeopardize the anonymity of $\mathcal{U}$. The threshold protocol is sketched in Figure 7. Some random values used for anonymizing the protocol are generated by a pseudorandom function (PRF). Distributing the PRF key allows generating commonly known pseudorandom values without reconstruction. The value B has, due to hashing, to be known by each $\mathcal{U}_i$, however, B is computed from x_1 and x_2, and not by the PRF. Therefore, it has to be reconstructed by $\mathcal{C}$. We blind B by ρ_B to maintain anonymity.

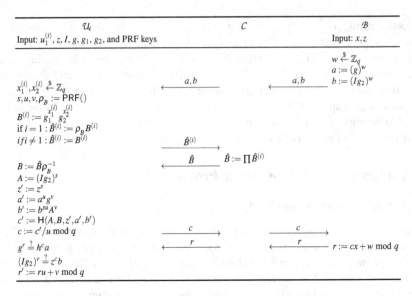

Fig. 7. Distributed version of the withdrawal protocol

If the adversary does not control any of $\mathcal{U}_1, \ldots, \mathcal{U}_n$ nor the combiner C, then the protocol is equivalent to the original protocol, and therefore has the same level of security in that case. In case of corruption, we do not ensure anonymity, nevertheless, no information regarding neither u_1, x_1 nor x_2 is leaked, and therefore, even after withdrawal with corrupted players, the adversary still has only negligible chance of paying afterward.

Spending coins. In this part of the original protocol $\mathcal{U}$ sends the coin $\langle A, B, sig(A, B) \rangle$ to S. $\mathcal{U}$ proves that the coin is valid, obtained by the user with secret key u_1, and that $\mathcal{U}$ has knowledge of u_1. This is basically a Σ-protocol proving representation of A with respect to g_1 and g_2, using x_1 and x_2 for blinding. Therefore, we can distribute it by the protocol from Section 3.1 (cf. Figure 1). Please note that B and not $B^{(i)}$ should be sent from each $\mathcal{U}_i$ to C. Otherwise, ρ_B would be leaked to C, and anonymity is revoked.

Theorem 1 summarizes the properties of our threshold version of Brands' scheme.

Theorem 1. *The threshold scheme preserves the following properties from the original scheme [5, Section 5]*

- **Anonymity of $\mathcal{U}$:** *The anonymity of the original scheme [5, Corollary 12] is preserved against a passive adversary controlling C, $\mathcal{B}$ and S.*
- **Security against double spenders, and forgery:** *Security for $\mathcal{B}$ and S against double spenders [5, Proposition 10] and against forged coins [5, Corollary 9, Proposition 7 and 13] is preserved.*
- **Security against theft:** *Security for $\mathcal{U}$ against theft of electronic coins [5, Proposition 14 and 15] is preserved against an adversary passively corrupting $n - 1$ of the user players, the combiner C, $\mathcal{B}$ and S.*

Proof. Security for $\mathcal{B}$ and $\mathcal{S}$ follows since it is oblivious for them that they execute the threshold version. Since u_1 is secret shared, the adversary cannot steal coins, and anonymity of $\mathcal{U}$ can be reduced to anonymity in the original scheme. See [28] for a detailed proof.

Robustness. To allow payments even in case some of the user players $\mathcal{U}_i$ are not present in the payment protocol, the following changes suffice. First the protocol for opening an account has to generate the users secret key u_1 as being shared with a linear secret sharing scheme that has lower threshold than the additive one. This can be done by using PRSS. The same has to be done with the blinding values x_1 and x_2 in the withdrawal protocol. In addition, C has to reconstruct the value of $\hat{B}$ taking into account that it is computed from the shares of x_1 and x_2, which is possible because the reconstruction of x_1 and x_2 is a linear operation. This enables a threshold version of the payment protocol where only a subset of the players $\mathcal{U}_i$ equivalent to the threshold value of the secret sharing scheme needs to be present.

4.2   Increasing the Security of Anonymous Credentials

Credentials are certificates of qualification (e.g., driver's licenses) or authorization of some kind (e.g., e-tickets) that are attached to a specific user. Credential systems allow their users ($\mathcal{U}$) to obtain credentials from organizations (O) and show possession of these credentials to verifiers ($\mathcal{V}$). In an anonymous credential system different transactions involving the same user cannot be linked.

Camenisch and Lysyanskaya [6, 30] show that an anonymous credential scheme can be immediately composed from a commitment scheme, a signature scheme, and efficient protocols for (1) proving the equality of two committed values, (2) obtaining a signature on a committed value (without opening the commitment), and (3) proving knowledge of a signature on a committed value. In [7] the same authors propose efficient pairing-based instantiations of the above building blocks. In the following we shortly describe these components and sketch threshold versions of the zero-knowledge protocols.

Let G and G_T be two cyclic groups of prime order q (both written multiplicatively in the following). A pairing $e : G \times G \rightarrow G_T$ is a function with the following properties:

- *Bilinearity*: $\forall (a,b) \in G^2$ and $(x,y) \in \mathbb{Z}_q^2$, it holds that $e(a^x, b^y) = e(a,b)^{xy}$.
- *Non-degeneracy*: $\exists a, b \in G$ such that $e(a,b) \neq 1$.
- e is efficiently computable.

The credential system in [7] makes use of Pedersen commitments [34] over G, which are information-theoretically hiding and computationally binding under the DL assumption. Here, given two generators $g, h \in G$, a commitment M to $m \in \mathbb{Z}_q$ is computed by choosing $r \xleftarrow{\$} \mathbb{Z}_q$ and setting $M := g^m h^r$. In the scope of the credential system, a commitment to a secret m chosen by a user serves as a pseudonym for the user when interacting with an organization. For different organizations, different pseudonyms are used. Usually, all pseudonyms of a user are required to be commitments to the *same* m, which is some master secret key (used outside the credential system).

Credentials are signatures on pseudonyms. To this end, the following signature scheme is proposed in [7], which is secure under the LRSW assumption.

- Gen samples a random generator g of G, $x,y,z \xleftarrow{\$} \mathbb{Z}_q$, and computes $X = g^x, Y = g^y, Z = g^z, W = Y^z$. It returns the signer's secret key $sk = (x,y,z)$ and public key $pk = (g,X,Y,Z,W)$.
- Sign$(sk,(m,r))$ chooses $\alpha \xleftarrow{\$} \mathbb{Z}_q$ and computes $a = g^\alpha$, $A = a^z$, $b = a^y$, $B = A^y$, $c = a^{x+xym}A^{xyr}$, where $(m,r) \in \mathbb{Z}_q^2$ is the given message. It returns the signature $\sigma = (a,A,b,B,c)$.
- Verify$(pk,(m,r),\sigma)$ returns 'accept', if the following equations are satisfied: $e(a,Z) = e(g,A)$, $e(a,Y) = e(g,b)$, $e(A,Y) = e(g,B)$, and $e(X,a)e(X,b)^m e(X,B)^r = e(g,c)$.

Let us now consider the protocols described above forming a credential system. For our threshold versions of these protocols we always distribute the user's side of the protocols over parties $\mathcal{U}_1,\ldots,\mathcal{U}_n$.

Proving the equality of two committed values. This is a zero-knowledge proof of knowledge of values (a_1,a_2,a_3) such that $C = g^{a_1}h^{a_2}$ and $C' = g^{a_1}h^{a_3}$, for given C and C'. Since (a_1,a_2,a_3) can be viewed as a preimage of (C,C') under the homomorphism $\psi : \mathbb{Z}_q^3 \to G^2$ where $\psi(\alpha_1,\alpha_2,\alpha_3) = (g^{\alpha_1}h^{\alpha_2},g^{\alpha_1}h^{\alpha_3})$, Figure 1 immediately yields a threshold version of this protocol for parties $\mathcal{U}_1,\ldots,\mathcal{U}_n$ acting as provers.

Obtaining a signature on a committed value (obtaining a credential). This is a protocol between $\mathcal{U}$ and O. The party $\mathcal{U}$ holds (m,r) and is given O's public signature key pk as input. O holds its secret signature key sk and is given commitment $M = g^m Z^r$ as input. The protocol consists of two steps. First, $\mathcal{U}$ proves in zero-knowledge its knowledge of a representation of M with respect to g and Z. Again, a threshold version of this subprotocol can be immediately obtained from the protocol in Figure 1. Second, if O accepts the previous proof, it generates a signature σ on (m,r) using the signature scheme described above. Since (m,r) is not given, the component c of the signature is computed only using M as $c = a^x M^{\alpha xy}$. Then, $\mathcal{U}$ checks the validity of σ according to Verify. Note that only for checking the last equation the knowledge of (m,r) is required. So to distribute the user's side of this subprotocol over $\mathcal{U}_1,\ldots,\mathcal{U}_n$, we only need to compute the left-hand side of this equation in a distributed way: $\mathcal{U}_i$ computes $w^{(i)} := e(X,a)e(X,b)^{m^{(i)}}e(X,B)^{r^{(i)}}e(g,g)^{\mathsf{PRZS}(i)}$, where $m^{(i)}$, $r^{(i)}$ are additive shares of m and r, respectively. Then it sends $w^{(i)}$ to the combiner C who computes the product of these shares and checks the corresponding equation. It is easy to see that the threshold protocol for obtaining a signature on a committed value is zero-knowledge with respect to adversaries passively corrupting O, C, and a static set of $n-1$ parties $\mathcal{U}_i$.

Proving knowledge of a signature on a committed value (showing a credential). This is a protocol executed between a user $\mathcal{U}$ and a verifier $\mathcal{V}$. $\mathcal{U}$ is given (m,r), a signature σ on these values, and the public key pk of the signer. $\mathcal{V}$ is only given pk. The player $\mathcal{U}$ first re-randomizes the given signature. To this end, it chooses $r_1,r_2 \xleftarrow{\$} \mathbb{Z}_q$, computes $\tilde{a} = a^{r_1}, \tilde{A} = A^{r_1}, \tilde{b} = b^{r_1}, \tilde{B} = B^{r_1}, \hat{c} = c^{r_1 r_2}$, and sends $\tilde{\sigma} = (\tilde{a},\tilde{A},\tilde{b},\tilde{B},\hat{c})$ to $\mathcal{V}$. $\mathcal{V}$ is now able to verify all equations for $\tilde{\sigma}$ defined in Verify except for the last which

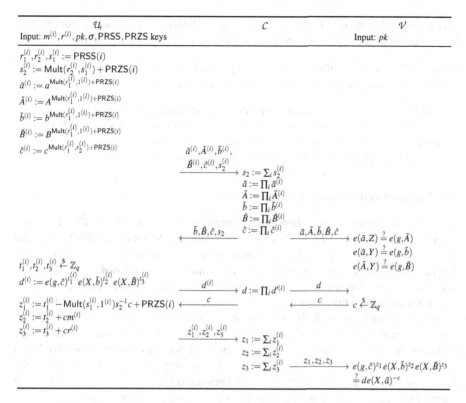

Fig. 8. Distributed version of the protocol proving knowledge of a signature on a committed value

involves (m, r). To assure $\mathcal{V}$ also of the validity of the last equation, $\mathcal{U}$ proves in zero-knowledge the knowledge of (r_2^{-1}, m, r) such that $e(X, \tilde{a})e(X, \tilde{b})^m e(X, \tilde{B})^r = e(g, \hat{c})^{r_2^{-1}}$. Note that this is equivalent to proving knowledge of a representation of $e(X, \tilde{a})^{-1}$ with respect to $e(X, \tilde{b})$, $e(X, \tilde{B})$, and $e(g, \hat{c})$. The threshold version of the whole protocol is shown in Figure 8. Note that in order to compute $\hat{c}$ a multiplicative secret sharing (e.g., Shamir's secret sharing) of r_1 and r_2 is needed. Furthermore, in order to compute an additive sharing of r_2^{-1} from a multiplicative sharing of r_2 (without reconstructing r_2), another trick is used: We choose a random value s_1 by means of PRSS and compute $s_2 := r_2 s_1$ in a distributed manner. Note that s_2 which is reconstructed by the combiner does not leak information about r_2. Then s_2 is given to every $\mathcal{U}_i$ who uses this value to compute its additive share $\mathrm{Mult}(s_1^{(i)}, 1^{(i)})s_2^{-1}$ of r_2^{-1}.

It is easy to see that the protocol in Figure 8 achieves completeness and special soundness. It is also zero-knowledge in the case of adversaries passively corrupting $\mathcal{V}$ and C. However, as soon as a single $\mathcal{U}_i$ is passively corrupted, the adversary knows σ and thus it is not a zero-knowledge proof of the signature anymore. But this does only affect the anonymity of a user, which we do not aim to increase here. More precisely, even if σ is known, the protocol does not leak information about (m, r) as long as not more than $n - 1$ of the players $\mathcal{U}_i$ are passively corrupted. So an adversary is not able to steal a user's identity or a credential in this case. Theorem 2 (informally) summarizes the properties which can be achieved using the proposed threshold protocols.

Theorem 2. *The threshold versions of the protocols described above can be used to build a credential system with the following main properties:*

- *Anonymity for users in presence of a passive adversary controlling C, O and V.*
- *Security of a user's master secret key against a static adversary passively corrupting $n-1$ of the user players U_i, the combiner C, O and V.*
- *Security for O and V against forgery of credentials.*

4.3   Forward and Backward Untraceability

In user-centric protocols we often want to preserve the untraceability of a user (i.e., different protocol executions involving the same user should not be linkable) even if the state of the device executing the user's side of the protocol is revealed at some point in time. This privacy notion is commonly called *backward and forward untraceability*. One usually considers an adversary who passively corrupts a user device at a certain time τ but otherwise may only eavesdrop communication at times $\tau' < \tau$ and $\tau'' > \tau$. Then by backward untraceability we mean that the adversary is not able to tell whether a protocol execution at time τ' involves this user device. By forward untraceability we mean that the adversary cannot decide whether the user device is involved in a protocol execution at time τ'' assuming that the adversary missed eavesdropping the communication of this device at least once between times τ and τ''. Unfortunately, a commonly accepted formal definition of these properties is still missing.

Nevertheless, it would be nice if threshold user-centric protocols, as introduced here, also satisfied the above properties, where we allow the passive corruption of up to $n-1$ devices of the same user and the combiner at time τ. However, the use of pseudorandom secret and zero sharing with *fixed* keys constitutes a problem. More precisely, PRSS and PRZS involves a PRF, whose past and future outputs can be computed once the key and the input to the function are known. In this way, an adversary revealing the state of some device at time τ can usually predict future and past messages and thus trace the device. For instance, it is easy to see that in this case in the protocol shown in Figure 8 all messages from U_i would be computable.

In order to achieve backward and forward untraceability one needs to update the keys of all PRFs involved in the protocol after every execution. For forward untraceability the idea is to use some external randomness like a challenge sent by the other party. To obtain backward untraceability the update function should be one-way. Hence, a simple solution could be the following: Let PRF be a pseudorandom function used for PRSS and PRZS and PRF' be another one whose output and key lengths correspond to the key length of PRF. A new key K_i for PRF (and PRF') could then be computed as $K_i := \text{PRF}'_{K_{i-1}}(c)$, where c is the challenge received. A more formal treatment of backward and forward untraceability for threshold protocols is left as future work.

Acknowledgments. The authors would like to thank Ivan Damgård for fruitful discussions and suggestions. The first two authors acknowledge the support by CFEM and CTIC at Aarhus University where most of the work was done.

References

1. Almansa, J.F., Damgård, I., Nielsen, J.B.: Simplified Threshold RSA with Adaptive and Proactive Security. In: Vaudenay, S. (ed.) EUROCRYPT 2006. LNCS, vol. 4004, pp. 593–611. Springer, Heidelberg (2006)
2. Ben-Or, M., Goldwasser, S., Wigderson, A.: Completeness theorems for non-cryptographic fault-tolerant distributed computation (extended abstract). In: STOC, pp. 1–10. ACM (1988)
3. Blum, M.: How to prove a theorem so no one else can claim it. In: Gleason, A.M. (ed.) Proceedings of the International Congress of Mathematicians, pp. 1444–1451 (1986)
4. Boudot, F.: Efficient Proofs that a Committed Number Lies in an Interval. In: Preneel, B. (ed.) EUROCRYPT 2000. LNCS, vol. 1807, pp. 431–444. Springer, Heidelberg (2000)
5. Brands, S.: Untraceable Off-Line Cash in Wallets with Observers (Extended Abstract). In: Stinson, D.R. (ed.) CRYPTO 1993. LNCS, vol. 773, pp. 302–318. Springer, Heidelberg (1994)
6. Camenisch, J.L., Lysyanskaya, A.: A Signature Scheme with Efficient Protocols. In: Cimato, S., Galdi, C., Persiano, G. (eds.) SCN 2002. LNCS, vol. 2576, pp. 268–289. Springer, Heidelberg (2003)
7. Camenisch, J.L., Lysyanskaya, A.: Signature Schemes and Anonymous Credentials from Bilinear Maps. In: Franklin, M. (ed.) CRYPTO 2004. LNCS, vol. 3152, pp. 56–72. Springer, Heidelberg (2004)
8. Chaum, D.: Blind signatures for untraceable payments. In: CRYPTO 1982, pp. 199–203 (1982)
9. Chaum, D.: Security without identification: Transaction systems to make big brother obsolete. Commun. ACM 28(10), 1030–1044 (1985)
10. Cramer, R., Damgård, I., Ishai, Y.: Share Conversion, Pseudorandom Secret-Sharing and Applications to Secure Computation. In: Kilian, J. (ed.) TCC 2005. LNCS, vol. 3378, pp. 342–362. Springer, Heidelberg (2005)
11. Cramer, R., Damgård, I., Schoenmakers, B.: Proof of Partial Knowledge and Simplified Design of Witness Hiding Protocols. In: Desmedt, Y.G. (ed.) CRYPTO 1994. LNCS, vol. 839, pp. 174–187. Springer, Heidelberg (1994)
12. Cramer, R., Fehr, S., Ishai, Y., Kushilevitz, E.: Efficient Multi-party Computation Over Rings. In: Biham, E. (ed.) EUROCRYPT 2003. LNCS, vol. 2656, pp. 596–613. Springer, Heidelberg (2003)
13. Damgård, I.: On Σ-protocols, Course Notes. Aarhus University (2010)
14. Damgård, I., Fujisaki, E.: A Statistically-Hiding Integer Commitment Scheme Based on Groups with Hidden Order. In: Zheng, Y. (ed.) ASIACRYPT 2002. LNCS, vol. 2501, pp. 125–142. Springer, Heidelberg (2002)
15. Damgård, I., Koprowski, M.: Practical Threshold RSA Signatures without a Trusted Dealer. In: Pfitzmann, B. (ed.) EUROCRYPT 2001. LNCS, vol. 2045, pp. 152–165. Springer, Heidelberg (2001)
16. Damgård, I., Mikkelsen, G.L.: On the Theory and Practice of Personal Digital Signatures. In: Jarecki, S., Tsudik, G. (eds.) PKC 2009. LNCS, vol. 5443, pp. 277–296. Springer, Heidelberg (2009)
17. Desmedt, Y.: Threshold Crypto Systems (Invited Talk). In: Zheng, Y., Seberry, J. (eds.) AUSCRYPT 1992. LNCS, vol. 718, pp. 3–14. Springer, Heidelberg (1993)
18. Desmedt, Y., Di Crescenzo, G., Burmester, M.: Multiplicative Non-Abelian Sharing Schemes and Their Application to Threshold Cryptography. In: Safavi-Naini, R., Pieprzyk, J.P. (eds.) ASIACRYPT 1994. LNCS, vol. 917, pp. 21–32. Springer, Heidelberg (1995)
19. Desmedt, Y.G., Frankel, Y.: Shared Generation of Authenticators and Signatures. In: Feigenbaum, J. (ed.) [22], pp. 457–469

20. Dodis, Y., Shoup, V., Walfish, S.: Efficient Constructions of Composable Commitments and Zero-Knowledge Proofs. In: Wagner, D. (ed.) CRYPTO 2008. LNCS, vol. 5157, pp. 515–535. Springer, Heidelberg (2008)

21. Feige, U., Shamir, A.: Witness indistinguishable and witness hiding protocols. In: STOC, pp. 416–426. ACM (1990)

22. Feigenbaum, J. (ed.): CRYPTO 1991. LNCS, vol. 576, pp. 457–469. Springer, Heidelberg (1992)

23. Fiat, A., Shamir, A.: How to Prove Yourself: Practical Solutions to Identification and Signature Problems. In: Odlyzko, A.M. (ed.) CRYPTO 1986. LNCS, vol. 263, pp. 186–194. Springer, Heidelberg (1987)

24. Fujisaki, E., Okamoto, T.: Statistical Zero Knowledge Protocols to Prove Modular Polynomial Relations. In: Kaliski Jr., B.S. (ed.) CRYPTO 1997. LNCS, vol. 1294, pp. 16–30. Springer, Heidelberg (1997)

25. Garay, J.A., MacKenzie, P.D., Yang, K.: Strengthening zero-knowledge protocols using signatures. J. Cryptology 19(2), 169–209 (2006)

26. Gennaro, R., Rabin, T., Jarecki, S., Krawczyk, H.: Robust and efficient sharing of RSA functions. J. Cryptology 13(2), 273–300 (2000)

27. Guillou, L.C., Quisquater, J.-J.: A Practical Zero-Knowledge Protocol Fitted to Security Microprocessor Minimizing Both Transmission and Memory. In: Günther, C.G. (ed.) EUROCRYPT 1988. LNCS, vol. 330, pp. 123–128. Springer, Heidelberg (1988)

28. Keller, M., Mikkelsen, G., Rupp, A.: Efficient threshold zero-knowledge with applications to user-centric protocols (full paper) (2012), Manuscript published at http://eprint.iacr.org/2012/306

29. Lipmaa, H.: On Diophantine Complexity and Statistical Zero-Knowledge Arguments. In: Laih, C.-S. (ed.) ASIACRYPT 2003. LNCS, vol. 2894, pp. 398–415. Springer, Heidelberg (2003)

30. Lysyanskaya, A.: Signature Schemes and Applications to Cryptographic Protocol Design. Ph.D. thesis. Massachusetts Institute of Technology (2002)

31. Maurer, U.: Unifying Zero-Knowledge Proofs of Knowledge. In: Preneel, B. (ed.) AFRICACRYPT 2009. LNCS, vol. 5580, pp. 272–286. Springer, Heidelberg (2009)

32. Okamoto, T.: Provably Secure and Practical Identification Schemes and Corresponding Signature Schemes. In: Brickell, E.F. (ed.) CRYPTO 1992. LNCS, vol. 740, pp. 31–53. Springer, Heidelberg (1993)

33. Pedersen, T.P.: Distributed Provers with Applications to Undeniable Signatures. In: Davies, D.W. (ed.) EUROCRYPT 1991. LNCS, vol. 547, pp. 221–242. Springer, Heidelberg (1991)

34. Pedersen, T.P.: Non-interactive and Information-Theoretic Secure Verifiable Secret Sharing. In: Feigenbaum, J. (ed.) [22], pp. 129–140

35. Rabin, T.: A Simplified Approach to Threshold and Proactive RSA. In: Krawczyk, H. (ed.) CRYPTO 1998. LNCS, vol. 1462, pp. 89–104. Springer, Heidelberg (1998)

36. Schnorr, C.-P.: Efficient Identification and Signatures for Smart Cards. In: Brassard, G. (ed.) CRYPTO 1989. LNCS, vol. 435, pp. 239–252. Springer, Heidelberg (1990)

37. Shamir, A.: How to share a secret. Commun. ACM 22(11), 612–613 (1979)

38. Simoens, K., Peeters, R., Preneel, B.: Increased Resilience in Threshold Cryptography: Sharing a Secret with Devices That Cannot Store Shares. In: Joye, M., Miyaji, A., Otsuka, A. (eds.) Pairing 2010. LNCS, vol. 6487, pp. 116–135. Springer, Heidelberg (2010)

Information-Theoretic Timed-Release Security: Key-Agreement, Encryption, and Authentication Codes

Yohei Watanabe, Takenobu Seito, and Junji Shikata

Graduate School of Environment and Information Sciences,
Yokohama National University, Japan
{watanabe-yohei-xs,takenobu.seito,shikata}@ynu.ac.jp

Abstract. In this paper, we study timed-release cryptography with information-theoretic security. As fundamental cryptographic primitives with information-theoretic security, we can consider key-agreement, encryption, and authentication codes. Therefore, in this paper, we deal with information-theoretic timed-release security for all those primitives. Specifically, we propose models and formalizations of security for information-theoretic timed-release key-agreement, encryption, and authentication codes, and we present constructions of those ones. In particular, information-theoretic timed-release encryption and authentication codes can be constructed from information-theoretic timed-release key-agreement in a generic and simple way. Also, we derive tight lower bounds of sizes of secret-keys and show an optimal construction for information-theoretic timed-release key-agreement. Furthermore, we investigate a relationship of mechanisms between information-theoretic timed-release key-agreement and information-theoretic key-insulated key-agreement. It turns out that there exists a simple algorithm which converts the former into the latter, and vice versa. In the sense, we conclude that these two mechanisms are essentially close.

1 Introduction

The security of most of present cryptographic systems is based on the assumption of difficulty of computationally hard problems such as the integer factoring problem or the discrete logarithm problem in finite fields or elliptic curves. However, taking into account recent rapid development of algorithms and computer technologies, such a system based on the assumption of difficulty of computationally hard problems might not maintain sufficient long-term security. In fact, it is known that quantum computers can easily solve the factoring and discrete logarithm problems. From these aspects, it is necessary and interesting to consider cryptographic techniques whose security does not depend on any computationally hard problems, especially for the long-term security.

Informally, the goal of timed-release cryptography is to securely send a certain information into the future. For instance, in timed-release encryption, a sender transmits a ciphertext so that a receiver can decrypt it when the time which the

A. Smith (Ed.): ICITS 2012, LNCS 7412, pp. 167–186, 2012.

sender specified has come, and the receiver cannot decrypt it before the time. The timed-release cryptography was first proposed by May [10] in 1993, and after that, Rivest et al. [12] developed it in a systematic and formal way. Since Rivest et al. gave a formal definition of timed-release encryption in [12], various researches on timed-release cryptography including timed-release signatures (e.g., [1,8,9]) and timed-release encryption have been done based on computational security. In particular, timed-release public key encryption (TR-PKE for short) has been recently researched intensively. Chan et al.[4] proposed the first TR-PKE scheme, but did not present a formal security definition. Cathalo et al.[2] and Chalkias et al.[3] proposed direct constructions of TR-PKE schemes based on number-theoretic assumptions in the random oracle model. Independently, Cheon et al. [6] proposed a generic construction of TR-PKE and it is efficient and provably secure in the standard model. And also, Fujioka et al.[7] proposed a generic construction of TR-PKE that guarantees strong security in the random oracle model. It also should be noted that Choen et al.[5] recently shows relationships between TR-PKE and key-insulated public-key encryption (KI-PKE for short) with computational security setting.

To the best of our knowledge, there is no paper which reports on the study of information-theoretic timed-release cryptography. If a sender wants to transmit a message far into the future, information-theoretic security will be helpful in constructing timed-release mechanism, since its security can provide the long-term security. In this paper, we study timed-release cryptography with information-theoretic security. As fundamental cryptographic primitives with information-theoretic security, we can consider information-theoretically secure key-agreement, encryption, and authentication codes. Therefore, in this paper, we deal with information-theoretic timed-release security for all those primitives. Specifically, the contribution of this paper is as follows.

- We propose a model and formalization of security for timed-release key-agreement (TR-KA for short) in information-theoretic security setting. We also derive tight lower bounds of entities' memory-sizes required for TR-KA. In addition, we propose an optimal direct construction of TR-KA based on multivariate polynomials over finite fields.
- We propose models and formalizations of security for timed-release encryption (TRE for short) and authentication codes (TRA-codes for short) in information-theoretic security setting. We also present simple generic constructions of TRE and TRA-codes: TRE can be constructed from TR-KA and the one-time pad; and TRA-codes can be constructed from TR-KA and traditional A-codes.
- We investigate and show relationship between TR-KA and key-insulated key-agreement (KI-KA for short) [13] in information-theoretic security setting. It turns out that there exists a simple algorithm which converts TR-KA into KI-KA, and vice versa. Therefore, we can conclude that the mechanisms of TR-KA and KI-KA are essentially close. Note that this relationship in information-theoretic security setting is analogous to that of TR-PKE and KI-PKE in computational security setting shown in [5].

2 TR-KA: Timed-Release Key-Agreement with Information-Theoretic Security

2.1 Model and Security Definition

In this section we show a model and a security definition of timed-release key-agreement (TR-KA for short) with information-theoretic security. This is done based on those of timed-release schemes with computational security and those of traditional key-agreement with information-theoretic security.

For simplicity, we assume that there is a trusted authority whose role is to generate and to distribute secret-keys of entities. We call this model the *trusted initializer model* as in [11]. In TR-KA, there are $n+2$ entities, n users $U_1, U_2, \ldots, U_n$, a time-server T for broadcasting *time-signals* and a trusted initializer TI, where n is a positive integer. In this paper, we assume that the identity of each user U_i is also denoted by U_i. In addition, when any two users communicate each other in a timed-release scheme (i.e., not only TR-KA but also TRE and TRA-codes in the following sections) under consideration in this paper, we call a user who specifies the time a *sender* and the other a *receiver* for convenience.

Informally, TR-KA is executed as follows. In the initial phase, TI generates secret-keys on behalf of U_i ($1 \leq i \leq n$) and the time-server T. After distributing these keys via secure channels, TI deletes them in his memory. Any user U_{i_1} can specify future time when U_{i_1} wants to share a common-key with a user U_{i_2}, and he computes a common-key in advance by using U_{i_1}'s secret-key and the identity U_{i_2}. And U_{i_1} tells U_{i_2} the future time which U_{i_1} specified. The time-server T periodically broadcasts a time-signal at each time which is generated by using T's master-key. When the specified time has come, U_{i_2} can compute a common-key shared with U_{i_1} by using U_{i_2}'s secret-key, the identity U_{i_1} and a time-signal of the specified time. Note that each user has two kinds of secret-keys: one is used for generating a common-key when he is a sender; and the other is used for deriving a common-key when he is a receiver. In TR-KA, we consider a non-interactive model where any two users can share a common-key without interactive communications.

Formally, we give the definition of TR-KA as follows.[1]

Definition 1 (TR-KA). A *timed-release key-agreement* (*TR-KA* for short) Π involves $n+2$ entities, TI, $U_1, U_2, \ldots, U_n$ and T, and consists of a four-tuple of algorithms (*Setup, Ext, KeyGen, KeyDer*) with five spaces, $\mathcal{TCK}, \mathcal{TUK}, \mathcal{TMK}, \mathcal{T}$, and $\mathcal{TI}$, where all of the above algorithms except *Setup* are deterministic and all of the above spaces are finite. In addition, Π is executed with four phases as follows.

---

[1] Note that our models of information-theoretically secure timed-release schemes (Definitions 1, 4 and 6) are almost the same as those of computationally secure timed-release schemes [2,4,5,6,7] except for considering the trusted initializer in our models.

- **Notation:**
  - *Entities*: TI is a trusted initializer, U_i $(1 \leq i \leq n)$ is a user and T is a time-server which broadcasts time-signals. Let $\mathcal{U} := \{U_1, U_2, \ldots, U_n\}$ be the set of all users.
  - *Spaces*: $\mathcal{TCK}$ is a set of possible common-keys, and $\mathcal{TMK}$ is a set of possible master-keys. $\mathcal{T} := \{1, 2, \ldots, \tau\}$ is a set of time. $\mathcal{TI}^{(t)}$ is a set of time-signals at time t. Let $\mathcal{TI} := \bigcup_{i=1}^{\tau} \mathcal{TI}^{(i)}$. Also, $\mathcal{TUK}_i^{(S)}$ is a set of possible U_i's secret-keys for common-key generation. And also, $\mathcal{TUK}_i^{(R)}$ is a set of possible U_i's secret-keys for common-key derivation. Then, $\mathcal{TUK}_i := \mathcal{TUK}_i^{(S)} \times \mathcal{TUK}_i^{(R)}$ is the set of possible secret-keys for U_i with an associated probability distribution P_{TUK_i}. Let $\mathcal{TUK}^{(S)} := \bigcup_{i=1}^{n} \mathcal{TUK}_i^{(S)}$, $\mathcal{TUK}^{(R)} := \bigcup_{i=1}^{n} \mathcal{TUK}_i^{(R)}$, and $\mathcal{TUK} := \bigcup_{i=1}^{n} \mathcal{TUK}_i$.
  - *Algorithms*: *Setup* is a key generation algorithm which on input a security parameter 1^k, outputs users' secret-keys and a time-server's master-key, *Ext*: $\mathcal{TMK} \times \mathcal{T} \to \mathcal{TI}$ is a time-signal generation algorithm for T, *KeyGen*: $\mathcal{TUK}^{(S)} \times \mathcal{T} \times \mathcal{U} \to \mathcal{TCK}$ is a common-key generation algorithm and *KeyDer*: $\mathcal{TUK}^{(R)} \times \mathcal{TI} \times \mathcal{U} \to \mathcal{TCK}$ is a common-key derivation algorithm.

1. **Key Generation and Distribution.** In the initial phase, TI generates the following keys by using *Setup*: a master-key $tmk^* \in \mathcal{TMK}$ for T; and a secret-key $tuk_i = (tuk_i^{(S)}, tuk_i^{(R)}) \in \mathcal{TUK}_i$ for U_i $(i = 1, 2, \ldots, n)$. These keys are distributed to corresponding entities via secure channels. After distributing these keys, TI deletes them from his memory. And, T and U_i keep their keys secret, respectively.

2. **Time-signal Generation.** For broadcasting a time-signal at each time, T generates a time-signal $tmk^{(t)} = Ext(tmk^*, t) \in \mathcal{TI}^{(t)}$ by using a master key tmk^* and time $t \in \mathcal{T}$. Then, T broadcasts it to all users via a (authenticated) broadcast channel.

3. **Common-key Generation.** If U_{i_1} wants to share a common-key with U_{i_2} at future time t, U_{i_1} computes a common-key to be shared with U_{i_2} in advance, $tck_{i_1, i_2}^{(t)} = KeyGen(tuk_{i_1}^{(S)}, t, U_{i_2}) \in \mathcal{TCK}$, by using his secret-key $tuk_{i_1}^{(S)}$, time t, and the receiver's identity U_{i_2}. And, U_{i_1} tells U_{i_2} the specified time t via an authenticated channel.

4. **Common-key Derivation.** On receiving the specified time t from U_{i_1}, and if the time t has come, U_{i_2} computes a common-key $tck_{i_1, i_2}^{(t)} = KeyDer(tuk_{i_2}^{(R)}, tmk^{(t)}, U_{i_1})$ by using his secret-key $tuk_{i_2}^{(R)}$, a time-signal $tmk^{(t)}$ at time t, and the sender's identity U_{i_1}.

In the model of TR-KA, we require the following equation holds: For all possible $t \in \mathcal{T}$, $i_1, i_2 \in \{1, 2, \ldots, n\}$, $tuk_{i_1}^{(S)} \in \mathcal{TUK}_{i_1}^{(S)}$, $tuk_{i_2}^{(R)} \in \mathcal{TUK}_{i_2}^{(R)}$, $tmk^{(t)} \in \mathcal{TI}^{(t)}$, we have $KeyGen(tuk_{i_1}^{(S)}, t, U_{i_2}) = KeyDer(tuk_{i_2}^{(R)}, tmk^{(t)}, U_{i_1})$DThe above requirement implies that any two users can share a common-key at the specified time without any error if they correctly follow the specification of TR-KA. In addition, $tck_{i_1,i_2}^{(t)}$ means a shared key between U_{i_1} and U_{i_2} at time t when U_{i_1} is the sender and U_{i_2} is the receiver, and we note that $tck_{i_1,i_2}^{(t)} \neq tck_{i_2,i_1}^{(t)}$ in general.

We now define several notation to formalize security of TR-KA as follows. For any finite set $\mathcal{Z}$ and any non-negative integer z, let $\mathcal{P}(\mathcal{Z}, z) := \{Z \subset \mathcal{Z} || Z| \leq z\}$ be the family of all subsets of $\mathcal{Z}$ whose cardinality is less than or equal to z. Let ω ($< n$) be the maximum number of possible colluders. For a set of colluders $W = \{U_{l_1}, U_{l_2}, \ldots, U_{l_j}\} \in \mathcal{P}(\mathcal{U}, \omega)$, $\mathcal{TUK}_W^{(S)} := \mathcal{TUK}_{l_1}^{(S)} \times \mathcal{TUK}_{l_2}^{(S)} \times \cdots \times \mathcal{TUK}_{l_j}^{(S)}$ denotes the set of possible W's secret-keys for common-key generation, and $\mathcal{TUK}_W^{(R)} := \mathcal{TUK}_{l_1}^{(R)} \times \mathcal{TUK}_{l_2}^{(R)} \times \cdots \times \mathcal{TUK}_{l_j}^{(R)}$ denotes the set of possible W's secret-keys for common-key derivation. And, let $\mathcal{TCK}_{i_1,i_2}^{(t)}$ be the set of possible common-keys shared between U_{i_1} and U_{i_2} at the time $t \in \mathcal{T}$. Furthermore, let $TCK_{i_1,i_2}^{(t)}, TMK, TUK_W^{(S)}, TUK_W^{(R)}$, and $TI^{(1)}, \ldots, TI^{(\tau)}$ be random variables which take values on $\mathcal{TCK}_{i_1,i_2}^{(t)}, \mathcal{TMK}, \mathcal{TUK}_W^{(S)}, \mathcal{TUK}_W^{(R)}$, and $\mathcal{TI}^{(1)}, \ldots, \mathcal{TI}^{(\tau)}$, respectively.

Next, we formalize a security definition of TR-KA based on the idea of timed-release security and traditional key-agreement with information-theoretic security. In TR-KA, we consider the following security goal and attacking model. First, the security goal which we consider is basically the same as that of the traditional key-agreement: an adversary (or a dishonest entity) cannot obtain any information on a common-key shared between two honest users. In addition to this, we want to require that even a legitimate receiver cannot obtain any information on a common-key to be shared before the specified time comes (i.e., before a time-signal at the specified time is received), since we consider timed-release security in this paper. Secondly, as an attacking model we consider the following three types of attacks: (1) an attack by a dishonest time-server; (2) an attack by colluders (i.e., dishonest users) not including a receiver; and (3) an attack by colluders including a receiver. By combining the security goal and attacks mentioned above, we formally define security of TR-KA as follows.

Definition 2. Let Π be TR-KA. Π is said to be (n, ω, τ)-*secure* if the following conditions are satisfied:

(1) For any $U_{i_1}, U_{i_2} \in \mathcal{U}$ and $t \in \mathcal{T}$, it holds that

$$H(TCK_{i_1,i_2}^{(t)} \mid TMK) = H(TCK_{i_1,i_2}^{(t)}).$$

(2) For any $W \in \mathcal{P}(\mathcal{U}, \omega)$, $U_{i_1}, U_{i_2} \in \mathcal{U}$ such that $U_{i_1}, U_{i_2} \notin W$, and for any $t \in \mathcal{T}$, it holds that

$$H(TCK_{i_1,i_2}^{(t)} \mid TUK_W^{(S)}, TUK_W^{(R)}, TI^{(1)}, \ldots, TI^{(\tau)}) = H(TCK_{i_1,i_2}^{(t)}).$$

(3) For any $W \in \mathcal{P}(\mathcal{U}, \omega)$, $U_{i_1}, U_{i_2} \in \mathcal{U}$ such that $U_{i_1} \notin W$ and $U_{i_2} \in W$, for any $t \in \mathcal{T}$, it holds that

$$H(TCK_{i_1,i_2}^{(t)} \mid TUK_W^{(S)}, TUK_W^{(R)}, TI^{(1)}, \ldots, TI^{(t-1)}, TI^{(t+1)}, \ldots, TI^{(\tau)})$$
$$= H(TCK_{i_1,i_2}^{(t)}).$$

Intuitively, the meaning of formalizations (1)-(3) in Definition 2 is explained as follows: (1) a dishonest time-server cannot obtain any information on a common-key shared between two honest users. However, we assume that the time-server correctly broadcasts a time-signal at each time; (2) No information on a common-key shared between two honest users is obtained by any colluding group W not including a legitimate receiver, even if W obtains time-signals at all the time; (3) No information on a common-key between two users at the specified time is obtained by any colluding group W including a legitimate (but dishonest) receiver, even if W obtains time-signals at all the time except the specified time.[2]

2.2   Lower Bounds

In this section, we derive lower bounds of entities' memory-sizes required for secure TR-KA as follows. The proof is given in Appendix.

Theorem 1. *Let Π be (n, ω, τ)-secure TR-KA, and we assume that all entropies on common-keys are equal, namely $H(TCK) = H(TCK_{i_1,i_2}^{(t)})$ for any $i_1, i_2 \in \{1, 2, \ldots, n\}$ and $t \in \mathcal{T}$. Then, we have*

(i) $H(TUK_i^{(R)}) \geq (\omega + 1)H(TCK)$,   (ii) $H(TUK_i^{(S)}) \geq (\tau + \omega)H(TCK)$,

(iii) $H(TI^{(t)}) \geq (\omega + 1)H(TCK)$,   (iv) $H(TMK) \geq \tau(\omega + 1)H(TCK)$.

As we will see in the next section, the above lower bounds are tight since our construction will meet all the above inequalities with equalities. Therefore, we define optimality of constructions of TR-KA as follows.

Definition 3. A construction of (n, ω, τ)-secure TR-KA is said to be *optimal* if it meets equality in every inequality of (i)-(iv) in Theorem 1.

2.3   Construction

We present a construction, which is provably secure TR-KA in our model, by using multivariate polynomials over finite fields. In addition, it is shown that the construction is optimal. The detail of our construction of TR-KA Π=(*Setup, Ext, KeyGen, KeyDer*) is given as follows.

1. **Setup.** For a security parameter 1^k, *Setup* outputs matching secret-keys tuk_i and tmk^* for U_i ($1 \leq i \leq n$) and T, respectively, as follows. *Setup* picks a k-bit prime power q, where $q > \max(n, \tau)$, and constructs the finite field $\mathbb{F}_q$ with q elements. We assume that the identity of each user U_i is encoded as $U_i \in \mathbb{F}_q \backslash \{0\}$. Also, we assume $\mathcal{T} = \{1, 2, \ldots, \tau\} \subset \mathbb{F}_q \backslash \{0\}$ by using appropriate encoding. And, *Setup* chooses uniformly at random

---

[2] In this sense, we have formalized the security notion stronger than the security that a dishonest receiver cannot obtain any information on a common-key to be shared before the specified time comes.

$f(x, y) := \sum_{i=0}^{\omega} \sum_{j=0}^{\omega} a_{ij} x^i y^j$, $tmk^*(x, z) := \sum_{i=0}^{\omega} \sum_{k=0}^{\tau-1} b_{ik} x^i z^k$ over $\mathbb{F}_q$ with three variables x, y and z in which each degree of x and y is at most ω, and the degree of z is at most $\tau - 1$. *Setup* also computes $tuk_i^{(S)}(y, z) := f(U_i, y) + tmk^*(U_i, z)$ and $tuk_i^{(R)}(x) := f(x, U_i)$ $(1 \le i \le n)$. Then, *Setup* outputs secret-keys $tuk_i := (tuk_i^{(S)}(y, z), tuk_i^{(R)}(x))$ $(1 \le i \le n)$ and $tmk^* := tmk^*(x, z)$ for U_i $(1 \le i \le n)$ and T, respectively.

2. **Ext.** For $tmk^* = tmk^*(x, z)$ and time $t \in \mathcal{T}$, *Ext* outputs a time-signal at time t, $tmk^{(t)}(x) := tmk^*(x, t)$.

3. **KeyGen.** For a secret-key $tuk_{i_1}^{(S)}$, the specified time t and an identity U_{i_2}, *KeyGen* generates a common-key shared between U_{i_1} and U_{i_2}, $tck_{i_1, i_2}^{(t)} := tuk_{i_1}^{(S)}(U_{i_2}, t)$, and outputs it.

4. **KeyDer.** For a secret-key $tuk_{i_2}^{(R)}$, a time-signal $tmk^{(t)}$ at the specified time t and an identity U_{i_1}, *KeyDer* outputs a common-key shared between U_{i_1} and U_{i_2}, $tck_{i_1, i_2}^{(t)} := tuk_{i_2}^{(R)}(U_{i_1}) + tmk^{(t)}(U_{i_1})$.

The security and optimality of the above construction is stated as follows. (See the full version of this paper [16] for the detailed proof.)

Theorem 2. *The resulting TR-KA Π by the above construction is (n, ω, τ)-secure and optimal.*

Proof Sketch. First, we show the construction satisfies the condition (1) in Definition 2. T cannot guess the information on a common-key $tck_{i_1, i_2}^{(t)}$ with probability larger than $1/q$, since he does not know at least one coefficient of $f(x, y)$. Thus, we have $H(TCK_{i_1, i_2}^{(t)}|TMK) = \log_2 q$. On the other hand, it is clear that $H(TCK_{i_1, i_2}^{(t)}) = \log_2 q$. Therefore, for any $U_{i_1}, U_{i_2} \in \mathcal{U}$ and $t \in \mathcal{T}$, $H(TCK_{i_1, i_2}^{(t)}|TMK) = H(TCK_{i_1, i_2}^{(t)})$.

Next, we show the construction satisfies the conditions (2) in Definition 2. Suppose a group of colluders W not including a targeted receiver gets all time-signals. Then, W can obtain $tmk^*(x, z)$. Also, W has $f(U_l, y)$ and $f(x, U_l)$ $(U_l \in W)$. However, since each degree of $f(x, y)$ with respect to x and y is at most ω, W cannot guess at least one coefficient of $f(x, y)$ with probability larger than $1/q$. Thus, we have $H(TCK_{i_1, i_2}^{(t)}|TUK_W^{(S)}, TUK_W^{(R)}, TI^{(1)}, \ldots, TI^{(\tau)}) = \log_2 q$. Therefore, for any $U_{i_1}, U_{i_2} \in \mathcal{U}$ such that $U_{i_1}, U_{i_2} \notin W$, and for any $t \in \mathcal{T}$, $H(TCK_{i_1, i_2}^{(t)}|TUK_W^{(S)}, TUK_W^{(R)}, TI^{(1)}, \ldots, TI^{(\tau)}) = H(TCK_{i_1, i_2}^{(t)})$.

Moreover, we show the construction satisfies the condition (3) in Definition 2. Without loss of generality, we suppose that U_{i_1} is a targeted sender, U_{i_2} is a targeted receiver, and τ is a specified time. Suppose a group of colluders W with $U_{i_2} \in W$ will guess a common-key $tck_{i_1, i_2}^{(\tau)}$. Note that W can get $f(U_{i_1}, U_{i_2})$ since $U_{i_2} \in W$. Thus, W tries to obtain $tmk^*(x, z)$ to know $f(U_{i_1}, U_{i_2}) + tmk^*(U_{i_1}, \tau)$. Although W can know $tmk^*(U_l, z)$ $(U_l \in W)$ and $tmk^*(x, t)$ $(1 \le t \le \tau - 1)$, W cannot guess at least one coefficient of $tmk^*(x, z)$ with probability larger than $1/q$ since the degrees of $tmk^*(x, z)$ with respect to x and z are at most ω and $\tau - 1$, respectively. Thus, we have $H(TCK_{i_1, i_2}^{(\tau)}|TUK_W^{(S)}, TUK_W^{(R)}, TI^{(1)},$

$TI^{(2)}, \ldots, TI^{(\tau-1)}) = \log_2 q$. Therefore, in general, for any $U_{i_1}, U_{i_2} \in \mathcal{U}$ such that $U_{i_1} \notin W$ and $U_{i_2} \in W$, and for any $t \in \mathcal{T}$, $H(TCK_{i_1,i_2}^{(t)}|TUK_W^{(S)}, TUK_W^{(R)}, TI^{(1)}, \ldots, TI^{(t-1)}, TI^{(t+1)}, \ldots, TI^{(\tau)}) = H(TCK_{i_1,i_2}^{(t)})$.

Finally, it is straightforward to see that the construction satisfies all the equalities of lower bounds in Theorem 1.   □

3   TRE: Timed-Release Encryption with Information-Theoretic Security

In this section, we show a model and a security formalization of timed-release encryption (TRE for short) with information-theoretic security. We also show that TRE can be constructed from TR-KA and the one-time pad in a generic and simple way.

3.1   Model and Security Definition

We propose a model and a security definition of TRE, based on that of timed-release encryption with computational security (e.g., [12]) and that of the traditional encryption with information-theoretic security (e.g., [14]). Formally, we give a definition of TRE in the TI-model as in the case of TR-KA.

Definition 4 (TRE). A *timed-release encryption* (*TRE* for short) Σ involves $n+2$ entities, TI, $U_1, U_2, \ldots, U_n$ and T, and consists of a four-tuple of algorithms (*EGen, EExt, Enc, Dec*) with six spaces, $\mathcal{C}, \mathcal{M}_E, \mathcal{USK}, \mathcal{EMK}, \mathcal{T}$, and $\mathcal{ETI}$, where all of the above algorithms except *EGen* are deterministic and all of the above spaces are finite. In addition, Σ is executed with four phases as follows.

- **Notation:**
    - Entities: TI, U_i ($1 \le i \le n$), T, and $\mathcal{U}$ are the same as those in Definition 1.
    - Spaces: $\mathcal{T}$ is the same as that in Definition 1. $\mathcal{C}$ is a set of possible ciphertexts, $\mathcal{M}_E$ is a set of possible plaintexts with a probability distribution P_M, $\mathcal{EMK}$ is a set of possible master-keys. $\mathcal{ETI}^{(t)}$ is a set of time-signals at time t. Let $\mathcal{ETI} := \bigcup_{i=1}^{\tau} \mathcal{ETI}^{(i)}$. Also, $\mathcal{EK}_i$ is a set of possible encryption-keys for U_i, $\mathcal{DK}_i$ is a set of possible decryption-keys for U_i, and $\mathcal{USK}_i := \mathcal{EK}_i \times \mathcal{DK}_i$ is a set of possible secret-keys for U_i. Let $\mathcal{EK} := \bigcup_{i=1}^{n} \mathcal{EK}_i$, $\mathcal{DK} := \bigcup_{i=1}^{n} \mathcal{DK}_i$ and $\mathcal{USK} := \bigcup_{i=1}^{n} \mathcal{USK}_i$.
    - Algorithms: *EGen* is a key generation algorithm which on input a security parameter 1^k, outputs each user's secret-key and a server's master-key, *EExt*: $\mathcal{EMK} \times \mathcal{T} \to \mathcal{ETI}$ is a time-signal generation algorithm for T, *Enc*: $\mathcal{M}_E \times \mathcal{EK} \times \mathcal{T} \times \mathcal{U} \to \mathcal{C}$ is an encryption algorithm, and *Dec*: $\mathcal{C} \times \mathcal{DK} \times \mathcal{ETI} \times \mathcal{U} \to \mathcal{M}_E$ is a decryption algorithm.
1. **Key Generation and Distribution.** In the initial phase, TI generates the following keys by using *EGen*: a master-key $emk^* \in \mathcal{EMK}$ for T; a secret-key $usk_i = (ek_i, dk_i) \in \mathcal{USK}_i$ for U_i ($i = 1, 2, \ldots, n$). These keys are distributed

to corresponding entities via secure channels. After distributing these keys, TI deletes them from his memory. And, T and U_i keep their keys secret, respectively.

2. **Time-signal Generation.** For broadcasting a time-signal at each time, T generates a time-signal $emk^{(t)} = EExt(emk^*, t) \in \mathcal{ETI}^{(t)}$ by using a master-key $emk^* \in \mathcal{EMK}$ and time $t \in \mathcal{T}$. Then, T broadcasts it to all users via a (authenticated) broadcast channel.

3. **Encryption.** U_{i_1} specifies time t when U_{i_2} can decrypt a ciphertext, and then U_{i_1} computes a ciphertext, $c_{i_1,i_2}^{(t)} = Enc(m, ek_{i_1}, t, U_{i_2}) \in \mathcal{C}$, by a plain-text $m \in \mathcal{M}_E$, an encryption-key $ek_{i_1} \in \mathcal{EK}$, the specified time t and the identity U_{i_2}. And, U_{i_1} sends a pair of the ciphertext and the specified time, $(c_{i_1,i_2}^{(t)}, t)$, to U_{i_2} via an authenticated channel.

4. **Decryption.** Suppose that U_{i_2} has received $(c_{i_1,i_2}^{(t)}, t)$ from U_{i_1}. After receiving a time-signal $emk^{(t)}$ at the specified time t, U_{i_2} recovers $m = Dec(c_{i_1,i_2}^{(t)}, dk_{i_2}, emk^{(t)}, U_{i_1})$ by a ciphertext $c_{i_1,i_2}^{(t)}$, a decryption-key dk_{i_2}, a time-signal $emk^{(t)}$, and the identity U_{i_1}.

In the model of TRE, we require the following equation holds: For all possible $t \in \mathcal{T}$, $i_1, i_2 \in \{1, 2, \ldots, n\}$, $ek_{i_1} \in \mathcal{EK}_{i_1}$, $dk_{i_2} \in \mathcal{DK}_{i_2}$, $emk^{(t)} \in \mathcal{ETI}^{(t)}$, we have $Dec(Enc(m, ek_{i_1}, t, U_{i_2}), dk_{i_2}, emk^{(t)}, U_{i_1}) = m$ The above requirement means correctness of TRE.

Next, we provide a security definition of TRE based on the idea of timed-release security and the traditional encryption with information-theoretic security. The choice of possible colluders $W \in \mathcal{P}(\mathcal{U}, \omega)$ is the same as that in TR-KA. For a set of colluders $W = \{U_{l_1}, U_{l_2}, \ldots, U_{l_j}\} \in \mathcal{P}(\mathcal{U}, \omega)$, $\mathcal{EK}_W := \mathcal{EK}_{l_1} \times \mathcal{EK}_{l_2} \times \cdots \times \mathcal{EK}_{l_j}$ is a set of W's encryption-keys, and $\mathcal{DK}_W := \mathcal{DK}_{l_1} \times \mathcal{DK}_{l_2} \times \cdots \times \mathcal{DK}_{l_j}$ is a set of W's decryption-keys. Also, let $\mathcal{C}_{i_1,i_2}^{(t)}$ be a finite set of possible ciphertexts sent from U_{i_1} to U_{i_2} such that it can be decrypted at the time t. Furthermore, let M, $C_{i_1,i_2}^{(t)}$, EMK, EK_W, DK_W, and $ETI^{(1)}, \ldots, ETI^{(\tau)}$ be random variables which take values on $\mathcal{M}_E$, $\mathcal{C}_{i_1,i_2}^{(t)}$, $\mathcal{EMK}$, $\mathcal{EK}_W$, $\mathcal{DK}_W$, and $\mathcal{ETI}^{(1)}, \ldots, \mathcal{ETI}^{(\tau)}$, respectively.

Similarly as in Definition 2 we consider the following three types of security notions for TRE: (1) A dishonest time-server cannot obtain any information on an underlying plaintext from a target ciphertext transmitted on the channel; (2) No information on an underlying plaintext from a target ciphertext is obtained by any colluding group W not including a legitimate receiver, even if W obtains time-signals at all the time; (3) No information on an underlying plaintext from a target ciphertext is obtained by any colluding group W including a legitimate (but dishonest) receiver, even if W obtains time-signals at all the time except the specified time.

The formalizations of the above security notions for TRE are given as follows.

Definition 5. Let Σ be TRE. Σ is said to be (n, ω, τ)-*secure* if the following conditions are satisfied:

(1) For any $U_{i_1}, U_{i_2} \in \mathcal{U}$ and any $t \in \mathcal{T}$, it holds that

$$H(M \mid C_{i_1,i_2}^{(t)}, EMK) = H(M).$$

(2) For any $W \in \mathcal{P}(\mathcal{U}, \omega)$, $U_{i_1}, U_{i_2} \in \mathcal{U}$ such that $U_{i_1}, U_{i_2} \notin W$, and for any $t \in \mathcal{T}$, it holds that

$$H(M \mid C_{i_1,i_2}^{(t)}, EK_W, DK_W, ETI^{(1)}, \ldots, ETI^{(\tau)}) = H(M).$$

(3) For any $W \in \mathcal{P}(\mathcal{U}, \omega)$, $U_{i_1}, U_{i_2} \in \mathcal{U}$ such that $U_{i_1} \notin W$ and $U_{i_2} \in W$, for any $t \in \mathcal{T}$, it holds that

$$H(M \mid C_{i_1,i_2}^{(t)}, EK_W, DK_W, ETI^{(1)}, \ldots, ETI^{(t-1)}, ETI^{(t+1)}, \ldots, ETI^{(\tau)})$$
$$= H(M).$$

3.2   Construction of TRE from TR-KA and One-Time Pad

We present a generic construction of TRE $\Sigma=(EGen, EExt, Enc, Dec)$ starting from TR-KA $\Pi=(Setup, Ext, KeyGen, KeyDer)$ and the one-time pad. In our construction, Π and Σ satisfy the following conditions: $\mathcal{EMK} = \mathcal{TMK}$; $\mathcal{ETI} = \mathcal{TI}$; $\mathcal{EK} = \mathcal{TUK}^{(S)}$; and $\mathcal{DK} = \mathcal{TUK}^{(R)}$.

1. **EGen.** For a security parameter 1^k, $EGen$ outputs matching secret-keys $usk_i = (ek_i, dk_i)$ and emk^* for U_i ($1 \leq i \leq n$) and T, respectively, as follows. $EGen$ calls $Setup$ with input 1^k. Suppose $(tuk_1^{(S)}, tuk_1^{(R)}, tuk_2^{(S)}, tuk_2^{(R)}, \ldots, tuk_n^{(S)}, tuk_n^{(R)}, tmk^*) \leftarrow Setup(1^k)$. Then, $EGen$ outputs secret-keys $ek_i := tuk_i^{(S)}$, $dk_i := tuk_i^{(R)}$, and $emk^* := tmk^*$ for U_i ($1 \leq i \leq n$) and T, respectively.

2. **EExt.** For a master-key $emk^* = tmk^*$ and time t, $EExt$ calls Ext, and suppose $tmk^{(t)} = Ext(tmk^*, t)$. Then, $EExt$ outputs a time-signal at the time t, $emk^{(t)} := tmk^{(t)}$.

3. **Enc.** For a plaintext m, an encryption-key $ek_{i_1} = tuk_{i_1}^{(S)}$, the specified time t and an identity U_{i_2}, Enc calls $KeyGen$, and suppose $tck_{i_1,i_2}^{(t)} = KeyGen(tuk_{i_1}^{(S)}, t, U_{i_2})$. Then, Enc outputs a ciphertext $c_{i_1,i_2}^{(t)} := m \oplus tck_{i_1,i_2}^{(t)}$.

4. **Dec.** For a ciphertext $c_{i_1,i_2}^{(t)}$, a decryption-key $dk_{i_2} = tuk_{i_2}^{(R)}$, a time-signal $emk^{(t)} = tmk^{(t)}$ at the specified time t and an identity U_{i_1}, Dec calls $KeyDer$, and suppose $tck_{i_1,i_2}^{(t)} = KeyDer(tuk_{i_2}^{(R)}, tmk^{(t)}, U_{i_1})$. Then, Dec outputs a plaintext $m := c_{i_1,i_2}^{(t)} \oplus tck_{i_1,i_2}^{(t)}$.

The security of the above construction is shown as follows. (See the full version of this paper [16] for the detailed proof.)

Theorem 3. *Given (n, ω, τ)-secure TR-KA Π in which common-keys are uniformly distributed over $\mathcal{TCK}$ (i.e., $H(TCK_{i,j}^{(t)}) = \log_2 |\mathcal{TCK}|$ for any i, j, and t), then the TRE Σ formed by the above construction based on Π is (n, ω, τ)-secure.*

Proof Sketch. The proof can be directly shown by the security of TR-KA and perfect secrecy of the one-time pad. First, we describe the outline of the proof for the condition (1) in Definition 5. From Definition 2, T cannot obtain any information on a common-key shared between two honest users even if T knows a master key. Therefore, by perfect secrecy of the one-time pad, $H(M \mid C_{i_1,i_2}^{(t)}, EMK) = H(M)$.

Next, we only describe the outline of the proof for the condition (2) in Definition 5, since the condition (3) can be shown by a similar idea. From Definition 2, any colluding group W such that $U_{i_1}, U_{i_2} \notin W$ cannot know a uniform common-key shared between U_{i_1} and U_{i_2} in TR-KA. Therefore, by perfect secrecy of the one-time pad, $H(M \mid C_{i_1,i_2}^{(t)}, EK_W, DK_W, ETI^{(1)}, \ldots, ETI^{(\tau)}) = H(M)$.   □

4   TRA-Codes: Timed-Release Authentication Codes

In this section, we show a model and a security definition of timed-release authentication codes (TRA-codes for short). We also show that TRA-codes can be constructed from TR-KA and the traditional authentication codes (A-codes for short) in a generic and simple way.

4.1   Model and Security Definition

We newly propose a model and a security definition of TRA-codes, based on that of timed-release signatures with computational security (e.g., [8]) and that of the traditional authentication code with information-theoretic security (e.g., [15]).

Formally, we give a definition of TRA-codes in the TI-model as in the case of TR-KA.

Definition 6 (TRA-codes). A *timed-release authentication code* (*TRA-code* for short) Λ involves $n + 2$ entities, TI, $U_1, U_2, \ldots, U_n$ and T, and consists of a four-tuple of algorithms (*TAGen, AExt, TAuth, TVer*) with six spaces, $\mathcal{M}_A$, $\mathcal{A}, \mathcal{E}, \mathcal{AMK}, \mathcal{T}$ and $\mathcal{ATI}$, where all of the above algorithms except *TAGen* are deterministic and all of the above spaces are finite. In addition, Λ is executed with four phases as follows.

- **Notation:**
    - Entities: TI, U_i $(1 \leq i \leq n)$, T, and $\mathcal{U}$ are the same as those in Definition 1.
    - Spaces: $\mathcal{T}$ is the same as that in Definition 1. $\mathcal{A}$ is a set of possible authenticators (or tags), $\mathcal{M}_A$ is a set of possible messages, $\mathcal{AMK}$ is a set of possible master-keys. $\mathcal{ATI}^{(t)}$ is a set of time-signals at time t. Let $\mathcal{ATI} := \bigcup_{t=1}^{\tau} \mathcal{ATI}^{(t)}$. Also, $\mathcal{E}_i^{(S)}$ is a set of possible U_i's authentication-keys, $\mathcal{E}_i^{(R)}$ is a set of possible U_i's verification-keys, and $\mathcal{E}_i := \mathcal{E}_i^{(S)} \times \mathcal{E}_i^{(R)}$ is a set of possible secret-keys for U_i. Let $\mathcal{E}^{(S)} := \bigcup_{i=1}^{n} \mathcal{E}_i^{(S)}$, $\mathcal{E}^{(R)} := \bigcup_{i=1}^{n} \mathcal{E}_i^{(R)}$, and $\mathcal{E} := \bigcup_{i=1}^{n} \mathcal{E}_i$.

- Algorithms: $TAGen$ is a key generation algorithm which on input a security parameter 1^k, outputs each user's secret-key and a time-server's master-key, $AExt \colon \mathcal{AMK} \times \mathcal{T} \to \mathcal{ATI}$ is a time-signal generation algorithm for T, $TAuth \colon \mathcal{M}_A \times \mathcal{E}^{(S)} \times \mathcal{T} \times \mathcal{U} \to \mathcal{A}$ is an authentication algorithm, and $TVer \colon \mathcal{M}_A \times \mathcal{A} \times \mathcal{T} \times \mathcal{E}^{(R)} \times \mathcal{ATI} \times \mathcal{U} \to \{true, false\}$ is a verification algorithm.

1. **Key Generation and Distribution.** In the initial phase, TI generates the following keys by using $TAGen$: a master-key $amk^* \in \mathcal{AMK}$ for T; a secret-key $e_i = (e_i^{(S)}, e_i^{(R)}) \in \mathcal{E}_i$ for U_i $(i = 1, 2, \ldots, n)$. These keys are distributed to corresponding entities via secure channels. After distributing these keys, TI deletes them from his memory. And, T and U_i keep their keys secret, respectively.

2. **Time-signal Generation.** For broadcasting a time-signal at each time, T generates a time-signal $amk^{(t)} = AExt(amk^*, t) \in \mathcal{ATI}^{(t)}$ by using a master-key $amk^* \in \mathcal{AMK}$ and time $t \in \mathcal{T}$. Then, T broadcasts it to all users via a (authenticated) broadcast channel.

3. **Authentication.** U_{i_1} specifies time t when U_{i_2} can verify validity of a message m, and then U_{i_1} computes an authenticator, $\alpha_{i_1, i_2}^{(t)} = TAuth(m, e_{i_1}^{(S)}, t, U_{i_2}) \in \mathcal{A}$, by the message $m \in \mathcal{M}_A$, an authentication-key $e_{i_1}^{(S)}$, the specified time t and the identity U_{i_2}. And, U_{i_1} sends $(m, \alpha_{i_1, i_2}^{(t)}, t)$ to U_{i_2} via an insecure channel.

4. **Verification.** Suppose that U_{i_2} has received $(m, \alpha_{i_1, i_2}^{(t)}, t)$ from U_{i_1}. After receiving a time-signal $amk^{(t)}$ at the specified time t, U_{i_2} checks the validity of $\alpha_{i_1, i_2}^{(t)}$ by a verification-key $e_{i_2}^{(R)}$, a time-signal $amk^{(t)}$ and the identity U_{i_1}: If $TVer(m, \alpha_{i_1, i_2}^{(t)}, t, e_{i_2}^{(R)}, amk^{(t)}, U_{i_1}) = true$, then U_{i_2} accepts $(m, \alpha_{i_1, i_2}^{(t)}, t)$ as valid, and rejects it otherwise.

In the model of TRA-codes, we require the following equation holds: For all possible $t \in \mathcal{T}$, $i_1, i_2 \in \{1, 2, \ldots, n\}$, $e_{i_1}^{(S)} \in \mathcal{E}_{i_1}^{(S)}$, $e_{i_2}^{(R)} \in \mathcal{E}_{i_2}^{(R)}$, $amk^{(t)} \in \mathcal{ATI}^{(t)}$, we have $TVer(m, TAuth(m, e_{i_1}^{(S)}, t, U_{i_2}), t, e_{i_2}^{(R)}, amk^{(t)}, U_{i_1}) = true$Ｄ The above requirement means correctness of TRA-codes.

Next, we provide a security notion and its formalization for TRA-codes based on the idea of timed-release security and the traditional authentication code with information-theoretic security. The choice of possible colluders $W \in \mathcal{P}(\mathcal{U}, \omega)$ is the same as that in TR-KA. For a set of colluders $W := \{U_{l_1}, U_{l_2}, \ldots, U_{l_j}\} \in \mathcal{P}(\mathcal{U}, \omega)$, $\mathcal{E}_W^{(S)} := \mathcal{E}_{l_1}^{(S)} \times \mathcal{E}_{l_2}^{(S)} \times \cdots \times \mathcal{E}_{l_j}^{(S)}$ is a set of W's authentication-keys, and $\mathcal{E}_W^{(R)} := \mathcal{E}_{l_1}^{(R)} \times \mathcal{E}_{l_2}^{(R)} \times \cdots \times \mathcal{E}_{l_j}^{(R)}$ is a set of W's verification-keys. In TRA-codes, we consider *impersonation attacks* and *substitution attacks* as follows. (a) *Impersonation attacks:* an adversary (or a dishonest entity) tries to generate a fraudulent authenticated message at time t, $(m, \alpha_{i_1, i_2}^{(t)}, t)$, that has not been legally generated by a sender U_{i_1} but will be accepted by a receiver U_{i_2}. (b) *Substitution attacks:* an adversary (or a dishonest entity) tries to generate a fraudulent authenticated message at time t_2, $(m', \alpha_{i_1, i_2}^{(t_2)}, t_2)$, that has not been legally generated by a

sender U_{i_1} but will be accepted by a receiver U_{i_2}, after observing a valid authen-
ticated message at time t_1, $(m, \alpha_{i_1,i_2}^{(t_1)}, t_1)$ with $(m, \alpha_{i_1,i_2}^{(t_1)}, t_1) \neq (m', \alpha_{i_1,i_2}^{(t_2)}, t_2)$.
Similarly as in Definition 2 we consider the following three types of security
notions for TRA-codes: (1) A dishonest time-server cannot succeed in each of
the *impersonation attack* and *substitution attack*; (2) Any colluding group W
not including a legitimate receiver cannot succeed in each of the *impersonation
attack* and *substitution attack*, even if W obtains time-signals at all the time; (3)
Any colluding group W including a legitimate (but dishonest) receiver cannot
check the validity of a target authenticated message without a time-signal at the
specified time, even if W obtains time-signals at all the time except the specified
time. To formalize this security notion, we consider it to be a kind of security
against impersonation attacks at the future specified time: Any colluding group
W including a receiver cannot succeed in impersonation attacks at the future
specified time, even if W obtains time-signals at all the time except the specified
time.

The formalizations of the above three types of security notions for TRA-codes
are given as follows.

Definition 7. Let Λ be a TRA-code. Λ is said to be $(n, \omega, \tau; \epsilon)$-*secure*, if $\max($
$P_{Server}, P_1, P_2) \leq \epsilon$, where P_{Server}, P_1 and P_2 are defined as follows.

(1) *Attacks by a dishonest time-server.* Let $P_{Server} := \max(P_{I_S}, P_{S_S})$, where P_{I_S}
and P_{S_S} are given as follows.

1-1) *Impersonation attacks.* The success probability of this attack denoted by
P_{I_S} is defined as follows: For any $U_{i_1}, U_{i_2} \in \mathcal{U}$ and any $t \in \mathcal{T}$, we define
$P_{I_S}(U_{i_1}, U_{i_2}, t)$ by

$$P_{I_S}(U_{i_1}, U_{i_2}, t) := \max_{(m, \alpha_{i_1,i_2}^{(t)}, t)} \max_{amk^*} \max_{amk^{(t)}}$$

$$\Pr(TVer(m, \alpha_{i_1,i_2}^{(t)}, t, e_{i_2}^{(R)}, amk^{(t)}, U_{i_1}) = true \mid amk^*).$$

The probability P_{I_S} is defined as $P_{I_S} := \max_{U_{i_1}, U_{i_2}, t} P_{I_S}(U_{i_1}, U_{i_2}, t)$.

1-2) *Substitution attacks.* The success probability of this attack denoted by
P_{S_S} is defined as follows: For any $U_{i_1}, U_{i_2} \in \mathcal{U}$ and any $t_1, t_2 \in \mathcal{T}$, we
define $P_{S_S}(U_{i_1}, U_{i_2}, t_1, t_2)$ by

$$P_{S_S}(U_{i_1}, U_{i_2}, t_1, t_2) := \max_{(m', \alpha_{i_1,i_2}^{(t_2)}, t_2)} \max_{(m, \alpha_{i_1,i_2}^{(t_1)}, t_1) \neq (m', \alpha_{i_1,i_2}^{(t_2)}, t_2)} \max_{amk^*} \max_{amk^{(t_2)}}$$

$$\Pr(TVer(m', \alpha_{i_1,i_2}^{(t_2)}, t_2, e_{i_2}^{(R)}, amk^{(t_2)}, U_{i_1}) = true \mid (m, \alpha_{i_1,i_2}^{(t_1)}, t_1), amk^*).$$

The probability P_{S_S} is defined as $P_{S_S} := \max_{U_{i_1}, U_{i_2}, t_1, t_2} P_{S_S}(U_{i_1}, U_{i_2}, t_1, t_2)$.

(2) *Attacks by colluders not including a legitimate receiver.* Let $P_1 := \max(P_{I_1},$
$P_{S_1})$, where P_{I_1} and P_{S_1} are given as follows.

2-1) *Impersonation attacks.* The success probability of this attack denoted
by P_{I_1} is defined as follows: For any set of colluders $W \in \mathcal{P}(\mathcal{U}, \omega)$, any

$U_{i_1}, U_{i_2} \in \mathcal{U}$ such that $U_{i_1}, U_{i_2} \notin W$ and for any $t \in \mathcal{T}$, we define $P_{I_1}(U_{i_1}, U_{i_2}, W, t)$ by

$$P_{I_1}(U_{i_1}, U_{i_2}, W, t) := \max_{(m,\alpha_{i_1,i_2}^{(t)},t)} \max_{e_W^{(S)}} \max_{e_W^{(R)}} \max_{amk^{(1)},...,amk^{(\tau)}}$$

$$\Pr(TVer(m, \alpha_{i_1,i_2}^{(t)}, t, e_{i_2}^{(R)}, amk^{(t)}, U_{i_1}) = true$$

$$\mid e_W^{(S)}, e_W^{(R)}, amk^{(1)}, \dots, amk^{(\tau)}).$$

The probability P_{I_1} is defined as $P_{I_1} := \max_{U_{i_1}, U_{i_2}, W, t} P_{I_1}(U_{i_1}, U_{i_2}, W, t)$.

2-2) *Substitution attacks.* The success probability of this attack denoted by P_{S_1} is defined as follows: For any set of colluders $W \in \mathcal{P}(\mathcal{U}, \omega)$, any $U_{i_1}, U_{i_2} \in \mathcal{U}$ such that $U_{i_1}, U_{i_2} \notin W$ and for any $t_1, t_2 \in \mathcal{T}$, we define $P_{S_1}(U_{i_1}, U_{i_2}, W, t_1, t_2)$ by

$$P_{S_1}(U_{i_1}, U_{i_2}, W, t_1, t_2) := \max_{(m',\alpha_{i_1,i_2}^{(t_2)},t_2)} \max_{(m,\alpha_{i_1,i_2}^{(t_1)},t_1) \neq (m',\alpha_{i_1,i_2}^{(t_2)},t_2)} \max_{e_W^{(S)}} \max_{e_W^{(R)}}$$

$$\max_{amk^{(1)},...,amk^{(\tau)}} \Pr(TVer(m', \alpha_{i_1,i_2}^{(t_2)}, t_2, e_{i_2}^{(R)}, amk^{(t_2)}, U_{i_1}) = true$$

$$\mid (m, \alpha_{i_1,i_2}^{(t_1)}, t_1), e_W^{(S)}, e_W^{(R)}, amk^{(1)}, \dots, amk^{(\tau)}).$$

And, P_{S_1} is defined as $P_{S_1} := \max_{U_{i_1}, U_{i_2}, W, t_1, t_2} P_{S_1}(U_{i_1}, U_{i_2}, W, t_1, t_2)$.

(3) *An attack by colluders including a legitimate (but dishonest) receiver.* The success probability of this attack denoted by P_2 is defined as follows: For any set of colluders $W \in \mathcal{P}(\mathcal{U}, \omega)$, any $U_{i_1}, U_{i_2} \in \mathcal{U}$ such that $U_{i_1} \notin W$ and $U_{i_2} \in W$, and for any $t \in \mathcal{T}$, we define $P_2(U_{i_1}, U_{i_2}, W, t)$ by

$$P_2(U_{i_1}, U_{i_2}, W, t) := \max_{(m,\alpha_{i_1,i_2}^{(t)},t)} \max_{e_W^{(S)}} \max_{e_W^{(R)}} \max_{amk^{(1)},...,amk^{(t-1)},amk^{(t+1)},...,amk^{(\tau)}}$$

$$\Pr(TVer(m, \alpha_{i_1,i_2}^{(t)}, t, e_{i_2}^{(R)}, amk^{(t)}, U_{i_1}) = true$$

$$\mid e_W^{(S)}, e_W^{(R)} amk^{(1)}, \dots, amk^{(t-1)}, amk^{(t+1)}, \dots, amk^{(\tau)}).$$

The probability P_2 is defined as $P_2 := \max_{U_{i_1}, U_{i_2}, W, t} P_2(U_{i_1}, U_{i_2}, W, t)$.

4.2   Construction of TRA-codes from TR-KA and A-Codes

We propose a generic construction of $(n, \omega, \tau; \epsilon)$-secure TRA-codes from TR-KA and the traditional A-codes (e.g., [15]). First, we briefly explain the traditional A-codes as follows.

A-codes. We consider a scenario where there are three entities, a sender S, a receiver R, and an adversary A. The A-code Θ consists of a three-tuple of algorithms ($AGen$, $Auth$, Ver) with three spaces, $\tilde{\mathcal{M}}$, $\tilde{\mathcal{A}}$ and $\tilde{\mathcal{E}}$, where they are finite sets of possible messages, possible authenticators (or tags) and possible secret-keys, respectively. $AGen$ is a key generation algorithm, which takes a security parameter on input and outputs a secret-key e. *Auth* is an algorithm for generating an authenticator. *Auth* takes a message $m \in \mathcal{M}$ and a secret-key $e \in \tilde{\mathcal{E}}$ on input and outputs an authenticator $\alpha \in \tilde{\mathcal{A}}$, and we write $\alpha = Auth(m, e)$ for it. On receiving (m, α), a receiver R can check the validity of it by using *Ver*. *Ver* takes a message m, an authenticator α and a secret-key e on input, and outputs *true* or *false*, and we write $true = Ver(m, \alpha, e)$ or $false = Ver(m, \alpha, e)$ for it. In A-codes, there are two kinds of attacks: *impersonation attacks* and *substitution attacks*. Here, Θ is said to be ϵ-*secure* if each of success probabilities of these attacks is at most ϵ (e.g., see [15] for details).

The detail of our generic construction of TRA-codes $\Lambda = (TAGen, AExt, TAuth, TVer)$ by using TR-KA $\Pi = (Setup, Ext, KeyGen, KeyDer)$ and A-codes $\Theta = (AGen, Auth, Ver)$ is given as follows. In our construction, Π, Θ and Λ satisfy the following conditions: $\mathcal{M}_A \times \mathcal{T} \subset \mathcal{M}$; $\mathcal{TCK} \subset \tilde{\mathcal{E}}$; $\mathcal{A} = \tilde{\mathcal{A}}$; $\mathcal{AMK} = \mathcal{TMK}$; $\mathcal{ATI} = \mathcal{TI}$; $\mathcal{E}^{(S)} = \mathcal{TUK}^{(S)}$; and $\mathcal{E}^{(R)} = \mathcal{TUK}^{(R)}$.

1. **TAGen.** For a security parameter 1^k, *TAGen* outputs matching secret-keys $e_i = (e_i^{(S)}, e_i^{(R)})$ and amk^* for U_i $(1 \leq i \leq n)$ and T, respectively, as follows. *TAGen* calls *Setup* with input 1^k, and suppose $(tuk_1^{(S)}, tuk_1^{(R)}, tuk_2^{(S)}, tuk_2^{(R)},$
   $\ldots, tuk_n^{(S)}, tuk_n^{(R)}, tmk^*) \leftarrow Setup(1^k)$. Then, *TAGen* outputs secret-keys $e_i^{(S)} := tuk_i^{(S)}, e_i^{(R)} := tuk_i^{(R)}$ and $amk^* := tmk^*$ for U_i $(1 \leq i \leq n)$ and T, respectively.

2. **AExt.** For a master-key $amk^* = tmk^*$ and time t, *AExt* calls *Ext*, and suppose $tmk^{(t)} = Ext(tmk^*, t)$. Then, *AExt* outputs a time-signal at time t, $amk^{(t)} := tmk^{(t)}$.

3. **TAuth.** For a message m, an authentication-key $e_{i_1}^{(S)} = tuk_{i_1}^{(S)}$, the specified time t and an identity U_{i_2}, *TAuth* calls *KeyGen*, and suppose $tck_{i_1, i_2}^{(t)} = KeyGen(tuk_{i_1}^{(S)}, t, U_{i_2})$. Then, *TAuth* calls *Auth*, and it computes an authenticator $\alpha = Auth((m, t), tck_{i_1, i_2}^{(t)})$. Finally, *TAuth* outputs an authenticator at time t, $\alpha_{i_1, i_2}^{(t)} := \alpha$.

4. **TVer.** For a message m, the specified time t, an authenticator $\alpha_{i_1, i_2}^{(t)}$, a verification-key $e_{i_2}^{(R)} = tuk_{i_2}^{(R)}$, a time-signal $amk^{(t)} = tmk^{(t)}$ at the specified time t and an identity U_{i_1}, *TVer* calls *KeyDer* with inputting them, and suppose $tck_{i_1, i_2}^{(t)} = KeyDer(tuk_{i_2}^{(R)}, tmk^{(t)}, U_{i_1})$. Then, *TVer* outputs *true* if $Ver((m, t), \alpha_{i_1, i_2}^{(t)}, tck_{i_1, i_2}^{(t)}) = true$, and outputs *false* otherwise.

The security of the above construction is shown as follows. (See the full version of this paper [16] for the detailed proof.)

Theorem 4. *Given an ϵ-secure A-code Θ and (n, ω, τ)-secure TR-KA Π in which common-keys are uniformly distributed over $\mathcal{TCK}$, then the TRA-code Λ formed by the above construction based on Θ and Π is $(n, \omega, \tau; \epsilon)$-secure.*

Proof Sketch. The proof can be directly shown by the security of TR-KA and that of the A-code. First, we describe the outline of the proof of $P_{S_S} \leq \epsilon$. From

Definition 2, T cannot obtain any information on a common-key shared between two honest users even if T knows a master key. Therefore, since the underlying A-code is ϵ-secure, success probability of substitution attacks is at most ϵ. Thus, we have $P_{S_S} \leq \epsilon$. In a manner similar to this, we can prove $P_{I_S} \leq \epsilon$. Therefore, we have $P_{Server} = \max(P_{I_S}, P_{S_S}) \leq \epsilon$.

Next, we describe the outline of the proof of $P_{S_1} \leq \epsilon$. From Definition 2, any colluding group W such that $U_{i_1}, U_{i_2} \notin W$ cannot know a uniform common-key shared between U_{i_1} and U_{i_2} in TR-KA. Therefore, since the underlying A-code is ϵ-secure, success probability of substitution attacks is at most ϵ. Thus, we have $P_{S_1} \leq \epsilon$. In a manner similar to this, we can prove $P_{I_1} \leq \epsilon$. Therefore, we have $P_1 = \max(P_{I_1}, P_{S_1}) \leq \epsilon$.

Finally, we describe the outline of the proof of $P_2 \leq \epsilon$. From Definition 2, even a colluding group W including a legitimate (but dishonest) receiver cannot obtain any information on a common-key at the future specified time. Hence, success probability of this attack can be reduced to that of impersonation attacks for the underlying A-code. Thus, we have $P_2 \leq \epsilon$.   □

5   Relation to Information-Theoretic Key-Insulated Security

In this section, we show relationship between TR-KA and key-insulated key-agreement (KI-KA for short) in information-theoretic security setting. We now start with describing the model of KI-KA as follows.

KI-KA. Recently, information-theoretically secure KI-KA is proposed by Seito and Shikata [13]. In KI-KA, there are $\tilde{n}$ users $U_1, U_2, \ldots, U_{\tilde{n}}$ where $\tilde{n}$ is a positive integer. And each user has two kinds of devices: a trusted device (e.g., a smart card, USB flash memory) which stores a master-key; and an insecure device in which a user's secret-key is stored. Here, the notion of a *secure device* implies that it is usually isolated from a network (e.g. the Internet or LAN) and that the attacker can neither wiretap nor substitute information stored in the device via the network. Here, we assume that the user U_i's secure device is expressed as H_i ($1 \leq i \leq \tilde{n}$). We also assume that the lifetime of systems is divided into discrete periods. And, at the beginning of each period j, U_i receives key-updating information from H_i by connecting with H_i, then U_i computes a secret-key at the period j by using the secret-key of the previous period and key-updating information. And then, any user U_{i_1} can share a common-key with any user U_{i_2} at a period j.

In KI-KA, if the trusted device is not compromised, then user's secret-keys of some periods can be exposed without losing security of systems. Additionally, even if the trusted device is exposed, the system will not be broken if no user's secret-key is exposed. The informal security requirement of KI-KA is as follows: the adversary does not obtain any information on a common-key shared between two honest users at a target period under each of the following adversarial models; (a) the adversary can obtain at most γ exposed target users' secret-keys; (b) the adversary can obtain target users' master-keys. In both cases, the adversary can also obtain exposed secret-keys and master-keys from at most $\tilde{\omega}$ corrupted users. Then, KI-KA is called to be $(\tilde{n}, \tilde{\omega}; N, \gamma)$-*secure* if the above requirement is satisfied.

Basic Idea of Generic Constructions. In KI-KA, any user cannot update a secret-key without using key-updating information which is generated by the master-key. That is to say, the user's key-updating process is *controlled* by the device's master-key and key-updating information. On the other hand, in TR-KA, no user (a receiver) can derive a common-key without using a time-signal corresponding to a designated period (time). Namely, the receiver's common-key derivation process is *controlled* by the time-server's master-key and the time-signal. As seen from the above observation, the mechanisms of KI-KA and TR-KA are similar in the point that a common-key (or a secret-key required for deriving a common-key) derivation process is *controlled* by a master-key.

The above statement is explicitly shown by proposing two generic constructions (or converters) in a simple way: one is a construction of KI-KA from TR-KA; and the other is a construction of TR-KA from KI-KA. More precisely, we can show the following theorem which states that the mechanisms of TR-KA and KI-KA are essentially close. The proof is shown in the full version of this paper [16].

Theorem 5. *There is a generic construction of KI-KA $\tilde{\Pi}$ from TR-KA Π in a simple way such that, if Π is (n, ω, τ)-secure, then the resulting $\tilde{\Pi}$ is $(\tilde{n}, \tilde{\omega}; N, \gamma)$-secure, where $\tilde{n} = n$, $\tilde{\omega} = \omega$, and $\gamma = \tau$. Conversely, there is a generic construction of TR-KA Π from KI-KA $\tilde{\Pi}$ in a simple way such that, if $\tilde{\Pi}$ is $(\tilde{n}, \tilde{\omega}; N, \gamma)$-secure, then the resulting Π is (n, ω, τ)-secure, where $n = \frac{1}{2}\tilde{n}$, $\omega = \frac{1}{2}\tilde{\omega}$, and $\tau = \gamma$.*

Acknowledgements. We would like to thank anonymous reviewers for their valuable comments.

References

1. Boneh, D., Naor, M.: Timed Commitments. In: Bellare, M. (ed.) CRYPTO 2000. LNCS, vol. 1880, pp. 236–254. Springer, Heidelberg (2000)
2. Cathalo, J., Libert, B., Quisquater, J.-J.: Efficient and Non-Interactive Timed-Release Encryption. In: Qing, S., Mao, W., López, J., Wang, G. (eds.) ICICS 2005. LNCS, vol. 3783, pp. 291–303. Springer, Heidelberg (2005)
3. Chalkias, K., Hristu-Varsakelis, D., Stephanides, G.: Improved Anonymous Timed-Release Encryption. In: Biskup, J., López, J. (eds.) ESORICS 2007. LNCS, vol. 4734, pp. 311–326. Springer, Heidelberg (2007)
4. Chan, A.C.-F., Blake, I.F.: Scalable, Server-Passive, User-Anonymous Timed-Release Public Key Encryption from Bilinear Pairing. In: 25th International Conference on Distributed Computing Systems, pp. 504–513. IEEE, Los Almitos (2005), The full version is available at, http://eprint.iacr.org/2004/211

5. Cheon, J.H., Hopper, N., Kim, Y., Osipkov, I.: Timed-Release and Key-Insulated Public key Encryption. In: Di Crescenzo, G., Rubin, A. (eds.) FC 2006. LNCS, vol. 4107, pp. 191–205. Springer, Heidelberg (2006), The full version is available at, http://eprint.iacr.org/2004/231

6. Cheon, J.H., Hopper, N., Kim, Y., Osipkov, I.: Provably Secure Timed-Release Public Key Encryption. ACM Trans. Information and System Security 11(2), 1–44 (2008)

7. Fujioka, A., Okamoto, Y., Saito, T.: Generic Construction of Strongly Secure Timed-Release Public-Key Encryption. In: Parampalli, U., Hawkes, P. (eds.) ACISP 2011. LNCS, vol. 6812, pp. 319–336. Springer, Heidelberg (2011)

8. Garay, J.A., Jakobsson, C.: Timed Release of Standard Digital Signatures. In: Blaze, M. (ed.) FC 2002. LNCS, vol. 2357, pp. 168–182. Springer, Heidelberg (2003)

9. Garay, J.A., Pomerance, C.: Timed Fair Exchange of Standard Signatures. In: Wright, R.N. (ed.) FC 2003. LNCS, vol. 2742, pp. 190–207. Springer, Heidelberg (2003)

10. May, T.C.: Timed-release crypto. manuscript (1993)

11. Rivest, R.: Unconditionally Secure Commitment and Oblivious Transfer Schemes Using Private Channels and a Trusted Initializer. manuscript (1999), http://people.csail.mit.edu/rivest/Rivest-commitment.pdf

12. Rivest, R., Shamir, A., Wagner, D.A.: Time-lock puzzles and timed-release crypto. MIT LCS Tech. Report. MIT LCS TR-684 (1996)

13. Seito, T., Shikata, J.: Information-Theoretically Secure Key-Insulated Key-Agreement. In: 2011 IEEE Information Theory Workshop (ITW), pp. 287–291. IEEE (2011)

14. Shannon, C.E.: Communication theory of secrecy systems. Bell System Technical Journal 28, 656–715 (1949)

15. Simmons, G.J.: Authentication Theory/Coding Theory. In: Blakely, G.R., Chaum, D. (eds.) CRYPTO 1984. LNCS, vol. 196, pp. 411–431. Springer, Heidelberg (1985)

16. Watanabe, Y., Seito, T., Shikata, J.: Information-Theoretic Timed-Release Security: Key-Agreement, Encryption, and Authentication Codes. the full version of this paper. To appear at Cryptology ePrint Archive, IACR (2012)

Appendix: Proof of Theorem 1

The proof follows from the following lemmas.

Lemma 1. $H(TUK_i^{(R)}) \geq (\omega + 1)H(TCK)$ for any $i \in \{1, 2, \ldots, n\}$.

Proof. For arbitrary $i \in \{1, 2, \ldots, n\}$, we take a subset $B := \{l_1, l_2, \ldots, l_{\omega+1}\} \subset \{1, 2, \ldots, n\}$ of indices of users such that $i \notin B$. Let $D_k := (l_k, i)$ and $W_k := \{l_1, l_2, \ldots, l_k\}$ for each k with $1 \leq k \leq \omega + 1$. Then, we have

$$H(TUK_i^{(R)}) \geq H(TUK_i^{(R)} \mid TI^{(t)})$$
$$\geq I(TCK_{D_1}^{(t)}, TCK_{D_2}^{(t)}, \ldots, TCK_{D_{\omega+1}}^{(t)}; TUK_i^{(R)} \mid TI^{(t)})$$
$$= H(TCK_{D_1}^{(t)}, TCK_{D_2}^{(t)}, \ldots, TCK_{D_{\omega+1}}^{(t)} \mid TI^{(t)})$$
$$\quad - H(TCK_{D_1}^{(t)}, TCK_{D_2}^{(t)}, \ldots, TCK_{D_{\omega+1}}^{(t)} \mid TI^{(t)}, TUK_i^{(R)})$$
$$= H(TCK_{D_1}^{(t)}, TCK_{D_2}^{(t)}, \ldots, TCK_{D_{\omega+1}}^{(t)} \mid TI^{(t)})$$
$$= \sum_{k=1}^{\omega+1} H(TCK_{D_k}^{(t)} \mid TI^{(t)}, TCK_{D_1}^{(t)}, TCK_{D_2}^{(t)}, \ldots, TCK_{D_{k-1}}^{(t)})$$
$$\geq \sum_{k=1}^{\omega+1} H(TCK_{D_k}^{(t)} \mid TUK_{W_{k-1}}^{(S)}, TI^{(t)})$$
$$= \sum_{k=1}^{\omega+1} H(TCK_{D_k}^{(t)}) \tag{1}$$
$$= (\omega + 1)H(TCK),$$

where (1) follows from the condition (2) in Definition 2. □

Lemma 2. $H(TUK_i^{(S)}) \geq (\tau + \omega)H(TCK)$ *for any* $i \in \{1, 2, \ldots, n\}$.

Proof. For arbitrary $i \in \{1, 2, \ldots, n\}$, we take a subset $B := \{l_1, l_2, \ldots, l_{\omega+1}\} \subset \{1, 2, \ldots, n\}$ of indices of users such that $i \notin B$. Let $D_k := (i, l_k)$ and $W_k := \{l_1, l_2, \ldots, l_k\}$ for each k with $1 \leq k \leq \omega+1$. Also, let $F_k^{(t)} := (TCK_{D_k}^{(1)}, TCK_{D_k}^{(2)}, \ldots, TCK_{D_k}^{(t)})$ and $G_k^{(t)} := (TCK_{D_1}^{(t)}, TCK_{D_2}^{(t)}, \ldots, TCK_{D_k}^{(t)})$ for $1 \leq k \leq \omega+1$ and $1 \leq t \leq \tau$. Then, we have

$$H(TUK_i^{(S)})$$
$$\geq H(F_1^{(\tau)}, G_{\omega+1}^{(t)})$$
$$= H(F_1^{(\tau)}) + H(G_{\omega+1}^{(t)} \mid F_1^{(\tau)})$$
$$= \sum_{t=1}^{\tau} H(TCK_{D_1}^{(t)} \mid F_1^{(t-1)}) + \sum_{k=2}^{\omega+1} H(TCK_{D_k}^{(t)} \mid F_1^{(\tau)}, TCK_{D_2}^{(t)}, \ldots, TCK_{D_{k-1}}^{(t)})$$
$$\geq \sum_{t=1}^{\tau} H(TCK_{D_1}^{(t)} \mid TUK_{D_1}^{(R)}, TI^{(1)}, \ldots, TI^{(t-1)})$$
$$\quad\quad + \sum_{k=2}^{\omega+1} H(TCK_{D_k}^{(t)} \mid TUK_{W_{k-1}}^{(R)}, TI^{(1)}, \ldots, TI^{(\tau)})$$
$$= \sum_{t=1}^{\tau} H(TCK_{D_1}^{(t)}) + \sum_{k=2}^{\omega+1} H(TCK_{D_k}^{(t)}) \tag{2}$$
$$= (\tau + \omega)H(TCK),$$

where (2) follows from the conditions (2) and (3) in Definition 2. □

Lemma 3. $H(TI^{(t)} \mid TI^{(1)}, \ldots, TI^{(t-1)}) \geq (\omega + 1)H(TCK)$ *for any* $t \in \mathcal{T}$. *In particular,* $H(TI^{(t)}) \geq (\omega + 1)H(TCK)$ *for any* $t \in \mathcal{T}$.

Proof. For arbitrary $i \in \{1, 2, \ldots, n\}$, we take a subset $B := \{l_1, l_2, \ldots, l_{\omega+1}\} \subset \{1, 2, \ldots, n\}$ of indices of users such that $i = l_1$. Let $D_k := (l_k, i)$ and $W_k := \{l_1, l_2, \ldots, l_k\}$ for each k with $1 \leq k \leq \omega + 1$. Then, we have

$$
\begin{aligned}
& H(TI^{(t)} \mid TI^{(1)}, \ldots, TI^{(t-1)}) \\
& \geq H(TI^{(t)} \mid TUK_i^{(R)}, TI^{(1)}, \ldots, TI^{(t-1)}) \\
& \geq I(TCK_{D_1}^{(t)}, TCK_{D_2}^{(t)}, \ldots, TCK_{D_{\omega+1}}^{(t)}; TI^{(t)} \mid TUK_i^{(R)}, TI^{(1)}, \ldots, TI^{(t-1)}) \\
& = H(TCK_{D_1}^{(t)}, TCK_{D_2}^{(t)}, \ldots, TCK_{D_{\omega+1}}^{(t)} \mid TUK_i^{(R)}, TI^{(1)}, \ldots, TI^{(t-1)}) \\
& \quad - H(TCK_{D_1}^{(t)}, \ldots, TCK_{D_{\omega+1}}^{(t)} \mid TUK_i^{(R)}, TI^{(1)}, \ldots, TI^{(t)}) \\
& = H(TCK_{D_1}^{(t)}, TCK_{D_2}^{(t)}, \ldots, TCK_{D_{\omega+1}}^{(t)} \mid TUK_i^{(R)}, TI^{(1)}, \ldots, TI^{(t-1)}) \\
& = \sum_{k=1}^{\omega+1} H(TCK_{D_k}^{(t)} \mid TUK_i^{(R)}, TI^{(1)}, \ldots, TI^{(t-1)}, TCK_{D_1}^{(t)}, \ldots, TCK_{D_{k-1}}^{(t)}) \\
& \geq \sum_{k=1}^{\omega+1} H(TCK_{D_k}^{(t)} \mid TUK_{W_{k-1}}^{(S)}, TUK_i^{(R)}, TI^{(1)}, \ldots, TI^{(t-1)}) \\
& = \sum_{k=1}^{\omega+1} H(TCK_{D_k}^{(t)}) \hspace{4cm} (3) \\
& = (\omega + 1)H(TCK),
\end{aligned}
$$

where (3) follows from the condition (3) in Definition 2. $\qquad \square$

Lemma 4. $H(TMK) \geq \tau(\omega + 1)H(TCK)D$

Proof. We have

$$
\begin{aligned}
H(TMK) & \geq I(TI^{(1)}, \ldots, TI^{(\tau)}; TMK) \\
& = H(TI^{(1)}, \ldots, TI^{(\tau)}) - H(TI^{(1)}, \ldots, TI^{(\tau)} \mid TMK) \\
& = H(TI^{(1)}, \ldots, TI^{(\tau)}) \\
& = \sum_{t=1}^{\tau} H(TI^{(t)} \mid TI^{(1)}, \ldots, TI^{(t-1)}) \\
& = \tau(\omega + 1)H(TCK),
\end{aligned}
$$

where the last equality follows from Lemma 3. $\qquad \square$

Optimum General Threshold Secret Sharing

Maki Yoshida[1], Toru Fujiwara[1], and Marc Fossorier[2]

[1] Osaka University, 1-5 Yamadaoka, Suita, Osaka, 560-0871, Japan
{maki-yos,fujiwara}@ist.osaka-u.ac.jp
[2] ETIS, ENSEA/UCP/CNRS UMR-8051, Cergy-Pontoise, 95014, France
mfossorier@ieee.org

Abstract. An important issue of threshold secret sharing (TSS) schemes is to minimize the size of shares. This issue is resolved for the simpler classes called (k, n)-TSS and (k, L, n)-threshold ramp secret sharing (TRSS). That is, for each of these two classes, an optimum construction which minimizes the share size was presented. The goal of this paper is to develop an optimum construction for a more general threshold class where the mutual information between the secret and a set of shares is defined by a discrete function which monotonically increases from zero to one with the number of shares. A tight lower bound of the entropy of shares is first derived and then an optimum construction is presented. The derived lower bound is larger than the previous one except for special functions such as convex and concave functions. The optimum construction encodes the secret by using one or more optimum TRSS schemes independently. The optimality is shown by devising a combination of TRSS schemes which achieves the new lower bound.

1 Introduction

A threshold secret sharing (TSS) scheme is a technique to encode a secret s into shares $v_1, v_2, \ldots, v_n$ so that the secret is recovered from the pre-defined number of shares. The mutual information between the secret and a set of shares is given by a monotonically increase function of the number of shares, which we call a mutual-information (MI) function. In other words, an arbitrary number of shares leaks out information about the secret according to the MI function. The TSS schemes are classified into three classes in terms of a MI function. The first class, called (k, n)-TSS scheme, was introduced in [4,12] for the simplest threshold MI functions that take exactly zero or one value. The second, called (k, L, n)-threshold ramp secret sharing (TRSS) scheme, was defined in [5,13] for the linear MI functions that can have rational values between zero and one. The final one, proposed in [14], further extends the MI functions to nonlinear ones.

In such TSS schemes, one of the most important issues is to minimize the size of shares. This issue is resolved for the simpler two classes, the (k, n)-TSS scheme and the (k, L, n)-TRSS scheme. That is, optimum constructions which minimize the size of each share have been presented [12,13]. Let $H(X)$ denote the entropy of a random variable X. Let S and V_i denote the random variables induced by s and v_i, respectively. For the first class (step functions), an optimum

A. Smith (Ed.): ICITS 2012, LNCS 7412, pp. 187–204, 2012.

construction in which the entropy of shares is equal to that of the secret, i.e., $H(V_i) = H(S)$ was presented in [12]. For the second class (linear functions), an optimum construction which makes the entropy of shares smaller than that of the secret was introduced in [13]. The entropy of shares is given by the gradient of the slope of the linear function. Specifically, a (k, L, n)-TRSS scheme satisfies $H(V_i) = \frac{1}{L}H(S) \le H(S)$. The results in [12,13] indicate that relaxing the privacy requirement improves the efficiency in terms of the share size.

For the third class (nonlinear functions), the previous constructions in [14,15] are either insecure [14] or inefficient [15] (the optimality of the construction in [15] is only shown for the class of convex and concave functions). In other words, for some general MI functions, the construction in [15] can make the entropy $H(V_i)$ smaller than $H(S)$, but cannot achieve the previously known lower bound of [11], which is derived for more general access structures including non-threshold ones and called a general lower bound. Some results in [11] suggest that the general lower bound may not be tight. Specifically, two examples of non-threshold access structures for which the entropy of some shares is larger than the general lower bound are given. Thus, it is not clear whether the general lower bound is tight for TSS, and whether the construction in [15] can remain optimum for general MI functions. The nonlinear class seems to further relax the privacy requirement in the sense that it allows any pattern of leakage. For applications whose main purpose is the recoverability of data, such as large scale distributed storage with data reliability, the efficiency is much more important.

Our contribution is the development of an optimum construction for the most general threshold class. The definition of TSS in this paper uses the entropy function as in [11,15] because the entropy-based definition originating from [9,6] is suitable for proving lower bounds, though some limitations have been shown for known techniques in [7,3]. We first derive a new lower bound of the entropy of shares and then show that the construction in [15] can achieve the derived lower bound for any MI function. The derived optimal bound is generally larger than the general lower one (which becomes a special case). As a result, the linear class is most efficient.

While the general lower bound is given by the maximum value of the gradient of the corresponding MI function, the derived tight lower bound is given not only by the maximum value of the gradient but also by the values called *local maximum/minimum* values of the gradient. It depends on the number of these local extrema and their respective values. As a result, the entropy of shares becomes larger if we allow more complicated control of the mutual information between the secret and the shares. Thus, except for special MI functions, the new lower bound becomes larger than the general one. We identify the class of MI functions for which the new lower bound is reduced to the general one. In addition, we also show the class of MI functions for which we cannot reduce the lower bound smaller than the entropy of the secret. That is, any scheme for this class is inefficient in terms of the share size.

Next, we show how to achieve the new lower bound by using the construction in [15]. The key idea of the construction in [15] is to divide a nonlinear MI

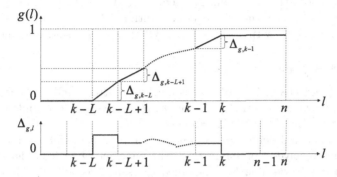

Fig. 1. Function in $\mathcal{F}$ and its gradient

function into linear functions and encode the secret by using the optimum TRSS (i.e., linear function) schemes. Generally, many divisions are possible and the entropy of shares depends on the divisions. Thus, we show how to divide a nonlinear MI function so that the division achieves the derived lower bound, i.e., minimizes the entropy of shares. The optimum division is given by dividing the MI function iteratively from the lowest slope.

The rest of this paper is organized as follows. In Section 2, we define a general TSS (GTSS) scheme which includes the previous threshold classes. The definition is based on that in [11,15]. In Section 3, the general lower bound in [11] is presented for a GTSS scheme. In Section 4, we derive a tighter lower bound for a GTSS scheme. In Section 5, the construction of [15] is reviewed and an optimum division for any MI function is devised. Concluding remarks are given in Section 6.

2   Notations and Definitions

2.1   Functions for GTSS Scheme

Let $\mathbb{Q}_{[0,1]}$ be the set of the rational numbers between 0 and 1. Let $\mathcal{F}$ be the family of monotonically increasing rational-valued discrete functions $g : \{0, 1, \ldots, n\} \to \mathbb{Q}_{[0,1]}$ with $g(0) = 0$ and $0 < g(n) \leq 1$. For $g \in \mathcal{F}$, define $\Delta_{g,l} \triangleq g(l+1) - g(l)$ with $0 \leq l < n$, where $\Delta_{g,l}$ is called the gradient of g on l. For any $g \in \mathcal{F}$, the gradients $\Delta_{g,l}$ with $0 \leq l < n$ satisfy

$$\begin{cases} \Delta_{g,l} = 0, \text{ for } 0 \leq l < k - L, \\ \Delta_{g,l} \geq 0, \text{ for } k - L \leq l < k, \\ \Delta_{g,l} = 0, \text{ for } k \leq l < n, \end{cases} \tag{1}$$

for some k and L with $k \geq L$ because g monotonically increases as depicted in Fig. 1. In the following, we call such k and L the end and the length of the slope of g, respectively. More precisely, we define the end k and the length L so that $k = \max\{l | 0 \leq l < n, \Delta_{g,l} \neq 0\} + 1$ and $L = k - \min\{l | 0 \leq l < n, \Delta_{g,l} \neq 0\}$.

Let $\Delta_{g,*}$ denote the maximum gradient, i.e., $\Delta_{g,*} = \max\{\Delta_{g,l}|0 \leq l < n\}$. We say that g is linear if the gradients $\Delta_{g,l}$ with $k - L \leq l < k$ are constant, i.e., $\Delta_{g,l} = \Delta_{g,*} = g(n)/L$ with $k - L \leq l < k$. Otherwise, g is said to be nonlinear.

2.2   GTSS Scheme

Let $H(X|Y)$ and $I(X;Y)$ denote the conditional entropy and the mutual information for two random variables X and Y, respectively. For a random variable X, $\hat{X}$ is defined as $\hat{X} \triangleq \{x|\Pr(X = x) > 0\}$.

The notations and definitions common to an SS scheme follow those in [11]. An SS scheme involves a probabilistic Turing machine D, called a dealer, whose input is a random variable S; $\hat{S}$ is called the set of secrets. On input $s \in \hat{S}$, the dealer produces $(v_1, v_2, \ldots, v_n)$ where v_i with $1 \leq i \leq n$ is called a share. Let $V_1, \ldots, V_n$ be the random variables induced by $v_1, \ldots, v_n$, respectively. Let $P \triangleq \{1, 2, \ldots, n\}$. For $A \subseteq P$, define $V_A \triangleq \{V_i|i \in A\}$. Let $|A|$ be the cardinality of a set A.

Definition 1. *A secret sharing (SS) scheme is a triplet* (S, D, P).

Intuitively saying, a GTSS scheme is an SS scheme defined for a function $g \in \mathcal{F}$ so that an arbitrary set of shares leaks out information about the secret based on g. The gradient of g indicates the leakage rate.

Definition 2. *For* $g \in \mathcal{F}$, *we say that* (S, D, P) *is a general threshold secret sharing (GTSS) scheme with mutual-information (MI) function* g (*g-GTSS scheme*) *if* (S, D, P) *is an SS scheme and for any* $A \subseteq P$,

$$I(S; V_A) = g(|A|)H(S), \tag{2}$$

or equivalently,

$$H(S|V_A) = (1 - g(|A|))H(S). \tag{3}$$

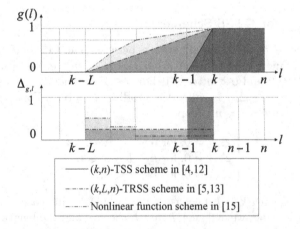

Fig. 2. MI functions of the previous TSS schemes in [4,5,12,13,15]

The previous TSS classes [4,5,12,13,15] are proper subclasses of the GTSS class. The MI functions of the previous schemes are shown in Fig. 2. The nonlinear function scheme in [15] restricts g to convex ($\Delta_{g,l} \leq \Delta_{g,l+1}$ with $k - L \leq l < k$) and concave ($\Delta_{g,l} \geq \Delta_{g,l+1}$ with $k - L \leq l < k$). The (k, L, n)-TRSS scheme in [5,13] is the special case of g being linear with $\Delta_{g,l} = \Delta_{g,*} = 1/L$ for $k - L \leq l < k$. The (k, n)-TSS scheme in [4,12] is the special case with $L = 1$.

3   Previous Lower Bound

In [11], for an SS scheme with a general access structure, a relation between $H(V_A|V_B)$ and $H(V_A|V_B S)$ with $A, B \subseteq P$ is derived in order to obtain a general lower bound of $H(V_i)$. In this section, for a GTSS scheme, we rederive the corresponding relation and lower bound in the threshold framework. The relation is also used to obtain a new lower bound in the next section. To derive the relation and these bounds, we use the following properties of the conditional entropy $H(\cdot|\cdot)$ for random variables $X, Y, Z,$ and W.

$$0 \leq H(X|Y) \leq H(X) \tag{4}$$
$$0 \leq H(X|ZW) \leq H(X|Z) \leq H(XY|Z) \tag{5}$$
$$H(XY|Z) = H(X|Z) + H(Y|XZ) = H(Y|Z) + H(X|YZ) \tag{6}$$

For a GTSS scheme, a useful relation between $H(V_A|V_B)$ and $H(V_A|V_B S)$ is given in the following lemma, which is the threshold version of Lemma 21 in [11].

Lemma 1. *For any g-GTSS scheme (S, D, P) with $g \in \mathcal{F}$ and any $A, B \subseteq P$,*

$$H(V_A|V_B) = H(V_A|V_B S) + (g(|A \cup B|) - g(|B|))H(S). \tag{7}$$

A proof is given in Appendix A.

For a GTSS scheme, a lower bound of $H(V_i)$ is given in the following corollary, which is the threshold version of Theorem 22 in [11].

Corollary 1. *For any g-GTSS scheme (S, D, P) with $g \in \mathcal{F}$ and any $i \in P$,*

$$H(V_i) \geq \Delta_{g,*} H(S).$$

A proof is given in Appendix B.

4   New Lower Bound

In this section, we derive a tighter lower bound on $H(V_i)$ than that of Corollary 1 for a g-GTSS scheme (S, D, P).

The gradient of MI function g (i.e., the leakage rate) iterates increase/decrease. The last gradient of successive increases (resp. decreases) is referred to as a local

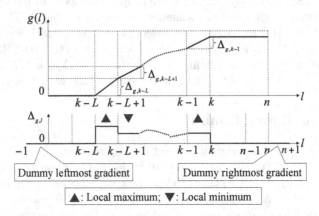

Fig. 3. Local minimum and maximum gradients of g

maximum (resp. local minimum). To define local maximum/minimum gradients precisely, we define two dummy leftmost/rightmost gradients $\Delta_{g,-1}$ and $\Delta_{g,n}$ by $\Delta_{g,-1} = \Delta_{g,n} = 0$. This implies that the gradient of g first increases from zero, then iterates decrease/increase, and finally decreases to zero as shown in Fig. 3. For $g \in \mathcal{F}$, $\Delta_{g,l}$ with $0 \le l < n$ is said to be a local maximum if $\Delta_{g,l'} < \Delta_{g,l'+1} = \cdots = \Delta_{g,l}$ for some l' with $-1 \le l' < l$ and $\Delta_{g,l} > \Delta_{g,l+1}$. In contrast, $\Delta_{g,l}$ with $0 \le l < n$ is said to be a local minimum if $\Delta_{g,l'} > \Delta_{g,l'+1} = \cdots = \Delta_{g,l}$ for some l' with $-1 \le l' < l$ and $\Delta_{g,l} < \Delta_{g,l+1}$. From this definition, the gradient of g first becomes a local maximum, then iterates local minimum/maximum, and finally decreases from the final local maximum to zero, but does not end up as a local minimum because $\Delta_{g,n-1} \ge \Delta_{g,n} = 0$ (i.e., the latter condition of a local minimum is not satisfied). Thus, for the number of local maximum gradients of g, denoted by $M > 0$, the number of local minimum gradients is $M - 1$. Note that the maximum gradient $\Delta_{g,*}$ is also local maximum.

The new lower bound on $H(V_i)$ of a g-GTSS scheme is given by the local maxima/minima of the gradient of g.

Theorem 1. *For $g \in \mathcal{F}$, let M denote the number of local maximum gradients of g and let $l_{\max,j}$ with $1 \le j \le M$ (resp. $l_{\min,j}$ with $1 \le j < M$) denote the point at which the gradient is the j-th local maximum (resp. the j-th local minimum). For any g-GTSS scheme (S, D, P) and any $i \in P$,*

$$H(V_i) \ge \left(\sum_{j=1}^{M} \Delta_{g,l_{\max,j}} - \sum_{j=1}^{M-1} \Delta_{g,l_{\min,j}} \right) H(S) \ge \Delta_{g,*} H(S). \qquad (8)$$

The equality in the second part of (8) holds if and only if $M = 1$.

Roughly speaking, a share needs information about the secret for every increase of the leakage rate (but not for any decrease). Thus, the total amount of necessary information about the secret is at least the summation of the first increasing amount $\Delta_{g,l_{\max,1}}$ and the j-th ones $\Delta_{g,l_{\max,j+1}} - \Delta_{g,l_{\min,j}}$ with $2 \leq j < M$. If the leakage rate increases only once (i.e., $M = 1$), then the share only needs the maximum leakage rate $\Delta_{g,*}$, which is the previous lower bound. Otherwise, to achieve the maximum value, the share needs additional information about the secret to increase a loss caused by decrease of the leakage rate. Thus, the new lower bound is larger than the previous one except for the case $M = 1$.

Proof. If the number of local maxima is only one (i.e., $M = 1$), then (8) is readily proved from Corollary 1 because the local maximum gradient is the maximum one. That is,

$$H(V_i) \geq \left(\sum_{j=1}^{M} \Delta_{g,l_{\max,j}} - \sum_{j=1}^{M-1} \Delta_{g,l_{\min,j}} \right) H(S) = \Delta_{g,*} H(S). \tag{9}$$

Next, we prove (8) for $M > 1$. For $i \in P$, we consider a sequence of $2M - 1$ subsets of $P \setminus \{i\}$ whose cardinalities are $l_{\max,j}$ and $l_{\min,j}$. Let $A^{(i)}_{\max,j} \subseteq P \setminus \{i\}$ with $1 \leq j \leq M$ and $A^{(i)}_{\min,j} \subseteq P \setminus \{i\}$ with $1 \leq j < M$ be subsets such that

$$|A^{(i)}_{\max,j}| = l_{\max,j}, \quad |A^{(i)}_{\min,j}| = l_{\min,j}, \tag{10}$$

$$A^{(i)}_{\max,1} \subset A^{(i)}_{\min,1} \subset \cdots \subset A^{(i)}_{\min,M-1} \subset A^{(i)}_{\max,M}. \tag{11}$$

We stress that

$$i \notin A^{(i)}_{\max,j}, A^{(i)}_{\min,j}. \tag{12}$$

There are such subsets because $l_{\max,1} < l_{\min,1} < \cdots < l_{\max,M} < n$. We claim that

$$H(V_i | V_{A_{\max,M}}) \geq \Delta_{g,l_{\max,M}} H(S), \tag{13}$$

$$H(V_i | V_{A_{\max,j}}) \geq H(V_i | V_{A_{\max,j+1}}) + (\Delta_{g,l_{\max,j}} - \Delta_{g,l_{\min,j}}) H(S), \text{ for } 1 \leq j < M, \tag{14}$$

$$H(V_i) \geq H(V_i | V_{A_{\max,1}}). \tag{15}$$

The first part of (8) is derived by summing (13), (14) for all j with $1 \leq j < M$, and (15).

The inequality (13) is proved from Lemma 1, (10), and (12) by

$$H(V_i | V_{A_{\max,M}}) \geq (g(|A_{\max,M} \cup \{i\}|) - g(|A_{\max,M}|)) H(S)$$
$$= \Delta_{g,l_{\max,M}} H(S).$$

Next, the inequality (14) is proved by

$$H(V_i | V_{A_{\max,j+1}})$$
$$\leq H(V_i | V_{A_{\min,j}}) \qquad \text{(from (5) and (11))}$$
$$= H(V_i | V_{A_{\min,j}} S) + \Delta_{g,l_{\min,j}} H(S) \quad \text{(from Lemma 1, (10), and (12))}$$
$$\leq H(V_i | V_{A_{\max,j}} S) + \Delta_{g,l_{\min,j}} H(S) \quad \text{(from (5) and (11))}$$
$$= H(V_i | V_{A_{\max,j}}) - \Delta_{g,l_{\max,j}} H(S) + \Delta_{g,l_{\min,j}} H(S).$$
$$\text{(from Lemma 1, (10), and (12))}$$

Then, it is readily seen that (15) follows from (4).

The second part of (8) is proved from the following relation between the adjacent local maximum/minimum gradients of g: Every local minimum gradient is smaller than its adjacent local maximum gradients, that is,

$$\Delta_{g,l_{\max,j}} - \Delta_{g,l_{\min,j}} > 0, \quad \text{for } 1 \leq j < M, \tag{16}$$

$$\Delta_{g,l_{\max,j}} - \Delta_{g,l_{\min,j-1}} > 0, \quad \text{for } 1 < j \leq M. \tag{17}$$

The maximum gradient $\Delta_{g,*}$ is also a local maximum, and its point is one of $l_{\max,j}$ with $1 \leq j \leq M$, denoted by $l_{\max,M'}$. Separating the sums of local maximum/minimum gradients in (8) by the point $l_{\max,M'}$ so that

$$\sum_{j=1}^{M} \Delta_{g,l_{\max,j}} - \sum_{j=1}^{M-1} \Delta_{g,l_{\min,j}}$$

$$= \sum_{j=1}^{M'-1} (\Delta_{g,l_{\max,j}} - \Delta_{g,l_{\min,j}}) + \Delta_{g,*} + \sum_{j=M'+1}^{M} (\Delta_{g,l_{\max,j}} - \Delta_{g,l_{\min,j-1}}),$$

it follows from (16) and (17) that

$$\left(\sum_{j=1}^{M} \Delta_{g,l_{\max,j}} - \sum_{j=1}^{M-1} \Delta_{g,l_{\min,j}} \right) H(S) > \Delta_{g,*} H(S). \tag{18}$$

From (9) and (18), the equality in the second part of (8) holds if and only if $M = 1$. □

This new lower bound is as small as the previous one of Corollary 1 for the class of functions with $M = 1$. We call this class the simplest class. Roughly speaking, the simplest class consists of functions which are either convex, concave, or a combination of convex and concave functions as depicted in Fig. 4. For these MI functions, a share only needs information about the secret for one increase of the leakage rate, which is given by the maximum leakage rate $\Delta_{g,*}$.

Corollary 2. *Let $\mathcal{F}_{\text{sim}} \subset \mathcal{F}$ be the class of functions whose gradient has only the one local maximum. For any g-GTSS scheme (S, D, P) and any $i \in P$,*

$$H(V_i) \geq \left(\sum_{j=1}^{M} \Delta_{g,l_{\max,j}} - \sum_{j=1}^{M-1} \Delta_{g,l_{\min,j}} \right) H(S) = \Delta_{g,*} H(S),$$

if and only if $g \in \mathcal{F}_{\text{sim}}$.

We also determine the class of functions for which the entropy of shares cannot be smaller than that of the secret, called the complicate class. Roughly speaking, the complicate class consists of functions which increase to one in a staircase pattern as depicted in Fig. 4.

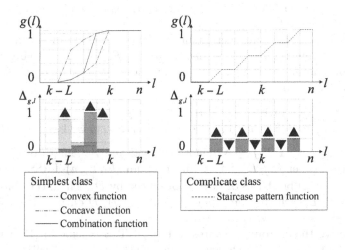

Fig. 4. Simplest and complicate classes

Corollary 3. *Let $\mathcal{F}_{\text{com}}$ be the class of functions whose slope consists of zero-gradient slopes and linear slopes with length one and $g(n) = 1$. For any g-GTSS scheme (S, D, P) and any $i \in P$,*

$$H(V_i) \geq H(S),$$

if and only if $g \in \mathcal{F}_{\text{com}}$.

A proof is given in Appendix C.

5   Optimum Construction

5.1   Division Based Construction

We review the construction of a g-GTSS scheme (S, D, P) in [15]. The basic idea is to divide the nonlinear MI function g into a set of linear functions $g_1, g_2, \ldots, g_N \in \mathcal{F}$ for some integer $N > 0$ so that $g(l) = \sum_{j=1}^{N} g_j(l)$ with $0 \leq l \leq n$. We call such a set a division of g. Based on this division, if $g(n) = 1$, then the secret is divided into the same number of subsecrets $s_1, s_2, \ldots, s_N$ so that the ratio of the entropy of each subsecret $H(S_j)$ and that of the original secret $H(S)$ is given by the total increasing amount of the linear function g_j, that is, $H(S_j) = g_j(n)H(S)$. Otherwise (i.e., $g(n) < 1$), the secret is divided into $N + 1$ subsecrets $s_1, s_2, \ldots, s_N, s_{N+1}$ where s_{N+1} is a temporal subsecret prepared to control the amount of information so that $H(S_{N+1}) = (1 - g(n))H(S)$. Then, for $1 \leq j \leq N$, the subsecret s_j is independently encoded by using the optimum linear function scheme (i.e., TRSS scheme) based on g_j while the sub-secret s_{N+1} is not encoded. The i-th share v_i of s is the set of the i-th shares of the encoded subsecrets $s_1, s_2, \ldots, s_N$.

More precisely, the construction in [15] assumes that for given S and g, there exist N linear functions $g_1, g_2, \ldots, g_N \in \mathcal{F}$, $N + 1$ mutually indepen-dent random variables $S_1, S_2, \ldots, S_{N+1}$, and a one-to-one mapping from $\hat{S}$ to $(\hat{S}_1, \hat{S}_2, \ldots, \hat{S}_{N+1})$ such that

- $g(l) = \sum_{j=1}^{N} g_j(l)$ with $0 \leq l \leq n$,
- $H(S_j) = g_j(n)H(S)$ with $1 \leq j \leq N$, and $H(S_{N+1}) = (1 - g(n))H(S)$.

Let k_j and L_j with $1 \leq j \leq N$ denote the end and the length of the slope of g_j, respectively. Let (S_j, D_j, P) be an optimum (k_j, L_j, n)-TRSS scheme. Let $(v_{j,1}, v_{j,2}, \ldots, v_{j,n})$ be shares of $s_j \in \hat{S}_j$ produced by D_j. Then, the construction in [15] defines D such that on input $(s_1, s_2, \ldots, s_N)$, D outputs $(v_1, v_2, \ldots, v_n)$ with $v_i = (v_{1,i}, v_{2,i}, \ldots, v_{n,i})$ for $i \in P$.

We rederive the entropy of shares in the g-GTSS scheme in [15] within the framework of this paper. The following theorem shows that the entropy of shares based on some division of g is given by the summation of the gradients of the slopes of g_j. This implies that the entropy is minimized if the division minimizes the summation of the gradients.

Theorem 2. *For $g \in \mathcal{F}$, the scheme (S, D, P) in [15] based on a division $\{g_1, g_2, \ldots, g_N\}$ of g is a g-GTSS scheme which satisfies*

$$H(V_i) = \sum_{j=1}^{N} \Delta_{g_j,*} H(S). \tag{19}$$

A proof is given in Appendix D.

5.2 Proposed Optimum Division

We now divide $g \in \mathcal{F}$ so that the division makes the entropy of shares given by Theorem 2 equal to the lower bound of Theorem 1, expressing in the process the tightness of this new bound. We call such division optimum.

The proposed optimum division is iteratively done by splitting the function into two parts, namely a linear part and the remaining nonlinear part. The idea of the optimum division is that, at each splitting step, we extend the divided slope as long as possible. This extension allows us to have lower gradients at subsequent steps, because the total increasing amount of the remaining part becomes smaller. This contributes to make later gradients smaller. To maximize the length of the divided slope, we divide the smallest slope of the function.

A linear function is characterized by the end, the length, and the gradient of its slope. Thus, we represent a linear function g_j by the triplet of the end k_j, the length L_j, and the gradient $\Delta_{g_j,*}$ of its slope.

The proposed procedure which outputs the optimum division for $g \in \mathcal{F}$, denoted by $\mathcal{F}_g$, is given in the following.

Initialization. Let h be the counter for the loop which represents the number of divided linear parts. Let g_h with $h \geq 1$ denote the h-th divided linear part and $g^{(h)}$ with $h \geq 0$ the remaining part after the h-th division. Set $\mathcal{F}_g := \emptyset$, $h := 0$, and $g^{(0)} := g$.

Repeat the following Steps 1–3 until $g^{(h)} = 0$. Then, output $\mathcal{F}_g$.

Step 1. Increment h by one ($h := h + 1$). Find the smallest positive gradient of the last remaining part $g^{(h-1)}$. If there are two or more points with the smallest positive gradient, then choose one of them. Let $l_{\min}$ be the chosen point. The smallest positive gradient is $\Delta_{g^{(h-1)}, l_{\min}}$.

Step 2. Extend the divided slope (i.e., the h-th divided linear part g_h) as long as possible by defining its end k_h and length L_h as follows.

$$k_h \triangleq \min\{l | \Delta_{g^{(h-1)}, l} = 0, l_{\min} < l\}, \tag{20}$$

$$L_h \triangleq k_h - \max\{l | \Delta_{g^{(h-1)}, l} = 0, l < l_{\min}\} - 1. \tag{21}$$

Thus, g_h is the linear function with $(k_h, L_h, \Delta_{g^{(h-1)}, l_{\min}})$.

Step 3. Divide g_h from $g^{(h-1)}$ by setting $g^{(h)} := g^{(h-1)} - g_h$ and $\mathcal{F}_g := \mathcal{F}_g \cup \{g_h\}$. □

We can show that the remaining part $g^{(h)}$ is always in $\mathcal{F}$ (i.e., monotonically increasing function) except for the case after the last division ($g^{(h)} = 0$). Considering the gradients of $g^{(h)}$ and $g^{(h-1)}$,

$$\Delta_{g^{(h)}, l} = \begin{cases} \Delta_{g^{(h-1)}, l} - \Delta_{g_h, *}, & \text{for } k_h - L_h \leq l < k_h, \\ \Delta_{g^{(h-1)}, l}, & \text{otherwise.} \end{cases} \tag{22}$$

While the gradient of $g^{(h-1)}$ on the just outside points of the divided linear part g_h is zero, i.e.,

$$\Delta_{g^{(h-1)}, k_h - L_h - 1} = \Delta_{g^{(h-1)}, k_h} = 0, \tag{23}$$

the gradient of $g^{(h-1)}$ in the divided range is no less than the gradient of g_h, that is,

$$\Delta_{g^{(h-1)}, l} \geq \Delta_{g^{(h-1)}, l_{\min}} = \Delta_{g_h, *}, \quad \text{for } k_h - L_h \leq l < k_h. \tag{24}$$

Thus, the gradients of $g^{(h)}$ is non-negative (i.e., monotonically increases).

It is readily seen that the above procedure has to terminate because the number of non-zero gradients decreases at least by one at each iteration. An example of the proposed procedure is given in Fig. 5.

The next theorem guarantees that the proposed division makes the entropy of shares equal to the derived lower bound.

Theorem 3. *For any $g \in \mathcal{F}$, the proposed division $\mathcal{F}_g$ satisfies*

$$\sum_{g_h \in \mathcal{F}_g} \Delta_{g_h, *} = \sum_{j=1}^{M} \Delta_{g, l_{\max, j}} - \sum_{j=1}^{M-1} \Delta_{g, l_{\min, j}}, \tag{25}$$

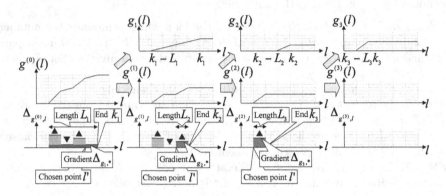

Fig. 5. Example of the proposed optimum division

where M denotes the number of local maximum gradients of g and $l_{\mathrm{max},j}$ with $1 \leq j \leq M$ (resp. $l_{\mathrm{min},j}$ with $1 \leq j < M$) denotes the point at which the gradient is the j-th local maximum (resp. the j-th local minimum) of g.

Proof. We prove (25) from relations on the maximum/minimum gradients of the remaining part between before and after each division. Let N be the total number of divisions, i.e., $N = |\mathcal{F}_g|$. For the remaining part $g^{(h)}$ after the h-th division with $0 \leq h < N$, let $M^{(h)}$ denote the number of local maximum gradients of $g^{(h)}$. Let $l^{(h)}_{\mathrm{max},j}$ and $l^{(h)}_{\mathrm{min},j}$ with $0 \leq h < N$ denote the point of the j-th local maximum gradient and that of the j-th local minimum gradient of $g^{(h)}$, respectively. Let $\Delta^{(h)}_{\mathrm{max-min}}$ denote the difference between the sum of the local maximum gradients and the sum of the local minimum gradients. That is,

$$\Delta^{(h)}_{\mathrm{max-min}} = \sum_{j=1}^{M^{(h)}} \Delta_{g^{(h)},l^{(h)}_{\mathrm{max},j}} - \sum_{j=1}^{M^{(h)}-1} \Delta_{g^{(h)},l^{(h)}_{\mathrm{min},j}}.$$

Since $g^{(0)} = g$, the initial value of this difference is given by

$$\Delta^{(0)}_{\mathrm{max-min}} = \sum_{j=1}^{M} \Delta_{g,l_{\mathrm{max},j}} - \sum_{j=1}^{M-1} \Delta_{g,l_{\mathrm{min},j}}. \tag{26}$$

We claim that after each division, this difference decreases by the gradient of the divided linear part so that

$$\Delta^{(h)}_{\mathrm{max-min}} = \Delta^{(h-1)}_{\mathrm{max-min}} - \Delta_{g_h,*}, \text{ for } 1 \leq h < N, \tag{27}$$

and that the difference finally equals the gradient of the last divided linear part, that is,

$$\Delta_{g_N,*} = \Delta^{(N-1)}_{\mathrm{max-min}}. \tag{28}$$

It is readily seen that (25) is derived by summing (26), (27) for all $1 \leq h < N$, and (28). In addition, (28) is easily proven from the fact that the final remaining part $g^{(N-1)}$ is divided as the last linear part g_N (i.e., $g_N = g^{(N-1)}$, $M^{(N-1)} = 1$, and $\Delta_{g^{(N-1)}, l_{\max,j}^{(N-1)}} = \Delta_{g_N,*}$).

Therefore, in the following, we prove (27) for $1 \leq h < N$. From (22), (27) is equivalent to

$$\Delta_{\max-\min}^{(h)} = \left(\sum_{j=1}^{M^{(h-1)}} \Delta_{g^{(h)}, l_{\max,j}^{(h-1)}} - \sum_{j=1}^{M^{(h-1)}-1} \Delta_{g^{(h)}, l_{\min,j}^{(h-1)}} + \Delta_{g_h,*} \right) - \Delta_{g_h,*}. \quad (29)$$

From the definition of $\Delta_{\max-\min}^{(h)}$, (29) follows from the following equivalences of sums,

$$\sum_{j=1}^{M^{(h)}} \Delta_{g^{(h)}, l_{\max,j}^{(h)}} = \sum_{j=1}^{M^{(h-1)}} \Delta_{g^{(h)}, l_{\max,j}^{(h-1)}}, \quad (30)$$

$$\sum_{j=1}^{M^{(h)}-1} \Delta_{g^{(h)}, l_{\min,j}^{(h)}} = \sum_{j=1}^{M^{(h-1)}-1} \Delta_{g^{(h)}, l_{\min,j}^{(h-1)}}. \quad (31)$$

Eqs. (30) and (31) are a direct consequence of the following fact: For any point l_0 with $0 \leq l_0 < n$ at which the gradient $\Delta_{g^{(h)}, l_0}$ of the remaining part $g^{(h)}$ is positive $(\Delta_{g^{(h)}, l_0} \neq 0)$,

(a) l_0 is a local minimum point of $g^{(h-1)}$ iff it is a local minimum point of $g^{(h)}$,
(b) l_0 is a local maximum point of $g^{(h-1)}$ iff it is a local maximum point of $g^{(h)}$.

A proof of this fact is given in Appendix E.   □

Theorem 4. *For any $g \in \mathcal{F}$, a g-GTSS scheme (S, D, P) of [15] based on the proposed division $\mathcal{F}_g$ minimizes $H(V_i)$ for any $i \in P$. Specifically,*

$$H(V_i) = \left(\sum_{j=1}^{M} \Delta_{g, l_{\max,j}} - \sum_{j=1}^{M-1} \Delta_{g, l_{\min,j}} \right) H(S), \quad (32)$$

where M denotes the number of local maximum gradients of g and $l_{\max,j}$ with $1 \leq j \leq M$ (resp. $l_{\min,j}$ with $1 \leq j < M$) denotes the point at which the gradient is the j-th local maximum (resp. the j-th local minimum).

Proof. From Theorems 2 and 3, it follows that $H(V_i)$ achieves the lower bound of Theorem 1.   □

6   Conclusion

In this paper, we have first derived a new lower bound on the entropy of shares in a GTSS scheme. This bound is generally higher than the previous lower bound.

Next, we have identified the class of functions for which the new lower bound is equal to the previous one. A function in this class is either convex/concave functions or a combination of convex and concave functions with one local maximum gradient. Then, we have also identified the class of functions for which the new lower bound is equal to that of the secret, in which case the control of the amount of leaked information is complicate so that the MI function has a staircase pattern. Finally, for the construction in [15], we have presented an optimum division of any MI function which makes the entropy of shares equal to the derived lower bound. The key idea is to divide the smallest slope at each splitting step so that its length is maximized. A possible future work is to derive a tighter lower bound than the previous one for an SS scheme with general access structures.

References

1. Bai, L.: A strong ramp secret sharing scheme using matrix projection. In: The 2006 Int'l Symp. on a World of Wireless, Mobile and Multimedia Networks, pp. 652–656 (2006)
2. Beimel, A.: Secret-Sharing Schemes: A Survey. In: Chee, Y.M., Guo, Z., Ling, S., Shao, F., Tang, Y., Wang, H., Xing, C. (eds.) IWCC 2011. LNCS, vol. 6639, pp. 11–46. Springer, Heidelberg (2011)
3. Beimel, A., Orlov, I.: Secret sharing and non-Shannon information inequalities. IEEE Trans. on Information Theory 57, 5634–5649 (2011)
4. Blakley, G.R.: Safeguarding cryptographic keys. In: AFIPS 1979 Nat. Comput. Conf. vol. 48, pp. 313–317 (1979)
5. Blakley, G.R., Meadows, C.: Security of Ramp Schemes. In: Blakely, G.R., Chaum, D. (eds.) CRYPTO 1984. LNCS, vol. 196, pp. 242–268. Springer, Heidelberg (1985)
6. Capocelli, R.M., De Santis, A., Gargano, L., Vaccaro, U.: On the size of shares for secret sharing schemes. J. of Cryptology 6, 157–168 (1993)
7. Csirmaz, L.: The size of a share must be large. J. of Cryptology 10, 223–231 (1997)
8. Iwamoto, M., Yamamoto, H.: Strongly secure ramp secret sharing schemes for general access structures. Inform. Processing Letters 97, 52–57 (2006)
9. Karnin, E.D., Greene, J.W., Hellman, M.E.: On secret sharing systems. IEEE Trans. on Information Theory 29, 35–41 (1983)
10. Kurosawa, K., Okada, K., Sakano, K., Ogata, W., Tsujii, S.: Nonperfect Secret Sharing Schemes and Matroids. In: Helleseth, T. (ed.) EUROCRYPT 1993. LNCS, vol. 765, pp. 126–141. Springer, Heidelberg (1994)
11. Okada, K., Kurosawa, K.: Lower Bound on the Size of Shares of Nonperfect Secret Sharing Schemes. In: Safavi-Naini, R., Pieprzyk, J.P. (eds.) ASIACRYPT 1994. LNCS, vol. 917, pp. 34–41. Springer, Heidelberg (1995)
12. Shamir, A.: How to share a secret. Comm. of the ACM 22, 612–613 (1979)
13. Yamamoto, H.: On secret sharing systems using (k, L, n) threshold scheme. IECE Trans. J68-A, 945–952 (1985) (in Japanese). English transl.: Electron. Comm. Japan Part I. 69, 46–54 (1986)
14. Yoneyama, K., Kunihiro, N., Santoso, B., Ohta, K.: Non-linear function ramp scheme. In: The 2004 Int'l Symp. on Inform. Theory and its Appli., pp. 788–793 (2004)
15. Yoshida, M., Fujiwara, T.: A secure construction for the nonlinear function threshold ramp secret sharing scheme. In: The 2007 Int'l Symp. on Inform. Theory, CD-ROM (2007)

A   Proof of Lemma 1

For any $A, B \subseteq P$,

$$
\begin{aligned}
H(V_A|V_B) &= H(S|V_B) - H(S|V_AV_B) + H(V_A|V_BS) &&\text{(from (6))}\\
&= (1 - g(|B|))H(S)\\
&\quad -(1 - g(|A \cup B|))H(S) + H(V_A|V_BS) &&\text{(from (3))}\\
&= H(V_A|V_BS) + (g(|A \cup B|) - g(|B|))H(S).
\end{aligned}
$$

B   Proof of Corollary 1

For any $i \in P$ and $B \subseteq P$ with $i \notin B$,

$$
\begin{aligned}
H(V_i) &\geq H(V_i|V_B) &&\text{(from (4))}\\
&= (g(|\{i\} \cup B|) - g(|B|))H(S) + H(V_i|V_BS) &&\text{(from Lemma 1)}\\
&\geq (g(|\{i\} \cup B|) - g(|B|))H(S) &&\text{(from (5))}\\
&= (g(|B| + 1) - g(|B|))H(S).
\end{aligned}
$$

Since $0 \leq |B| < n$,

$$
\begin{aligned}
H(V_i) &\geq \max\{(g(l+1) - g(l))H(S)|0 \leq l < n\}\\
&= \max\{\Delta_{g,l}H(S)|0 \leq l < n\}\\
&= \Delta_{g,*}H(S).
\end{aligned}
$$

C   Proof of Corollary 3

If $g \in \mathcal{F}_{\text{com}}$, all the nonzero gradients $\Delta_{g,l}$ are local maxima because $\Delta_{g,l-1} = \Delta_{g,l+1} = 0$ (i.e., $\Delta_{g,l-1} < \Delta_{g,l}$ and $\Delta_{g,l} > \Delta_{g,l+1}$). Thus, every local minimum gradient has zero value. Therefore,

$$
\left(\sum_{j=1}^{M} \Delta_{g,l_{\max,j}} - \sum_{j=1}^{M-1} \Delta_{g,l_{\min,j}} \right) = g(n) - 0 = 1.
$$

Thus, if $g \in \mathcal{F}_{\text{com}}$, then the new lower bound on $H(V_i)$ equals $H(S)$.

On the other hand, if $g \notin \mathcal{F}_{\text{com}}$, then $g(n) < 1$ or there exist some successive positive gradients. If $g(n) < 1$, then it holds

$$
\left(\sum_{j=1}^{M} \Delta_{g,l_{\max,j}} - \sum_{j=1}^{M-1} \Delta_{g,l_{\min,j}} \right) < \sum_{j=1}^{M} \Delta_{g,l_{\max,j}} < \sum_{l=0}^{n-1} \Delta_{g,l} = g(n) < 1.
$$

Otherwise (i.e., $g(n) = 1$), there exists successive positive gradient. For each successive positive gradient, at least one of them (denoted by $\Delta_{g,l}$) is a local maximum and its adjacent positive gradient (i.e., $\Delta_{g,l-1}$ or $\Delta_{g,l+1}$) is not local maximum. Thus, the summation of the local maximum gradients is smaller than the total increasing amount of g, i.e, is smaller than $g(n) = 1$. Thus, if $g \notin \mathcal{F}_{\text{com}}$, then the new lower bound on $H(V_i)$ is smaller than $H(S)$.

D   Proof of Theorem 2

First, we prove that (S, D, P) is a g-GTSS scheme. Since it is readily seen that (S, D, P) is an SS scheme, we prove that (3) holds. For $A \subseteq P$, we have

$$H(S|V_A) = \sum_{j=1}^{N} H(S_j|V_A) + H(S_{N+1}), \tag{33}$$

since S_j's for $1 \leq j \leq N + 1$ are mutually independent.

A (k_j, L_j, n)-TRSS scheme (S_j, D_j, P) is a GTSS scheme for a linear MI function with the end k_j, the length L_j, and the gradient $1/L_j$, denoted by g'_j. Thus,

$$H(S_j|V_A) = (1 - g'_j(|A|))H(S_j). \tag{34}$$

Note that $g'_j(l) = \frac{1}{g_j(n)}g_j(l)$ for any l with $0 \leq l \leq n$ because the gradient of g'_j is $1/L_j$ and the gradient of g_j is $g_j(n)/L_j$. From (33) and (34), it follows

$$H(S|V_A) = \sum_{j=1}^{N}(1 - g'_j(|A|))H(S_j) + H(S_{N+1})$$

$$= \sum_{j=1}^{N}\left(1 - \frac{1}{g_j(n)}g_j(|A|)\right)g_j(n)H(S) + (1 - g(n))H(S)$$

$$= \left(\sum_{j=1}^{N}g_j(n) - \sum_{j=1}^{N}g_j(|A|)\right)H(S) + (1 - g(n))H(S)$$

$$= (1 - g(|A|))H(S).$$

Thus, (3) is satisfied.

Next, we prove (19). Since S_j's for $1 \leq j \leq N$ are mutually independent,

$$H(V_i) = \sum_{j=1}^{N} H(V_{j,i}), \tag{35}$$

where $V_{j,i}$ denote the random variable induced by the i-th share $v_{i,j}$ of $s_j \in S_j$. By using the optimum construction of (k_j, L_j, n)-TRSS scheme proposed in [13],

$$H(V_{j,i}) = \Delta_{g'_j,*}H(S_j). \tag{36}$$

From (35) and (36), it follows

$$H(V_i) = \sum_{j=1}^{N} \Delta_{g'_j,*}H(S_j) = \sum_{j=1}^{N} \Delta_{g'_j,*}g_j(n)H(S).$$

Since the gradients of g'_j and g_j are given by $\Delta_{g'_j,*} = 1/L_j$ and $\Delta_{g_j,*} = g_j(n)/L_j$ as described in the above, the value $\Delta_{g'_j,*}g_j(n)$ equals the gradient of g_j. Therefore, (19) holds.

E   Proof of Fact in Proof of Theorem 3

We prove the following fact: For any point l_0 with $0 \leq l_0 < n$ at which the gradient $\Delta_{g^{(h)},l_0}$ of the remaining part $g^{(h)}$ is positive (i.e., $\Delta_{g^{(h)},l_0} \neq 0$),

(a) l_0 is a local minimum point of $g^{(h-1)}$ iff it is a local minimum point of $g^{(h)}$,
(b) l_0 is a local maximum point of $g^{(h-1)}$ iff it is a local maximum point of $g^{(h)}$.

Proof for (a): For the $\Rightarrow$-direction, assume l_0 is a local minimum point of $g^{(h-1)}$. That is,

$$\Delta_{g^{(h-1)},l'} > \Delta_{g^{(h-1)},l'+1} = \cdots = \Delta_{g^{(h-1)},l_0}, \text{ for some } l' \text{ with } l' < l_0,$$
$$\Delta_{g^{(h-1)},l_0} < \Delta_{g^{(h-1)},l_0+1}.$$

We first consider the case that l_0 is in the h-th divided range (i.e., $k_h - L_h \leq l_0 < k_h$). In this case, both l' and $l_0 + 1$ are also in the h-th divided range, because $\Delta_{g^{(h-1)},l'}$ and $\Delta_{g^{(h-1)},l_0+1}$ are larger than $\Delta_{g^{(h-1)},l_0} (> \Delta_{g^{(h)},l_0} > 0)$, which is not smaller than the gradient $\Delta_{g^{(h-1)},l_{\min}}$. On the other hand, considering the case that l_0 is not in the h-th divided range, l_0 is either at the left side ($l_0 < k_h - L_h$) or at the right side ($k_h \leq l_0$). For the left-side case, it holds that $l_0 < k_h - L_h - 1$ because $\Delta_{g^{(h-1)},l_0}(= \Delta_{g^{(h)},l_0})$ should be positive but $\Delta_{g^{(h-1)},k_h-L_h-1} = 0$ from (23). Thus, both l' and $l_0 + 1$ are also at the left side. For the right-side case, it holds that $k_h < l'$ because $\Delta_{g^{(h-1)},l'}$ should be positive but $\Delta_{g^{(h-1)},k_h} = 0$ from (23). Thus, both l' and $l_0 + 1$ are also at the right side. Thus, for any case, from (22), the same relation between the gradients holds after the h-th division,

$$\Delta_{g^{(h)},l'} > \Delta_{g^{(h)},l'+1} = \cdots = \Delta_{g^{(h)},l_0},$$
$$\Delta_{g^{(h)},l_0} < \Delta_{g^{(h)},l_0+1}.$$

This means that l_0 is a local minimum point for $g^{(h)}$. The other direction (i.e., $\Leftarrow$-direction) can be shown in a similar way.

Proof for (b): For the $\Rightarrow$-direction, assume l_0 is a local maximum point of $g^{(h-1)}$. That is,

$$\Delta_{g^{(h-1)},l'} < \Delta_{g^{(h-1)},l'+1} = \cdots = \Delta_{g^{(h-1)},l_0}, \text{ for some } l' \text{ with } l' < l_0,$$
$$\Delta_{g^{(h-1)},l_0} > \Delta_{g^{(h-1)},l_0+1}.$$

We first consider the case that l_0 is in the h-th divided range (i.e., $k_h - L_h \leq l_0 < k_h$). In this case, it holds that $k_h - L_h - 1 \leq l'$ because $\Delta_{g^{(h-1)},k_h-L_h-1}$ equals zero from (23) and is smaller than $\Delta_{g^{(h-1)},l_0}(> \Delta_{g^{(h)},l_0} > 0)$. Thus, $k_h - L_h - 1 \leq l' < l_0 < l_0 + 1 \leq k_h$. After the h-th division, while the gradient between $k_h - L_h$ and $k_h - 1$ decreases by $\Delta_{g_h,*}$, the gradient on $l' + 1$ remains positive as the gradient on l_0 does. Thus, regardless whether $l' = k_h - L_h - 1$ (outside of the divided range) or $l' \leq k_h - L_h$ (inside of the divided range), it holds that

$$\Delta_{g^{(h)},l'} < \Delta_{g^{(h)},l'+1} = \cdots = \Delta_{g^{(h)},l_0},$$
$$\Delta_{g^{(h)},l_0} > \Delta_{g^{(h)},l_0+1}.$$

This means that l_0 is a local maximum point of $g^{(h)}$.

On the other hand, considering the case that l_0 is not in the h-th divided range, l_0 is either at the left side ($l_0 < k_h - L_h$) or at the right side ($k_h \leq l_0$). For the left-side case, it holds that $l_0 < k_h - L_h - 1$ because $\Delta_{g^{(h-1)},l_0} > \Delta_{g^{(h-1)},k_h-L_h-1} = 0$ from (23). Thus, $l' < l_0+1 \leq k_h - L_h$. For the right-side case, it holds that $k_h \leq l'$ because $\Delta_{g^{(h-1)},k_h}$ equals zero from (23) and is smaller than $\Delta_{g^{(h-1)},l_0} (> 0)$. Thus, $k_h \leq l' < l_0+1$. Thus, for any side, from (22) and the fact that the gradient on the just outside points of the divided range equals zero ($\Delta_{g^{(h-1)},k_h-L_h-1} = \Delta_{g^{(h-1)},k_h} = 0$), the same relation between the gradients holds after the h-th division,

$$\Delta_{g^{(h)},l'} < \Delta_{g^{(h)},l'+1} = \cdots = \Delta_{g^{(h)},l_0},$$
$$\Delta_{g^{(h)},l_0} > \Delta_{g^{(h)},l_0+1}.$$

This means that l_0 is a local maximum point for $g^{(h)}$.

The other direction (i.e., the $\Leftarrow$-direction) can be shown in a similar way. □

Share Conversion and Private Information Retrieval (Abstract)[*]

Amos Beimel[1], Yuval Ishai[2], Eyal Kushilevitz[2], and Ilan Orlov[1]

[1] Dept. of Computer Science, Ben Gurion University of the Negev, Beer Sheva, Israel
[2] Dept. of Computer Science, Technion, Haifa, Israel

Abstract. An information-theoretic *private information retrieval* (PIR) protocol allows a client to retrieve the i-th bit of a database, held by two or more servers, without revealing information about i to any individual server. Information-theoretic PIR protocols are closely related to *locally decodable codes* (LDCs), which are error correcting codes that can simultaneously offer a high level of robustness and sublinear-time decoding of each bit of the encoded message. Recent breakthrough results of Yekhanin (STOC 2007) and Efremenko (STOC 2009) have led to a dramatic improvement in the asymptotic complexity of PIR and LDC. We suggest a new "cryptographic" perspective on these recent constructions, which is based on a general notion of *share conversion* in secret-sharing schemes that may be of independent interest.

Our new perspective gives rise to a clean framework which unifies previous constructions and generalizes them in several directions. In a nutshell, we use the following two-step approach: (1) apply *share conversion* to get a low-communication secure multiparty computation protocol $\mathcal{P}$ for a nontrivial class $\mathcal{F}$ of low-depth circuits; (2) use a lower bound on the *VC dimension* of $\mathcal{F}$ to get a good PIR protocol from $\mathcal{P}$. Our framework reduces the task of designing good PIR protocols to that of finding powerful forms of share conversion which support circuit classes of a high VC dimension.

Motivated by this framework, we study the general power of share conversion and obtain both positive and negative results. Our positive results improve the concrete complexity of PIR even for very feasible real-life parameters. They also lead to some improvements in the asymptotic complexity of the best previous PIR and LDC constructions. For 3-server PIR, we improve the asymptotic communication complexity from $O(2^{146\sqrt{\log n \log \log n}})$ to $O(2^{6\sqrt{\log n \log \log n}})$ bits, where n is the database size. Our negative results on share conversion establish some limitations on the power of our approach.

---

[*] The paper was presented in the 27th IEEE Conference on Computational Complexity, 2012 at Porto, Portugal. This research was supported by ERC Starting Grant 259426. The first and fourth authors are additionally supported by ISF grant 938/09 and by the Frankel Center for Computer Science. The second and third authors are additionally supported by ISF grant 1361/10 and BSF grant 2008411.

Almost-Everywhere Secure Computation with Edge Corruptions (Abstract)*

Nishanth Chandran[1],[**], Juan Garay[2],[***], and Rafail Ostrovsky[3],[†]

[1] Microsoft Research, Redmond
[2] AT&T Labs – Research
[3] Departments of Computer Science and Mathematics, UCLA

Abstract. We consider secure multi-party computation (MPC) in a setting where the adversary can separately corrupt not only the parties (nodes) but also the communication channels (edges) in the network. We consider this question in the information-theoretic setting, and require security against a computationally unbounded adversary.

In a fully connected network the above question is simple (and we also provide an answer that is optimal up to a constant factor). What makes the problem more challenging is to consider the case of sparse networks. Partially connected networks are far more realistic than fully connected networks, which led Garay and Ostrovsky [Eurocrypt'08] to formulate the notion of (unconditional) *almost-everywhere (a.e.) secure computation* in the node-corruption model, i.e., a model in which not all pairs of nodes are connected by secure channels and the adversary can corrupt some of the nodes (but not the edges).

In this work we introduce the notion of *almost-everywhere secure computation with edge corruptions*, which is exactly the same problem as described above, except that we additionally allow the adversary to completely control some of the communication channels between two correct nodes—i.e., to "corrupt" edges in the network. While it is easy to see that an a.e. secure computation protocol for the original node-corruption model is also an a.e. secure computation protocol tolerating edge corruptions (albeit for a reduced fraction of edge corruptions with respect to the bound for node corruptions), no polynomial-time protocol is known in the case where a **constant fraction** of the edges can be corrupted (i.e., the maximum that can be tolerated) and the degree of the network is sub-linear.

We make progress on this front, by constructing graphs of degree $O(n^\epsilon)$ (for arbitrary constant $0 < \epsilon < 1$) on which we can run a.e. secure computation protocols tolerating a constant fraction of adversarial edges.

---

* A version of this paper entitled "Edge Fault Tolerance on Sparse Networks" appears in the Proceedings of the 39th *International Colloquium on Automata, Languages and Programming* (ICALP 2012). The full version of this paper is available at http://eprint.iacr.org/2012/221.
** Email: nish@microsoft.com. Part of this work was done at UCLA.
*** Email: garay@research.att.com.
† Email: rafail@cs.ucla.edu.

Improving the Quality of Santha-Vazirani Sources (Abstract)

Roger Colbeck and Renato Renner

Institute for Theoretical Physics, ETH Zurich, 8093 Zurich, Switzerland

Abstract. Is it possible to generate perfectly random bits, using only a source of weakly random bits? A well-known result by Santha and Vazirani [1] shows that this is impossible if the only guarantee one has about the initial randomness is that the bias of each bit (that is, the difference between the probability of the most likely bit value and $\frac{1}{2}$), conditioned on all previous ones, is upper bounded by a (known) constant ε. However, this impossibility result only applies to classical methods. Here we show that it is in fact possible to improve the quality of a Santha-Vazirani source using a quantum protocol provided the randomness source has a sufficiently low ε. Furthermore, the randomness of the resulting bits can be certified without relying on the correctness or completeness of quantum theory; the result holds in any non-signalling theory.

This has implications for cryptography, where honest users are often assumed to have trusted sources of perfect randomness. Our result implies that this assumption can be weakened: using our protocol, any task that can be securely performed using perfect randomness can in principle be securely performed using imperfect randomness (provided it is not too weak).

Although the present technique only works for a source with a sufficiently small bound on ε, we conjecture that with an alternative method this bound can be increased. More precisely, we conjecture that, given a source with any non-trivial bound on ε (i.e. with ε strictly smaller than $\frac{1}{2}$), there exists a protocol that uses only this source to generate bits with an arbitrarily small bias.

The full version of this work can be found in [2].

References

1. Santha, M., Vazirani, U.V.: Generating quasi-random sequences from slightly random sources. In: Proceedings of the 25th IEEE Symposium on Foundations of Computer Science (FOCS 1984), pp. 434–440 (1984)
2. Colbeck, R., Renner, R.: Free randomness can be amplified. Nature Physics 8, 450–453 (2012); also available as arXiv:1105.3195

David & Goliath Oblivious Affine Function Evaluation (Abstract)

Asymptotically Optimal Building Blocks for Universally Composable Two-Party Computation from a Single Untrusted Stateful Tamper-Proof Hardware Token

Nico Döttling*, Daniel Kraschewski, and Jörn Müller-Quade

Institute of Cryptography and Security, Department of Informatics,
Karlsruhe Institute of Technology, Germany
{doettling,kraschewski,mueller-quade}@kit.edu

Abstract. Cryptographic assumptions regarding tamper-proof hardware tokens have gained increasing attention. Even if the tamper-proof hardware is issued by a party that is not trusted by the other(s), many tasks become possible: Tamper proof hardware is sufficient for universally composable protocols, for information-theoretically secure protocols, and even allows to create software that can only be used once (one-time programs).

In a two-party setting, where only *one single* tamper-proof token is issued, we present secure constructions for multiple one-time memories (OTMs), and reusable and bidirectional commitment and oblivious transfer (OT) primitives. Our approach in its primary variant comes along without any computational assumptions, but allows only for limited, yet arbitrary token reuse. However, unlimited token reusability can be achieved straightforwardly by using a pseudorandom number generator. All our constructions have only linear communication complexity (i.e. per implemented instance of k-bit OTM/commitment/OT only $O(k)$ bits are transferred) and are thus asymptotically optimal. Moreover, the computation complexity of our protocols for k-bit OTMs/commitments/OT is dominated by $O(1)$ finite field multiplications with field size 2^k, what is considerably more efficient than any other known construction based on untrusted tamper-proof hardware alone.

The central part of our contribution is a construction for oblivious affine function evaluation (OAFE), which can be seen as a generalization of the well known oblivious transfer primitive: Parametrized by a finite vector space $\mathbb{F}_q^k$, the OAFE primitive allows a designated sender party to choose an arbitrary affine function $f : \mathbb{F}_q \to \mathbb{F}_q^k$, such that hidden from the sender party a designated receiver party may learn $f(x)$ for exactly *one* function argument $x \in \mathbb{F}_q$ of its choice. All our abovementioned results build on this primitive and it may also be of particular interest for the construction of garbled arithmetic circuits.

See http://eprint.iacr.org/2012/135 for a public version of the full paper.

---

* Supported by IBM Research & Development Germany within the HomER project.

A Unified Approach to Deterministic Encryption: New Constructions and a Connection to Computational Entropy (Abstract)

Benjamin Fuller[1], Adam O'Neill[2], and Leonid Reyzin[2]

[1] Boston University and MIT Lincoln Laboratory
[2] Boston University

Abstract. We propose a general construction of deterministic encryption schemes that unifies prior work and gives novel schemes. Specifically, its instantiations provide:

- A construction from any trapdoor function that has sufficiently many hardcore bits.
- A construction that provides "bounded" multi-message security from lossy trapdoor functions.

The security proofs for these schemes are enabled by three tools that are of broader interest:

- A weaker and more precise sufficient condition for semantic security on a high-entropy message distribution. Namely, we show that to establish semantic security on a distribution M of messages, it suffices to establish indistinguishability for all conditional distribution $M|E$, where E is an event of probability at least $1/4$. (Prior work required indistinguishability on *all* distributions of a given entropy.)
- A result about computational entropy of conditional distributions. Namely, we show that conditioning on an event E of probability p reduces the quality of computational entropy by a factor of p and its quantity by $\log_2 1/p$.
- A generalization of leftover hash lemma to correlated distributions.

We also extend our result about computational entropy to the average case, which is useful in reasoning about leakage-resilient cryptography: leaking λ bits of information reduces the quality of computational entropy by a factor of 2^λ and its quantity by λ.

A conference version of this work appeared in Theory of Cryptography 2012 [2] and a full version is available online at [1].

References

1. Fuller, B., O'Neill, A., Reyzin, L.: A unified approach to deterministic encryption: New constructions and a connection to computational entropy. Cryptology ePrint Archive, Report 2012/005, http://eprint.iacr.org/2012/005
2. Fuller, B., O'Neill, A., Reyzin, L.: A Unified Approach to Deterministic Encryption: New Constructions and a Connection to Computational Entropy. In: Cramer, R. (ed.) TCC 2012. LNCS, vol. 7194, pp. 582–599. Springer, Heidelberg (2012)

Bounds for Secure Two-Party Sampling from a Generalization of Common Information (Abstract)⋆

Vinod M. Prabhakaran[1] and Manoj M. Prabhakaran[2]

[1] Tata Institute of Fundamental Research, India
[2] University of Illinois at Urbana-Champaign, USA

Abstract. Secure multi-party computation is a central problem in modern cryptography. An important sub-class of this are problems of the following form: Alice and Bob desire to produce sample(s) of a pair of jointly distributed random variables. Each party must learn nothing more about the other party's output than what its own output reveals. To aid in this, they have available a *set up* — correlated random variables whose distribution is different from the desired distribution — as well as unlimited noiseless communication. We upper-bound how efficiently a given set up can be used to produce samples from a desired distribution.

The key tool we develop is called *tension* – or more precisely, the *region of tension* – which measures how well the correlation between a pair of random variables can be (or rather, cannot be) resolved as a piece of common information and other independent pieces of information. We show various properties of this region, including a crucial monotonicity property: *a protocol between two parties can only lower the tension between their views.* Then we derive state-of-the-art bounds on the rate at which samples from one distribution can be produced per sample of a set up, by comparing the regions of tension of the two distributions.

Another important contribution of this work is to generalize the notion of common information of two dependent variables introduced by [Gács-Körner, 1973]. They defined common information of (X, Y) as the largest entropy rate of a common random variable that two parties observing X^n and Y^n respectively, can agree upon. It is well-known that this captures only a limited form of dependence between X and Y, and is zero in most cases of interest. Our generalization, which we call *Assisted Common Information*, lets us take into account "almost common" information ignored by Gács-Körner common information. In the assisted common information system, a genie assists the parties in agreeing on a more substantial common random variable; we characterize the trade-off between the amount of communication from the genie and the quality of the common random variable produced. We show that the optimal trade-off is essentially given by the region of tension. Connections to the Gray-Wyner system and Wyner's common information are also studied.

⋆ Based partly on papers at IEEE International Symposia on Information Theory (ISIT) 2010 and 2011. Full version available at http://arxiv.org/abs/1206.1282. Supported in part by a Ramanujan Fellowship of the Department of Science and Technology, Government of India, and NSF CAREER award 07-47027.

An Information-Theoretic Approach to Privacy (Abstract)[*]

Lalitha Sankar[1], S. Raj Rajagopalan[2], and H. Vincent Poor[1]

[1] Dept. of Electrical Engineering, Princeton University, Princeton, NJ 08544, USA
[2] HP Labs, Princeton, NJ 08540, USA

Abstract. Ensuring the usefulness of electronic data sources while providing necessary privacy guarantees is an important unsolved problem. This problem drives the need for an analytical framework that can quantify the safety of personally identifiable information (privacy) while still providing a quantifiable benefit (utility) to multiple legitimate information consumers. State of the art approaches have predominantly focused on privacy. Utility of a data source is potentially (but not necessarily) degraded when it is restricted or modified to uphold privacy requirements. The central problem of this paper is a precise quantification, using information theoretic tools, of the tradeoff between the privacy needs of the *respondents* (individuals represented by the data) and the utility of the *sanitized* (published) data for any data source. The central contribution of this work is a precise quantification of the tradeoff between the privacy needs of the individuals represented by the data and the utility of the *sanitized* (published) data for any data source using the theory of rate distortion with additional privacy constraints. Utility is quantified (inversely) via *distortion* (accuracy), and privacy via *equivocation* (entropy). We expose an essential dimension of information disclosure for the first time via an additional constraint on the disclosure rate which is a measure of the precision of the sanitized data. We translate the rate-distortion-equivocation formalism of information theory to the utility-privacy problem and develop a framework that allows us to model data sources, including multi-dimensional databases and data streams, develop application independent utility and privacy metrics, quantify the fundamental bounds on the utility-privacy tradeoffs, and develop a side-information model for dealing with questions of external knowledge. We demonstrate the application of this framework for both numerical and categorical examples [1]. We have also applied this framework to privacy applications with time-series sources and organizational data disclosure.

References

1. Sankar, L., Rajagopalan, S.R., Poor, H.V.: An information-theoretic approach to privacy. In: Proc. 48th Allerton Conference on Communication, Control, and Computing, Monticello, IL, pp. 1220–1227 (September 2010)

[*] This research is supported in part by the U. S. NSF under Grant CCF-1016671 and the Air Force Office of Scientific Research under Grant FA9550-09-1-0643. This research described here first appeared as [1].

Author Index